Person-Centred Approach
and Client-Centred Therapy
Essential Readers
series editor Tony Merry

Person-Centred Approach and Client-Centred Therapy
Essential Readers is a new series of books making important and
exciting contributions to international person-centred literature by
authors who have already made distinuguished additions to the
development of the person-centred approach.

The series is edited by **Tony Merry**, Senior Lecturer,
Department of Psychology, University of East London, A person-
centred counsellor, trainer and supervisor, and author of several
person-centred books and articles.

Other books in this series:

Person-Centered Therapy: A Revolutionary Paradigm.
Jerold Bozarth

Experiences in Relatedness: Groupwork and the Person-
Centred Approach.
Colin Lago and Mhairi MacMillan (Eds)

Women Writing in the Person-Centred Approach.
Irene Fairhurst (Ed)

Understanding Psychotherapy: Fifty years of client-centred theory and practice

C. H. Patterson

PCCS BOOKS
Ross-on-Wye

First published in 2000

PCCS BOOKS
Llangarron
Ross-on-Wye
Herefordshire
HR9 6PT
United Kingdom
Tel (01989) 77 07 07

**Understanding Psychotherapy:
Fifty years of client-centred theory and practice**

ISBN 1 898059 28 4

Cover design by Denis Postle.
Printed by Redwood Books, Trowbridge, Wiltshire, United Kingdom

Contents

(CONTINUED OVER . . .)

FOREWORD

It is a special pleasure, as well as a reflective personal experience, to 'forward' my old friend Cecil Holden Patterson. How old is this friendship?

Fifty eight years ago, we met at an air force base in Texas, as 'aviation psychologists' — a new classification invented to describe newly inducted soldiers assigned to the new task of selecting army air force cadets for training as pilots, navigators, bombardiers. We never knew him as 'Cecil' — I never have called him by that name. Only 'Pete', or 'Pat'. His professional persona belies a warm and friendly man.

The psychologists in those 'Psychological Research Units' were mainly trained in learning theory, experimental and statistical methods. Some of the younger men were interested in other aspects of psychology, even including counseling and clinical. Someone in the Unit had a copy of Carl Rogers' book. Pat says that he did not see it (nor did I, who had not even heard of Rogers) but we both heard his ideas reported scornfully — 'dumb treatment for dumb people', and 'let the patient keep his secrets until the pain of keeping is worse than the shame of confessing'. (This from the large New York contingent. It sat well enough with me — a midwestern novice who knew nothing but the intriguing case studies and psychoanalytic interpretations of Freud and Jung.)

Later, the unit was re-assigned; Pat and I went separate ways, but our lives have criss-crossed on paths that came close, had many similiarities, yet missed connections. Toward the end of the war, the military was being converted to meet the oncoming problems of the armed forces — millions of men and women — being re-intergrated into civilian society. Not only hospitals for cases of injury and combat related trauma, but problems of new careers, jobs, education — all needing a vast corps of counseling psychologists. Pat was one of those 'directly commissioned' before the end of the war, to start delivery of such services. Thus he became an officer, a gentleman, and a 'clinical psychologist' (exactly the title) all at once, and by order of the President of The United States!

Note that he, (Pat) was in Sociology at the University of Chicago in 1938, several years before Rogers arrived there, and had not been trained in psychotherapy. But his wartime appointment carried over into the Veteran's Administration, the 'VA', a powerful political force with huge sums of money and influence. It was the main source of support for university training programs and practicum placements. In fact, many of us were in school thanks to the 'GI Bill of Rights', which just by itself created a need, a staff, and new justification for Counseling Centers. This 'VA' was the source and the impetus for a growing profession, now the 'mental health industry'.

Citizen Patterson worked in that government-civilian service enterprise for roughly a decade, (1947–56) a period of intensive practical clinical experience.

By 1947, Rogers was a special force in many ways. For instance, he and colleagues started a program of training, (VA supported), later reported in the small book, 'Counseling Returned Servicemen'. Around 1948, Pat was sent there for that very training. I was nearby, just starting my first year of graduate school. We were in the same vicinity, but unbeknownst. That was the pattern for years. Here, too, Pat came close to knowing Rogers, but the press of affairs was so great that Rogers delegated most of the program to younger colleagues. One of them, E. L. Porter, was Pat's special faculty, and a few years later, was my first practicum supervisor.

So what? The 'what' is, how close the parallels — how separated our connection. It was several years before we met again, and discovered — happily but much to our surprise — that we had both become 'Rogerians'. Who would have predicted? Not I. Why, with the range of possibilities available, did we choose this? That must be a question for many who will read this book. For any of us, what is or was the attraction? Not for easy entry, but for commitment? Perhaps to sincerely held convictions, based on ethical, political or moral principles? Where did we learn, how did we know enough to recognize the voice Rogers gave to our thoughts and feelings?

And the other 'what' is that Patterson, becoming the academic, with Distinguished Professorships appointed, and large contributions made, and honors received, and high offices held, did all this at somewhat remote move from the 'center', or the 'inner circle' — Chicago, Wisconsin, California — wherever Rogers was. Contrast this with the many who rested on sought-after personal affiliation with 'Carl', and some of those who made their reputations by renegade departures, or by proclaiming that they had never read Rogers at all. Reading Patterson's book, you will see how true to principle and theme (but far from copy-cat) is his published work. Central, but independent — probably somewhat lonely for Pat. Given the volume and quality, that situation of distance might be recommended.

Later he traveled and taught in distant places — in Turkey, at the Chinese University in Hong Kong, in Ireland, the UK. In Turkey, I met some of his former students. We visited the site of Tarsus, home of Saul of Tarsus, the '13th disciple' who became St. Paul. In writing this foreword, I had thought to suggest the likeness of Pat to Paul (not so much to Saul, a brute) — but it seemed a bit too weird. While reading Patterson's acceptance of the Leona Tyler Award, one finds that he has made that comparison himself! Not too far out, not a bad fit.

This weighty volume, collection of a life time of work, constitutes a whole course of instruction in theory and practice. But how does it look, feel, sound, in action? There is at hand a wonderful answer.

Beside his occupational productions, Pat has a family of loving adult children. Not only his, but the issue of his beloved wife, and of their own creation. One of them, Francine ('Penny' to her familiars) came with Pat to visit us in Big Sur. An exquisite person in every way, she is famous in her own right, for her research in human-primate communication, and for the establishment of the Gorilla Foundation. You may have seen televised *Conversations with Koko*. In one, really a profound example of 'grief counseling', this is the scene — Koko, a large, childless female gorilla, had been given a kitten, a baby to love. Kitten has died. Koko cradles the lifeless infant in her arms; she does not want to let it go. With unmistakeable expressions of anguish, she communicates her grief to Penny, who is providing every condition — whether three, six, or even seven — that Rogers ever proposed as the essence of the therapeutic relationship. When you hear Penny say to Koko, 'Oh, Honey', you will know the full meaning of 'empathic understanding'. And it flows right across all the boundaries we often see as impediments; race, class, color, culture, country and language of origin — it is unforgettable. Then, take the course.

John Shlien
Cambridge, Mass.

PREFACE

The papers included in this collection cover a period of over 50 years. They were selected from some 200 journal articles and book chapters. They represent a half century of study, practice, research, teaching and writing in the field of client-centered counseling or psychotherapy (the terms are used interchangeably). The first paper was published a year after my brief period of study with Carl Rogers and his staff at the University of Chicago. I have said that it was then that I was inoculated against directive counseling, and that I have never needed a booster shot. I have also suggested that I have tried to be to Carl Rogers as Paul was to Christ: I have preached one gospel, the gospel of Carl Rogers. In recent years, with the falling out of favor of client-centered counseling, I have felt more like John the Baptist — a voice crying in the wilderness. Not all of the papers focus on client-centered therapy, but they are all relevant in some way to the theory and practice of client-centered therapy.

As I have re-read these articles in preparing this book, I have been struck by their current relevance. They deal with problems and issues that are still present but have been neglected in the current literature in psychotherapy. They will eventually have to be addressed — certainly when client-centered therapy becomes recognized, as I believe it must, as the universally effective form of psychotherapy. The presumption on which these papers are based, and the motive for reprinting them at this time, is that client-centered therapy will be again accepted. The basic principles of client-centered therapy are the essential common elements of all the major systems of psychotherapy. These elements are currently recognized by most therapists as being necessary, but not sufficient for successful psychotherapy. Yet the research evidence for their sufficiency as well as necessity is compelling. But many, if not most, therapists are resistant to giving up the belief that there are techniques that are also necessary. Curiously, psychotherapy has been moving toward and active, interventionist approach, while at the same time medicine is moving toward minimally invasive processes.

The papers are not in chronological order, but have been grouped in three sections on the basis of similar content. There is inevitably some repetition of content, but it occurs in different contexts.

To Tony Merry and Pete Sanders who made this book possible.

C.H.Patterson
May 2000

ON COUNSELING AND PSYCHOTHERAPY

Is Psychotherapy Dependent upon Diagnosis?

1

At first glance, such a question as that posed in the title of this paper may seem absurd. The tendency would be to answer immediately: 'Yes, of course', and to refer to the field of medicine, where it is quite apparent that therapeutic measures are determined by differential diagnosis. Thorne writes in this connection: 'It seems elemental that rational treatment cannot be planned and executed until an accurate diagnosis has been made' (Thorne 1945, p. 319).

On the other hand, Rogers has just as positively stated that 'diagnostic knowledge and skill is not necessary for good therapy' (Rogers, 1946, p. 421).

Before proceeding further it should be made clear that we are concerned with the so-called functional disorders in which psychotherapy is applicable. It is recognized that there are mental disorders of definite organic origin, involving neurological disease, physiological disturbances, toxic conditions, and traumatic injury. There are also certain mental disorders which are possibly organic in nature, on a constitutional or endocrinological basis, e.g. the so-called endogenous depressions. Diagnosis of organic factors is an important medical function in these cases (assisted often by the use of psychological tests), and obviously influences therapy. Such diagnosis is, however, often difficult, and sometimes inconclusive, and psychotherapy should not be denied pending decision as to the presence or absence of organic pathology. Moreover, although psychotherapy may not be indicated for a purely organic disorder, there are often mixtures of organic and psychological components in which psychotherapy is beneficial. In addition, the presence of a purely organic condition may, and often does, result in psychological reactions to which psychotherapy may be directed. However, the present discussion is primarily concerned with the recognized functional disorders, including psychosomatic dysfunctions, of psychogenic origin, which are regarded as suitable for psychotherapy.

It might seem that a logical analogy could be drawn between internal medicine and psychiatry. Psychiatry, it might be maintained, is a branch of medicine, and therefore the principles, methods and techniques which are applicable in internal medicine apply also, of necessity, to mental disease and maladjustment. This

First published in *American Psychologist*, 1948, pp.155–9.

approach is the basis of a recent article by Thorne (1947a), in which clinical psychologists are urged to learn from medicine by adopting its methods.

If one looks a little more closely into the matter, however, a question might be raised regarding the validity of the analogy between physical disease and mental disease. The two are, as a matter of fact, entirely different in many respects. In the first place, the nature of the primary malignant process is entirely different. In one case it involves primarily the physiological and chemical processes of bodily functioning; in mental disease of a functional type the disorder is primarily one of psychological and social behavior. Two distinct levels of functioning are represented which are different enough to raise considerable doubt as to the validity of any analogy between them. Again, physical disease is the result of specific experimentally verifiable foreign agents, whether chemical, bacteriological, or virus in nature. Such a statement cannot be made regarding functional mental disease, although it is the hope of some that eventually it will be possible to do so. Finally, in physical medicine there exists a wide variety of specific and experimentally or empirically verified remedies. Again, this is not the case in the field of mental disease. In other words, while in physical medicine accurate differential etiological diagnosis is possible, leading to the selection of specific remedies, in the field of mental disease no such specific etiological diagnosis is possible, nor are there specific, discrete psychotherapies which have differential effects from which to choose.

As a matter of practice, psychiatric diagnosis has little rational connection with choice of psychotherapy. Methods of therapy depend more upon the specific training, experience, and preferences of the therapist than upon the diagnosis. Those who feel that psychotherapy should be selective and specific, and thus 'rational', chosen on the basis of diagnosis, have been unable to relate specific therapies to specific diagnoses, in terms of indications and contraindications, except possibly on the basis of severity of the condition. Attempts to list indications or contraindications are more often in terms of symptomatic or basic treatment or the depth of therapy desired or possible, the time available, etc. In other words, the distinctions are based upon the limits of the therapist and therapeutic situation rather than being related to the diagnosis or etiology of the disorder.

The difficulty, according to the usual argument, is chiefly with the diagnostic system of classifying mental disorders. Perhaps if we could develop a system of diagnosis based upon etiology we could apply specific types of therapy (provided they exist or could be differentiated) to specific types of mental disease. The idea sounds intriguing, particularly when we consider what has been accomplished in physical medicine, but the prospects are not promising (Malalmud, 1946). But granted that the classification of mental disorders is not possible in the present state of our knowledge, it might be expected that a thorough study of the individual case would yield an understanding of the etiological factors, and lead to a rational choice of therapy. Thorne, in his use of the term 'diagnosis', refers to 'the description of the organism and its behavior by a variety of methods whose basic purpose is to discover the personality dynamics of each individual case. It is implied that the more complete the description, the more complete will be our understanding of why, when, where, and how the individual got that way' (Thorne, 1947a, p. 161). Elsewhere he states that 'no rational plan of treatment can be accomplished without detailed knowledge of each individual case history' (Thorne, 1945, p. 320).

Rogers, however, maintains that a case history is not a prerequisite for therapy (Rogers, 1942, pp. 80–4). It is rather common experience that, given a detailed case study of an individual, wide differences and disagreements concerning its analysis and interpretation, in terms of etiology and personality dynamics, occur, not only between different professional groups, but within these groups. Indeed, the number of diagnoses on the basis of such material is about as great as the number of analysts (Elkin, 1947). Rational or specific therapy is obviously impossible in such a situation. If we are unable to agree upon the etiology and specific dynamics of individual cases, we certainly cannot set up diagnostic classification based upon etiology or dynamics.

Part of the difficulty no doubt lies in the fact that behavior is multiply determined — there is no single cause which can be isolated, to the extent that this is possible in physical medicine. But also, in terms of basic etiology there may be no fundamental or essential differences which will allow us to distinguish classes of mental disorder on an etiological basis. All maladjustments may be essentially alike in terms of basic etiology, and the various behavior, or symptomatic, manifestations which appear to distinguish various types of disorder may be determined by contingent influences. In that event, specific therapy would not be possible, necessary, or desirable, except on the basis of severity of the disorder, and the presence or absence of organic disease or insult.

That there is a common basic etiology of all functional mental disorder is not a new idea. In fact, most discussions of maladjusted behavior take such a point of view. Work on experimental neuroses in animals, e.g. that of Masserman (1946), indicates that the same experimental procedure results in widely different types of maladjusted behavior in different animals of the same species. Moreover, a variety of apparently different procedures are capable of inducing maladjusted behavior. The variety of manifestations of mental disorder, leading first to a symptomatic classification, has perhaps blinded us to the common origin of all maladjustment.

In the field of psychological testing, the failure to find diagnostic test-signs to differentiate the various classifications of mental disease may be as much the result of the absence of basic differences as of the inadequacy of the present primarily symptomatic classification. In fact, the obtained overlapping of the various diagnostic categories in terms of test results would tend to support the theory of a basic common etiology, with differences being relatively unessential or determined by other contingent factors.

Instead of assuming that we need a new classification, based not upon symptomatology but upon some other more fundamental difference such as a genetic origin, we should develop a rational therapy directing attention to the basic elements of maladjustment common to all mental disorder. If we found that there is a common basic etiology, then, rather than being concerned about developing specific therapies, a rational psychotherapy would be concerned with principles and techniques which are most effective in reaching and remedying the underlying causes of maladjustment.

As a suggestion of the line such an approach might take, the following discussion is offered in outline. It involves first a statement of a theory of behavior and its maladjustment, followed by a statement of therapeutic principles and practices which arise from a consideration of the nature of maladjustment. The discussion draws from the work of many people including that of Masserman (1946), Mowrer and Kluckhohn (1944), Rogers (1946, and in lecture notes), and many others who have written in the field of personality and its disorders.

Outline of a theory of behavior and its aberrations
I. *Assumptions:*
1. The living organism, by definition, is never at rest but in a state of constant activity, with physiological tendencies to approach or withdraw, contract or expand.
2. It is characteristic of living matter that it tends to seek a state of equilibrium, both within itself and in relation to its environment, and to maintain its organization when threatened.
3. In the realm of personality and behavior, this characteristic is exemplified by the tendency of the individual to become and remain integrated and consistent within itself.
4. Since the organism is constantly subject to stimuli, both from within and from without, equilibrium is never maintained for long, but is dynamic and unstable.
5. This dynamic equilibrium allows for change, so that all living organisms are normally characterized by change, or growth and development, from lesser to greater complexity, from immaturity to maturity, from dependence to independence, from irresponsibility to responsibility.

II. *Principles*:
1. Although the organism is constantly active, this activity is not random, but is directed or motivated by needs, drives, etc., on a physiological level, and by wishes, desires, etc., on the psychological and social levels.
2. The organism reacts to its environment or to a stimulus as it is perceived and experienced, not as it may actually exist. Interpretive or symbolic (meaningful) processes thus intervene between the stimulus and the response of the organism.
3. Motives are directed toward the preservation and enhancement of the organism (Assumptions 2 and 3).
4. All behavior is thus goal-directed, or a purposeful attempt to satisfy the needs of the organism, either through the approach toward beneficial stimuli, or the avoidance of noxious stimuli.
5. Behavior which succeeds in satisfying a need or desire is rewarded by the reduction of tension, or an approach to equilibrium or integration. Such behavior tends to be repeated again in similar circumstances, and if it continues to be successful in reducing tension it becomes fixated, or is learned, so that it becomes habitual.
6. The presence of unsatisfied drives or desires creates a state of physiological and/or psychological tension or disequilibrium.

7. When a need or desire is frustrated, either by external conditions or by conflict with another incompatible drive or desire, tension is not reduced, and the organism seeks for substitute or compromise satisfactions.
8. Such substitute satisfactions may or may not result in complete reduction of tension, and may or may not lead to the creation of additional tensions by arousing other antagonistic motives.
9. Behavior becomes maladjusted when substitute satisfactions do not result in sufficient tension reduction, and/or violate the integrity of the organism's organization, or result in behavior which is not acceptable to the (social) environment of the organism.
10. The repression of conflicts, or of unsatisfied needs and desires, occurs as the result of the tendency to maintain the integration and organization of the organism or personality. Conflicts and tensions may thus exist on an unconscious level.
11. Substitute satisfactions are retained because they supply partial satisfaction of needs. Since they thus become fixated they prevent further growth and development and lead to immature, dependent, maladjusted behavior.

Principles of psychotherapy
1. Since all maladjustment is similar in origin, diagnosis in terms of symptomatology or etiology or dynamics is not essential to therapy. Similarly, knowledge of the content of the conflict involved is unessential as a prerequisite of therapy, since the technique of therapy does not depend on the nature or content of the conflict but upon the presence of conflict and the resulting tensions.
2. Since the functions of the formal case history (Thorne, 1945) can be satisfied, insofar as is desirable, during the process of therapy, such a history is not a prerequisite of therapy. During therapy pertinent material will be brought out. Whether or not these data are factually correct is unessential, since it is the patient's interpretation of them which is important for his adjustment.
3. Since the basic etiology of maladjustment is the presence of unrelieved tensions as a result of conflict and inadequate substitute satisfactions (which constitute the symptoms of maladjustment), a rational therapy should aim at providing an opportunity for the individual to attain more satisfactory, acceptable, and direct satisfaction of his needs. Therapy should therefore be more than symptomatic, palliative, supportive, etc.
4. Therapy should result in bringing to consciousness the repressed conflicts so that they may be resolved in a more adequate manner, with consciously selected goals and methods of satisfying needs, and resulting reintegration of the self and more adjusted behavior.
5. Since the aim of development in the individual is ability to adapt and adjust to the demands of the environment in a mature, independent manner, therapy should avoid creating dependence. Therapy should therefore be directed toward aiding the patient to solve his own problems and developing problem-solving ability rather than solving his immediate problems for him.

6. Since one of the characteristics of the organism is the capacity for growth, this capacity should be capitalized on in therapy. Therapy should be directed toward freeing this positive energy in the individual so that more constructive, integrative, and adjusted behavior develops.

7. The therapeutic situation is a learning situation and the principles of learning apply. This means that the patient will learn what he is taught in therapy, whether dependence or independence, immaturity or maturity, where to go to have his problems solved, or how to solve his own problems.

The practice of psychotherapy

1. The positive growth forces will manifest themselves in the individual if:
   a. He is given responsibility for himself,
   b. He is allowed the freedom to explore his own conflicts, attitudes, and feelings,
   c. The drive toward maturity and independence is recognized, and the opportunity to practice and learn independence through experience is provided.

2. Repressed conflicts and attitudes may be brought into consciousness by:
   a. The conveying of a sense of understanding and acceptance in a noncritical, nonjudgmental relationship, conducive to the expression of negative attitudes, with resulting release of tension, and the assimilation of negative feelings by the patient,
   b. The creation by the therapist of a free, permissive atmosphere in which the client can explore his problems and conflicts and develop a conscious awareness of the elements of the conflicts,
   c. The clarification of expressed attitudes and feelings, enabling the patient to see himself in a somewhat different light, leading to insight into himself and the interrelationships among his attitudes and conflicts.

3. As a result of the application of these techniques a favorable situation for learning is supplied, in which the patient discovers and proposes alternative solutions for his conflicts and more adequate satisfactions for his needs. Insight, choice, and positive action arrived at by the client then follow, with resulting tension reduction.

4. Symptomatic or palliative therapy, involving suggestion, persuasion, reassurance, support, sympathy, etc., is admittedly ineffective in reaching at conflicts and tensions involved in maladjustment. In addition, these techniques, together with questioning, probing, advice, and interpretation, restrict the freedom of the patient and foster dependence, which are inimical to his progress in solving his own problems.

The practical significance of the foregoing is that the present emphasis on differential diagnosis is unnecessary for therapy. It would also follow that for purposes of therapy, neither extensive nor intensive case-history techniques nor so-called diagnostic testing is necessary.

   For therapeutic purposes all that is necessary is that the patient come for help and be in sufficient contact to be able to verbalize his behavior and attitudes and feelings. As long as the motivation to change or grow exists, the application of the principles and techniques of therapy outlined above is possible. The point at which this motivation is lost is possibly a function of the severity of the disorder; i.e., one of the characteristics of a severe psychotic disorder appears to be the loss, perhaps only temporarily, of the positive growth forces, so that the struggle has been given up, with a complete rejection or denial of drives or desires which disturb the integration of the individual.

If in the course of this type of psychotherapy a severe psychotic or organic condition becomes evident, no harm will have been done, and psychotherapy may be abandoned as being ineffective or inapplicable — although of course such therapy might be an adjunct and continuation of other chemical or physical therapies which might reactivate motives and conflicts which could then be expressed or verbalized. A lack of awareness of conflict and need for therapy in a nonpsychotic individual may preclude the use of psychotherapy, since it is generally recognized that such awareness and desire for help is necessary. In some individuals this may develop with continuing experience in which their behavior leads to discomfort and unhappiness. It is possible that an awareness of maladjustment can be developed by the therapist by the induction of conflict, as suggested by Thorne (1947b). It would be desirable that such a technique be used by an individual other than the therapist who aids the patient in the solution of the conflicts, since it is inconsistent with the attitudes and principles of therapy discussed here, and is a preparation for, rather than a part of, therapy.

References

Elkin, F. (1947) Specialists interpret the case of Harold Holzer. *Journal of Abnormal and Social Psychology*, 42, 99–111.

Malalmud, D. I. (1946) Objective measurement of clinical status in psycho-pathological research. *Psychological Bulletin*, 43, 240–58.

Masserman, J. H. (1946) *Principles of dynamic psychiatry.* Philadelphia: W. B. Saunders and Co.

Mowrer, O. H., and Kluckhohn, C. (1944) Dynamic theory of personality. Chapter 3 in Hunt, J. McV. (Ed): *Personality and the behavior disorders.* New York: The Ronald Press Co. Pp. 12–42.

Rapaport, D. (1947) The future of research in clinical psychology and psychiatry. *American Psychologist*, 2, 167–72.

Rogers, C. R. (1942) *Counseling and psychotherapy.* Boston: Houghton Mifflin.

Rogers, C. R. (1946) Significant aspects of client-centered therapy. *American Psychologist*, 1, 415–22.

Rogers, C. R. Lecture notes.

Thorne, F. C. (1945) Directive psychotherapy: IV. The therapeutic implications of the case history. *Journal of Clinical Psychology*, 1, 318–30.

Thorne, F. C. (1947a) The clinical method in science. *American Psychologist*, 2, 159–66.

Thorne, F. C. (1947b) Directive psychotherapy: XI. Therapeutic use of conflict. *Journal of Clinical Psychology,* 3, 168–79.

A Unitary Theory of Motivation and its Counseling Implications

2

One of the most frequent problems posed by those working with people, including counselors, is represented by such questions as: What do we do with the unwilling, the involuntary client, the so-called unmotivated individual? How can we instill motivation into people? How can we get people to want to be helped, to want to do what they should do, tp want to do what is obviously good for them?

The problem of motivating people is a ubiquitous one. It is present in all situations where one person desires to affect or influence the behavior of others, including child training, education, politics, advertising, courtship, counseling and psychotherapy, and brainwashing. What can the psychology of motivation contribute to the solution of this problem? It is the purpose of this paper to review briefly the development of a unitary concept of motivation, and to discuss its implications for the counseling relationship.

Development of a unitary concept of motivation

Many motives or none

The concept of motivation has been a central aspect of so-called dynamic systems of psychology, from Freudian psychoanalysis to neobehaviorism. However, there has been little agreement upon identifying the motives underlying behavior, with the result that there have been as many lists of motives as there were of instincts, the precursors of motives. As in the case of instincts, the question may be raised as to whether motives are necessary, and the question might well be answered in the same way, that is, in the negative. Postman (1956), reviewing one of the volumes of the Nebraska Symposium on Motivation, expressed the hope that at a future symposium someone would devote a paper to this question. His wish was in part granted by Kelly (1962), who stated in opening his discussion: 'I have no use for the concept of motivation . . . Motivation is an invented construct' (pp. 83–4). Jones (1962), in the introduction to this tenth symposium, noted that 'There seems to be increasing evidence over the years that the motivational concept as such has reached the end of its usefulness as a scientific concept' (p. viii).

First published in *Journal of Individual Psychology,* 1964, 10, pp. 17–31.
© 1964 Journal of Individual Psychology. Reprinted with permission.

English and English (1958) define motivation as follows:
(1) the non-stimulus variables controlling behavior; the general name for the fact that an organism's acts are partly determined in direction and strength by its own nature (or enduring structure) and/or internal state. (2) a specific hypothesized process that energizes differentially certain responses, thus making them dominant over other possible responses to the same situation.

This is a rather vague and loose definition, but even so it is not generally accepted by psychologists. The lack of agreement as to what motivation is, and the inability to answer such questions as how many motives (or drives, impulses, desires, needs, etc.) there are, how they operate, how they are aroused (Jones, 1958), could well suggest that there may not be any validity or utility to the concept.

Littman (1958) attempted to find common elements among 52 motivational terms. Motivation as an energizing function or as an instigator of behavior was not present in all terms, nor was the concept of selection or direction of activity. Persistence in behavior, suggested by some as a characteristic of motivation, did not appear in most terms or definitions. Littman proposed, facetiously, a definition of motivation which would include all the aspects proposed by various writers. This definition turned out to include all of behavior, and thus all of psychology.

Littman's definition may not be as facetious as he supposed. It points to something which has not been adequately recognized by many psychologists, and which, when recognized, changes the whole problem of motivation. This is the fact that activity, or behavior, does not have to be energized, or stimulated, either from within or from without. This disposes of the necessity for a concept of motivation to account for activity, or to look for sources of energy which give strength to motives or drives.

The living organism is continuously active, continuously behaving. Life is activity, so that motivation, in its energizing aspect, is living activity. It is a given, and does not have to be accounted for except as a property of living matter. As Littman (1958) expresses it: 'It is not necessary that there be psychological actives (motives) to set behavioral systems into motion; systems may be so constructed that they already have the property of motion or activity'.

Kelly (1962, p. 85) suggests that we begin
. . . by assuming that the fundamental thing about life is that it goes on. It isn't that something makes it go on; the going on is the thing itself. It isn't that motives make man come alert to do things; his alertness is an aspect of his very being. Talking about activating motives is simply redundant talky-talk, for once you've got a human being on your hands, you already have alertness and movement, and sometimes a lot more of it than you know what to make of (p. 85).

And Skinner, a strict behaviorist, makes the same point. 'No one,' he says, 'asks how to motivate a baby. A baby naturally explores everything it can get at, unless restraining forces have been at work. And this tendency doesn't die out, it's not wiped out . . . We don't need to create motives' (1948, pp. 101–2).

But does this dispose of the concept of motivation? Is motivation entirely redundant, and useless, as Kelly (1958) claims? What about the direction of activity? Motivation is frequently considered as the directional influencing of behavior by nonstimulus, or internal, variables. These variables are usually called drives or needs.

In the effort to understand the great variety of behavior manifested by the human organism, long lists of physiological, psychological and social drives and needs have been proposed. A basic problem in motivation then becomes the organization of these needs into a system. The solution most frequently proposed is the ordering of needs in a hierarchy. Maslow's (1954) hierarchy is perhaps the most adequate attempt at such a solution. Problems arise in any ordering of needs, however, and no hierarchy appears to be invariant, with the so-called more basic or prepotent needs always taking precedence over less 'higher' needs. For example, it is not always true that the lower, more basic physiological need of self-preservation will take precedent over a 'higher' less prepotent need such as belongingness or esteem needs, to use Maslow's terms.

Is there no way of resolving this problem? Must we, with Littman (1958), accept the conclusion that 'there are many different kinds of motivational phenomena', all separate, unique, specific, unintegrated? There have been, and are, many who feel that we do not. These are the psychologists, and others, who seek to understand the organism or the individual as an organized, integrated whole, who feel that there must be an organizing or unifying element or factor.

Unitary concept of motivation
There have been a number of unitary theories of motivation and the first to propose such a theory probably lived before recorded history. Contemporary psychology includes many well-known figures who have arrived, more or less independently, at the conclusion that there is one single, dominating need or motive behind all behavior.

Freud for a time was a monist, basing all behavior upon eros or the libido, or the pleasure principle. But he then added a second instinct or motive, the ego. His theory of instincts went through many stages (Bibring, 1958), but the dualism persisted. He became impressed by the destructive and aggressive elements in behavior, and felt that they needed to be accounted for on an instinctual basis. His final theory continued the dualism, with life instincts (self-preservation and preservation of the species) on the one hand, and the death instinct (aggression and destructiveness) on the other.

The existence of aggression has been a stumbling block to many who have been concerned with human motivation. Its strength and practical universality have led to its being considered instinctive or innate. But there have been many who have suggested that this is not the case, that 'it may be that what has often been considered instinctive or natural aggressiveness is always a reaction to threat, a reaction which is universal because threat, in some form or other, is universal' (Patterson, 1962, p. 115). Bibring (1958) in his discussion of Freud's theories suggests this solution also. He raises the question 'whether there are any phenomena of aggression at all outside the field of the ego-preservative functions', and notes 'the empirical fact that aggressiveness appears only or almost only when the life instincts or the ego instincts are exposed to harm'. Ashley Montagu (1962) contends that 'the view that aggressiveness is instinctual is not scientifically corroborated'. 'In fact,' he states, 'all the available evidence gathered by competent investigators indicates that man is born without a trace of aggressiveness', but that aggression or hostility results from deprivations or the frustration of needs (cf. Maslow, 1949). Support for this is also provided by Dollard and his associates (Dollard, Doob, Miller, Mowrer, & Sears, 1939) in their discussion of the frustration-aggression hypothesis.

The influence of the aggressive aspect of behavior has been so strong that in some cases it has been accepted as the basic and single motivation for behavior. Adler, who was one of the first in contemporary psychology to propose a unitary concept of motivation, originally accepted aggression as the unifying principle (Ansbacher & Ansbacher, 1956, p. 34). But he seems to have recognized that aggression occurs 'when one of the primary drives is prevented from satisfaction', or as a result of neurotic feelings of inferiority, and soon abandoned this principle. (An interesting development of this thesis is found in Golding's 'Lord of the Flies' [Golding, 1959].)

Adler then sought the unifying concept elsewhere, and over a period of time used varying terms to designate the basic striving and the 'fictional' (because unattainable) goal of such striving. An early term was the striving 'to be a real man' of the masculine protest. Other early terms were the striving for superiority, for power, for security, for self-esteem. Such striving was a compensatory process developing out of a feeling of inferiority. As Adler turned from the neurotic to the normal or healthy individual, he turned from compensatory strivings to more positive concepts: completion and perfection. While the neurotic strives to overcome personal deficiencies, the normal individual is less self-centered and strives for a goal which includes the welfare of others. Adler saw no need for positing special forces as the source of energy for motivation:

> The striving for superiority . . . is an intrinsic necessity of life itself
> . . . The striving for perfection is innate in the sense that it is a part of
> life, a striving, an urge, or something without which life would be
> unthinkable' (Ansbacher & Ansbacher, 1956, pp. 103, 104).

Many others have reached this solution to the problem of motivation, apparently independently and using somewhat differing terminology.

Goldstein (1939, p. 186), on the basis of extended experience with brain-injured veterans, came to the conclusion that self-actualization is the single basic motive of all behavior: 'We can say an organism is governed by a tendency to actualize, as much as possible, its individual capacities, its nature in the world'.

Angyal, defining life as 'a process of self-expansion' (Angyal, 1941), goes on to say that 'We can say that the tendency of the organism is toward increased autonomy' (p. 47), or a tendency toward self-determination. He also refers to self-realization as being the intrinsic purpose of life (p. 354).

Lecky, impressed by the integration and organization of the self, felt that a need for self-consistency and its preservation is the single basic need of the organism: 'The goal for which the individual strives is the maintenance of a unified organization' (Lecky, 1945, p. 45).

Rogers sees the organism, or the individual, as being inherently growing and forward-moving. The basic tendency of the maintenance and enhancement of the organism and of the self provides the motive force for therapy and personality change (Rogers, 1951, p. 195). 'The organism has one basic tendency and striving — to actualize, maintain, and enhance the experiencing organism' (p. 487). Other terms which Rogers uses include independence, self-determination, integration, self-actualization. In his presentation of his theoretical position, Rogers (Rogers, 1959) refers to self-actualization as an aspect of a general actualizing tendency. The self becomes differentiated as part of the actualizing tendency, and a need for positive regard from others and for positive self-regard develops. Rogers here considers the need for positive regard from others and of oneself as secondary or learned needs. However, although they may develop on the basis of and be shaped by experience, these needs may be potential in the general actualizing tendency.

Combs and Snygg (1959) adopt the same terminology, and were in fact influential upon the development of Rogers' thinking. They state that

> From birth to death the maintenance of the phenomenal self is the
> most pressing, the most crucial, if not the only task of existence . . .
> Man seeks not merely the maintenance of a self . . . Man seeks both
> to maintain and enhance his perceived self (p. 45).

Their book is probably the most systematic and detailed development of the implications of a unitary theory of motivation.

White's (1959) concept of competence, which he defines as 'an organism's capacity to interact effectively with its environment,' may appear to be a unitary approach to motivation, and he does refer to motivation as the urge toward competence. But White's concept is actually much narrower. Competence does not supplant or subsume the primary drives. It is an attempt to integrate many apparently spontaneous activities such as exploration, manipulation, sensing, mastery, etc. But while pleasure or satisfaction is not the goal, the feeling of efficacy as a goal seems limited and hardly acceptable as a basic, general goal of life.

Woodworth (1958) does elevate similar interaction with the environment to the status of a single motivating principle, however. He states that '. . . the direction of receptive and motor activity toward the environment is the fundamental tendency of animal and human behavior', and 'is the all-pervasive primary motivation of behavior' (pp. 124–5). Again, however, this would appear to be a limited and rather meager concept of life.

Even those who would repudiate the whole concept of motivation appear to be unable to avoid dealing with the problem of the direction or goal of behavior, and develop concepts which are essentially motivational. Kelly (1958) declares that the concept of motivation is not needed to explain directionality of movement.

Yet his theory of personal constructs assumes a motive or goal which is quite similar to those discussed above: 'A person chooses for himself that alternative in a dichotomized construct through which he anticipates the greater possibility for extension and definition of his system' (p. 59).

It appears, then, that a number of workers have come, more or less independently, to the position that the assumption of a single basic, dominant, integrating motive, or goal, is more useful in understanding behavior than an indefinite multiplicity of separate, independent, or even hierarchically arranged motives or needs. Whether this is an overemphasis upon the love of parsimony, or itself evidence of the need for integration, unity, perfection or completeness, is a matter for the future to decide. Suffice it to say that the concept seems to be increasingly accepted in psychology, and may lead to the solution of the age-old problem of motivation and the understanding of behavior.

The concept of a single, basic motive clarifies, or eliminates, the confusion which we face when we try to understand and order or integrate the multiplicity of specific drives and motives, often contradictory or opposed to each other, which are attributed to human beings. There is no need to attempt to order drives in a hierarchy. There *is* no hierarchy, except in the sense that all the specific needs or drives are subservient to the basic tendency for the preservation and enhancement of the self. Specific needs take priority in terms of their current relation to the basic tendency. The concept has the virtues of simplicity and parsimony, and offers an organizing principle for the understanding of individual behavior. To illustrate this, we shall apply the concept to the process of counseling and psychotherapy. First, however, some criticisms of the concept will be briefly considered.

Some objections to a unitary concept
The unitary concept of motivation has not of course achieved complete acceptance. Three objections may be briefly noted and disposed of.

Hilgard (1962), discussing the concept of a master motive and referring to some of the writers presented above, concludes, 'Because these theorists disagree among themselves as to the one master motive, we are on safer grounds to think of a group of *ego-integrative* motives, that is, motives with some sort of self-reference' (p. 144). It is of course true that many terms have been used by various writers — self-enhancement, self-actualization, self-fulfillment, self-realization, self-esteem, completeness, perfection, etc. But as far as the concept is concerned the diversity is more apparent than real. There appears to be a basic commonality which would require only agreement as to its designation.

A second objection may be formulated in the question whether the maintenance and the enhancement of the self are not a dualism. Are these not two independent motives, which may actually oppose one another at times, rather than a single motive? Preservation of the physical organism may mean the sacrifice of the psychological self, or its actualization, fulfillment, or realization. Conversely, preservation of the psychological self may require the sacrifice of the physical organism. Maslow (1955) apparently was influenced by some such considerations in his concept of deficiency motivation and growth motivation.

But preservation or maintenance, and enhancement or actualization may be seen as two aspects of the same motive, operating in different situations. Adler (Ansbacher & Ansbacher, p. 114) recognized the different expression of the same basic motive in neurotics and normals. The neurotic, threatened and compensating for a deep feeling of inferiority, reacts to preserve or restore his self-esteem, to overcome his inferiority with superiority through the striving for power. The normal individual, on the other hand, free of threat, can strive for completeness or perfection. In the unhealthy individual, in the individual under stress who is threatened, enhancement or positive striving is impossible. He must defend himself against attack or threat of attack, and strive to safeguard, defend or secure what he has. His energies are absorbed in preservation. Goldstein (1939) makes the same point. He considers the drive for self-preservation a pathological phenomenon. The drive for self-actualization, he suggests, undergoes a change in the sick (or threatened) individual in whom the scope of life is reduced, and he is driven to maintain (or defend) a limited state of existence. Preservation or maintenance of the self is thus a pathological form of self-actualization, the only form of self-actualization left to the threatened individual.

A third objection to a unitary concept of motivation as self-actualization or self-enhancement is that it leads to a self-centered, selfish, antisocial or asocial individual. This objection appears to be based upon the assumption that man is innately bad or antisocial, that the needs of the individual are antithetical to society. A more adequate assumption is that man, as Aristotle noted, is a political (social) animal, and in order to exist needs the group. In order to actualize himself, man needs others. Moreover, man lives in a society, and as a social being he

> must necessarily adjust to the demands of society or remove himself from it. If he identifies himself with society he cannot deny it, for to do that is to deny himself. Since he lives in and is dependent upon society for his welfare, his own maintenance and enhancement will lead to that of the members of society as well, providing he is free to make adequate differentiations and to accept these into his concept of self (Combs & Snygg, 1959, p. 260).

Rogers (1951) notes that, in the long run, enhancement of the self 'inevitably involves the enhancement of other selves as well . . . The self-actualization of the organism appears to be in the direction of socialization, broadly defined' (pp. 150, 488; see also pp.177–78).

Implications for client-centered counseling
There is no unmotivated client
There is no such thing as lack of or absence of motivation. To be alive is to be motivated, to be unmotivated is to be dead. Thus we cannot say that a client is unmotivated.

Marguerite Dickey (1959), in summarizing the Cleveland Symposium on Behavioral Research in Rehabilitation, noting that while perhaps no more difficult problem exists for the rehabilitation worker than how to deal with the so-called nonmotivated patient, points out that 'the label 'nonmotivated' attached to such a patient is not only erroneous but is not likely to lead into the kinds of behavioral or conceptual analyses which would increase our understanding of the problem'.

Recognizing that clients are not unmotivated is the first step in recognizing positive aspects in them, in attempting to understand how their motivation is directed, i.e., toward what goals or objectives. For the client does have goals and objectives, although they may not be the same which the counselor has for him, or would like him to have. This shift from a negative to a positive view of the client is the beginning of an understanding of him. Instead of viewing a client as resistant, uncooperative, unreasonable because he does not seem to be interested in commonly accepted goals, we may see him as concerned about other things, which are of importance to him in achieving adequacy or enhancing his self. We recognize then, that in many cases the problem is not lack of motivation, but motivation toward goals not accepted by the counselor or others concerned with the client. They are not lacking in motivation. Indeed, the problem often is that the client is too highly motivated! There are also those individuals who refuse and resist counseling, and are thus 'uncooperative' because they are strongly motivated to go it alone and remain independent.

Motivation is in terms of the self-concept
The motivation toward personal adequacy or self-enhancement is always in terms of the concept one has of himself. The self-concept is the center around which behavior is organized. Essentially the world is given meaning in terms of its significance for the maintenance and enhancement of the self, for the development of a sense of personal adequacy or self-esteem. This orientation leads to a consideration of motivation in terms of the implementation of the self-concept.

To understand the client and his motivation, one must know what his concept of himself is. It does not help to know what others think of him, how others see him. The perceptions which others have about one, may influence one's self-concept, but the pictures which others paint of a particular individual are not necessarily his 'real' self.

The self-concept is the organization of the perceptions of the self. It includes all the perceptions and conceptions which the individual has about himself, his attitudes and beliefs about himself. It influences his perceptions of the world about him. If he sees himself as weak and inadequate, the world is a threatening place. The self is the central part of the individual's phenomenal field, about which the world is organized. 'All perceptions . . . derive their meaning from their relation to the phenomenal self' (Combs & Snygg, 1959, p. 131). 'What a person thinks and how he behaves are largely determined by the concepts he holds about himself and his abilities' (p. 122).

We can only attempt to understand the self-concept of the particular client with whom we are working. It is not easy to put oneself in the place of another and to see himself and the world as he does, because each individual is unique. If we were able to do this more successfully, perhaps we would have less of a problem with so-called uncooperative and nonmotivated clients.

Clients may have perceptions of themselves and the world which are not consistent with the perceptions others have of them and the world. I do not say reality, here, since no one knows what reality really is. What we call reality is no more than the agreement of the perceptions of a number of observers. Nor do I speak of 'distorted' perceptions, since this also implies a known reality. A person's perceptions are not distorted to himself, but are so only from the frame of reference of another whose perceptions differ. This constitutes a problem in understanding. The client may perceive his personality, with its positive aspects and its limitations, differently than the counselor. He may perceive his abilities and aptitudes differently than they are indicated by tests or other evidence of performance. He may perceive the opportunities available to him quite differently than does the counselor. He may perceive the attitudes of others toward him in an entirely different way than does the counselor or others, or even different from the way in which others would express their attitudes toward him. It is the client's perceptions, however, which determine his conceptions of what he can or cannot do, what he should or should not do, what his goals should be.

Behavior change must be preceded by change of perception
The third implication of this point of view has to do with the way in which change in the direction or goals of the client may be facilitated or made possible. The basic assumption is that perception determines behavior. The individual behaves as he does because of the way he perceives his environment, his world, particularly in relation to himself and his need for enhancing his personal adequacy. The problem of changing behavior, then, is not one of 'motivating' people, but of changing their perceptions of themselves and of the world around them. This is to some a startling and apparently inadequate approach to behavior change. Yet it is a basic and effective method which is recognized and used in much advertising, for example.

How do perceptions change? We know that they do change, that change actually is the normal state of living. Change sometimes occurs suddenly and dramatically, although more frequently it is slow and even painful. The fact that perceptions may change suddenly is attested by experiences which all of us have had of suddenly seeing things in a new light, a new perspective. It is the ah-hah experience of insight. It is also illustrated in the phenomenon of figure-ground reversal.

In the area of interpersonal relationships, the ability to put oneself in the place of another, and in effect to look at oneself through the eyes of the other, is a source of new perceptions of oneself. The loss of this ability seems to be a characteristic of the severely emotionally disturbed person.

While it is not clear just why and how perceptions, including perceptions of the self, change, there is evidence regarding the conditions which are conducive for such change. Combs and Snygg (1959) suggest that there must be a stimulus, from within or without, the impingement of a new feeling or experience, a disturbance or change in the internal or external environment. Thus experiences with which an individual is confronted present him with inconsistencies or discrepancies or raise questions about his way of looking at himself and his environment. These authors list three factors which are important in determining the likelihood of change in the perceived self:

1. 'The place of the new concept in the individual's present self-organization' (p. 63). Central concepts of the self will be more resistant to change than more peripheral ones.
2. 'The relation of the new concept to the person's basic need . . . Other things being equal, change in the self is most likely to occur in situations which do not force the individual to self-defense' (pp. 63–4).
3. 'The clarity of the experience of the new perception . . . The more vivid such experience, the more likely is it to result in changes in self-perception' (p. 64).

There is resistance to change, however, due to the need to maintain the self as well as to enhance it. This leads to a clinging to the current self and its perceptions. Threat further restricts perception, rigidifies it, prevents the open acceptance of new perceptions, or leads to altering or denying them. Under threat, the organism reacts to defend its organization, its present perceptions. As Combs and Snygg (1959) note, 'To resolve a threatening situation requires exactly the opposite of suppression and tunnel vision. It requires freedom to examine and to differentiate any and all aspects of the field in a search for a more adequate self' (p. 188).

It is apparent that the absence of threat is the prime condition for change, whether in psychotherapy or in other interpersonal relations. Where the client feels threatened, whether by the counselor, or others in his environment, or by nonpersonal aspects of the environment, he will show behavior which is commonly designated as lack of motivation. Actually he is strongly motivated, motivated to resist change, to defend what he is and has against possible loss. He prefers the security of the present, the known, for the insecurity of the unknown future.

Now it is also true that behavior does change under threat. We have already indicated that the individual retreats, withdraws, becomes defensive or aggressive. He changes from open, positive self-enhancing behavior to restricted, negative self-preservative behavior. And if the threat or actual force is great enough — or perceived as great enough — the individual will comply with the demands made upon him, and will submit and conform. This is, of course, a change in behavior. But it is not the kind of change in which we are interested. We are concerned here with positive change, self-enhancing change, with voluntary rather than enforced change, with change which will be lasting and persist when force, or the threat of force, is no longer present.

So we come to a conclusion which is not new, not startling, and not a panacea. We deal with the so-called unmotivated client exactly as we do with any other client. He is not different from any other client, or from ourselves. He has the same basic need, the need for the maintenance and enhancement of himself. This is his basic motivation, a strong motivation. He manifests it in the only way he can in the situation as he perceives it. In a situation which by its nature has threatening aspects, he defends his concept of himself and his perceptions of the environment. The counselor can help him to change his perceptions, and thus his behavior, only by understanding him and providing an atmosphere free of threat.

However, even though the counselor is not threatening, success is not possible with every client. The responsibility of the counselor cannot go beyond the providing of the opportunity for the client to accept and use the counseling relationship. If the client cannot accept it, it cannot be forced upon him. If he chooses not to accept it, that is his right. The possibility of future acceptance will be greater if pressure, coercion and threat are not used in the false belief that such devices are motivating.

Summary

We have compared various formulations of unitary motivation. These showed a substantial commonality in spite of different designations. The assumption of such a single basic integrative motive or goal is more useful in theory and practice than traditional multiplicities, dualities, or hierarchies of drives or needs. The understanding of the direction and goals of behavior is possible only when we recognize that behavior is determined by the one basic need for the preservation and enhancement of the self or the self-concept. The goal is always conceived in terms of the individual's perception of himself and his environment. The counselor, then, is one who is skilled in understanding human beings and their perceptions and who provides the conditions under which change in perceptions, and then self-initiated behavior change, can occur.

References

Angyal, A. (1941) *Foundations for a science of personality*. New York: Commonwealth Fund.

Ansbacher, H. L., and Ansbacher, R. R. (Eds.) (1956). *The Individual Psychology of Alfred Adler*. New York: Basic Books.

Bibring, E. (1958) The development and problems of the theory of instincts. In C. L. Stacy and M. F. DeMartino (Eds.), *Understanding human motivation*. Cleveland, Ohio: Howard Allen. Pp. 474–98.

Combs, A. W., and Snygg, D. (1959) *Individual behavior.* Rev. ed. New York: Harper and Row.

Dickey, M. (1959) Behavioral research in rehabilitation: a report on the Cleveland Symposium, Highland View Hospital, November 4–6, 1959. Cleveland, Ohio: Highland View Hospital. Mimeographed.

Dollard, J., Doob, L. W., Miller, N. E., Mowrer, O. H., and Sears, R. R. (1939) *Frustration and aggression*. New Haven: Yale University Press.

English, H. B., and English, A. C. (1958) *Comprehensive dictionary of psychological and psychoanalytic terms*. New York: Longmans, Green.

Golding, W. (1959) *Lord of the flies*. New York: Capricorn Books.

Goldstein, K. (1939) *The organism*. New York: World Book.

Hilgard, E. R. (1962) *Introduction to psychology.* 3rd ed. New York: Harcourt, Brace and World.

Jones, M. R. (Ed.) (1958) *Nebraska symposium on motivation, 1958*. Lincoln, Nebr.: University of Nebraska Press.

Jones, M. R. (Ed.) (1962) *Nebraska symposium on motivation, 1962*. Lincoln,

Nebr.: University of Nebraska Press.

Kelly, G. A. (1958) Man's construction of his alternatives. In G. Lindzey (Ed.), *The assessment of human motives*. New York: Rinehart. Pp. 33–64.

Kelly, G. A. (1962) Europe's matrix of decision. In M. R. Jones (Ed.), *Nebraska symposium on motivation, 1962*. Lincoln, Nebr.: Univer. Nebraska Press. Pp. 83–123.

Lecky, P. (1945). *Self-consistency: a theory of personality*. New York: Island Press.

Littman, R. A. (1958) Motives, history and causes. In M. R. Jones (Ed.), *Nebraska Symposium on Motivation, 1958*. Lincoln, Nebr.: Univer. Nebraska Press. Pp. 114–68.

Maslow, A. H. (1949) Our maligned human nature. *Journal of Psychology, 28*, pp. 273–8.

Maslow, A. H. (1954) *Motivation and personality*. New York: Harper & Row.

Maslow, A. H. (1955) Deficiency motivation and growth motivation. In M. R. Jones (Ed.), *Nebraska symposium on motivation, 1955*. Lincoln, Nebr.: Univer. Nebraska Press. Pp. 1–30.

Montagu, A. (1962) *The humanization of man*. Cleveland, Ohio: World Publishing.

Patterson, C. H. (1962) *Counseling and guidance in schools: a first course*. New York: Harper and Row.

Postman, L. (1956) Is the concept of motivation necessary? Review of M. R. Jones (Ed.), Nebraska symposium on motivation, 1955. *Contemporary Psychology, 1*, pp. 229–30.

Rogers, C. R. (1951) *Client-centered therapy*. Boston: Houghton Mifflin.

Rogers, C. R. (1959) A theory of therapy, personality, and interpersonal relationships, as developed in the client-centered framework. In S. Koch (Ed.), *Psychology: a study of a science*. Vol. 3. New York: McGraw-Hill.

Rogers, C. R. (1961) *On becoming a person*. Boston: Houghton Mifflin.

Skinner, B. F. (1948) *Walden two*. New York: Macmillan.

White, R. W. (1959) Motivation reconsidered: the concept of competence. *Psychological Review, 66*, pp. 287–333.

Woodworth, R. S. (1958) *Dynamics of behavior*. New York: Holt.

DIVERGENCE AND CONVERGENCE IN COUNSELING AND PSYCHOTHERAPY

3

A survey of the major theories or approaches to psychotherapy (Patterson, 1966) reveals considerable diversity. Various points of view appear to differ widely in philosophy and concepts, in goals or objectives, and in methods or techniques. Not only do the points of view differ as presented by their principal proponents, but there are often schools within schools. And in addition there are differences among individual practitioners. Every psychotherapist considers himself different or unique in some respects.

This diversity, and even disagreement, has led some observers to despair about the state of psychotherapy. Ungersma (1961, p. 55) writes as follows:

> The present situation in psychotherapy is not unlike that of a man who mounted his horse and rode off in all directions. The theoretical orientation of therapists is based upon widely divergent hypotheses, theories and ideologies . . . Individual practitioners of any art are expected to vary, but some well-organized schools of therapy also seem to be working at cross-purposes with other equally well-organized schools. Nevertheless, all schools, given favorable conditions, achieve favorable results: the patient or client gets relief and is often enough cured of his difficulties. This equal success of apparently widely different approaches constitutes a problem requiring some explanation.

Rogers (1961), who admits to having had hopes that therapists would be able to come to agreement on what constitutes psychotherapy, has recently expressed his disillusionment. Whereas he had felt that 'we were all talking about the same experiences', he now feels that 'we differ at the most basic levels of our personal experience'. He concludes that 'the field of psychotherapy is in a mess', although he also feels that the present confusion is a healthy climate for new ideas, theories, methods, and concepts.

According to an old adage, 'Where there are many medicines the illness is incurable'. Does this divergence in various points of view, and attempt to sift out

Published here with permission of the Association for the Advancement of Psychotherapy. First published in *American Journal of Psychotherapy*, 1967, XXI, pp. 4–17.

convergences to arrive at an integrated approach to psychotherapy, apply to the field of psychotherapy? Is there no agreement, no commonality, among the diverse approaches, no way of integrating them into a unified approach? This paper will review the basic divergences in various points of view, and attempt to sift out convergences to arrive at an integrated approach to psychotherapy.

Divergences

While there are numerous specific differences among theories of psychotherapy relating to the nature of man, these may be reduced to a single basic difference in what Allport (1965) refers to as the image of the nature of man. Allport describes three models. The first is that of man as a reactive being. Here man is viewed as a biologic organism reacting to stimuli from his environment. He is determined by his experiences, by his past learning or conditioning and by potential reconditioning. The concepts representing this point of view include the following: reaction, reinforcement, reflex, respondent, reintegration, reconditioning. This is the image of man assumed by the behavior theorist and by psychotherapists who take a learning or behavior theory approach to psychotherapy.

Allport's second image of the nature of man sees man as a reactive being in depth. Rather than man being conceived as a being reacting to his environment, he is seen as reacting to his innate drives, motives, and needs, and is influenced by their past frustrations and satisfactions. The concept includes repression, regression, resistance, abreaction, reaction formation, and recall and recovery of the past. This is the view of depth psychology, including psychoanalysis.

These two images are similar in basic respects. Both see man as reacting to forces or stimuli, in the one case from within, in the other from without. In the one case man is a victim of his environment, in the other of his innate needs and drives. They may thus be combined to constitute a single model of man as a reactive being.

In contrast to this image is a second (Allport's third) model. Allport designates this as man as a being in the process of becoming. This model sees man as personal, conscious, future oriented. It includes such concepts as tentativeness and commitment. This is the model of existentialism.

These two models appear to underlie differing approaches to psychotherapy, with behavior therapy, learning theory approaches, and psychoanalysis in one group, and client-centered and existential approaches in the other.

In addition to differences in philosophy, the therapy process is viewed differently by the various approaches. The writer (1966), reviewing various theories, adopted a continuum varying from highly rational approaches at one end to strongly affective approaches at the other end. In rational approaches, the process tends to be planned, objective and impersonal. In the affective approach it is emphasized as being warm, personal, and spontaneous. One emphasizes reason and problem solving, the other affect and experiencing. It appears that there may be two divergent trends in psychotherapy, one toward a more cognitive approach, and another toward a more affective approach, so that there may be a bimodal distribution, or a dichotomy in the making.

Another classification of approaches in terms of process is the insight-action dichotomy of London (1964). London includes under the insight therapies client-centered therapy and existential analysis, as well as the various schools of psychoanalysis. Although there are differences among the insight approaches, London sees these as insignificant in comparison to their commonalities. Action therapies, or behavior therapies, unlike insight therapies, are not concerned with verbalizations, or talk, but with behavior, actions, or symptoms. Ullmann and Krasner (1965) propose essentially the same dichotomy in their distinction between evocative or expressive therapies and behavior therapy, although they recognize that there are overlappings in techniques.

If one examines the goals of different approaches, one finds an amazing range and variety. Some therapists speak of personality reorganization, others of curing a disease or illness, others of adjustment to the environment, society, or the culture. Still others are concerned with the development of independence, responsibility, or assisting the client to use his potentialities or to actualize himself. Still others are concerned with helping the client feel better, or with removing disturbing symptoms.

Recent research provides evidence of differences among psychotherapists. Sundland and Barker (1962) studied differences in orientation in a group of 139 psychotherapists who were members of the American Psychological Association, using a Therapist Orientation Questionnaire containing 16 subscales. These scales included, among others, Frequency of Activity, Type of Activity, Emotional Tenor of the Relationship, Spontaneity, Planning, Conceptualization of the Relationship, Goals of Therapy, Theory of Personal Growth, Theory of Neurosis, Theory of Motivation, and Criteria for Success. The therapists distributed themselves over the range of scores from 'strongly agree' to 'strongly disagree' on most of the scales. When the therapists were classified into three groups — Freudians, Sullivanians, and Rogerians — the three groups differed significantly on nine of the 16 scales, with the Sullivanians being in the middle position in eight of these comparisons. The Freudian group, compared to the Rogerian group, believed that the therapist should be more impersonal, plan his therapy, have definite goals, inhibit his spontaneity, use interpretation, conceptualize the case, and recognize the importance of unconscious motivation. Only one difference was found between therapists grouped by levels of experience.

A factor analysis of the 16 scales yielded six factors. A general factor cut across most of the scales, providing a major single continuum upon which therapists vary. One end is labeled 'analytic' (not simply 'psychoanalytic') and the other is designated as 'experiential' by Sundland and Barker. The 'analytic' therapist emphasizes conceptualizing, planning therapy, unconscious processes, and restriction of spontaneity. The 'experiential' therapist emphasizes nonverbal, nonrationalized experiencing, the personality of the therapist, and therapist spontaneity. More therapists tended toward the 'analytic' approach than toward the 'experiencing' approach.

Wallach and Strupp (1964) obtained similar results from factor analysis of ratings of two groups of therapists on a scale of Usual Therapeutic Practices. The major factor was called the maintenance of personal distance. Four groupings of therapists — Orthodox Freudians, Psychoanalytic General, Sullivanian and Client-centered — were compared, with the first group being highest in the personal distance factor, the second group next highest, and the remaining two about the same but lower than the other two.

McNair and Lorr (1964) studied the reported techniques of 192 male and 73 female psychotherapists (67 psychiatrists, 103 psychologists, and 95 social workers) in 44 Veterans Administration Mental Hygiene Clinics, using an instrument developed on the basis of the Sundland and Barker Therapist Orientation Scale. They hypothesized three dimensions to be measured by the AID scales: (A) psychoanalytically oriented techniques, (I) impersonal versus personal approaches to the patient, and (D) directive, active therapeutic methods. All three dimensions emerged in the factor analysis of the 49 scales included in the analysis. High scores on the A factor represent traditional psychoanalytic techniques. High scores on the I factor represent a detached, objective, impersonal approach, while low scores represent emphasis on therapist personality and the therapist-patient relationship. High scores on the D factor indicate therapist setting of goals and planning of treatment, leading of the interview, and acceptance of social adjustment as a major goal. Low scores indicate therapist lack of direction of the interview and belief in patient determination of therapy goals. While the three factors are intercorrelated, McNair and Lorr consider them independent.

The Sundland and Barker study provides support for the rational-affective continuum or dichotomy. The McNair and Lorr study also supports this ordering or classifying of approaches or techniques. These studies would not support London's classification of client-centered and existential approaches with psychoanalysis in a homogeneous insight therapy group. However, none of these studies included behavior therapists, and the results would, no doubt, have been different if they had. With the advent of behavior therapy, a new dimension has been added to psychotherapy, and it is the difference between this approach and all other approaches which now seems to present the major problem for the future.

It is here that the greatest differences in philosophy, methods, and goals appear. The behavior therapists are apparently interested in specific, immediate, concrete results. To obtain them, the therapist takes responsibility for the process, and controls and manipulates the situation. He may disavow any ethical implications of his control by contending that he is a technician in the service of the client, who determines what the goals of the process should be.

The experiential therapist is concerned about more general, long-range goals. He gives the client the responsibility for the direction and the pace of the counseling process. While he may be very active, his activity is not the directing, manipulative activity of the behavior therapist, but the activity of empathizing with and understanding the client and communicating that understanding. Paradoxically, however, he may not accept the specific goals of the client, but may impose his own goals of self-understanding, self-realization, or self-actualization on the client. But implicit, if not explicit, in this goal is greater freedom for the client in his specific behavior. By choosing the goal of maximum future freedom for the client, a goal which is presumably that of our society, he resolves the value issue of imposing his own specific goals on the client.

Convergences

With all the differences among approaches, are there no commonalities or similarities among all, or even some, of the major systems? The search for common elements is stimulated by the observed fact that all approaches report successes.

It would seem to be difficult to find a common philosophy, or even a single common concept, among the many points of view which exist. There would seem to be little, if anything, in common between a concept of man as determined by his environment, or by his internal needs and drives, on the one hand, and the concept of man as a person capable of making choices and free to do so on the other hand, or between the concept of man as essentially an organism to be manipulated by rewards and punishments, on the one hand, and on the other as having the potential for growth and development in the process of self-actualization. There are, however, some agreements. All approaches recognize that neurosis, disturbance, maladjustment, conflict, the presence of an unsolved problem, and so on, are (a) unpleasant and painful for the client, and (b) such a state of affairs is undesirable and warrants attempts to change it. Secondly, all approaches regard man as capable of changing, or at least of being changed. He is not hopelessly predetermined, but at any stage may still be pliable.

A third common element is the recognition of the influence of the future, or of anticipations, hopes, or expectations related to the future, on present behavior. This is an element that appears to tie together approaches as different as operant conditioning and existentialism. In other words, the recognition that behavior is not entirely 'caused' by the past, but is also influenced by future consequences, or expectation of consequences, seems to be accepted by most points of view. Lindsley (1963) states it as follows, referring to operant conditioning: 'The discovery that such [voluntary] behavior is subject to control by its consequences makes it unnecessary to explain behavior in terms of hypothetical antecedents'. May (1958), presenting the existentialist position, writes that 'The future, in contrast to the present or past, is the dominant mode for human beings'.

Therapists of different persuasions have common characteristics. All therapists expect their clients to change. This expectation may vary in its degree, in some instances approaching a highly optimistic or even enthusiastic expectation, while in others it may be minimal. But it is always present. There is always an attitude of hope and expectation of change. Not only do counselors or therapists accept the possibility and desirability of client change, but they are genuinely and strongly interested in being the agent of change in their clients. If they were not, they would not be engaged in counseling or psychotherapy.

An element which appears to be common to the process in all approaches is given various designations. In the client-centered approach it is referred to as therapist genuineness or self-congruence. Others refer to it as sincerity, honesty, or openness. The existentialists use the term 'authenticity'. Some approaches do not refer specifically to this characteristic, but it is apparent in their discussions, and particularly in their protocols, that this element is present.

One final characteristic unites therapists of widely differing approaches — the fact that each therapist believes in, or has confidence in, the theory and method which he uses. Again, if he did not feel it was the best method or approach, he would not use it, but would adopt a different one.

The most widely known studies of commonalities of the therapy process are those of Fiedler (1950a, 1950b, 1951). Fiedler found that therapists from different schools agreed upon the nature of the ideal therapeutic relationship, and that factor analysis yielded one common factor of goodness of therapeutic relationships. But how are these results to be interpreted in view of the studies referred to above which found important differences? The solution seems to lie in the nature of the instruments used in the studies. Sundland and Barker developed their instrument by eliminating items upon which therapists agreed. Fiedler, on the other hand, appears to have assembled a group of items on which therapists agree. Sundland and Barker point out that items which they discarded because they did not result in a distribution of responses were similar to items in Fiedler's studies. These items were concerned with empathy. There appears to be evidence, therefore, that therapists agree upon the importance of empathy and understanding. The behavior therapists seem to deny or minimize the presence and importance of empathy. Nevertheless, it would appear that a minimum of empathic understanding is necessary for the continuation of the interaction of therapist and the client, as well as being a factor in effecting change. It appears that a relationship characterized at least to some extent by interest, acceptance, and understanding is basic to influencing others therapeutically. Other factors may direct change along the lines the therapist desires, but the relationship makes possible any change.

Most, if not all, approaches therefore seem to include a relationship which on the part of the counselor or therapist is characterized by a belief in the possibility of client change, an expectation that the client will change, interest in and concern for the client, including a desire to help, influence, or change him, sincerity and honesty in the process, and confidence in the approach which is used to achieve client change.

It is necessary to add one other point, namely, that the crucial aspect of the therapist's impact or contribution is not his actual personality or behavior, nor even his intent, in the relationship. It is the client's perception of the therapist which determines the therapist's characteristics and contribution. Thus the client's characteristics, his attitudes and set, are important aspects of the relationship.

There are apparent some common aspects of individuals who come to therapists for help. In the first place, they 'hurt' — they are suffering, or are unhappy, because of conflicts, symptoms, unfulfilled desires or aspirations, feeling of failure or inadequacy, or lack of meaning in their lives. They thus are motivated to change.

Second, clients also believe that change is possible, and expect to change, to be helped. Frank (1961, Rosenthal & Frank, 1956) has emphasized the universality of this factor in clients.

Third, the client must be active in, or participate in, the process. He is not a passive recipient, as is the physically ill patient being treated by a physician. All learning (behavior change) appears to require activity (whether motor, verbal, or thinking) on the part of the learner. This kind of behavior in psychotherapy includes self-analysis or self-exploration. Truax and Carkhuff (1965) refer to it also as intrapersonal exploration or self-disclosure. Jourard (1964) and Mowrer (1964) also speak of self-disclosure. It appears that the client as well as the therapist must be genuine, open, and honest in the process. Thus, all approaches appear to deal with clients who are in need of help, recognize this need, believe they can change, believe that the counselor can help them change, and engage in some activity in the attempt to change.

It may be more difficult to find commonalities among goals than among concepts and techniques. The differences may not be as great as they at first appear, however. The behavior therapists, though they emphasize the removal of symptoms as an objective goal, also appear to recognize a broader goal. They seem to expect the client to feel better, to function better in life and its various aspects, to achieve at a higher level — in short to live up to his potential. Salter (1961, p. 24), for example, speaks of freeing the individual by 'unbraking' him. There is a similarity here to the concept of self-actualization, which is accepted in one or another form, in varying terminology, by most other approaches. The conditioning therapists also appear to see increasing freedom and expressiveness as desirable results of therapy. This is similar to the spontaneity and openness to experience of Rogers. There also seems to be general acceptance of the desirability of responsibility and independence as outcomes of counseling or psychotherapy.

There thus appears to be a good deal in common among the various and diverse approaches to counseling or psychotherapy. To some extent the various theories or points of view represent different ways of describing or explaining the same phenomena. Differences are in part related to the use of different emphases, to different perceptions of the same events, to differences in comprehensiveness of formulation. To some extent differences may appear greater than those that actually exist. This may be due in part to the use of different terminology to refer to the same or similar concepts. Differences may also be exaggerated by the propensity to emphasize differences rather than similarities.

The question to which we now turn is whether it is possible to develop a tentative integration of the common aspects which appear to exist, and to propose, in very general form, an approach which will include the necessary and sufficient conditions for psychotherapy.

An attempt at integration

Perhaps the greatest divergence is that between the behavior therapies on the one hand, and the experiential or relationship approaches on the other. In spite of the similarities or agreements noted above, it appears that these points of view are perceived by their adherents and by others as inconsistent and contradictory. The behavior therapies appear to be objective, impersonal, technique oriented, mechanical. The relationship approaches may be seen as subjective, personal, and not concerned with technique. Is it possible to reconcile these apparently inconsistent approaches? Rogers (1961, p. 85), recognizing these divergent trends, not only in psychotherapy but in psychology, states that they 'seem irreconcilable because we have not yet developed the larger frame of reference that would contain them both'.

A possible reconciliation is suggested. It derives from a consideration of the different models of man delineated by Allport. Allport (1965) writes: 'The trouble with our current theories of learning is not so much that they are wrong, but that they are partial'. It may be said, then, that the trouble with the behavior therapy approach is not that it is wrong, but that it is incomplete as a description or theory of the nature of man and of his behavior and its modification. There can be no question about the existence of conditioning, about man as a reactive being, who can be conditioned and reconditioned. But man is more than this; he is also a being in the process of becoming. He is not merely a mechanism, or organism, who is controlled by objective stimuli in his environment. He is also a being who lives, or exists, who thinks and feels and who develops relationships with other beings.

The essential nature or characteristic of psychotherapy is that it is a relationship. It is a complex relationship, with various aspects. It is not simply a cognitive, intellectually impersonal relationship, but an effective, experiential, highly personal relationship. It is not necessarily irrational, but it has nonrational aspects. The behavior therapists appear to be unconcerned about or to minimize the relationship. However, it appears that the relationship is of greater significance in their methods than they admit. It should be apparent that the characteristics of the therapist and of the client discussed above are manifested in, or manifest themselves in, a relationship.

The therapy relationship always involves, or includes, conditioning aspects. The accepting, understanding, nonthreatening atmosphere offers the opportunity for the extinction of anxiety, or for desensitization of threatening stimuli. In this relationship, where external threat is minimized, anxiety-arousing ideas and words, images, and feelings are free to appear. Moreover, they appear in a sequence in the kind of hierarchy which Wolpe establishes, that is, from least anxiety arousing to more anxiety arousing. Thus, in any nonthreatening therapy relationship, desensitization occurs naturally in the manner achieved artificially by Wolpe (1958). The relationship, by minimizing externally induced anxiety, makes it possible for the client to experience and bring out his internally induced anxieties, or anxiety-arousing experiences, at the time and rate at which he can face and handle them in the accepting relationship.

In addition, operant conditioning serves to reinforce the production of verbalizations which the therapist believes are therapeutic, or necessary for therapy to occur. The therapist rewards these verbalizations by his interest and attention, or by explicit praise and approval. At the beginning of therapy, negative elements may be rewarded — for example, the expression of problems, conflicts, fears, and anxieties, negative self-references, and so forth. As therapy progresses, the therapist may reinforce positive elements — for example, problem-solving efforts, positive thoughts, attitudes and feelings, and positive self-references. The therapist expects progress of this kind, and is sensitive to its expression in the client.

Conditioning principles have thus contributed to an understanding of the nature of the therapeutic process and the therapy relationship. But the conditioning which occurs is not the mechanical conditioning of a rat in a Skinner box. The conditioning is an aspect of, takes place in, and is influenced by the relationship. There is considerable evidence that the rate and extent of conditioning is influenced by the personality and attitudes of the experimenter and his relationship to the subject (Ullmann & Krasner, 1965). This relationship involves characteristics of the client — his interest, motivations, thoughts, attitudes, perceptions, and expectations — as well as those of the counselor.

It also is affected by the total situation or setting in which the relationship occurs — what are called the demand characteristics in a research experiment. As Ullman and Krasner (1965, p. 43) note, 'both the subject's and the examiner's expectancies, sets, and so forth, have major effect on the individual's response to the situation', and 'the best results are obtained when the patient and the therapist form a good interpersonal relationship'. The relationship, therefore, cannot be ignored even in behavior therapy. The most powerful influencers of behavior, or, in conditioning terms, reinforcers, are the respect, interest, concern, and attention of the therapist. The demonstration by research of the effects of these generalized reinforcers supports the importance of the relationship in counseling or psychotherapy.

A further point emphasizes the importance of the relationship. Many if not most of the problems or difficulties of clients involve interpersonal relationships. It is being increasingly recognized that good interpersonal relationships are characterized by honesty, openness, sincerity, spontaneity. Psychotherapy is an interpersonal relationship having these characteristics. It is therefore a place where the client can learn good interpersonal relationships. In fact, therapy would be limited if it tried to influence the client's interpersonal relationships by providing a different kind of relationship. If it attempted to influence interpersonal relationships by avoiding establishing a therapeutic relationship, psychotherapy would seem to be inefficient. Teaching, or conditioning individual behavior in a mechanical manner, would not appear to offer much hope of generalization to personal relationships outside of therapy.

There is thus no basic or necessary contradiction between behavior therapy and relationship therapy. One emphasizes shaping or changing specific aspects of behavior by specific rewards or reinforcers. The other emphasizes more general behavior changes (including attitudes and feelings), using generalized reinforcers. Both utilize the principles of learning, one rather narrowly, emphasizing conditioning, the other more broadly, emphasizing what might be called a social learning approach (Murray, 1963). The behavior therapists are, as Ullmann and Krasner (1965, p. 37) point out, systematic in their application of specific learning concepts. But it might also be said that relationship therapists are also systematic in the application of generalized reinforcers. The conditioning or behavior therapy approach is supported by research evidence, including laboratory or experimental research. The relationship approach is also supported by research, including some of the research on conditioning. It is interesting, and significant, that both groups are coming to the same conclusions, one from laboratory work in conditioning, the other from experience and research in counseling or psychotherapy. It is important, however, that behavior therapists come to recognize the complexity and the social or relationship aspects of the learning process, and also that relationship therapists be aware of the conditioning that is an aspect of psychotherapy. The therapist's behavior is most effective when it is sincere and spontaneous, not when it is a contrived technique.

Two questions

The conclusion that the essence of psychotherapy consists of a genuine human relationship characterized by interest, concern, empathic understanding, and genuineness on the part of the therapist leads to two questions:

1. What is there unique about this relationship? How does it differ from all good human relationships? If the answer is, as should be obvious, that there is nothing unique or different, then what is there special about the practice of counseling or psychotherapy? Fiedler (1950) concluded from his studies that 'a good therapeutic relationship is very much like any good interpersonal relationship'.

This view may be opposed by those who feel that it deprives therapists of unique powers, who fear that 'it leaves the practitioner without a specialty' (Mowrer,1964, p. 235). But it should not be surprising that the characteristics of psychotherapy should be the characteristics of good human relationships. Nor does it follow that, if they are not limited to psychotherapy, they are not relevant or specific. The essence of emotional disturbances is disturbed human relationships. The client's relationships with others have become ruptured or have been placed on an insecure, false, or untenable basis. He needs to re-establish good relationships with others.

Therapy offers the opportunity for learning how to relate to others in a different, more effective way. It utilizes or embodies the principles of good human relationships, which, although they appear to be simple, are not widely practiced outside of therapy. While there is merit in Schofield's (1964) analysis of psychotherapy as the purchase of friendship, therapy is, however, more than the offering of friendship, at least in the usual sense of the word. While viewing psychotherapy as something dark and mysterious classifies the therapist with magicians and witch doctors, viewing it as bought friendship places him in the same category as taxi-dancers, gigolos, and call girls.

2. The characteristics of psychotherapy which have been developed above have frequently been considered nonspecific elements. It is often assumed that they are not related to the specific nature of the disturbance present in clients, and that, while they may be considered as necessary conditions, they are not sufficient. Further, such characteristics as attention, interest, concern, trust, belief, faith, expectation are part of what is designated as the placebo effect in the treatment of physical diseases. While it is not usual to insist that these effects be eliminated from counseling or psychotherapy, it is generally accepted that these factors, as nonspecific, are not sufficient and that other methods or techniques must be included to deal with the specific aspects of the disturbance. It is generally argued that any method or technique must produce greater effects than those obtained by placebo elements in order to be considered useful.

The placebo effect is a psychologic effect. Where the interest or concern is with determining the physical or physiologic effect of a drug or medication, on a known physical disease or disturbance, it is reasonable to consider this effect as extraneous and nonspecific. But this reasoning may not be applicable in psychotherapy. Here, the disorder or disturbance is psychologic. Is it not logical that the specific treatment for a psychologic condition should be psychologic? Is it not reasonable to suggest that the specific treatment for disturbed human relationships is the providing of a good relationship? Is the placebo effect, then, as Rosenthal and Frank (1956) claim, 'a nonspecific form of psychotherapy?'

It is strange that, with all the evidence of the power of the placebo effect, it has not been recognized as the most effective approach to the treatment of psychologic problems. As Krasner and Ullmann (1965, p. 230) put it, 'Whereas the problem had previously been conceptualized in terms of eliminating the "placebo effects", it would seem reasonable to maximize placebo effects in the treatment situation to increase the likelihood of client change'.

Necessary and sufficient conditions for psychotherapy

Are there any necessary and sufficient conditions of psychotherapy, and if there are, what are they? Ellis (1959), criticizing the necessary and sufficient conditions proposed by Rogers (1957), concludes that there are no necessary conditions but there are a number of sufficient conditions. With the wide variety of approaches and methods in psychotherapy, all of them claiming success with some apparent justification, this would appear to be a reasonable position to take.

But if there is a common element in all methods and approaches, it would also be reasonable to conclude that this would be the necessary and sufficient condition of psychotherapy. We have attempted to show that this common element is the relationship between the client and the therapist. This relationship is a complex one, and it is possible that we do not understand it completely and are thus not able to specify all its aspects. But at least some of its aspects are known, and include those enumerated above. They have been demonstrated to be sufficient conditions for therapeutic personality change (Truax, 1963; Truax & Carkhuff, 1965a; Truax & Carkhuff, 1965b). In addition to the research on psychotherapy, there is considerable evidence of the positive influences these conditions have on behavior when they are incorporated into the programs of institutions ranging from industry to schools to mental hospitals. The effects of the use of environmental treatment in the form of the therapeutic milieu in mental hospitals seem to be evident, and to come essentially from the change in human relationships between staff and patients.

If these conditions are necessary as well as sufficient, then it must be shown that therapeutic personality change not only occurs when they are present, but that it does not occur when they are absent. It can, of course, be demonstrated that changes in behavior can be obtained when they are not present, as in simple conditioning, which may not involve the presence of another person, or in instances of coercion by the use of threat or physical force, including punishment. But it can be questioned whether such changes are therapeutic.

There is some evidence from research on psychotherapy that, in the absence of these conditions in psychotherapy, positive change does not occur. Truax (1963) found that while the (schizophrenic) patients of therapists evidencing high conditions of accurate empathy, unconditional positive regard, and self-congruence improved, patients of therapists evidencing low levels of these conditions showed negative personality change. Similar results have been found with clients in college counseling centers, according to Truax. There also appears to be considerable evidence that the absence of these conditions in other situations leads to psychologic disturbance. This evidence includes studies on the influence of schizophrenogenic mothers, the effects of the double bind, the effects of an institutional environment lacking in human attention on infants and children, the results of sensory isolation, and the effects of imprisonment.

There seems to be evidence that the elements of the therapeutic relationship described in this paper are common to all approaches to psychotherapy, and that, where they are absent, positive change or development does not occur. There thus appears to be a basis for considering them the necessary and sufficient conditions for psychotherapeutic change.

Summary

An examination of various schools or approaches to psychotherapy indicates differences in philosophy, in the psychotherapy process, and in goals which appear to be irreconcilable. Nevertheless, there are some basic commonalities. These commonalities contribute to a relationship between therapist and client which is shared, to some extent at least, by all therapists or schools. Perhaps not surprisingly, the characteristics of this relationship are the characteristics of all good human relationships. But they also involve what is commonly called the placebo effect. It is concluded that this relationship is the specific treatment for psychologic disturbances, and includes the necessary and sufficient conditions for psychotherapy.

References

Allport, G. W. (1965) Psychological Models for Guidance. In *Guidance: An Examination*, Mosher, R. L., Carle, R. F., and Kehas, C. D. (Eds.) New York: Harcourt, Brace and World. Pp. 13–23.

Ellis, A. (1959) Requisite Conditions for Basic Personality Change. *Journal of Consulting Psychology*, 23, pp. 538.

Fiedler, F. (1950a) The Concept of An Ideal Therapeutic Relationship. *Journal of Consulting Psychology*, 14, pp. 235.

Fiedler, F. (1950b) A Comparison of Therapeutic Relationships In Psychoanalytic, Non-directive and Adlerian Therapy. *Journal of Consulting Psychology*, 14, pp. 436.

Fiedler, F. (1951) Factor Analyses of Psychoanalytic, Non-directive, and Adlerian Relationships. *Journal of Consulting Psychology*, 15, pp. 32 .

Frank, J. D. (1961) *Persuasion and Healing*. Baltimore: Johns Hopkins Press.

Jourard, S. M. (1964) *The Transparent Self*. Princeton, N. J.: Van Nostrand.

Krasner, L., and Ullmann, L. P., Eds. (1965) *Research in Behavior Modification.* New York: Holt, Rinehart & Winston.

Lindsley, O. (1963) Free Operant Conditioning and Psychotherapy. In *Current Psychiatric Therapies*, Masserman, J. and Moreno, J. J., Eds. New York: Grune and Stratton.

London, P. (1964)*The Modes and Morals of Psychotherapy*. New York:Holt, Rinehart and Winston.

May, R. (1958) Contributions of Existential Psychotherapy. In *Existence*. May, R. Angel, E. and Ellenberger, H. F., Eds. New York: Basic Books.

McNair, D. M. and Lorr, M. (1964) An Analysis of Professed Psychotherapeutic Techniques. *Journal of Consulting Psychology*, 28, pp. 265.

Mowrer, O. H. (1964) *The New Group Therapy*. Van Nostrand, Princeton, N. J.

Murray, E. J. (1963) Learning Theory and Psychotherapy: Biotropic Versus Sociotropic Approaches. *Journal of Counseling Psychology*, 10, pp. 251.

Patterson, C. H. (1966) *Theories of Counseling and Psychotherapy*. New York: Harper and Row.

Rogers, C. R. (1957) The Necessary and Sufficient Conditions of Therapeutic Personality Change. *Journal of Consulting Psychology*, 21, pp. 95.

Rogers, C. R. (1961) Divergent Trends. In *Existential Psychology*, May, R., Ed. New York: Random House.

Rosenthal, D., and Frank, J. D. (1956) Psychotherapy and the Placebo Effect. *Psychological Bulletin*, 53, pp. 294.

Salter, A. *Conditioned Reflex Therapy*. (1961) New York: Capricorn Books.

Schofield, W. (1964) *Psychotherapy: The Purchase of Friendship*. Englewood Cliffs, N. J.: Prentice-Hall.

Sundland, D. M., and Barker, E. N. (1962) The Orientations of Psychotherapists. *Journal of Consulting Psychology*, 26, pp. 201.

Truax, C. B. (1963) Effective Ingredients in Psychotherapy: an Approach to Unraveling the Patient-Therapist Interaction. *Journal of Counseling Psychology*, 10, pp. 256.

Truax, C. B., and Carkhuff, R. R. (1965a) Client and Therapist Transparency in the Psychotherapeutic Encounter. *Journal of Counseling Psychology*, 12, pp. 3.

Truax, C. B., and Carkhuff, R. P. (1965b) The Old and the New: Theory and Research in Counseling and Psychotherapy. *Personnel & Guidance Journal*, 12: 3.

Ullmann, L. P., and Krasner, L., Eds. (1965) *Case Studies in Behavior Modification*. New York: Holt, Rinehart and Winston.

Ungersma, A. J. (1961) *Search for Meaning*. Westminster Press, Philadelphia.

Wallach, M. S., and Strupp, H. H. (1964) Dimensions of Psychotherapists' Activities. *Journal of Consulting Psychology*, 28, pp. 120.

Wolpe, J. (1958) *Psychotherapy by Reciprocal Inhibition*. Stanford, Calif.: Stanford University Press.

RELATIONSHIP THERAPY AND/OR BEHAVIOR THERAPY?

4

Leonard Krasner (1966) begins his review of Eysenck and Rachman's 'The Causes and Cures of Neurosis' with the statement: 'A quiet yet dramatic revolution is underway in the field of psychotherapy'. Krumboltz (1966c) entitled the proceedings of the Cubberly Conference, 'Revolution in Counseling'. A quiet revolution seems to me to be a contradiction in terms. The current development of behavior therapy, I would like to suggest, is neither quiet nor a revolution. The behavior therapists are far from being quiet. They are highly vociferous, dominating our professional journals with their cases and claims, exhibiting all the characteristics of a school or cult which they rail against. Rather than being a revolution, behavior therapy is a revival, a rediscovery of the story of Peter and the Rabbit first told by Mary Cover Jones (1924) under the tutelage of Watson. Once before, behavior modification was going to save the world, through the practice of conditioning in the home and the nursery school. It might be instructive to study the reasons for its eclipse. One reason might be that parents could not maintain the objectivity required for the proper dispensation of rewards and punishments, but I suspect there were others, such as the limitations and limited effectiveness of the method. It might be well to temper current enthusiasm for behavior therapy by a look at the history of all new therapies. Many, if not most, of them appear to be highly successful at first, when they are used by enthusiastic believers, but then are found to be less effective, or noneffective, after the enthusiasm wanes. Faith, or the so-called placebo effect, may have more to do with the success of the behaviorists than the techniques themselves. But more will be said about this later.

There is more than one way to change behavior. Two such ways are through various conditioning procedures and through the more usual methods of psychotherapy, including client-centered therapy. The question of which method to use in particular instances hinges upon a number of factors, such as the nature of the change desired, the conditioning of the client, patient, or subject whose behavior it is desired to change, and the implications of the change in terms of concomitant changes or side effects. Efficiency is only one, and sometimes a minor

First published in *Psychotherapy: Theory, Research, and Practice,* 1968, 5, pp. 226–33. Reprinted by permission of the publisher.

factor, though it would appear to be the major factor to many behavior therapists. But if change could be obtained either through conditioning or through client-centered therapy, even though the specific change desired might be more easily and quickly changed through conditioning, it might be preferable to seek the change through client-centered therapy. It might be argued, with some justification, I think, that change occurring by the latter method might have certain advantages, at least in terms of certain values held and long-term effects desired by many counselors and others. These effects might include more active participation of the client in the change, the assuming of more responsibility by the client for the change with increasing learning of taking responsibility for himself, a greater sense of satisfaction and of achievement when the change has occurred in this way, greater independence and confidence in himself, perhaps a greater generalization and persistence of change or even greater induced change in other behaviors or total functioning or well-being.

There is now considerable evidence that client-centered or relationship therapy is effective. But it is also claimed that behavior therapy is effective. I would agree that this is so, although I do not believe the behavior therapists have demonstrated this by any acceptable research as yet. So far, there are no adequately controlled studies. Reports of individual cases abound, but the behaviorists do not accept this as evidence for the effectiveness of any other approach. Nor would they accept from others the evidence Wolpe presents for his effectiveness, which consists of his own ratings or evaluations of selected cases.

But accepting the effectiveness of these two apparently quite different approaches to counseling or psychotherapy, there are two questions which must be considered. First, are the results achieved by both methods the same or similar? Do they have the same goals? Second, are these approaches really different? Do they have nothing in common? Are there really two (or more) basically different methods of changing behavior in a counseling or therapy situation, that is, the changing of significant behavior above the reflex level, where a change is voluntarily desired or sought by the subject or client?

The goals of counseling have been variously stated to include such things as self-acceptance, self-understanding, insight, self-actualization, self-enhancement, adjustment, maturity, independence, responsibility, the solving of a specific problem or the making of a specific choice, learning how to solve problems or to make decisions, and the elimination of or the performance of specified acts or behaviors. Some, usually those who state the more general goals at the beginning of the list, feel that the goals of counseling should be the same for all clients. Others, including the behaviorists (Krumboltz, 1966, a,b,d), believe that goals should be specific for each client. The behaviorists see general goals as vague, undefinable, unmeasurable, and neglecting individual differences. Some would see many of the specific goals of the behaviorists as trivial, partial, limited in significance or meaning, selected mainly because they are concrete and measurable, as by increasing frequency of performance of a specific act. The behaviorists may seem to be unconcerned about the meanings of their goals, or with any general criterion for determining the desirability of specific goals.

Can any agreement between these two points of view be achieved? I believe that it can be. As a matter of fact, the criteria actually used in studies of the effectiveness of client-centered therapy are specific. They include responses on the Rorschach, the MMPI, the TAT, the Wechsler Adult Intelligence Scale, Q-sorts, and other tests and rating scales, including ratings of clients or patients by others. The significance of test responses in terms of other behavior may, of course, be questioned. A question may also be raised about the relationship of these measures to the general goals expressed by client-centered therapists. There have been some attempts to utilize or develop instruments related to these goals, however, such as Q-sorts, the Personal Orientation Inventory (Shostrom, 1963) and the Problem Expression Scale (van der Veen and Tomlinson, 1962).

The behaviorists, on the other hand, do seem to be concerned with broader, more general goals or outcomes — greater freedom, more expressiveness, the more effective use of potential — or self-actualization. But because they cannot count or measure these goals, they do not talk about them.

There need be no inconsistency between specific, immediate goals and more general, long-term goals. In fact, there should be a relationship or consistency. Specific goals may be, or should be, steps toward, or aspects of, a more general goal. Those who advocate the more general goals might accept some of the specific goals of the behaviorists. The behaviorists might accept a general goal if it could be specified how its attainment could be demonstrated. Self-actualization may be considered as the goal or purpose of life, or, from another point of view, as the unitary motivation of all behavior (Goldstein, 1949; Patterson, 1964).

There is no reason why self-actualization cannot be defined, its characteristics or manifestations described, and instruments developed to measure its attainment. Maslow's (1956) study of self-actualizing persons is relevant here, since it attempts to define and describe the manifestations of self-actualization. Rogers' (1959, 1961) specifications of the fully functioning person are also relevant as a step in this direction.

The acceptance of a general goal for all clients does not mean that individual differences are ignored. Different individuals actualize themselves in different ways. The point is that it seems desirable to have some criterion to apply in the selection of specific, limited goals. These specific behaviors are aspects of a total individual, a person, who is more than a bundle of separate behaviors established through mechanical reinforcements. It is probably the case at present that, while the client-centered counselors are interested in goals that are too general or vague, at least in terms of present ability to define and measure them, the behaviorists seem to be too specific, lacking in any general theory or criterion for selecting their goals.

If, as I think is possible, we can gain some agreement on goals, both general and specific, are these goals attainable by widely differing means? Or are client-centered therapy and behavior therapy essentially the same?

The essence of the client-centered approach is that it is a relationship. Several aspects of the relationship have been identified and measured, and shown to be related to outcome (Truax and Carkhuff, 1964, a,b, 1967). These aspects include empathic understanding, nonpossessive warmth, genuineness, and concreteness. It is a complex relationship with various aspects. It is not simply a cognitive, intellectual, impersonal relationship, but an affective, experiential, highly personal relationship. It is not necessarily irrational, but it has nonrational aspects. Evidence seems to be accumulating that the effective element in counseling or psychotherapy is the relationship. Goldstein (1962, p.105), after reviewing the literature on therapist-patient expectancies in psychotherapy, concluded: 'There can no longer be any doubt as to the primary status which must be accorded the therapeutic relationship in the overall therapeutic transaction'.

Now the behavior therapists appear to be unconcerned about the relationship, or perhaps it would be more accurate to say that they minimize its importance, treating it as a general rather than a specific condition for therapy. Wolpe (1958) recognizes it as a common element in therapy, but not a sufficient condition for change in most cases. He does recognize its effectiveness in some cases, however, when he notes: 'I have a strong clinical impression that patients who display strong positive emotions toward me during the early interviews are particularly likely to show improvement before special methods for obtaining reciprocal inhibition of anxiety are applied' (Wolpe, 1958, p. 194). Krumboltz (1966d) also recognizes the relationship as a necessary but not sufficient condition.

Examination of the functioning of behavior therapists such as Wolpe, makes it very clear that the behavior therapist is highly interested in, concerned about, and devoted to helping the client. He is genuine, open, and congruent. He is understanding and empathic, though perhaps not always to a high degree. He respects his client, though he may not rate extremely high on unconditional positive regard. There is no question but that a strong relationship is present. Behavior therapists are human; they are nice people, not machines.

Now I would like to suggest that the relationship is not only a necessary but the sufficient condition for therapeutic personality change. Wolpe concedes that it is in some cases. I suggest that it is in all cases. Let me try to indicate why this is so.

I noted earlier that the relationship is complex. It almost certainly includes more significant aspects than the four mentioned earlier although these themselves are complex. Some of the other aspects can be mentioned. Every therapy relationship is characterized by a belief on the part of the therapist in the possibility of client change, by an expectation that the client will change, by a desire to help, influence or change him, and, highly important, confidence in the approach or method which is used to achieve change. The client, for his part, also contributes to the relationship. He needs and wants help, recognizes this need, believes that he can change, believes that the counselor or therapist, with his methods, can help him change, and finally he puts forth some effort or engages in some activity in the attempt to change. These characteristics are all present in behavior therapy. Their presence alone produces change. One might say, with good evidence to support such a statement, that it almost does not matter what *specific* behavior the therapist engages in as long as these conditions are present.

The consideration of the nature and importance of the relationship leads to the necessity for caution in accepting the claims of the behavior therapists that their results are due to their specific techniques rather than to the relationship, or that their results are greater than could be achieved by means of the relationship alone. One aspect of this is the well-known fact that any new approach, applied with enthusiasm and confidence, and accompanied by faith in its efficacy on the part of the therapist and the client, is always successful when first applied, and continues to be successful to some extent as long as the confidence and faith in it continue. A second implication of the known power of the relationship is that in order to demonstrate the efficacy of the specific techniques of behavior therapy, their effects must be tested apart from or independent of the relationship. As a matter of fact, these techniques have been tested in the laboratory although not entirely apart from the influence of the relationship between the subject and the experimenter, as Orne (1962) points out in his discussion of the social psychology of the psychological experiment. (The work of Rosenthal [1964] on the effect of the experimenter on the results of psychological research is relevant here also.) The results of such research, that is, laboratory research on conditioning, indicate that (a) generalization is difficult to obtain and (b) in every situation (with one possible exception which cannot be considered here), when the reinforcement is discontinued, the conditioned behavior ceases, or is extinguished. If this is the case, why does the behavior conditioned in behavior therapy persist? Either there are other factors operating, or the reinforcement is continued outside of therapy. If the latter is the case, what is the nature of this reinforcement?

Perhaps it is too stringent a requirement to insist that behavior therapists eliminate the relationship to demonstrate the effectiveness of their specific methods. After all, they do recognize that the relationship is necessary. But at least they ought to control the relationship; they ought to test the added effects due to their specific methods, instead of simply stating that since other methods emphasizing the relationship achieve only about 60 percent success, and since they achieve (so they claim) 90 percent success, the difference is due to their specific methods. This is obviously unacceptable evidence, for several reasons which cannot be enumerated here.

The laboratory research on conditioning itself demonstrates the importance of the relationship between the experimenter and the subject for obtaining conditioning. The development of conditioning, the rate of conditioning, and the extent and persistence of conditioning are related to and influenced by the personality and attitudes of the experimenter and his relationship to the subject (Ullmann and Krasner, 1965, p. 43). The essential point is that the relationship is more important than the behavior therapists recognize, and their claims that the effects they produce are greater than those which can be attributed to the relationship alone have not been demonstrated.

But there is another aspect of the counseling relationship, an inherent element in the relationship, which must be recognized. Simply stated, the counseling relationship (and every good human relationship) is reinforcing. Reinforcement, and conditioning, are an inherent part of the therapeutic relationship. It is by now generally recognized that all therapists reinforce, by one means or another, the production of the kinds of verbalization in their client in which they are interested, i.e., the kind they feel are therapeutic, whether it is talk of sex, inferiority feelings, self-concepts, or of decision making. The therapist rewards the appropriate verbalizations by his interest, his attention, or by implicit or explicit indications of praise or approval.

The therapeutic relationship also, as a number of writers, including Shoben (1949) and Dollard and Miller (1950) have noted, provides by its accepting, understanding, nonthreatening atmosphere, a situation where anxiety may be extinguished. Further than this, I would like to suggest that, in such a relationship, where external threat is minimized, desensitization occurs. Anxiety-arousing thoughts, ideas, images, words, and feelings are free to appear. Moreover, I believe that they appear in a hierarchal sequence which is the same as that laboriously established by Wolpe (1958), that is, from the least anxiety arousing to the more anxiety arousing. Thus, in any good (nonthreatening) therapy relationship, desensitization occurs in the manner produced by Wolpe. The relationship, by minimizing externally induced anxiety, makes it possible for the client to experience and bring out his internally induced anxieties, or anxiety-arousing experiences, at the time and rate at which he can face and handle them in the accepting relationship. Ullmann and Krasner (1965, p. 37) state that the behavior therapists are systematic in their application of specific learning concepts. But it might also be said that client-centered or relationship therapists are systematic in the application of these principles, though not in the same conscious or deliberate manner.

We might conclude that there are not two different kinds of therapy; relationship therapy and behavior therapy. All counseling or psychotherapy involves both a relationship and conditioning. The difference between relationship therapy and behavior therapy is essentially one of emphasis. The behavior therapist emphasizes conditioning techniques, which he applies systematically, and is not systematic in his development of a relationship. The relationship therapist systematically develops a relationship, but is not so consciously systematic in applying conditioning techniques. Which is better? Or should both the relationship and the conditioning techniques be used systematically?

The behavior therapist, by providing a relationship, unsystematically treats other, perhaps underlying or more general problems than the specific ones he focuses upon with his particular techniques. The relationship therapist, on the other hand, influences more specific behaviors by his reinforcement of client behavior.

It would seem reasonable to believe that, where we are concerned with specific behaviors, we apply methods of training or relearning which are most effective. For example, where a particular kind of behavior is desired, or required, we apply the most effective reward when such behavior is performed, and continue this reinforcement until the behavior is 'learned' to a desired criterion, or until the client receives reinforcement by others in his life to assure its continuance.

But for some kinds of behavior the most potent reinforcement is a good human relationship. Some clients are not seeking to change specific behaviors, but to develop different attitudes and feelings toward themselves and others, to find a meaning in life, to develop long-term or life goals, to determine who and what they are, to develop a self-concept. The behaviorist would presumably attempt to reduce these goals or desires of clients to specific behaviors, or perhaps decide that such clients were not appropriate for them, or even not in need of counseling. But the attempt to reduce such concerns or problems to specifics may lead to breaking up the total person, to dealing with specific aspects of behavior which may not be particularly relevant to the client as a whole. It appears that some behavior therapists, if one may judge from their approach, refuse to accept any client statement of a problem which is not a specific one with which they can deal. It is interesting in this respect to note what Wolpe does in his demonstration tape (Wolpe, 1965). He refuses to accept any problems presented by the client, but defines her problem in his own terms. Behavior therapists, if not always overtly forcing the client to accept their definition of his problem, perhaps teach or condition their clients to have the kinds of problems for which their techniques are applicable.

Moreover, some behaviors *are* symptoms — not necessarily symptoms of a presumed underlying pathology in a medical sense, but indications of a more widespread problem or disturbance. The client may not be able to express this. The presenting problem is not always the real or total problem. The behavior therapists seem to deny or refuse to accept any problem which is not concrete or specific. London (1964) notes that the behavior therapist must 'drastically curtail the range of persons or problems he attacks. Courting specificity [he] risks wedding triviality.' If he widens the concept of 'symptom', until it includes meaning, his position becomes scientifically tenuous, according to London. One might ask the behavior therapist how he would decondition the pain or suffering of the client who suffers from a realization that he is not functioning up to his potential or aspiration level, who has a concept of himself as a failure, or who experiences a lack of meaning in his life. I am not convinced that the specific behaviors which might be derived from such complaints by a behaviorist would actually represent or include the problem. And if the behaviorist would deny that such complaints are real problems, then he would seem to be taking the narrow behaviorist position that nothing exists which cannot be dealt with by his specific techniques.

The specificity and concreteness of the behaviorist, as it appears to be represented in those concerned with clients in an educational setting, such as Krumboltz, seems to me to be moving from counseling or psychotherapy toward teaching. There seems to be some confusion about what is counseling and what is teaching. (Parenthetically, it is interesting that those who most strongly insist that there is a difference between counseling and psychotherapy tend not to distinguish between counseling and teaching.) Much emphasis has been placed upon the similarity between counseling and teaching, illustrated by the statement that counseling is deeper teaching, or that counseling or psychotherapy is learning. To counteract this tendency to identify teaching and counseling, I have sometimes suggested that the greatest similarity may be that both utilize a 50-minute hour. There are, of course, similarities and as in many other situations, the major difference may be one of emphasis. It would appear to me that the emphasis in teaching is upon cognitive problems or aspects of behavior, while the emphasis on counseling is — or should be — upon affective problems or aspects of behavior.

As Krumboltz (1966d) notes, classical conditioning is important in emotional learning. But most of Krumboltz's concern is with operant conditioning, imitative learning and cognitive learning, and the concerns of the Cubberly Conference on which he was reporting included

> . . . procedures for encouraging college accomplishment among disadvantaged youth, minimizing classroom learning and discipline problems, developing decision-making ability, modifying the behavior of autistic children, reducing test anxiety, building an environment conducive to school achievement, increasing attentive behavior, encouraging career exploration, improving testwiseness, improving child-rearing techniques, using computers in counseling, increasing the assertive behavior of shy children, and improving study habits (Krumboltz, 1966c, p. VIII).

These are worthy concerns, and things to which the learning techniques of behavior modification have much to contribute, but, I wonder, how many of these problems and their treatment would be considered as involving counseling? In this conference also, Bijou (1966) presents an excellent paper which is entitled 'Implications of behavioral science for counseling and guidance', but which has nothing to do with counseling, but rather with the modification of the environment to shape the behavior of children.

The broad goals desired by the relationship therapists are perhaps those most consistent with the emphasis upon the therapeutic relationship.

This approach, it seems to me, has several advantages.

1. It does not restrict counseling to one or a few specific problems determined by the client or the client and therapist early in the counseling process.
2. It does not attempt to deal with specific problems independently of each other, but deals with the total person of the client.
3. The nonthreatening atmosphere created not only makes possible client self-exploration, but also the desensitization and anxiety extinction accomplished in behavior therapy.
4. It places more responsibility on the client for the process of therapy, thus reinforcing independence and responsibility.
5. Its goals of self-exploration, responsibility, and independence, outside of and following therapy as well as within therapy, allow the client maximum freedom in making choices and decisions regarding specific goals or behavior changes.
6. Insofar as self-exploration, independence, and responsibility are aspects of or lead to self-actualization, this ultimate goal is promoted.

Specific behaviors must be considered in terms of the perspective of their meaning for life; they may be considered as means to the end of living a meaningful life, of actualizing one's potentialities as much as possible.

The question is not one of whether we should accept behavior therapy or become behavior therapists. For the individual counselor there are alternatives, in terms of what clients he works with or what kinds of problems he accepts to work with, and the way in which he works with clients. He can choose to deal with clients with specific problems or kinds of behavior which the client and counselor agree should be changed, and apply specific conditioning techniques to achieve these changes. Or he can choose to select and work with clients who express broader, more general problems and desire an opportunity to explore feelings and attitudes about these problems, and consider values, goals, and objectives for their lives, in which case he will offer the kind of relationship which appears to help the client explore himself. I believe there are many clients who want to experience a relationship, to be accepted and understood, to be allowed to explore themselves in order to find themselves. One's theory and method, of course, affect one's perceptions, and there is also selection of clients, and of counselors by clients based on knowledge of the methods and the reputation of the counselor. Clients have been known to present the problems which the counselor likes or prefers to deal with.

The application of behavior modification techniques is not likely to be the cure-all that some enthusiasts seem to imply. Monkeys can be taught, by conditioning, to do many things — such as picking olives. These and other employable skills can no doubt be taught to socially and economically disadvantaged and chronically unemployed humans. But there is a question as to whether this is sufficient, even if we accept it as desirable, if we are concerned with them as people and potential full members of society rather than simply as workers. Sanford (1966, pp. 3–4), discussing the program of the women's Job Corps Centers, suggests that

> . . . it seems likely that, in order to teach these girls the skills and social competencies that would make them employable, it would first be necessary to change attitudes, to develop different self-conceptions — indeed to undertake socialization on a broad scale . . . as a minimum it would be necessary to build up whatever was necessary in order for a girl to hold a job . . . such a girl would not be likely to hold a job unless she could see some point in it, and this would require that she develop in herself capacities for enjoying its benefits and taking satisfaction in it . . . The residential centers, then, would have to be conceived as institutions for personality development.

Now the behaviorists claim that by conditioning behaviors, such complex behavior can be built up. But the evidence for the claim is lacking.

Behavior therapists emphasize the efficiency of their methods, the small number of interviews required to achieve success with specific symptoms. This could be because they may be dealing with simple, isolated, restricted behavior disturbances. But there may be an even more efficient way of dealing with such behaviors. At a VA hospital one of the patients was irritating the staff by sticking his tongue out at them. The staff was responding nontherapeutically. A student trainee decided to use aversive conditioning in the interview. After a few interviews, the patient said: 'Say, Doc, if you're trying to get me to stop sticking my tongue out, just say so and I'll stop.' If we want clients or students to engage in certain specific behaviors, such as some techniques of problem solving, asking questions, exploring alternatives, perhaps the most efficient way is to ask them openly, or suggest it to them, or teach them in the usual way, rather than resort to lengthy conditioning procedures, which in effect may be a sort of guessing game in which the client has to find out what you want him to do. This is an indication of the confusion between counseling and teaching. Since the relationship is not so important in teaching, which is more cognitively oriented, it is understandable why behavior therapists consider the relationship as relatively unimportant.

References

Bijou, S. W. (1966) Implications of behavioral science for counseling and guidance. In Krumboltz, J. D. (Ed.) *Revolution in counseling*. Boston: Houghton Mifflin.

Dollard, J., and Miller, N. E. (1950) *Personality and psychotherapy*. New York: McGraw-Hill.

Goldstein, A. P. (1962) *Therapist-patient expectancies in psychotherapy*. New York: Macmillan.

Goldstein, K. (1949) *The organism*. New York: World Book.

Hart, J. (1960) *The evolution of client-centered therapy*. Unpublished Paper.

Jones, Mary C. (1924) A laboratory study of fear: the case of Peter. *Pedagogical Seminary*, 31, 308–15. Reprinted in Eysenck, H. J. (Editor) (1960) *Behavior therapy and the neuroses*, New York: Pergamon Press.

Krasner, L. (1966) Review of Eysenck, H. J. and Rachman, S., The causes and cures of neuroses; an introduction to modern behavior therapy based on learning theory and the principles of conditioning. *Contemporary Psychology*, 11, pp. 341–4.

Krumboltz, J. D. (1966a) Behavioral goals for counseling. *Journal of Counseling Psychology*, 1, 13, pp. 153–9.

Krumboltz, J. D. (1966b) Stating the goals of counseling. *Monograph No. 1, California Personnel and Guidance Association.*.

Krumboltz, J. D. (Ed) (1966c) *Revolution in counseling*. Boston: Houghton Mifflin.

Krumboltz, J. D. (1966d) Promoting adaptive behavior. In Krumboltz, J. D. (Editor) *Revolution in counseling*. Boston: Houghton Mifflin.

Maslow, A. H. (1956) Self-actualizing people: a study of psychological health. In Moustakas, C. E. (Ed.) *The self: explorations in personal growth*. New York: Harper and Row, pp. 160–94.

Orne, M. T. (1962). On the psychology of the psychological experiment. *American Psychologist*, 17, 776–83.

Patterson, C. H. (1964) A unitary theory of motivation and its counseling implications. *Journal of Individual Psychology*, 20, pp. 17–31.

Patterson, C. H. (1966). *Theories of counseling and psychotherapy*. New York: Harper and Row.

Rogers, C. R. (1959). A theory of therapy, personality, and interpersonal relationships, as developed in the client-centered framework. In Koch, S. (Ed.)

Psychology: a study of a science. Study 1. Conceptual and systematic. Vol. 3. Formulations of the person and the social context. New York: McGraw-Hill, pp. 184–256.

Rogers, C. R. (1961) The therapist's view of the good life: The fully functioning person. In *On becoming a person.* Boston: Houghton Mifflin, pp. 183–96.

Rosenthal, R. (1961) *Experimenter effects in behavioral research.* New York: Appleton-Century-Crofts.

Rosenthal, R. (1964) The effect of the experimenter on the results of psychological research. In Maher, B. (Ed.) *Progress in experimental research*, Vol. I. New York: Academic Press.

Sanford, N. (1966) *Self and Society.* New York: Atherton Press.

Shoben, E. J. Jr. (1949) Psychotherapy as a learning problem. *Psychological Bulletin*, 46, pp. 366–92.

Shostrom, E. L. (1963) *The Personal Orientation Inventory.* San Diego, California: Educational and Industrial Testing Service.

Truax, C. B. and Carkhuff, R. R. (1964a) Concreteness: a neglected variable in research in psychotherapy. *Journal of Clinical Psychology*, 20, 264–267.

Truax, C. B. and Carkhuff, R. R. (1964b). The old and the new: theory and research in counseling and psychotherapy. *Personnel & Guidance Journal*, 42, pp. 860–6.

Truax, C. B. and Carkhuff, R. R. (1967) *Toward effective counseling and psychotherapy: Training and practice.* Chicago: Aldine.

Wolpe, J. (1958) *Psychotherapy by reciprocal inhibition.* Stanford: Stanford University Press.

Wolpe, J. (1965). *The case of Mrs. Schmidt.* Typescript and record published by Counselor Recordings and Tests, Box 6184, Acklen Sta., Nashville, Tennessee.

Ullmann, L. P. and Krasner, L. (Eds). (1965). *Case studies in behavior modification*, New York: Holt, Rinehart and Winston.

Van Der Veen, F. and Tomlinson, T. M. (1962). *Problem Expression Scale.* Madison, Wisconsin: Wisconsin Psychiatric Institute, University of Wisconsin.

SOME NOTES ON BEHAVIOR THEORY, BEHAVIOR THERAPY AND BEHAVIORAL COUNSELING

5

There have been a number of critiques of behavior theory as applied to counseling and psychotherapy (Breger and McGaugh, 1965, 1968; Kiesler, 1966; Murray, 1963; Weitzman, 1967), whose purpose has been, to some extent, to cut away the underpinnings. While these critiques have in turn been criticized (Rachman and Eysenck, 1966; Wiest, 1967; Yates, 1970), questions still remain regarding the theoretical and experimental bases of behavior therapy or behavioral counseling (these terms are used interchangeably in this paper). However, it is not proposed here to reiterate these criticisms, or to question the (demonstrated) effectiveness of what is called behavior therapy. Rather, the purpose here is to raise questions regarding the nature of what happens in behavior modification, behavior therapy, and behavioral counseling, and to suggest that this area of activity is not as simple and clear-cut as is often assumed to be the case, and that it is not as different from so-called 'traditional' counseling or therapy as it has often been made to appear to be. Limitations of space prevent the detailed documentation of the points discussed. Further documentation of many of the points will be found in Murray and Jacobson (1970).

My comments will therefore not be restricted to Hosford's paper[1], which is elementary and avoids the issues and problems involved in behavior therapy. I shall pass by the use of the word 'revolution' with only the comment that if the use of this term enhances the self-concept of behavior therapists, I am willing to allow them to use it. Hosford provides no justification for the use of the word, acknowledging that behavior modification goes back to Jones in 1924.

Is behavior therapy the only scientific therapy?
Behaviorists emphasize that their approach is based upon 'scientific research findings' (is there also nonscientific research?); that it is 'laboratory-based', uses 'experimentally-derived methods', and is based on 'modern learning theory'. The implication clearly is that other methods differ in these respects. The simple facts are that: (1) Other methods are supported by research; (2) The procedures used by

First published in *The Counseling Psychologist,* 1969, 1, 4, pp. 44–56.
© 1969 Division oif Counseling Psychology. Reprinted by permission of Sage Publications/Corwin Press, Inc.

1. Hosford, unpublished paper.

behaviorists are not always based upon prior research demonstrating their effectiveness (not that this should necessarily be the case) but are often developed on the basis of clinical experience; (3) The research evidence for the validity of their methods is far from conclusive, and in fact, as more research data have accumulated, the more complex the apparently simple methods appear to be; (4) The methods are not necessarily explainable only by so-called modern learning theory (whatever that is) but can be rationalized in other ways. The recognition that counseling or psychotherapy is a learning process existed before the current revival of behavior theory, and other explanations involving learning theory have been proposed (Shoben, 1949; Dollard and Miller, 1950). Furthermore, the methods of behavior therapy are not invariably successful. In spite of the recognized fact that negative results are under-reported in professional and scientific publications, there are reports of failures, which may even be increasing — a phenomenon common as any new method begins to be used by other than its early, enthusiastic proponents. This will be referred to later in another connection.

Contrary to the impression often given that the methods are simple and clear-cut, and that their methods of operation are clearly understood, it is becoming evident that they are highly complex and not clearly understood, as some behaviorists are willing to admit. Moreover, there is no integrating theory to tie together the many methods or techniques. 'While there are many techniques, there are few concepts or general principles involved in behavior therapy' (Ullmann and Krasner, 1969, p. 252). Weitzman (1967) suggests that behavior therapy is actually 'a nontheoretical amalgam of pragmatic principles'. The behaviorists make a virtue out of necessity in expressing their willingness to try anything that seems to work or that might work. Behaviorists will try anything, and of course, sometimes (particularly under the right conditions, which will be considered later), with some clients, anything will work. Thus specific techniques are being tried and recommended and accepted on a superstitious basis until extinguished after enough failures. Wolpe (1968) refers to a case of Guthrie's in which a girl was locked in a car and driven around until her phobia of riding in cars was 'apparently' overcome. This, of course, is a good 'common sense' approach, analogous to throwing a nonswimmer in the water to teach him how to swim. This would be claimed by many behaviorists to be inconsistent with learning theory as exemplified in desensitization (Hogan and Kirchner, 1967; 1968; Levis and Carrera, 1967; Murray and Jacobson, 1970; Stampfl and Levis, 1967; Wolpin, 1968; Wolpin and Raines, 1966).

There is no general agreement on the nature and conditions of learning, and thus no generally accepted, proven principles or methods which can be automatically applied in behavior therapy. An examination of desensitization (see e.g. Weitzman, 1967, and Murray and Jacobson, 1970) as well as of other techniques, indicates that they cannot be reduced to the simple principles advanced by the behaviorists.

Are behavior therapy goals specific?
Two points may be made about goals: (1) the behaviorists have no monopoly on goals which are specific; and (2) the behaviorists are interested in general,

nonspecific, or what I have called 'ultimate' goals (Patterson, 1970). Other counselors or therapists are of course concerned about specific behaviors of their clients, but the question which the behaviorists ignore or minimize is the meaning or significance of specific behaviors. The choice, or acceptance, of particular specific goals involves a value decision. The question is, what is the criterion which the behaviorists use in determining the appropriateness of specific goals? Michael and Meyerson (1962) say that this question has been decided by society. But one might well question whether society has made the decisions which they claim it has. At any rate, the criterion problem must ultimately be faced and resolved by the behaviorists. Ullmann and Krasner appear to be caught up in the problem of goals and values. On the one hand they state that 'The stress throughout this volume has been that any behavior by itself is neither good nor bad' (Ullmann and Krasner, 1969, p. 589). Yet, they recognize that this is not so in any real or social sense: 'if, on the other hand, the role of the therapist is to directly and actively change behavior (which in itself is neither normal nor abnormal) and to arrange environmental contingencies, then what the therapist considers socially appropriate becomes crucial' (p. 593). The need for a criterion is obvious. Miller (1969), in his 1969 APA Presidential Address dealing with the question of the role of psychology in human welfare, states that 'Changing behavior is pointless in the absence of any coherent plan for how it should be changed . . . Too often, I fear, psychologists have implied that acceptable uses for behavior control are either self-evident, or can be safely left to the wisdom and benevolence of powerful men.' A solution to this problem has been suggested in terms of an ultimate goal of self-actualization (Patterson, 1970).

Now before this goal is rejected out of hand by the behaviorists, two points should be considered. The first is that although self-actualization cannot yet be adequately measured, in principle it is measurable. As a matter of fact, considerable progress has been made in this direction (Patterson, 1970). The behaviors constituting the process of self-actualization can be defined objectively, and can be observed and measured.

It might be noted here that the behaviorists at least imply, if they do not state specifically, that nonbehavioral counselors ignore the problem for which the client seeks help. One might be equally justified in arguing that it is the behaviorists who refuse to accept the client's stated problem, and insist that he reduce it to the kind of problem with which the behaviorist prefers to deal.

Secondly, the behaviorists are interested in broad general goals, although they apparently consider these as side effects. Yet the explicit consideration of side effects has been ignored by the behaviorists. Pavlov noticed that, in addition to the specific conditioning which he produced in his dogs, other changes in their behavior occurred. He recognized that the total organism was affected by the conditioning procedure. Most current behaviorists are not aware of or have forgotten this aspect of Pavlov's work. They focus their attention upon a single specific result and ignore the possibility that significant other effects (or side effects) may occur. It has been suggested that one possible such effect of a highly structured, counselor-therapist-directed treatment may be increased client dependency.

Behaviorists could, of course, respond that, if greater independence is desired, they could achieve this. But the point is that the behaviorists have not been concerned about possible effects other than the specific one with which they are concerned. In addition, there appears to be an inconsistency between methods of behavior modification and independence which should be explored. Moreover, it has not been demonstrated that behavior modification techniques are more effective for achieving independence or responsible behavior than other approaches such as client-centered or relationship therapy.

Side effects need not, of course, be unfavorable, though this is the usual connotation of the term. There appears to be some evidence that behavior therapy, in addition to its specific effects, has general, or less specific effects, which are favorable, and these effects are accepted by behavior therapists as evidence of their effectiveness. Wolpe, for example, used as criteria of improvement not only symptom removal, but 'increased productiveness, improved adjustment and pleasure in sex, improved interpersonal relationships and ability to handle psychological conflict and reasonable stresses' (Wolpe, 1958, p. 200). He does not explain how these results were measured, how they were achieved, or how they are related to the specific technique of behavior therapy. Murray and Jacobson (1970) note that 'rather than the symptom substitution feared by dynamic therapists, published and unpublished reports by the therapists indicate that when a symptom is removed, it is often followed by a general, nonspecific improvement in the individual's daily life'. They cite a study by Gelder et al. (1967), in which it was found that systematic desensitization

> not only decreased the main phobias and related fears more effectively than individual and group therapy, but had generalized effects in areas that had little connection with the focus of treatment. Thus, the systematic desensitization group showed greater improvements in adjustment to work and leisure-time activities than either of the other two treatments, and as much improvement in general social relationships as those patients in group therapy (Murray and Jacobson, 1970).

The concept of symptom substitution is relevant here, and we now turn to this.

Do behaviorists treat symptoms?

The issue of what behaviorists treat is clouded by the concept of 'symptoms' used in a medical sense. If the results of behavior therapy go beyond the specific behaviors about which the behaviorists make so much fuss, just what is it that they are treating? The specificity of effect which many behaviorists insist on is apparently a myth.

The behaviorists have an explanation. It is that the change in specific behaviors of the client leads to changes in the way in which he is responded to by others in his environment, which leads in turn to changes in other aspects of the client's behavior. This is, of course, no doubt the case. But it also appears that the client's behavior may change in other respects prior to his experiences with others, and in ways which cannot be accounted for as generalization from the specific behavior effect. Such generalization, in the strict sense of the term, is recognized by the behaviorists as limited, even in terms of phobias other than the one treated.

Murray and Jacobson (1970) suggest that such changes are the result of changes in the belief system of the client, so that he believes, or has confidence that, he can cope with the situation, and other situations as well. In effect, there has been a change in his self-concept (see also Wolpin, 1968).

Murray and Jacobson (1970) refer to Leff's review of studies utilizing operant techniques with children, in which there were nonspecific effects which could not be accounted for, by either the authors or the reviewer, in terms of the procedures used, or in terms of stimulus generalization. They suggest that 'it is difficult to see how such widespread effects can be attributed to the specific reinforcement procedure employed unless one assumes that it resulted in some basic change in the patients' attitudes and conceptions about themselves and their interpersonal environment', They also refer to the study of Valins and Ray (1967), in which a decrease in overt phobic behavior occurred following the giving of falsified information to the subjects about their autonomic reactions to snakes. They suggest that 'the study indicates dramatically that the critical factor in systematic desensitization therapy is the change in beliefs about the self — similar to that occurring in traditional therapy — rather than the mechanics of relaxation, hierarchies, images, and so on'.

These general changes in the client have significance for the position of the behaviorists with regard to the symptom removal controversy as well as the specificity of results. If there are general changes in the client, this suggests, if it does not actually prove, that the client's problem goes beyond the specific complaint which the behaviorists treat, and includes a general low level of 'adjustment', for want of a better term. Thus, in a nonmedical sense, the complaint is a 'symptom', or an indicator, of a more general problem. This is not surprising, since the individual is an integrated whole, whose parts are all interrelated, so that a change in one part — or one aspect of behavior — leads to or induces changes in others. The behaviorists appear to ignore the wholeness and integrity of the organism, although it is an obvious factor in explaining the generality of their results and an important theoretical support for their approach. Weitzman (1967) notes that the concept that 'systematic desensitization does, as a technique, in some way affect the total psychological matrix, has not been given due theoretical consideration by behavior therapists or psychotherapists'. In terms of a systems or cybernetic approach to human behavior, the entrance into or the modification of the system at any point leads to changes in the total system. However, this view also suggests that entering the system at the point, or level, of the belief system would also be useful or effective.

Many behaviorists, of course, accept the interaction of behaviors within the individual, and do not reject a causal interpretation, although their emphasis is upon external causes (i.e. in terms of contingencies). Yates (1970, pp. 398–9) indicates that even 'some notion corresponding to the term "symptom substitution" is acceptable to most (but not all) behavior therapists, though the use of a different term would probably be preferable . . . ' He refers with approval to Cahoon's (1968) concept of symptoms and symptom substitution, a concept similar to that used here.

It is not our purpose, again, to question the results or the effectiveness of behavior therapy, but to question whether the explanations of the behaviorists are adequate to account for the nature and kinds of changes which appear to occur.

Counseling or guessing game?

The narrowness of the concept of learning accepted by many behavioral therapists or counselors is illustrated by the methods used in many studies. In these studies, the counselor — or behavior modifier — actually sets up and engages in a guessing game with the client, or subject. This is essentially what Krumboltz and Thoreson (1964) did in their highly regarded study which demonstrated the effectiveness of reinforcement of information-seeking behavior with eleventh-grade students. It would be interesting to compare the results of such treatment with simply telling 'clients' what it is you wish them to do, such as 'If you want to obtain educational-vocational information, you should seek such information by talking with people who are working in the occupation, look up materials in the library, visit schools and places of employment, etc.' Such an approach would appear to be more simple and efficient than a reinforcement approach. In fact, there is some evidence that suggests that such a cognitive structuring method is as effective as reinforcement (Baker, 1966; Maurath, 1966; Rubin, 1968; Serber, 1968). Gilbert (1967, p. 32) presents an interesting anecdote relevant to this comparison. A psychology student in a mental hospital decided to attempt to eliminate by aversive conditioning certain antagonizing behavior which consisted of the patient sticking his tongue out at the staff. After several interviews, the patient said: 'Say Doc, if you're trying to get me to stop sticking my tongue out, just tell me and I'll be glad to.' As Murray and Jacobson (1970) put it, 'if the critical factor in verbal conditioning is the communication of information, it would appear that there are more efficient means of achieving this goal than the protracted process of response shaping and extinction'.

The problem of awareness in conditioning studies obviously arises here. It will probably come as a surprise to most behavioral counselors that the effects of operant conditioning do not occur without awareness on the part of the subject. Ericksen, evaluating the research on human operant conditioning, concluded that 'in none of these situations is impressive or unequivocal evidence of learning without awareness obtained' (Ericksen, 1962, p. 11). If awareness is necessary for such learning then it is fair to ask whether it is conditioning in the strict sense of the term, or whether it is not, in fact, cognitive learning. If the latter is the case, as certainly it seems to be, the conditioning paradigm is inappropriate, and indeed, inefficient for such learning. Certainly the question may be raised, in the light of negative results in studies of conditioning without awareness, as to whether human beings are susceptible to operant conditioning. Parenthetically, the recognition of awareness as a cognitive aspect of what has been called conditioning leads to a suggested cognitive explanation for the resistance of behavior established by intermittent reinforcement to extinction, which has never been adequately explained by conditioning principles. Apparently, intermittent reinforcement sets up expectations which persist through nonreinforced trials. Reinforcement, rather than operating in a mechanical manner, is essentially informational feedback.

Again, the question is not whether learning is involved in behavior modification, but whether the learning which takes place can be accounted for in the simple model of conditioning which the behaviorists propose. Counseling is not simply operant conditioning in an interview situation. The learning principles accepted by the behaviorists are limited and neglect or minimize cognitive, emotional, and social learning. In this respect, behavior modification is not current with the state of learning theory and research (Murray and Jacobson, 1970).

Counseling or instruction?

Related to the confusion of 'behavioral counseling' with the use of reinforcement in an interview situation is the confusion of counseling with teaching. I have recently reviewed, as an editorial board member, several studies which involve this confusion. A study involving the comparison of different approaches to dealing with study problems will illustrate this. Such a study might involve a group in which group discussion (not counseling) with reinforcement of positive statements and attitudes toward study would be one treatment. A control group might be designated a 'placebo' group, in which undirected discussion would be permitted (in one such study this group was called a 'nondirective counseling group'). The criterion might consist of a test of knowledge about study habits and methods. When, as obviously would result, it is found that the first group does better than the second group, the conclusion could be (and was in a similar study) drawn that behavioral counseling is more effective than nondirective or client-centered counseling! Such studies exhibit ignorance of what over 50 years of research in educational psychology has clearly demonstrated — that direct discussion and teaching in a subject-matter area results in better scores on tests of achievement in that area than discussion not so directed or limited. It should be apparent that a measure of the acquisition of specific information or behavior is not a fair test to compare an approach specifically directed to the development of such behavior with one which does not deal with such behavior. Yet this is typical of many studies purporting to compare behavioral counseling with 'traditional' counseling.

In addition to the obvious illegitimacy of such conclusions, there is the matter of the confusion of didactic instruction with counseling. Behavioral counselors engage in such instruction and call it counseling. It is not possible to examine this problem in detail here, but if there is a distinction between counseling and teaching, even though both are learning, then behavioral counselors should be clear about what they are doing. This failure to make a distinction is the source of confusion. In fact, much of what behaviorists call counseling or psychotherapy is direct instruction or teaching, or in some cases, indirect teaching through others. Bijou (1966), for example, uses the term counseling to refer to the latter kinds of activities. Goldiamond and Dyrud (1968, p. 70) note the possibility of confusion when they say that 'Whether the appropriate programming [or treatment] is to be academic [education] or therapeutic, or both, depends on the nature of the problem'.

Even where the instruction is not direct, the cognitive aspects of behavior therapy are more important than is recognized. Ullmann and Krasner (1969, p. 189) appear to reject the concept of cognition as a factor in abnormal behavior, in favor of 'specific stimuli contingent upon behavior'. Nevertheless, they recognize that the therapist teaches (p. 593), although they separate education and psychotherapy, even though they eventually merge (p. 597).

While the experimental psychologists have increasingly recognized the importance of cognitive, emotional (personality) and interpersonal factors in conditioning, behavior therapists have in general ignored these factors, although they are now beginning to discover their existence.

Is modeling behavior therapy?

One of the methods widely used in behavior therapy which would appear to involve cognitive learning is modeling. Modeling is a highly complex, yet universal form of learning, which cannot be reduced to simple S-R learning. It was not derived from so-called 'modern learning theory', but was appropriated by the behaviorists when it was recognized as an effective method of behavior modification. Bandura's work (e.g. 1965) has indicated that modeling is not a simple process and that social (interpersonal) factors are extremely important.

It is interesting to note that modeling is turning out to be perhaps the most useful and most important method of behavior therapy. It has recently been found to be more effective than desensitization in the treatment of phobias, for which desensitization has been felt to be the specific treatment. This leads to the question of specificity of methods.

Is behavior therapy specific?

It has been noted in passing that there is no single method of behavior therapy. In fact, behavior therapy has appropriated or incorporated every conceivable method or technique in addition to those methods generally associated with it, that is, desensitization and various forms of conditioning and reconditioning. In addition to modeling, these include simple relaxation, presentation of information, hypnosis, direct instruction, encouragement, suggestion, advice giving, persuasion, and indoctrination, often in various combinations. Klein, Dittman, Parloff and Gill (1969), after observing Wolpe and Lazarus, noted:

> From our acquaintance with the literature, we knew intellectually at least that behavior therapists do not work in a unitary fashion and indeed take pains to vary their approach from case to case. We were surprised to find, however, that within most cases, too, a number of manipulations were routinely employed . . . It is appropriate . . . to note the apparent contradiction between the proliferation of methods in behavior therapy and the popular conception, based partly on hope, partly on the behavior therapists' writings, that this is a simple and straightforward treatment for the neuroses.

There appears to be some evidence that all of these methods lead to behavior change. However, the claims of some behaviorists that specific methods are most effective for specific results have not been demonstrated. In fact, evidence to the contrary seems to be accumulating. Although efforts are made in research to isolate specific techniques for study, most studies involve the confounding of several methods which makes it difficult to determine to just what the results may be attributed. The problem of relationship factors is especially noted here, since few, if any, studies have adequately controlled these factors. While it may be laudable for a therapist to do anything which may appear to be necessary or desirable to help the client, it then becomes impossible to attribute results to any specific treatment.

Techniques or relationship?
The matter of the relationship in behavior therapy has long been a topic of dispute. Most behavior therapists admit the existence, even the necessity, of the relationship, but view it as a nonspecific factor. It is becoming clear, however, that the relationship is much more significant than has been admitted, and some behaviorists are recognizing this (Wolpe and Lazarus, 1966; Wilson, Hannan and Evans, 1968).

The relationship factor is extremely complex. An aspect of this is the so-called placebo. While it is not possible to examine this effect in detail, it appears that there is a difference of opinion regarding the desirability of eliminating the placebo effect from therapy. Some behavior therapists appear to feel that it should be avoided. Others, however, would accept it and exploit it (Krasner and Ullmann, 1965, p. 44).

Suggestion is a main aspect of the placebo effect. Klein, Dittman, Parloff and Gill (1969) comment: 'Perhaps the most striking impression we came away with was of how much use behavior therapists make of suggestion .and of how much the patient's expectations and attitudes are manipulated.' They quote Lazarus as stating: 'Both Wolpe and I have explicitly stated that relationship variables are often extremely important in behavior therapy. Factors such as warmth, empathy, and authenticity are considered necessary but often insufficient.' He continues later: 'If suggestion enables the person to attempt new responses, these may have positive effects. One thus endeavors quite deliberately to maximize the "placebo effect".' And he agrees that 'even the results of a specific technique like systematic desensitization cannot be accounted for solely in terms of graded hierarchies and muscle relocation'.

Efforts have been made in research to eliminate the effects. Lang, Lazovik and Reynolds (1965) conducted a study from which they concluded that suggestion and the relationship were not responsible for the results. However, they note that 'the possibility of error in a procedure can never be completely discounted'. While they found no relationship between suggestibility and results, it is quite possible that suggestibility operated (differentially perhaps) on all subjects. Grossberg (1964) notes that 'It is not logically possible to prove the absence of an effect such as suggestion'. The attempt to eliminate the relationship by using a device for automatic desensitization (DAD) (Lang, et al., no date) is also open to criticism.

Although the desensitization process can be handled mechanically with a programmed tape, at least three elements of an interpersonal relationship were present. First, the tape utilized a human voice. Even if the usual printed tape were used, the likelihood of the subjects perceiving the machine as a person, or attributing personal characteristics to it by the process of anthropomorphism is present (Schwitzgebel and Traugott, 1968). Second, the total experiment involved relationships with the experimenters. Third, it is possible that the use of a machine enhances the expectation of help, which is a psychological or 'placebo' effect.

The work of behaviorists with psychotic and autistic children (Leff, 1968; Lovaas, 1968a, 1968b) has involved intense personal relationships, clearly using the personal interest, concern and attention of the therapists as reinforcers. Incidentally, the nonspecific results cannot be attributed to stimulus generalization or any other clear cause. Lovaas (1968a), referring to these changes, states:

> As children improve, and their behaviors become increasingly complex, requiring increasingly complex environments, we face certain methodological and theoretical problems which we have been unable to handle within the present structure. Ricky, for example, can now verbalize that he makes 'crazy faces' to scare away fears. Such verbalization demands empathy, and I see no easy way, at the present time, to handle this interaction within a reinforcement theory paradigm (see also Lovaas, 1968b, p. 119).

It is also interesting to speculate whether, if the therapist's behavior were based upon reinforcement in terms of results of his efforts, he would have persisted so long with no apparent effects. The total context of the situation, with its interpersonal factors, seems to be ignored by the behaviorists. While the Hawthorne effect is well known, and while experimental psychologists have become sensitive to what have been called the demand characteristics of the experiment (Orne, 1962; Rosenthal,1966), the behaviorists, in both their research and practice, appear in general to be oblivious to the effect. (Kanfer,1965; Krasner,1965 and Sarason, 1965 are exceptions.) Hunt and Dyrud (1968, pp. 144–5) write:

> In general, the social psychology of the situation receives too little attention [in behavior therapy research]. Placebo control are comparatively rare, and even more rarely do we have a firm basis for knowing how 'believable' the placebo controls were to the subject. Also, 'Hawthorne effects' need to be guarded against, as expectations and responsiveness may be enhanced when the subjects are given the opportunity to participate in an experiment on a promising new treatment.

Orne and Scheibe (1964) have suggested that expectancy factors on the part of the subjects have been involved in the results of sensory deprivation studies, and they concluded that 'the effects of sensory deprivation are almost universally interaction phenomena'; i.e. the result of the nature of the relationship. Similarly, it might be maintained that the results of the techniques of behavior modification are essentially or mainly interaction phenomena, involving the demand characteristics of the situation including beliefs, expectancies and enthusiasm of the experimenter or therapist on the one hand, and the set, expectancies, belief and faith of the subject or client on the other. Perhaps it does not matter too much what you do, as long as these factors (and other relationship factors) are present. As Ullmann and Krasner (1969, p. 408) note, 'With tact, sensitivity and genuine respect for the person as an individual, there is little that is not possible; without these, little can be accomplished'. Reich's orgone box was effective, and so are the methods of so-called quacks in medicine and psychology, because of these factors.

The criticism of behavior modification as mechanical, dehumanizing, and coldly manipulative is mistaken. It is just because behavior therapy is not impersonal that its claimed reasons for success, that is, its specific techniques, must be questioned.

Charcot recognized the role of suggestion in hypnosis but minimized it, insisting that hypnosis was a neurological phenomenon. The behaviorists recognize the role of suggestion (and more broadly the relationship) in behavior therapy, but minimize it, insisting that behavior therapy is a simple, objective learning phenomenon. History is likely to show that they, like Charcot, are wrong. Ullmann and Krasner (1969, p. 124n), commenting on Charcot's hypothesis, note that the null hypothesis that hypnosis is due to neural weakness cannot be proven. 'All one can do is illustrate that every hypnotic phenomenon can be instigated without reference to trance or neurological weakness.' Similarly, one cannot prove that the results of behavior therapy are not due to the specific mechanical techniques. All one can do is show that every result can be instigated without reference to these specific techniques. Evidence is accumulating that this is indeed the case. The emergence of modeling as the most important method of behavior change, a method in which complex relationship factors are present, supports this conclusion.

The evidence seems to indicate that, as the importance of relationship factors becomes evident, behavior therapy is moving closer to traditional therapy. The common element in all the various methods of the behaviorists is the relationship. The relationship itself can be viewed as a reinforcer for the kinds of human behavior which appear to be desirable as outcomes of counseling or psychotherapy. Ullmann and Krasner (1965, p. 56) refer to relationship factors as generalized reinforcers which 'may be the most important factor in the control of behavior because they are so powerful.' But these reinforcers are powerful only when they are genuine, and are not artificially offered and withdrawn or withheld. One of the reasons that the behavioral approach died out prior to its recent revival may be that the providing of praise, attention, interest and concern were used as techniques. The old motto that you can fool some of the people all of the time and all of the people some of the time, but you can't fool all of the people all of the time, applies here. It might even be questioned whether you can fool anyone all of the time.

The behaviorists have suggested that traditional therapy uses or involves reinforcement, but have insisted that it is unsystematic and that the behaviorists are systematic in their use of reinforcement. Ullmann and Krasner (1965) write that 'the traditional therapist does influence his patients and we think that he should do so consciously and systematically (p. 38). However, the procedure [of the traditional or expressive therapist] is not overtly systematic' (p. 37).

Is behavior therapy more systematic than traditional therapy in the use of reinforcement?

The behavior therapists are, presumably, systematic in the application of specific reinforcers. But it might also be said that relationship therapists are systematic in the application of generalized reinforcers — interest, concern, warmth respect, understanding.

In fact, it might be questioned how systematic the behaviorists actually are. Research on the conditioning of verbal behaviors, such as positive self-references, indicates that it is difficult to establish such conditioning. It has been contended that this is because the time periods in such therapy analog studies are brief, and that not enough reinforcements are provided to establish the conditioned response. But another factor appears to be present. Experimenters (including some of my own students) who have worked on such studies have noted how difficult it is to identify each member of the response class to be conditioned and to reinforce every occurrence of the response (or operant). This indicates that such conscious reinforcement is not continuous, that it is not highly systematic. Skinner recognizes this:

> In the experimental study of learning it has been found that the contingencies of reinforcement which are most efficient in controlling the organism cannot be arranged through the personal mediation of the experimenter . . . Mechanical and electrical devices must be used . . . Mechanical help is also demanded by the sheer number of contingencies which may be used efficiently in a single experimental session . . . Personal arrangement of the contingencies and personal observation of the results are quite unthinkable (1968, pp. 21–2).

This may be true when one is concerned with reinforcing a highly specific response or response class on an artificial basis or even in the classroom, the situation to which Skinner is referring here. On the other hand, it is possible that the relationship therapist, in concentrating upon his own behavior and upon the general rather than highly specific behavior of the client (client self-talk, self-exploration rather than particular kinds of self-talk), is highly systematic in providing the generalized reinforcers of his approach. As Ullmann and Krasner note, 'The therapist has a "theory" that helps him respond rapidly to patient behavior' (1965, p. 37).

A point which students raise here is that not reinforcing every response is not a problem because intermittent reinforcement is more effective than continuous reinforcement. This is an illustration of the lack of understanding of the conditioning process shown by many who accept and attempt to use it. Skinner answers that simply:

> If you devise an apparatus which reinforces every hundredth response, and put an organism in it, the organism will starve because it will not make the required one hundred responses. But if you

reinforce every response, then every second response, then every fifth, then every tenth, twenty-fifth, fiftieth, and hundredth, you can get a pigeon to go on indefinitely, responding one hundred times for each small measure of food. Actually, you can build up to ten thousand responses for each small measure of food. But it takes programming. You can't reach the final stage without going through intervening stages. In most studies of learning, organisms are plopped down into terminal contingencies of reinforcement and allowed to struggle through. They may reach the terminal behavior or they may not (Evans, 1968).

Summary

The purpose of these comments is not to question the effectiveness of those techniques grouped under the terms behavior therapy, behavioral counseling, or behavior modification, nor to question that the process involved is learning. However, the following points appear to be in order:

1. The learning process involved in the methods of behavior therapy is more complex, and perhaps even different, than the conceptualization of the behaviorists. 'Research has begun to make it increasingly clear that the learning occurring in the behavioral therapies involves complex cognitive, emotional and motivational changes operating within a social context' (Murray and Jacobson, 1970), or in an interpersonal relationship.
2. Conditioning as an automatic, mechanical process without the awareness or without involving cognitive activities on the part of the subject, is rare or nonexistent in human behavior.
3. The existence of methods or techniques which are specific treatments for specific problems is questionable.
4. Much of what is called behavior therapy or behavioral counseling is simply standard teaching or instruction, applying principles and methods which are neither new nor unique.
5. Experience and research have indicated that the relationship variables, including those referred to as the placebo effect, the Hawthorne effect and demand characteristics of the experiment or situation, are much more important in behavior therapy than has been generally admitted.
6. Perhaps a major difference between behavior therapy and 'traditional' or relationship therapy is that the relationship therapist has more confidence in the ability of the client to resolve his own problems — assuming that he is not lacking in information, knowledge or skills. Behavioral methods are useful where these are lacking and are essentially teaching or instruction. An apparent conflict exists between the view of the behaviorists that the client learns only when his learning is directed or controlled from without, and the view that the client is capable of learning on his own.

The early workers in behavior therapy oversimplified the approach, overgeneralized, and were overconfident and overoptimistic. Equating behavior therapy with learning techniques, they claimed the whole area of psychotherapy as a technology of learning. More recent work indicates that the situation is much more complex and less clear-cut than a simple application of laboratory techniques. Behavior therapists are rediscovering the complexity of learning of which the experimental psychologists in learning have long been aware, and are also discovering the significance of human relationship factors.

7. The recognition of the significance of the relationship, involving the complexities of social learning, brings behavior therapy close to the so-called 'traditional' therapies.

8. This provides the basis and opportunity for analyzing problems in learning in terms of those for which the relationship alone is the necessary and sufficient condition and those which require, in addition, information, direct instruction or training. The former, it is suggested, is psychotherapy, while the latter is teaching.

References

Alexander, F. (1963) The dynamics of psychotherapy in the light of learning theory. *American Journal of Psychiatry,* 201, pp. 440–8.

Baker, J. N. (1966) *Reason versus reinforcement in behavior modification.* Unpublished doctoral dissertation, University of Illinois.

Bandura, A. (1961) Psychotherapy as a learning process. *Psychological Bulletin,* 58, pp. 143–59.

Bandura, A. (1965) Behavioral modification through modeling procedures. In L. Krasner and L. P. Ullmann (Eds.), *Research in behavior modification.* New York: Holt, Rinehart and Winston. Pp. 310–40.

Bandura, A. (1968) On empirical disconfirmations of equivocal deductions with insufficient data. *Journal of Consulting and Clinical Psychology,* 1968, 32, pp. 247–9.

Bijou, S. W. (1966) Implications of behavior science for counseling and guidance. In J. D. Krumboltz (Ed.) *Revolution in counseling.* Boston: Houghton Mifflin. Pp. 27–48.

Breger, L., and McGaugh, J. L. (1965) Critique and reformulation of 'learning theory' approaches to psychotherapy and neuroses. *Psychological Bulletin,* 63, pp. 338–58.

Breger, L. and McGaugh, J. L. (1968) Learning theory and behavior therapy: A reply to Rachman and Eysenck. *Psychological Bulletin*, 65,pp. 170–3.

Cahoon, D. D. (1968) Symptom substitution and the behavior therapies: Reappraisal. *Psychological Bulletin*, 69, pp. 149–56.

Dollard, J., and Miller, N. E. (1950) *Personality and psychotherapy.* New York: McGraw-Hill.

Ericksen, C. W. (1962) *Behavior and awareness.* Durham: Duke University Press.

Ericksen, C. W. (1962) Figments, fantasies, and follies: A search for subconscious mind. In C. W. Ericksen (Ed.), *Behavior and awareness.* Durham: Duke University Press. Pp. 3–26.

Evans, R. (1968) B. F. Skinner: The man and his ideas. Excerpted in *Psychiatry and Social Science Review*, 12, 2, pp. 12.

Gelder, M. G., Marks, J. M. and Wolff, H. M. (1967) Desensitization and psychotherapy in the treatment of phobic states: A controlled study. *British Journal. of Psychiatry*, 1113, pp. 53–73.

Gilbert, W. (1967) Discussion In J. M. Whitely (Ed.) *Research in counseling.* Columbus, Ohio: Merrill. Pp. 30–5.

Goldiamond,I., and Dyrud, J. E. (1968) Some applications and implications of behavior analysis for psychotherapy. In J. M. Shlien (Ed.), *Research in psychotherapy*, Vol. III. Washington: American Psychological Association, pp. 54–89.

Goldstein, A. P. (1962) *Therapist-patient expectancies in psychotherapy.* New York: Pergamon Press.

Grossberg, J. M. (1964) Behavior therapy: A review. *Psychological Bulletin*, 62, pp. 73–88.

Hogan, R. A. and Kirchner, J. H. (1967) Preliminary report of the extinction of learned fear in a short-term implosive therapy. *Journal of Abnormal Psychology,* 72, pp. 106–9.

Hogan, R. A., and Kirchner, J. H. (1968) Implosive, eclectic verbal and bibliotherapy in the treatment of fears of snakes. *Behavior Research and Therapy*, 6, pp. 167–71.

Hunt, H. F. and Dyrud, J. (1968) Commentary: Perspective in behavior therapy. In J. M. Shlien (Ed.) *Research in psychotherapy*, Vol. III. Washington American Psychological Association. Pp. 140–54.

Kanfer, F. H. (1965) Vicarious human reinforcements: A glimpse into the black box. In L. Krasner and L. P. Ullmann (Eds.), *Research in behavior modification.* New York: Holt, Rinehart and Winston. Pp. 244–67.

Kiesler, D. J. (1966) Some myths of psychotherapy research and the search for a paradigm. *Psychological Bulletin*, 65, pp. 110–36.

Klein, M., Dittman, A. J., Parloff, M. B. and Gill, M. M. (1969) Behavior therapy: Observations and reflections. *Journal of Consulting and Clinical Psychology,* 33, pp. 259–66.

Krasner, L. (1965) Verbal conditioning and psychotherapy. In L. Krasner and L. P. Ullmann (Eds.), *Research in behavior modification.* New York: Holt, Rinehart and Winston. Pp. 211–28.

Krasner, L., and Ullmann, L. P. (Eds.) (1965) *Research in behavior modification.* New York: Holt, Rinehart and Winston.

Krumboltz, J. D., and Thoreson, C. E. (1964) The effect of behavioral counseling in group and individual settings on information-seeking behavior. *Journal of Counseling Psychology,* 11, pp. 324–33.

Lang, P. J. (1966) The transfer of treatment. *Journal of Consulting Psychology*, 30, pp. 375–8.

Lang, P. J., Lazovik, A. D., and Reynolds, D. J. (1965) Desensitization, suggestibility, and pseudotherapy. *Journal of Abnormal Psychology*, 70, pp. 395–402.

Lang, P. J., Melomed, Barbara G., and Hart, J. (No Date) *Automating the desensitization procedure: A psychophysiological analysis of fear modification.* Mimeographed paper.

Leff, R. (1968) Behavior modification and the psychoses of childhood: A review. *Psychological Bulletin*, 69, pp. 3, 46–409.

Levis, D. I., and Carrera, R. (1967) Effects of ten hours of implosive therapy in the treatment of outpatients: A preliminary report. *Journal of Abnormal Psychology,*72, pp. 504–8.

London, P. (1964) *The modes and morals of psychotherapy.* New York: Holt, Rinehart and Winston.

Lovaas, O. I. (1968a) Learning theory approach to the treatment of childhood schizophrenia. In A. B. Mills (Ed), *Behavior theory and therapy.* California Mental Health Research Symposium, No. 2. Sacramento: Bureau of Research, Department of Mental Hygiene.

Lovaas, O. I. (1968b) Some studies on the treatment of childhood schizophrenia. In J. M. Shlien (Ed.), *Research in Psychotherapy.* American Psychological Association. Pp. 108–21.

Maurath, J. D. (1966) Selective reinforcement versus cognitive structuring: Effects on 'motivational' behavior. Unpublished doctoral dissertation, University of Illinois.

Michael, J., and Meyerson, L. (1962) A behavioral approach to counseling and guidance. *Harvard Educational Review*, 32, pp. 382–402.

Miller, G. A. (1969) Psychology as a means of promoting human welfare. *American Psychologist,* 24, pp. 1063–75.

Murray, E.J.(1963) Learning theory and psychotherapy: Biotropic versus sociotropic. *Journal of Counseling Psychology*, 10, pp. 250–5.

Murray, E.J. (1968) Verbal reinforcement in psychotherapy. *Journal of Consulting and Clinical Psychology*, 32, pp. 243–6.

Murray E. D., and Jacobson, L. T. (1970) The nature of learning in traditional and behavioral psychotherapy. In A. B. Bergin and S. L. Garfield (Eds.), *Handbook ofpsychotherapy and behavior change.* New York: Wiley.

Orne, M. T. (1962) On the social psychology of the psychology experiment: With particular reference to demand characteristics and their implications. *American Psychologist.* 17, 776–83.

Orne, M. T., and Scheibe. (1964) The contribution of nondeprivation factors in the production of sensory deprivation effects: The psychology of the panic button. *Journal ofAbnormal and Social Psychology*, 68, pp. 3–12.

Patterson, C. H. (1970) A model for counseling and other interpersonal relationships. In W. Van Hoose and J. Pietrofesa (Eds.), *Counseling and guidance in the twentieth century.* Boston: Houghton Mifflin. Pp. 169–90.

Rachman, S. and Eysenck, H. J. (1966) Reply to 'a critique and reformulation' of behavior therapy. *Psychological Bulletin,* 65, pp. 165–9.

Rosenthal, R. (1966) *Experimenter effects in psychological research.* New York: Appleton-Century-Crofts.

Rubin, S. (1968) Direct reinforcement, vicarious reinforcement and reason in behavior modification. Unpublished doctoral dissertation, University of Illinois.

Sarason, I. G. (1965) The human reinforcer in verbal behavior research. In L. Krasner and L. P. Ullmann (Eds.), *Research in behavior modification.* New

York: Holt, Rinehart and Winston. Pp. 229–43.

Schwitzgebel, R. K. and Traugott, M. (1968)Initial note on the placebo effect of machines. *Behavioral Science*,13, pp. 267–72.

Serber, J. (1968) Instructions versus reinforcement in generalization of positive self-references. Unpublished masters thesis, University of Illinois.

Shoben, B. J. (1949) Psychotherapy as a problem in learning theory. *Psychological Bulletin*, 46, pp. 366–92.

Skinner, B. F. (1968) *The technology of teaching. New* York: Appleton-Century-Crofts.

Spielberger, C.D. (1962) The role of awareness in verbal conditioning. In C.W. Erickson (Ed.), *Behavior and awareness*. Durham: Duke University Press. Pp. 73–101.

Stampfl, T. G. and Levis, D. J. (1967) Essentials of implosive therapy: A learning theory based psychodynamic behavioral therapy. *Journal ofAbnormal Psychology,* 72, pp. 496–03,

Ullmann, L. P. and Krasner, L. (1969) *A psychological approach to abnormal behavior.* New York: Prentice-Hall.

Ullmann, L. P. and Krasner, L. (Eds.). (1965) Introduction, *Case studies in behavior modification*. New York: Holt, Rinehart and Winston.

Valins, S., and Ray, A. A. (1967) Effects of cognitive desensitization of avoidance behavior. *Journal of Personality and Social Psychology*, 7, pp. 345–50.

Weitzman, B. (1967) Behavior therapy and psychotherapy. *Psychological Review*,1, pp. 300–17.

Wiest, W. M. (1967) Some recent criticisms of behaviorism and learning theory with special references to Breger and McGaugh and to Chomsky. *Psychological Bulletin*, 67, pp. 214–25.

Wilson, G. T., Hannon, A.E,. and Evans, W. I. M.(1968) Behavior therapy and the therapist-patient relationship. *Journal of Consulting and Clinical Psychology*, 32, pp. 103–9.

Wolpe, J. (1958) *Psychotherapy by reciprocal inhibition*. Stanford: Stanford University Press.

Wolpe, J. (1968) Some methods of behavior therapy. In A. B. Mills (Ed.), *Behavior theory and therapy.* California Mental Health Research Symposium, No. 2. Sacramento: Bureau of Research, Department of Mental Hygiene.

Wolpe, J., and Lazarus, A. A. (1966) *Behavior therapy techniques*. New York: Pergamon.

Wolpin, M. (1968) Guided imagining in reducing fear and avoidance behavior. In A. B. Mills (Ed.), *Behavior theory and therapy*. California Mental Health Research Symposium, No. 2. Sacramento: Bureau of Research, Department of Mental Hygiene. Pp. 37–49.

Wolpin, M., and Raines, J. (1966) Visual imagery, expected roles and extinction as possible factors in reducing fear and avoidance behavior. *Behavior Research and Therapy*, 4, pp. 25–37.

Yates, A. J. (1970) *Behavior therapy.* New York: Wiley.

CONTROL, CONDITIONING AND COUNSELING

6

Psychology, as the science of behavior, is concerned with the understanding, prediction, and control of such behavior. Counseling and psychotherapy, it is asserted, have as goals the changing of behavior. An individual who is unproductive, unhappy, frustrated, dependent, irresponsible, overly submissive or overly aggressive, et cetera, is expected to become productive, happy, independent, responsible, able to function without undue submissiveness or aggressiveness or other undesirable or self-defeating behavior. In the school situation, we hope that counseling will produce a well-behaved student, one who shows the proper degree of dependence and independence, who is attentive, interested, motivated, and achieves up to his ability level, in other words, the ideal student. And often teachers and administrators are not concerned about how the counselor achieves this result, as long as he achieves it.

Control of behavior a fact

Psychology, as the science of behavior, should be able to tell us something about methods of changing or modifying human behavior. What does psychology provide in the way of techniques of changing or controlling human behavior?

Although the achievements of psychology are quite modest, and do not measure up to the conceptions of the man in the street, considerable progress has been made in the prediction and control, if not the understanding, of behavior. Although there are differing conceptions of the process and of its operation, the control of behavior through the administering of rewards and punishment has been possible to some extent for a long time (Schlosberg, Skinner, Miller, & Hebb, 1958). The whole field of education has, of course, benefited from the contributions of psychology to the teaching-learning process, with the current teaching machines being only the most recent application of psychology to education.

Perhaps the most recent and spectacular method of changing behavior is by the use of subliminal stimulation (McConnell, Cutler, & McNeil, 1958). Attitudes, opinions, and behavior can apparently be controlled, at least to some extent under some conditions, without the individual being aware of it. While there is some

First published in *Personnel & Guidance Journal*, 1963, 41, pp. 680–6. © ACA.
Reprinted by permission of the American Association for Counselling and Development. No further reproduction authorised without written permission of ACA.

question as to how effective this method is, so that it is belittled by some psychologists, yet we cannot discount the possibilities of its becoming highly effective.

A method about which there is no question regarding its effectiveness is that known as operant conditioning (Schlosberg, et al, 1958). Operant conditioning is the shaping of behavior through the reinforcement of spontaneous behavior approximating the desired response, and gradually eliciting and rewarding responses which are closer and closer to the desired response. Skinner developed this method, beginning with pigeons, which were taught, among other things, to bowl.

Using this method, an experimenter, or interviewer, can, by his reactions to the verbalizations of the subject, or client, influence verbal behavior. The first study in this area was that of Greenspoon (1950, 1955). He instructed subjects to say all the words they could think of, not using sentences or phrases. Plural nouns were reinforced by the examiner saying 'mmm' and 'huh-uh'. The first expression resulted in an increase in plural responses, while the second led to a decrease, but both expressions resulted in increases when applied to nonplural responses. Numerous studies done since have confirmed the fact that verbal behavior can be influenced by this method of operant conditioning (Cohen, et al, 1954; Hildum & Brown, 1956; Sapolsky, 1960; Salzinger & Pisoni, 1958, 1960; Quay, 1959; Rogers, 1960; Wilson & Verplanck, 1956).

While none of the studies has reported results in actual counseling or psychotherapy, some have approached this. Rogers (1960) found that he could increase negative self-reference statements by saying ' mmm-hmmm' and nodding. Although positive self-references were not increased, they remained the same when responded to, while decreasing when not responded to. Schizophrenic patients, as well as normals, have been found to increase the number of statements referring to affect, when the interviewer reinforced such statements by agreement (Salzinger & Pisoni, 1958, 1960). Isaacs, Thomas and Goldiamond (1960) report that psychotics can be 'taught' to verbalize by operant conditioning after years of muteness. All of these results can be brought about without the awareness of the subject, although awareness may be present.

The technique may be said to be still in the experimental stage. The effectiveness of the procedure in terms of the extent and duration of the changes produced is not known. There is also the possibility that verbal behavior may be changed without any change in other aspects of the individual's behavior. As Hildum and Brown (1956) note: 'Perhaps a patient could even be brought to an appearance of mental health through the encouragement of "healthy" responses'. Delusional patients have been known to conceal or deny their delusions in order to achieve the reward of favorable consideration for discharge from the hospital.

That the attitudes and theories of the therapist can affect the responses of the client has been suspected for some time. The way in which this occurs now seems apparent, that is, through the operant conditioning of the responses of the patient by the verbal and nonverbal behavior of the therapist, without either the therapist or client being aware of the process. In this way, clients talk about what interests the therapist, and produce support for his theories. As Hildum and Brown (1956) put it, 'the therapist who believes in the importance of the Oedipus complex could elicit Oedipal content by means of selective reinforcement'. Quay (1959) has experimentally demonstrated this by increasing the discussion of family memories through reinforcement of such material.

The implications of the operant conditioning of verbal behavior thus have significance for counseling and psychotherapy. It might appear that counseling, as a method for controlling and changing behavior, is in for a revolutionary change. It might seem that we have at least the beginnings of objective, practical techniques which can take counseling and psychotherapy out of what many consider to be the realm of fumbling trial and error, flying by the seat of the pants, or intuitive behavior, and bring it into the realm of a scientific procedure involving the application of known objective techniques with known, objective results. 'For those interested in such things there appears a glittering new prospect for human manipulation' (Hildum & Brown, 1956).

Control for what?
This, it would seem, is a goal to be devoutly desired, and anything which promises this should be seized upon. But before we become too confident that we are approaching the millennium, let us consider the implications of this approach to the modification of human behavior. First, we must recognize that science provides us with techniques, but does not determine the goals toward which we use the technique. What are the results of this approach to changing behavior? What are the indirect as well as the direct results? What are the implications for a philosophy of human life and behavior?

There are many who are concerned, if not alarmed, at the potentialities for evil inherent in the use of these and other techniques, such as the use of drugs, for changing and controlling behavior. Aldous Huxley (1959) is one of these. Another is Paul Tillich (1961), the theologian, who points out that science is corrupting the religion and philosophy of modern man by giving him means without ends. Skinner, an advocate of control, nevertheless recognizes that 'There is good reason to fear those who are most apt to seize control' (1953, p. 438). These techniques of control may be, and are, used in propaganda and indoctrination, and are an important element in the process of brainwashing (Farber, Harlow, & West, 1957).

But it is not only the specter of Orwell's 1984 (Orwell, 1949), which some discount as a possible or probable result of the application of these techniques, which faces us. Skinner, in his novel *Walden Two* (Skinner, 1948), presents the possibilities of operant conditioning for controlling human behavior in a way which would be acceptable to many. He outlines a utopia based upon the shaping and control of human behavior by operant conditioning without the awareness of the subjects that they are being controlled. He notes that 'if it's in our power to create any of the situations which a person likes or to remove any situation he doesn't like, we can control his behavior. When he behaves as we want him to behave, we simply create a situation he likes, or remove one he doesn't like. As a result, the probability that he will behave that way again goes up, which is what we want' (p. 216). He continues: 'We can achieve a sort of control under which the controlled, though they are following a code much more scrupulously than was ever the case under the old system, nevertheless feel free. They are doing what they want to do, not what they are forced to do . . . there's no restraint and no revolt. By a careful cultural design, we control not the final behavior, but the inclination to behave — the motives, the desires, the wishes' (p. 218). To the charge of despotism, Skinner replies: 'I don't think anyone should worry about it. The despot must wield his power for the good of others. If he takes any step which reduces the sum total of human happiness, his power is reduced by a like amount. What better check against malevolent despotism could you ask for?' (p. 220). He presents the possibilities of molding personality. 'What do you say to the design of personalities? . . . The control of temperament? Give me the specifications, and I'll give you the man! What do you say to the control of motivation, building interests which will make men most productive and most successful?' (p. 243). This is reminiscent of J. B. Watson.

In the utopia described by Skinner everyone is well-behaved, productive, secure, happy. But is this utopia? Is this a sufficient and desirable goal for man? The goals are chosen by the benevolent despot, not by the people, who are not free, even though they have the sense of freedom. Skinner argues that man is not free in any event. But nevertheless, there is a degree of freedom, and in Skinner's utopia even this is eliminated. Some would feel that if we can make people productive and happy, with a sense of freedom, by methods which do not use force or threat of force, this would be a utopia. Some reason that since positive reinforcement is sought by the individual, there is a freedom or choice present.

Who selects the goals?
But we cannot get away from the fact that the goals are selected by another, that there is control and manipulation of behavior even if the subjects are not aware of it and are happy. Indeed, these results are achieved because the control and manipulation is so complete. People become automatons. As Tillich (1961) puts it, the manipulation of conditioned reflexes by social and psychological engineering reduces man to the status of an object rather than a subject.

This is not the place to enter into a discussion of free will versus control. There are obviously various kinds and degrees of control, by different sources of control. A word might be said about the word 'manipulation', however, to which there has been some objection. The writer has used this word elsewhere (Patterson, 1958, 1959) to designate a highly controlled approach to human behavior and human relations. It is recognized, as has been frequently pointed out, that the concept of manipulation or control represents a continuum, that there is no state of absence of manipulation, and that everyone, including the client-centered counselor, as we shall see, manipulates. But again, it is equally obvious that there are extremes to any continuum, and the difference between the extremes — a matter of five or six standard deviations — is significant, both statistically and practically. The word is used for want of a better. The matter of degree of manipulation, or control, of the behavior of one person by another is something that must be faced. Is a state of complete control even for the goal of happiness, security, and contentment, desirable? And is the conditioning method the only method for changing behavior? We shall consider the last question first, and then return to the first.

Fortunately for mankind, in the opinion of some, there is another way of changing human behavior, a way which is also supported by scientific research. It is a method of changing behavior without depriving the individual of freedom. In fact, its purpose and result is to free the individual as much as possible from the control of external circumstances and to enable him to achieve control of himself and his environment. The goal of this approach — a goal which is outside of, and not determined by, science — is self-direction and self-actualization. For simplicity, we shall refer to this as the understanding approach to human behavior. There is no implication that it is one extreme of the manipulation or control continuum; it may be a qualitatively different approach, although it does represent a minimum of control.

We now know the conditions under which constructive personality change can occur without the introduction of control and manipulation of the responses of the individual. These are the conditions of client-centered counseling. We shall not here consider these conditions. But we should dispose of a question which arises from an apparent contradiction in client-centered counseling. On the one hand, we emphasize the independence, responsibility, self-determination, and freedom of choice of the individual. On the other hand we refer to the conditions of counseling and the techniques of the counselor, which are imposed on the client, with little that he can do about it. Isn't the client-centered counselor being manipulative here?

In a broad sense of the term, the answer is yes. The counselor is attempting to influence the behavior of the client — this is obvious; otherwise he wouldn't be engaged in counseling. We must recognize that anything we do, in or out of counseling, has some influence on others; that it is not possible, in this sense to avoid some control or manipulation of the behavior of others. It is important, however, to recognize this and to determine what kind of an influence we wish to have upon others. The client-centered counselor is aware of this influence and is clear upon the kind of influence he desires to have upon the client. The objective of this manipulation distinguishes it from other kinds of manipulation. The nature of the behavior changes desired, and which the conditions are designed to bring about, are not the changes occurring under the conditions of direct conditioning of behavior as outlined under the manipulative approach discussed above. The goal of counseling, and the result of the conditions established, is the freeing of the client for self-direction or self-actualization. As Rogers recently phrased it, 'We have established by external control conditions which we predict will be followed by internal control by the individual, in pursuit of internally chosen goals ... by less dependence upon others, an increase of expressiveness as a person, an increase in variability, flexibility, and effectiveness of adaptation, an increase in self-responsibility and self-direction' (Rogers, 1961). The difference, then, is one of directly conditioning behavior which is desired by the manipulator on the one hand, and on the other providing the conditions under which the individual is enabled to make his own choices and decisions regarding his specific behavior. We freely admit that the latter is a choice of the counselor as the goal of counseling, and thus represents his values and philosophy.

We cannot deny that the counselor's behavior, and his responses to the client, do influence the client's verbalizations, and in this sense the counselor utilizes operant conditioning. The techniques which the counselor uses may be considered as the operant conditioning of the client's behavior in the interview. It is necessary that the client talks, if he is to make progress in counseling. Listening by the counselor, and the showing of interest and concern in what the client is saying, encourage the client to talk and to continue talking. In addition, the client must talk about certain things in certain ways if he is to progress in understanding of himself. The counselor encourages the client to talk about himself and his relations with others, about his feelings and attitudes toward himself and others, by responding to self-statements and feelings, and by not responding to comments or statements about the weather, current events, or other impersonal material. The research on operant conditioning helps us to understand what we do in counseling. But the important point is that the counselor uses such a technique not to control or manipulate the client's behavior toward specific counselor-chosen goals, but to encourage client behavior which will lead to the development of a situation in which the client gains in self-understanding, self-reliance, and the ability to take responsibility for himself and his behavior. In other words, the counselor's techniques may be viewed as operant conditioning which creates the conditions for achieving the goal of counseling which is self-determination and self-actualization.

Underneath techniques

But the application of the technique merely to get the client to talk about himself is apparently not sufficient for continued progress on the part of the client. More than this appears to be necessary. There seems to be reason to believe that only when there is genuine interest in and understanding of the client when he responds to these techniques that he can make progress. The counselor must be genuine and offer a relationship into which the client can enter, rather than being a detached, objective, uninvolved outsider applying a carefully planned conditioning technique. That is, it seems that the optimum condition for personality development on the part of the client — the most powerful reinforcer, in conditioning terms — is the genuine, spontaneous concern, interest and understanding of the counselor. This, rather than dispensing simple rewards, either of candy or cigarettes by a machine or verbal rewards or behavior such as smiling or nodding, is apparently necessary for real growth in the client. The study of Sapolsky (1960) lends some support to the importance of other factors than the routine administration of reinforcement. In two experiments he showed that the effectiveness of reinforcement depended upon the relationship between the experimenter and the subject. Subjects who were given instructions which pictured the experimenter as attractive conditioned well, while those who were led to perceive the experimenter as unattractive did not condition during the experimental period, although there was evidence of delayed conditioning. Similarly, subjects who were matched with experimenters for similarity (compatibility) on the basis of a personality test conditioned better than those who were incompatible.

Summary

Recent developments in psychology relating to the control of human behavior raise some problems and issues of significance to counseling and psychotherapy.

They require us to examine the goals and techniques of counseling, as well as the goals of society. The issues have been stated, and a resolution, recognized as only tentative, has been attempted.

We may summarize by suggesting that there are two basically different approaches to counseling, or indeed to any human relationship. The first of these, designated as manipulation, is characterized by the shaping or molding of the behavior of others in directions determined by the counselor. The direction, or the resulting behavior, may be for the presumed good of the person being directed — his adjustment, integration, happiness, freedom from symptoms, etc. But this is as defined by the counselor. The essence of the approach is that the counselor is an outside, external force determining rather specific behavior outcomes by his activities. As the control of the counselor increases, as his goals become more specific in terms of behavior outcomes, the freedom of the client becomes restricted.

The second approach has been termed understanding. Here the counselor has as his goal not specific behavior outcomes or actions; the goal is for the client to become a responsible, independent, self-actualizing person capable of determining his own behavior.

Perhaps the terms manipulation and understanding are not the best ones to use here. It has been pointed out that the counselor using the understanding approach manipulates. He manipulates or controls the counseling environment. But the control is for the purpose of creating a situation which will result in a freeing of the client from the more detailed, restrictive controls not only of the counselor but of others in his environment, so that he may become, insofar as possible, a responsible, self-controlled individual rather than an automaton or puppet, even a happy one, dancing to the tune of the counselor or of others in his environment. It is the goal of the counseling process, perhaps more than a complete difference in techniques, which distinguishes the two approaches.

Nevertheless, the understanding approach is more than the application of techniques. The essential nature of this approach is the establishing of a human relationship in which the emphasis is upon the expression of certain attitudes, rather than the rigid, wooden, standardized application of techniques. The condition for personality change of the kind desired in the understanding approach is an atmosphere of acceptance, interest, and understanding, a genuine relationship rather than a controlled application of a technique in a cold, objective, detached manner.

References

Cohen, B. D., Kalish, H. I., Thurston, J. R., and Cohen, E. (1954) Experimental manipulation of verbal behavior. *Journal of Experimental Psychology*, 47, pp. 106–10.

Farber, I. E., Harlow, H. F., and West, L. J. (1957) Brainwashing, conditioning, and DDD (debility, dependency, and dread). *Sociometry*, 20, pp. 271–85.

Greenspoon, J. S. (1950) The effect of a verbal stimulus as a reinforcement. *Proceedings of the Iowa Academy of Science*, 59, p. 287.

Greenspoon, J. (1955). The reinforcing effect of two spoken sounds on the frequency of two responses. *American Journal of Psychology*, 68, pp. 409–16.

Hildum, D. C., & Brown, R. W. (1956) Verbal reinforcement and interviewer bias. *Journal of Abnormal and Social Psychology*, 53, pp. 108–11.

Huxley, A. (1959) In Featherstone, R. M., & Simon, A. (Eds.) *A pharmacologic approach to the study of the mind.* Springfield, Illinois: Thomas.

Isaacs, W., Thomas, J., and Goldiamond, I. (1960) Application of operant conditioning to reinstate verbal behavior in psychotics. *Journal of Speech & Hearing Disorders.* 25, pp. 8–12.

Krasner, L. (1958) Studies of the conditioning of verbal behavior. *Psychological Bulletin*, 55, pp. 148–70.

Lindsley, O. R. (1956) Operant conditioning methods applied to chronic schizo-phrenic patients. *Psychiatric Research Reports. No. 5. Research techniques in schizophrenia.* Washington, D. C., American Psychiatric Association. Pp. 118–53.

Lindsley, O. R., and Skinner, B. F. (1954) A method for experimental analysis of the behavior of psychotic patients. *American Psychologist*, 9, pp. 419–20.

McConnell, J. V., Cutler, R. L., and McNeil, E. B. (1958) Subliminal stimulation: an overview. *American Psychologist*, 13, pp. 229–42.

Orwell, G. (1949). *1984.* New York: Harcourt, Brace.

Patterson, C. H. (1958) Two approaches to human relations. *American Journal of Psychotherapy*, 12, pp. 691–708.

Patterson, C. H. (1959. *Counseling and psychotherapy: Theory and practice.* New York: Harper.

Quay, H. (1959) The effect of verbal reinforcement on the recall of early memories. *Journal of Abnormal and Social Psychology*, 59, pp. 254–7.

Rogers, C. R. (1961) The place of the person in the world of the behavioral sciences. *Personnel & Guidance Journal*, 39, pp. 444–51.

Rogers, M. J. (1960) Operant conditioning in a quasi-therapy setting. *Journal of Abnormal and Social Psychology*, 60, pp. 247–52.

Salzinger, K., and Pisoni, Stephanie. (1958) Reinforcement of affect responses of schizophrenics during the clinical interview. *Journal of Abnormal and Social Psychology*, 57, pp. 84–90.

Salzinger, K., and Pisoni, S. (1960) Reinforcement of verbal affect responses of normal subjects during the interview. *Journal of Abnormal and Social Psychology*, 60, pp. 127–30.

Sapolsky, A.(1960) Effect of interpersonal relationships upon verbal conditioning. *Journal of Abnormal and Social Psychology*, 60, pp. 241–6.

Schlosberg, H., Skinner, B. F., Miller, N. E., and Hebb, D. O. (1958) Control of behavior through motivation and reward. *American Psychologist*, 13, pp. 93–113.

Skinner, B. F. (1948) *Walden two.* New York: Macmillan, .

Skinner, B. F. (1953) *Science and human behavior.* New York: Macmillan.

Tillich, P. (1961) Report of a speech given at Massachusetts Institute of Technology in *Time*, April 21, p. 57.

Verplanck, W. S. (1955) The control of the content of conversation: reinforcement of statements of opinion. *Journal of Abnormal and Social Psychology*, 51, pp. 688–76.

Wilson, W. C., and Verplanck, W. S. (1956) Some observations on the reinforcement of verbal operants. *American Journal of Psychology,* 69, pp. 448–51.

Is Cognition Sufficient?

7

On May 14–17, 1967 a conference on Counseling Theories and Counselor Education was held at Onamia, Minnesota. George A. Kelly was scheduled to present his position on psychotherapy. He had requested that I respond to his paper. However, shortly before the conference he died. Leon H. Levy replaced him. This paper is a response to Dr Levy's paper titled 'Fact and Choice in Counseling and Counselor Education: A Cognitive Viewpoint'. Levy's paper is published in the book reporting the conference edited by Clyde Parker — see references. It is felt that my paper can stand alone, so it is included here.

The paper by Dr Levy presenting a cognitive viewpoint in counseling created in me a state of cognitive dissonance. The viewpoint is inconsistent with my theory and approach to counseling. And since I abhor inconsistency (which I do not believe must be pathognomonic or pathogenic), I must do something about it. There must be some way of reconciling (apparent) differences between honest and intelligent individuals; after all, neither can be wrong.

But was it cognitive dissonance that I experienced, or was it affect arousal? Is cognitive dissonance entirely cognitive, or is it always associated with, or followed by, affect?

Is man a rational being, or is he essentially a rationalizing being, using reason in the service of affect and emotion? Are choices and decisions essentially rational, based upon logical analysis of the problem and alternative solutions, or are choices and decisions influenced by feelings and emotions? Are psychological problems the same as scientific problems, to be solved through logical analysis?

The answers to these questions should be obvious. At least they are to me although I do not claim to be a completely rational being and admit to rationalizing. It would seem to me obvious that counseling is not a rational or logical process, or the application of rational, logical procedures with a client and his problems. Nevertheless, this is a widely held concept, at any rate among a certain segment of counselors. Perhaps — and this may be a new insight to me — it is this concept of counseling which leads to the insistence on differentiating between counseling

First published in Clyde A. Parker (Ed.) *Counselor Theory and Counselor Education.* Boston: Houghton Mifflin Company, 1968 (pp. 85–96). © University of Minnesota Office of the General Council. Reprinted by permission.

and psychotherapy. But if counseling is differentiated from psychotherapy on the basis of being a process of rational problem solving and decision making — or, as Weitz (1964) proposes, developing problem-solving skill — then it becomes difficult if not impossible to differentiate counseling from teaching, or individual tutoring. If counseling is not psychotherapy, is counseling then not teaching? It appears that the concept of counseling as a cognitive or rational process is prevalent among academically oriented counselors and counselor educators, including the University counseling center staff, and counselor educators whose background is in education, with little or no psychology. Levy seems to accept this concept of counseling when he says that counseling becomes 'another exercise in problem solving and creativity. It becomes educational rather than remedial or clinical . . .' What about the client who requires no education, or even re-education, but needs to find out who he is, what the meaning of life is or could be for him, how to reduce the discrepancy between what he is and what he wants to be or can be, how to get rid of crippling feelings and attitudes?

It is, of course, true that cognition is receiving increasing attention. Perhaps it has, in the recent past, been underemphasized in the study of behavior and in education. But, in the characteristic manner of human beings, the pendulum may be swinging too far in this direction. Some counselors may be so sensitive to trends and so fearful of being left behind that, to mix a metaphor, they are jumping on the pendulum and being swung into outer space.

Now, of course, psychologists, as scientists, claim to be rational and objective. But it is interesting to note the affective strength with which this claim is defended. I have been impressed, incidentally and parenthetically, with the feeling with which editorial reviewers of psychological journals condemn an author for showing his feelings and values.

The neocognitivists, to coin a word, have the new look. That is, they recognize the influence of perception (which has affective elements) on cognition, and Levy makes it clear that 'the facts' are not the objective facts sought by Sergeant Friday. His is not a 'naïve realism' but actually a phenomenological viewpoint: 'to either understand, predict, or modify the behavior of an individual in a situation, it is necessary to know the meaning of that situation to him. To know the facts of a person's existence, that is, we must first know the ways in which he codes his experience.' Facts do not, then, exist in some external world or constitute an external reality; they are constructed, or created, by the individual. Facts are the perceptions, concepts, meanings, attitudes, constructs, beliefs, etc., held by the individual. This is a phenomenological position. If one understands that 'fact', as used by Levy in his description of the counseling process, is the meaning of the situation to the client, one can accept, at least in part, his statement that 'The counselor is expected to help the client consider all the facts, distinguishing between relevant and irrelevant facts, accept them, and make the most of life in the face of these facts'. One might substitute 'meanings' or 'perceptions', then, for 'facts'. But when one does that, it becomes apparent that the statement does not describe all of counseling, since it is possible, and perhaps desirable, that meanings and perceptions should change as a result of counseling. Thus, counseling does not accept facts as immutable, to be accepted and adjusted to by the client.

Cognitions and 'facts'

The question which arises when one uses the term 'facts' in this way is whether counseling is, or can be, a purely cognitive process. To apply the term 'fact' may give it the appearance of a cognitive process, but the definition of fact given by Levy suggests that it is only an appearance, based upon the use of a word associated with cognition but not, as defined, necessarily a purely cognitive term, as witness the cognates which are suggested: 'meanings', 'concepts', 'perceptions', etc. Are such 'facts', or perceptions or meanings, affect free, or rationally determined? The new 'look' in perception, dating back to the study of Postman, Bruner, and McGinnies (1948) on personal values as selective factors in perception, makes it clear that perception is not a purely cognitive process but involves affect as well. Facts are not entirely objectively determined and thus cannot be treated as objective and impersonal, or apart from the emotions of the individual. Levy, of course, recognizes this.

Man is not a rational being, living in a 'real' world of 'facts', He is an affective, rationalizing being living in a phenomenological world which he in a sense created and to which he gives meanings — and the meanings are influenced by his feelings and emotions. The fact of man's nonrationality is clearly demonstrated in his persistent claim to being rational in the face of overwhelming evidence that he is not rational.[1]

The individual is a unitary organism, with cognitive, conative, and affective aspects, none of which can be divorced from each other and dealt with separately. Therefore, any approach to counseling or psychotherapy must recognize the affective nature of man.

This view, long accepted in education, is epitomized in the statements that the whole child comes to school and that teachers teach pupils, not subject matter. If the affective factors are important in subject-matter learning, are they not more important in the learning that occurs in counseling or psychotherapy, with its infinitely greater ego involvement? The difference is belittled by those who attempt to emphasize the similarity of teaching and counseling. Representative of their attitude is the slogan that teaching and counseling are alike except that the subject matter of teaching consists of academic disciplines while the subject matter of counseling is the client himself, the implication being that this difference is not significant. I have sometimes suggested, perhaps minimizing similarities for the sake of emphasizing the differences, that the greatest similarity of counseling and teaching is that both make use of a 50 minute hour.

---

1. Nicholas Hobbs ('Sources of gain in psychotherapy', *American Psychologist*, 1962, 17, 18-34), in discussing the strength of the belief in the efficacy of insight, relates it to 'our strong general commitment to rationality in problem solving'. As F. S. C. Northrop has pointed out, Western culture (in spite of its immense irrationalities) has a deeply ingrained rational component. For us, reason is a faith. From earliest childhood we are taught to apply rational principles to the solution of many kinds of problems.

There are, of course, similarities, since both deal with a total human being. Education recognizes the importance of the affective aspect of the person. Perhaps it may be contended that many approaches to counseling or psychotherapy do not adequately recognize the cognitive aspects. The difference between teaching and psychotherapy may be essentially one of emphasis, with teaching emphasizing cognitive learning while recognizing the influence of affective factors, and psychotherapy emphasizing affective change while recognizing cognitive factors. In the client with deep personal problems, however, affective factors overshadow cognitive factors, and the counselor must recognize and deal with these. Rational thinking and behavior may be a goal of counseling, but it may be that, once the affective factors are dealt with, the client will need little if any help in working through the cognitive aspects of his problems. Yet peculiarly Levy seems not to accept greater rationality as a goal of counseling: '. . . it is not rationality that the counselor is after in helping his client, but a better conceptual scheme'. A rational approach to counseling or psychotherapy must be one which recognizes and deals with the affective and nonrational nature of man. Counselors must *feel* with their clients rather than *think* with them.

The importance of the atmosphere in counseling is its relationship to the affective aspects of the client's problem. The therapeutic atmosphere is anxiety reducing, desensitizing the client's emotional reactions to his experiences. It is nonthreatening, leading to self-exploration, or dealing with affect-laden ego-involving ideas. Absence of threat, and the accompanying reduction of anxiety, has been demonstrated to lead to greater exploration and improved problem solving in noncounseling situations and to client self-exploration and therapeutic personality change in counseling (Truax, 1963). Thus, Levy's statement that the client will be more receptive to the facts of his life and be guided by them in an unthreatening, accepting, and warm atmosphere, though intuitively plausible, but apparently not demonstrated, is simply not true.

The virtues of inconsistency seem to be overrated by Levy. If, as the aphorism says, consistency is the virtue of simple minds, then our greatest scientists have been simpletons. Inconsistencies certainly exist, and we must accept some, but the acceptance of all can lead to passivity. Refusal to accept inconsistencies is the source of discovery and scientific advancement. Levy misreads history if he feels that it is inconsistency which reflects growth. It is the refusal to accept inconsistency itself, and certainly not its acceptance, that results in growth. There is a need for consistency in human beings, perhaps constituting or including the need for self-consistency or the need for integration. The striving for consistency, the reduction of apparent contradictions, leads to the development of theories and systems which in turn spur investigations and experiments designed to test hypotheses of consistencies. In addition, while a moderate amount of inconsistency may constitute a challenge and lead to growth, great inconsistency may constitute a threat and lead to disturbance.

Interestingly, Levy presents a dualism in his approach to counseling. On the one hand, he points out that the client needs help because he has run out of alternatives, which the counselor must supply. Yet, at the same time, he states that

'Most importantly, [the client] needs to learn a new stance in relation to his experience, a different perspective so that he can find his way out of the box he is in'. Thus, it seems, it is not so much new knowledge as new perceptions which are necessary; counseling is not the suggestion of new alternatives by the counselor but the emerging of new alternatives in the client as a result of his new perceptions. Again, 'it is not additional information that is required as often as it is additional ways of interpreting information'. While Levy apparently considers this a highly cognitive process, it appears to be one involving feelings and emotions.

Counselor and client

The problem of counseling or psychotherapy, then, is not getting the client to think differently but getting him to feel differently. In fact, it may be suggested that the way to get people to think differently is to get them to feel differently, and thus to perceive differently. One need only consider the different thinking of the depressed and the manic individual to recognize the influence of affect on perception and thinking. One does not try to change thinking in counseling, therefore, but to change feelings and perceptions. The achievement of this change is not by means of information giving, analysis of alternatives, teaching problem solving, or applying logic, but through providing a safe, secure, nonthreatening relationship in which self-exploration and changes in perception can occur. The counselor does not — indeed, cannot — change the facts or perceptions of the client. Only the client can do so. The counselor can facilitate — or hinder — the process, however. Intervention of the cognitive kind, I suggest, hinders rather than facilitates perceptual change. It may facilitate the solution of essentially cognitive problems, or assist in the making of choices in which affective factors are minimal. But this, it is proposed, is not counseling, but teaching, and probably not what most clients who need and want counseling require.

The cognitive approach apparently has little confidence in the client. The client cannot be depended on to solve his own problems or effect his own change. The providing of an atmosphere or conditions for client self-exploration and changes in perception is not considered sufficient. Levy states that 'If the counselor sees the world as his client does, he has little to offer him'. He must 'provide the new and different inputs necessary to help his client move forward'. Yet the counselor must see the 'client's problem as the result of how he has coded or construed events', which Levy feels is a cognitive process. But this is empathic understanding, achieved by adopting the internal frame of reference of the client, and hardly a purely cognitive process. The solution to a client's problem is, as Levy notes, helping him find different ways of construing (or perceiving) events. But this is not achieved, except possibly on an intellectual or verbal level, by a cognitive approach. It is not verbalizations about the events which must change, but the perceptions of the events.

Again and again in counseling I have found that the client can and does change his perceptions — or his personal constructs — when the counselor enters his frame of reference and sees things as the client does. When a client says, 'Things are completely black,' the counselor may simply respond, 'Everything is completely black.' Then the client is enabled to say, 'Well, perhaps not everything,' or, 'Well, perhaps not completely.' But if the counselor responds by saying, 'Things can't be completely black,' or 'Everything can't be completely black,' the client will probably reiterate his statement or defend it, thus leading to resistance to changing his perception. I recently supervised a student who was working with a child. For several interviews the child reported incident after incident of being picked on, discriminated against, misunderstood, etc. The student counselor felt that no progress was being made, so we looked closely at what he was doing. It became apparent that he was not in the client's frame of reference but was seeing the child as being somewhat paranoid or showing ideas of reference. The client did not feel he was being understood or accepted and persisted in trying to get the counselor to see things as he did.

Now, seeing things as the client sees them does not mean, as Levy seems to say, that the counselor agrees with the client and accepts the client's perceptions as being unchangeable or not in need of change. On the other hand, it is not necessary for the counselor to keep reminding himself and the client that there is a difference between the client's perception and the counselor's, or that understanding of the client's perceptions does not mean acceptance of them as fixed. And it does appear to be sufficient that the counselor see how the client perceives things for the client to begin to change his perceptions. This is what empathic understanding is. The new perceptions are those of the client; he must change his perceptions. The counselor cannot offer or provide new perceptions, which are his own, and which cannot become those of anyone else. Kelly apparently recognizes this when he notes that the counselor does not attempt to pass his own constructs on to the client; if he should do so, the client would translate and change them to fit his own construct system (Kelly, 1955, pp. 593–4). Thus does Levy fuse concepts and percepts, reason and affect, logic and psychologic, and the behavior of the scientist with the process of developing personal constructs.

The scientist qua scientist is not functioning as an ordinary human being in relationship to his environment. Although he is not entirely able to shed his humanity to become an objective observer and analyzer, in the pursuit of science he strives to do so. That it is not a natural, ordinary, or easy thing is attested to by the difficulty, and incompleteness, with which it can be achieved. Therefore, the analogy of the development of the individual's personal construct system with the practice of the scientist is misleading. True objectivity would make of man an (almost) affectless human being. It would, or should, lead to more homogeneity and less conflict between the personal construct systems of individuals. Scientists also, if they were successful in achieving rationality, would evidence less disagreement (often accompanied by considerable feeling) than they do.

The difficulty seems to lie in not assigning affect the place it should have in the development of personal construct systems and in their change. Affect seems to be implicit in Kelly's system, certainly as an underlying factor in the rigidity and resistance to change of personal constructs. But peculiarly it is not recognized and dealt with, at least overtly and explicitly, in counseling. In the same way, emotion seems to permeate personal constructs, which determine one's facts or one's perceptions, yet no overt recognition is given to the emotional component pervading the personal construct system. Personal constructs are said to be responsive to validating and invalidating evidence, but the resistance to such evidence indicates their emotional component. And it is, of course, known that one's hypotheses can be confirmed by manipulation of events and data in response to strong emotions or belief or desire to see certain results.

If there is one thing that experience and experiment in psychology has demonstrated, it is that attitudes, beliefs, perceptions (and personal constructs) are not altered easily if at all by logic, reason, and argument — that is, by rational approaches. Yet cognitive counseling proposes to do exactly this. To quote Levy, 'the activity he [the counselor] and his client are engaged in is no different from that of the scientist and theorist'. This activity, he says, leads to 'changes in the nature of the client's construct repertoire and . . . belief system. Feelings, needs, and motives are not ignored, but they are viewed as part of the context in which solutions are to be sought and as subject to reconstruction themselves,' presumably by the same cognitive approach. The resulting changes — indeed, all changes — are apparently regarded as cognitive changes. Yet they are not 'insights', which are 'equated with the discovery of Truth', but are simply alternative ways of construing or perceiving events.

It is interesting how strongly theorists resist the acceptance of the relationship as the effective element in counseling. They view it instead as the substratum, the nonspecific context, or, as Levy terms it, the medium. There is probably no doubt that what is added to the basic relationship has some influence on the outcome, but questions may be raised as to the necessity or desirability of this influence. However, if one defines counseling as teaching, as many, including Levy, apparently do, perhaps something more than the relationship must be provided, something of the kind Levy describes.

The statement that 'it would be grossly inefficient if we failed to make use of man's symbolic processes and relied solely upon the experiential component of the counseling relationship in trying to communicate with clients and modify their cognitive structures' needs some experimental support, particularly when it has been pretty clearly demonstrated that the relationship alone does lead to change, and to change from more emotional to more rational behavior.

The cognitive counselor in action

The difficulty with the cognitive approach as outlined by Levy is not necessarily its goals, nor its description (at least in broad outline) of the process of change in counseling. The goal of counseling is change in perceptions or the personal construct system, leading to changes in behavior. The counseling process involves exploration by the client of new ways of perceiving or construing events, choices, decisions, etc. The difficulty is the methods by which change is induced, the techniques of counseling. Can change be achieved by the methods proposed by the cognitivists, even when applied in a warm, nonthreatening relationship, if the latter can actually be provided using these methods? The reason for doubt and questioning is that perceptions and personal constructs are not purely, or even mainly, cognitive. It appears that Levy equates cognitions with perceptions or personal constructs. This equating is deceptive and lends plausibility to his argument which it does not merit. The research he cites provides evidence for the importance of perceptions, with their affective components, rather than for cognition, which is, or has always been, contrasted with affect.

If there is cause to believe that cognitive counseling is not effective with emotional problems, how does one account for the (apparent) success of the approach? The answer is relatively simple. Cognitive counselors do not do what they say they do — or, perhaps better, they do not limit themselves to cognitive counseling. They can and do offer a relationship. Like the behavior therapists, they state that this is not the effective element, but they have not demonstrated their claim. Their effectiveness may be, and probably is (as with behavior therapy) more the result of the relationship than added specific techniques. It is high time, especially in view of the evidence we have for the effectiveness of the relationship alone, that those who claim added effects from specific methods or techniques demonstrate the effects rather than assuming them. We cannot accept success as evidence for the effectiveness of the approach unless it is shown that the success is not or cannot be achieved by the relationship alone.

The implications for counselor education suggested by Levy do not appear to be closely related to the cognitive approach to counseling which he outlines. His methods are not highly cognitively oriented. There are no courses in logic, reasoning, pitfalls in thinking, argument and persuasion, or in social, cultural, educational, occupational, and other information, which should be very much part of the background of a cognitive counselor. There may be an overemphasis on learning and cognition as compared to personality and emotion. Few, if any, would disagree with the comments on the milieu of counselor education, however. The practicum, on the other hand, may seem to reflect the cognitive approach, with much time spent in 'discussing the client's cognitive structure and how it may account for his present behavior'. But if one reads 'perceptual structure' or 'personal construct system' for 'cognitive structure', there would probably be little objection. It is interesting that Levy places little emphasis upon technique and specific interventions, whether in terms of analysis of the student's past interviews or with reference to what he should do in future interviews. 'Technique is surely discussed, but it is secondary to understanding.' There can be scant disagreement with the general discussion of supervision.

The foregoing discussion may be obscured by terminology. Levy uses the term 'cognitive' in its generally accepted meaning as covering all aspects and means of knowing, including perceiving as well as recognizing, judging, reasoning, and conceiving. Difficulty and confusion arise, however, in that the view of the nature of perception has changed. Perception is no longer seen as being determined by, or isomorphic with, external stimuli or the excitation of sensory receptions. In other words, perception is not purely cognitive but has affective aspects or components, as well as cognitive elements. Thus the old classification of mental processes into cognitive, affective, or conative is no longer possible. All mental or psychological events or processes, and all behavior, as indicated earlier, partake of all three aspects. Levy includes affective elements in his cognitive approach through recognizing their influence on perception. His approach is accordingly not purely cognitive in the old sense of being separate from or excluding affect. His cognitive viewpoint is clearly not a solely intellectual or rational approach to counseling.

My criticism, therefore, is directed to the relative emphasis on a rational, logical, intellectual approach as compared to an emphasis on an affective, experiential, relationship approach to counseling. To me, the former is an overemphasis on the nonaffective aspects of psychological problems, or a lack of recognition of the affective influences on behavior. The question is not one of either-or, but of more or less. The difference, however, is not to be minimized. The emphasis in dealing with psychology and problems in counseling or psychotherapy should, in my opinion, be heavily on the affective, experiential side. The development of skill or effectiveness in this area should be the focus in counselor education. The stress on the rational and the logical in all other areas of education should be sufficient to assure that the cognitive (nonaffective) aspects of counseling will not be neglected. In fact, the greatest problem in counselor education, I believe, is getting counseling students to reduce the cognitive factor and attend to the affective aspects of the client, his problems, and the relationship.

References

Kelly, G. A. (1955) *The psychology of personal constructs. Vol. II: Clinical diagnosis and psychotherapy.* New York: Norton.

Levy, L. H. (1968) Fact and choice in counseling and counselor education: A cognitive viewpoint. In C. A. Parker (Ed.) *Counseling theories and counselor education.* Boston: Houghton Mifflin.

Postman, L., Bruner, J. S., and McGinnies, E. (1948). Personal values as selective factors in perception. *Journal of Abnormal and Social Psychology,* 43, pp. 142–54.

Truax, C. B. (1963) Effective ingredients in psychotherapy: An approach to unraveling the patient-therapist interaction. *Journal of Counseling Psychology,* 10, pp. 256–64.

Weitz, H. (1964) *Behavior change through guidance.* New York: Wiley.

Eclecticism in Psychotherapy: is Integration Possible?

8

Interest in eclectic psychotherapy, and in the integration of various systems of psychotherapy, have been increasing in recent years. Goldfried and Safran (1986, p. 463) note that 'the indications are very clear that the field of psychotherapy in the 1980s is highlighted by a rapid developing movement toward integration and eclecticism'. The extent of this interest is indicated by Norcross's (1986) edited book. Included are chapters by authors of the major eclectic positions including Beutler (1983, 1986), Garfield (1980, 1986), Hart (1983, 1986), Lazarus (1981, 1986), and Prochaska and DiClementi (1984, 1986). Goldfried and Newman (1986) provide a historical background, and Dryden (1986), Goldfried and Safran (1986), Messer (1986) and Murray (1986) provide critical comments. Perusal of these presentations and other writings, in the process of preparing a paper on 'Foundations for a Systematic Eclectic Psychotherapy' (Patterson,1989), suggested a number of issues that have not been adequately recognized or considered.

1. The objective of any movement toward eclecticism or integration in psychotherapy must be the development of a single comprehensive system of psychotherapy including philosophical and theoretical foundations, the derivative principles guiding practice, and the implementation of these principles. Norcross (1986b, p.11) notes that 'the promise of eclecticism is the development of a comprehensive psychotherapy based on a unified and empirical body of work'. At the present time, nothing of this sort has been proposed (with the exception of my paper). The existing proposals for an eclectic psychotherapy are independent of each other. Each incorporates limited combinations of methods, strategies and techniques from existing theories or approaches, with little attention to any philosophy or theory. What appears to be happening is the development of a number of new approaches on the way to becoming schools. Dryden (1986, p. 374), evaluating the contributions in the Norcross volume, writes: 'There is little evidence at present that the contributors . . . are drawing upon one another's work to a significant degree. This surprises and troubles me.' Goldfried and Safran (1986, p. 466) make the same point:

First published in *Psychotherapy*, 1989, 26, pp. 157–61. Reprinted by permission of the publisher.

Although there is an increasing acknowledgement of the need to develop a more integrative approach to psychotherapy, we are far from having any consensus as to exactly what that approach should be . . . there exists a real danger that . . . we may ultimately end up with as many eclectic models as we currently have schools of psychotherapy.

It seems that the present situation does not provide any basis for optimism about achieving the goal of a comprehensive unified system. Norcross (1986, p. 6) writes: 'The ideal of integrating all available psychotherapy systems is not likely to be met'. London (1988, p. 10) recognizes that integration may not be possible but does not suggest any reasons: 'Integration involving conceptual continuity across all techniques is still missing, and it is missing for a good reason, I think. It may not be possible.'

2. Current eclectic attempts neglect theory. Murray (1986, p. 405) writes: 'in the contributions of the eclectic therapists in this volume, theoretical orientations play a relatively small role.' He continues: 'However, true integration requires a coherent theoretical structure, which does not yet exist. We are still waiting for our theoretical integration' (p. 413).

3. Not only is theory neglected, but there is little concern with research support. Eclectic writers emphasize the empirical bases of their proposals, but this is essentially nothing more than their own individual clinical experience, or at most one or a few limited studies whose results agree with their system. Also, as Dryden (1986, p. 373) notes, the research literature is interpreted differently by different authorities.

4. Clearly, we are at a very early stage in the development of a truly systematic eclectic psychotherapy. Many writers have noted obstacles in the way. The nature and seriousness of these obstacles do not seem to be adequately acknowledged or recognized. The result is that optimism about progress is perhaps greater than is warranted. Two major problems are considered.

Incompatible theoretical orientations

The neglect of theory appears in part to represent the apparent perception of many writers that (a) theory is not important in the practice of psychotherapy, or (b) there are no irreconcilable elements in the various theories, or (c) theories are too abstract and complex to attempt to integrate. Goldfried's proposal that integration should be attempted at the level of strategies rather than at the level of techniques or theory (Goldfried, 1980; Goldfried and Padawer, 1982; Goldfried and Safran, 1986), however, is based on the belief that 'In the search for commonalities, it is unlikely that we can ever hope to reach common ground at either the theoretical or the philosophical level' (Goldfried, 1980, p. 984). Further, Goldfried and Safran (1986, p. 468) suggest that

There is always the danger that comparative analysis [of the psychotherapy process] at the higher levels of abstraction [philosophical and theoretical] will obscure important similarities in [the] psychotherapy process, both because of differences in theoretical language and because of abstract philosophical differences that never really translate into clinical reality.

But focusing on strategies rather than theories does not avoid the theoretical incompatibilities. Strategies involve goals, and goals involve theory. Casting the therapist as a strategist puts him/her in the role of expert, the planner and director of therapy. (Strategies also imply conflict — generals plan strategies in war; and chess players plan strategies in the game of chess.) While this concept of the therapist is widely, if not generally, accepted, it is not the only concept of the therapist.

Thirty years ago the writer suggested that there are two conflicting approaches to psychotherapy (and to human relations in general) (Patterson, 1958, 1959). One approach, the manipulative approach, casts the therapist as an expert, controlling and directing the therapy process. The second, or understanding, approach places the locus of control with the client, with the therapist facilitating the therapy process through empathic understanding. London (1964) has also noted these two major approaches to psychotherapy. These two approaches represent two different views of human beings, described by Allport (1962) as on the one hand reactive beings, controlled from without (behaviorism) or within (psychoanalysis), and on the other hand as a being in the process of becoming. That these two opposed, and irreconcilable, approaches still exist was apparent at the 1985 Phoenix Conference at which 26 of the world's leading therapists lectured and demonstrated before an audience of some 7000 (Zweig, 1987). The conference was a veritable Tower of Babel. Yet Margo Adler, reporting on the conference for PBS radio, said that there were two different kinds of therapists present: the manipulators and the enablers, or, as more commonly termed, the facilitators.

Until we can reach agreement on the nature of human beings, no agreement on a philosophy or theory of psychotherapy is possible. And until some agreement on philosophy and theory is achieved, no agreement on the practice of psychotherapy is possible.

The paradigm for eclectic psychotherapy

The basis for eclectic practice is the contention that different clients and different problems require different treatments.

This paradigm was stated clearly by Paul (1967, p. 111): 'In all its complexity, the question toward which all outcome research should ultimately be directed is the following: *What* treatment, by *whom*, is most effective for this individual with *that* specific problem, and under *which* set of circumstances'. Krumboltz (1966) had phrased it: 'What we need to know is which procedures and techniques, when used to accomplish what kinds of behavior change, are most effective with what kind of client when applied by what kind of counselor'. Blocher (1968, p. 16) writes: 'The old question of "Is counseling effective?" or "Which counseling theory is correct?" are (*sic*) largely seen as rhetorical. They give way to questions of "What treatment in the hands of which counselors can offer what benefit to particular clients?"' Strupp and Bergin (1969, pp. 19–20), in an extensive review of research in psychotherapy, wrote:

> We have become convinced that the therapy of the future will consist of a set of specific techniques that can be applied under specifiable conditions to specific problems, symptoms or cases . . . the problem of psychotherapy research, in its most general terms, should be reformulated as a standard scientific question: What specific therapeutic interventions produce what specific changes in specific patients under specific conditions?

This has been the model for much of the research by behaviorists in psychotherapy. Some 20 years later, no progress seems to have been made in specifying different treatment for different clients with different problems. A consideration of the requirements for adequate research following this paradigm should reveal the basis for lack of success. The model requires (a) a taxonomy of client problems (a reliable, relevant diagnostic system), (b) a taxonomy of therapist qualities, (c) a taxonomy of therapeutic interventions (strategies and techniques), (d) a taxonomy of relevant circumstances, conditions, situations, or environments in which therapy is provided, and (e) principles or empirical rules for matching all these variables. Given, for simplicity, that there are five classes of variables, each with ten levels, the resulting research design would have so many cells as to be unrealistic; this is probably what led Kisch and Kroll (1980, p. 406) to note that 'the compelling question of what aspects of therapy work for what kinds of problems when practiced by what kinds of therapists for what kinds of patients is probably empirically unanswerable because it is methodologically unsolvable'.

Yet the paradigm is still held to. Goldfried (1986) embraces this model, as do Omer and London (1988). Norcross (1986b) emphasizes that 'eclecticism addresses a central concern of mental health professionals', and 'the optimal match between the intervention, the patient, the problem, and the setting'. Murray (1986, p. 414) still hopes that 'the use of techniques that fit the particular client, problem, and situation may result in an improved product'.

This is, however, not the only paradigm. There is an alternative. As Ford and Urban (1967, p. 340) noted most theories 'have characterized all behavior disorder as resulting from a common nucleus . . . it follows that one psychotherapeutic approach will suffice for all'. It is the concept of the unitary nature of emotional disturbance (Angyal, 1941; Menninger et al. 1958; Menninger et al. 1963; Patterson, 1948, 1949, 1958, 1974, 1985). Functional emotional disturbance is a problem in interpersonal relationships, resulting from the lack or inadequacy of an understanding, caring, respecting, warm (unconditional positive regard), and honest, genuine personal environment. The providing, by the therapist, of empathic understanding, respect and genuineness is the specific treatment for this condition. It is a manifestation of the philosophy and theory of the understanding approach to human relations. Such an approach enables the client to take responsibility for himself/herself and make the choices, decisions and behavior changes that lead to becoming a more self-actualizing person — the goal of this approach to human behavior and of its system of psychotherapy.

The application of this approach is spelled out in this writer's work cited above, and, of course in the work of Carl Rogers. It is not currently a popular or widely practiced approach. The therapist conditions are, of course, widely recognized and accepted, but are seldom practiced consistently and without added strategies or techniques — they are accepted as important, even necessary for effective psychotherapy, but not as sufficient. The relationship that they constitute is considered as either preliminary to the beginning of 'real' therapy or as providing a basis from which the therapist operates to actively intervene with other strategies and techniques. Empathic understanding, for example, is a technique, to be used to provide a basis for diagnosis and interpretation.

Summary
Current eclectic approaches and attempts at integration in psychotherapy have not been successful. Obstacles to integration have been noted (e.g. Dryden, 1986; Goldfried and Safran, 1986; Messer, 1986; Murray, 1986). But there exist at least two sources of irreconcilable differences: (a) in philosophies and theories of human nature; and (b) in views of the nature of functional emotional disturbances and its treatment. The currently accepted paradigms in each of these areas appear to preclude the achievement of an integrative, comprehensive system of psychotherapy. It is suggested that a paradigm shift is necessary before this can be achieved. Prospects for this are not good. Mook (1988, p. 5) quotes Max Planck, the physicist: 'a new scientific truth does not triumph by convincing its opponents . . . but rather because its opponents eventually die, and a new generation grows up that is familiar with it'. Mook continues: 'Paradigms change by attrition as well as, or instead of, by persuasion. But the process can also work the other way: A paradigm can be *locked in* by attrition as we lose, first, those who hold alternative views, and later, those who even remember that there are any.' There is a danger that this is what is happening in the present situation in psychotherapy.

References
Allport, G. W. (1962) Psychological models for guidance. *Harvard Educational Review*, 32, 373–81.

Angyal, A. (1941) *Foundations for a science of personality*. New York: Commonwealth Fund.

Beutler, L. E. (1983) *Eclectic psychotherapy: A systematic approach*. New York: Pergamon.

Beutler, L. E. (1986) Systematic eclectic psychotherapy. In J. C. Norcross (Ed.), Handbook of Eclectic Psychotherapy, (Pp. 94–131). New York: Brunner/Mazel.

Blocher, D. (1968) What can counseling offer clients? In J. M. Whitely (Ed.), *Research in counseling*, (Pp. 5–20). Columbus, OH: Merrill.

Dryden, W. (1986) Eclectic psychotherapies: A critique of leading approaches. In J. C. Norcross (Ed.), *Handbook of eclectic psychotherapy*, (Pp. 353–75). New

York: Brunner/Mazel.

Ford, D. H., and Urban, H. B. (1967) Psychotherapy. *Annual Review of Psychology,* 18.

Ford, D. H., and Urban, H. B. (1971) Some historical and conceptual perspectives on psychotherapy and behavior change. In A. E. Bergin and S. L. Garfield (Eds.), *Handbook of psychotherapy and behavior change.* New York: Wiley.

Garfield, S. L. (1980) *Psychotherapy: An eclectic approach.* New York: Wiley.

Garfield, S. L. (1986) An eclectic psychotherapy. In J. C. Norcross (Ed.), *Handbook of eclectic psychotherapy,* (Pp. 132–62) New York: Brunner/Mazel.

Goldfried, M. R. (1980) Toward the delineation of therapeutic change principles. *American Psychologist,* 35, 991–9.

Goldfried, M. R. (Ed.) (1982) *Converging themes in psychotherapy.* New York: Springer.

Goldfried, M. E., and Newman, C. (1986) Psychotherapy integration: An historical perspective. In J. C. Norcross (Ed.), *Handbook of eclectic psychotherapy,* (Pp. 25–61). New York: Brunner/Mazel.

Goldfried, M. R., and Padawer, W. (1982) Current status and future directions in psychotherapy. In M. R. Goldfried (Ed.), *Converging themes in psychotherapy.* New York: Springer.

Goldfried, M. R., and Safran, J. D. (1986) Future directions in psychotherapy integration. In J. C. Norcross (Ed.), *Handbook of eclectic psychotherapy,* (Pp. 463–83). New York: Brunner/Mazel.

Hart, J. T. (1983) *Modern eclectic therapy: A functional orientation to counseling and psychotherapy.* New York: Plenum.

Hart, J. T. (1986) Functional eclectic therapy. In J. C. Norcross (Ed.), *Handbook of eclectic psychotherapy,* (Pp. 201–25). New York: Brunner/Mazel.

Kisch, J., and Kroll, J. (1980) Meaningfulness vs effectiveness. *Psychotherapy: Theory, Research and Practice,* 17, 401–13.

Krumboltz, J. D. (1966) Promoting adaptive behavior. In J. D. Krumboltz (Ed.), *Revolution in counseling,* (Pp. 3–26). Boston: Houghton-Mifflin.

Lazarus, A. A. (1981) *The practice of multimodal therapy.* New York: McGraw-Hill.

Lazarus, A. A. (1986) Multimodal therapy. In J. C. Norcross (Ed.), *Handbook of eclectic psychotherapy,* (Pp. 65–93). New York: Brunner/Mazel.

London, P. (1964) *The modes and morals of psychotherapy.* New York: Holt, Rinehart and Winston.

London, P. (1988) Metamorphosis in psychotherapy: Slouching toward integration. *Journal of Integrative and Eclectic Psychotherapy,* 7 (1), 3–12.

Menninger, K., Ellenberger, H. F., Pruyser, P., and Mayman, M. (1958). The unitary concept of mental illness. *Bulletin of the Menninger Clinic,* 22, 4–12

Menninger, K., Mayman, M., and Pruyser, P. (1963) *The vital balance.* New York: Viking Press.

Messer, S. R. (1986) Eclecticism in psychotherapy: Underlying assumptions, problems, and trade-offs. In J. C. Norcross (Ed.), *Handbook of eclectic psychotherapy,* (Pp. 379–97). New York: Brunner/Mazel.

Messer, S. B., and Winokur, N. (1980) Some limits to the integration of psychoanalytic and behavior therapy. *American Psychologist*, 35, 818–27.

Mook, D. G. (1988) The selfish paradigm. [Review of the battle for human nature: Science, morality and modern life.] *Contemporary Psychology*, 33, 5–7.

Murray, E. J. (1986) Possibilities and promises of eclecticism. In J. C. Norcross (Ed.), *Handbook of eclectic psychotherapy*, (Pp. 398–415). New York: Brunner/Mazel.

Norcross, J. C. (Ed.) (1986b) *Handbook of eclectic psychotherapy*. New York: Brunner/Mazel.

Norcross, J. C. (1986b) Eclectic psychotherapy: An introduction and overview. In J. C. Norcross (Ed.), *Handbook of eclectic psychotherapy*, (Pp. 3–24). New York: Brunner/Mazel.

Omer, H., and London, P. (1988) Metamorphosis in psychotherapy: End of the systems era. *Psychotherapy*, 25, 171–80.

Patterson, C. H. (1948) Is psychotherapy dependent on diagnosis? *American Psychologist*, 3, 155–9.

Patterson, C. H. (1949) Diagnosis and rational psychotherapy. *Journal of Nervous and Mental Disease*, 109, 440–50.

Patterson, C. H. (1958) Two approaches to human relations. *American Journal of Psychotherapy*, 12, 691–708.

Patterson, C. H. (1959) *Counseling and psychotherapy: Theory and practice*. New York: Harper and Row (Chapter 6).

Patterson, C. H. (1974) *Relationship counseling and psychotherapy*. New York: Harper Row.

Patterson, C. H. (1985) *The therapeutic relationship*. Belmont, CA: Brooks/Cole.

Paul, G. L. (1967) Strategy of outcome research in psychotherapy. *Journal of Consulting Psychology*, 31, 109–19.

Prochaska, J. O., and DiClementi, C. C. (1984) *The transtheoretical approach: Crossing the traditional boundaries of therapy*. Homewood, IL: Dow Jones-Irvin.

Prochaska, J. O., and DiClementi, C. C. (1986) The transtheoretical approach. In J. C. Norcross (Ed.), *Handbook of eclectic psychotherapy*, (Pp. 163–200). New York: Brunner/Mazel.

Strupp, H. H., and Bergin, A. E. (1969) Some empirical and conceptual bases for coordinated research in psychotherapy. *International Journal of Psychiatry*, 7 (7), 18–90.

Wachtel, P. L. (1977) *Psychoanalysis and behavior therapy: Toward an integration*. New York: Basic Books.

Zweig, J. K. (Ed.) (1987) *The evolution of psychotherapy*. New York: Brunner/Mazel.

FOUNDATIONS FOR A SYSTEMATIC ECLECTIC PSYCHOTHERAPY

9

Two topics are currently prominent in discussions of psychotherapy: (1) eclecticism, and (2) integration. These are not synonymous terms. Goldfried (1982b), and Goldfried and Newman (1986) provide useful histories of attempts at therapeutic integration. Current formulations of eclectic psychotherapy are not really integrative. They consist of a congeries of disparate techniques from many different — and often disparate and inconsistent — theoretical approaches, with little attempt at systematic integration. They pay little, if any, attention to the common elements in the major theories. The idea of common elements in different approaches has a long history, briefly reviewed here. Two classes of common elements are distinguished: (1) nonspecific elements, i.e., those elements not specifically related to the nature of client disturbance or therapy outcomes (the placebo), and (2) specific elements, directly related to client disturbance and therapy outcomes. The second group of common elements is proposed as a basis for a systematic eclecticism.

The rise of eclecticism
Eclecticism is not a new development. Most therapists were probably eclectic in the first half of the century, before the development of the current major theories. Psychoanalysis and its derivatives were the first theories to develop and most of those therapists who were not eclectic adhered to some form of psychoanalysis or psychoanalytic (dynamic) therapy. The so-called Minnesota point of view (Patterson, 1966, 1973, 1980) was an eclectic position. Thorne (Patterson, 1966, 1973, 1980, 1986) was perhaps the first to adopt the term eclecticism to designate a detailed, systematically developed position.

The number and percentage of psychologists (therapists) who considered themselves eclectic during the 1940s and 1950s is not known. Thorne (Personal communication, June 2, 1967) gives a figure of zero for members of the American Psychological Association who identified themselves as eclectic, but the source of this figure is not known. Kelly (1961) reported a survey in which 40% of those responding in 1960 identified themselves as eclectic. Since then numerous surveys

First published in *Psychotherapy*, 1989, 26, pp. 427–35. Reprinted by permission of the publisher.

have found the percentage of psychologists (therapists) accepting the designation ranging from 30% to 65%, and fluctuating around 50% (Garfield and Kurtz, 1974, 1976; Swan and MacDonald, 1978; Larson, 1980; Fee, Elkins and Boyd, 1982; Smith, 1982; Norcross and Prochaska, 1982; Prochaska and Norcross, 1983; Watkins, Lopez, Campbell and Himmell, 1986; Mahoney, Norcross, Prochaska and Nissar, unpublished manuscript, 1986).

It appears that the popularity of eclecticism may be declining; it is too early to sound the death knell for schools or theories. Eclecticism, while the most frequently chosen label by therapists (clinical and counseling psychologists), still claims less than 50% of those responding to surveys. The statement by Lambert, Shapiro, and Bergin (1986, p. 202) that '. . . the vast majority of therapists have become eclectic in orientation' is an overstatement. An important point not addressed adequately in surveys is just what eclecticism means.

What is eclectic psychotherapy?

There is an increasing literature on eclecticism in psychotherapy, including the *Journal of Integrative and Eclectic Psychotherapy*. Various kinds of eclecticism have been proposed: theoretical eclecticism, technical eclecticism (Lazarus, 1981), prescriptive eclecticism (Dimond, Havens, and Jones, 1978), strategic eclecticism (Held, 1984), radical eclecticism (Robertson, 1979), and perhaps others. Most discussions of eclectic therapy involve combining two theories or approaches, usually psychoanalysis and behavior therapy (e.g. Wachtel, 1977). A number of books go beyond this, however: Beutler (1983), Garfield (1980), Hart (1983), Lazarus (1981), Norcross (1986a), Palmer (1979) and Prochaska and DiClementi (1984). The general impression from all this literature is one of confusion. It is not clear just what eclectic therapy is. Those who call themselves eclectic appear to have little in common. They do not subscribe to any common set of principles. While they may not be anti-theoretical or even atheoretical, there is nothing that could be called an eclectic theory. Garfield and Bergin (1986) note that 'there is no single or precise definition of an eclectic orientation . . . it is exceedingly difficult to characterize an eclectic approach in terms of either theory or procedures' (p. 8). Garfield's (1982) earlier characterization still holds: 'Eclecticism is perceived as the adherence to a nonsystematic and rather haphazard clinical approach' (p. 612). Strupp and Binder (1984) make a similar statement: 'The term eclectic, which many therapists use to describe their orientation and practices, is so fuzzy it defies definition' (p. xii). In effect, there are as many eclectic approaches as there are eclectic therapists. Each operates out of his or her unique bag of techniques, on the basis of his or her particular training, experiences, and biases, on a case-by-case basis, with no general theory or set of principles as guides.

Prochaska and Norcross (1983) note that:

> The need for theoretical orientation has been frequently recognized, but few, if any, adequate models of systematic eclecticism have been created . . . Beyond its conceptual relativity and personal appeal, eclecticism in its current state may not possess adequate clinical utility or validity for increasing numbers of therapists (p. 171). The real

challenge for synthetic eclectic therapists and theorists alike is to construct models of systematic eclecticism that have both empirical validity and clinical utility (p. 168).

A true eclecticism is neither nonsystematic nor haphazard.

English and English (1958) define it as follows:

Eclecticism. n. In theoretical system building, the selection and orderly combination of compatible features from diverse sources, sometimes from incompatible theories and systems; the effort to find valid elements in all doctrines or theories and to combine them into a harmonious whole. Eclecticism is to be distinguished from unsystematic and uncritical combination, for which the name is syncretism.

This definition of eclecticism is accepted for the purposes of this paper. In addition, the object of the paper is not to attempt to support another kind of eclecticism, but to suggest the basis for a single, all-encompassing system, which is presumably the ultimate goal of all those concerned with psychotherapy.

Common elements in pychotherapy

The confusing state of eclectic (actually syncretic) psychotherapy is due to two factors: (1) in rejecting various theories, theory has been ignored or downplayed in the eclectic stance, and (2) in the attempt to include as many diverse methods or techniques as possible, there is little concern with their compatibility or orderly integration. Most eclectic approaches have been built upon the differences among the various approaches rather than upon similarities.

Yet it has been recognized for at least 50 years (Rosenzweig, 1936) that there are basic common factors or elements in the diverse approaches to psychotherapy. Following Rosenzweig, numerous writers have suggested various common factors.

The common factors noted have been numerous and varied. (Our concern here is with therapist variables only, and not with client variables.) At the simplest and most concrete level, therapy consists of two persons talking to each other. At the most abstract level, therapy is an interpersonal relationship, in which the therapist's personality (undefined) is the most important element. In between are such therapist behaviors or characteristics as status or superiority, authority, expertise, rapport, and support. More current terms are therapist credibility, trustworthiness, and attractiveness. Other writers have listed more specific techniques: catharsis, suggestion, reassurance, persuasion, advice, guidance, and direction. These are not present, however, in all theories or approaches. Still other factors noted are acceptance and understanding of the client, permissiveness, nonjudgmentalness, respect, honesty or genuineness.

Frank (1982), who has been writing about common elements for nearly 25 years, has focused on a group of components more complex than simple lists, centering on his concept of therapy as a 'means of directly or indirectly combating demoralization' (p. 19). His first component is 'an emotionally charged confiding relationship with a helping person', involving the therapist's status or reputation but also including the communication of caring, competence, and the absence of ulterior motives (p. 19). Second, is a healing setting that heightens the client's expectation of help from a healer and that provides safety. Third, is 'a rational, conceptual scheme or myth that provides a plausible explanation for the patient's symptoms and prescribes a ritual or procedure for resolving them' (p. 20). The fourth is 'a ritual that requires active participation of both patient and therapist and that is believed by both to be the means of restoring the patient's health' (p. 20). Though developed in detail over a period of time, Frank's elements are abstract and not operationalized. Yet they have apparently had wide acceptance. They bear a striking resemblance to Fish's (1973) delineation of placebo therapy.

In 1967 Truax and Carkhuff, after reviewing the major theoretical approaches to psychotherapy, in a chapter titled 'Central Therapeutic Ingredients: Theoretic Convergence', found three sets of characteristics: (1) 'the therapist's ability to be integrated, mature, genuine or congruent', (2) 'the therapist's ability to provide a non-threatening, trusting, safe or secure atmosphere by his acceptance, non-possessive warmth, unconditional positive regard, or love', and (3) the therapist's ability to be 'accurately empathic, be with the client, be understanding, or grasp the patient's meaning' (Truax and Carkhuff, 1967, p. 25). Accurate empathy, respect or nonpossessive warmth, and genuineness are 'aspects of the therapist's behavior that cut across virtually all theories of psychotherapy and appear to be common elements in a wide variety of approaches to psychotherapy and counseling' (p. 25). Truax and Carkhuff note that these are the therapist conditions for client therapeutic personality change posited by Rogers (1957).

Recently there has been considerable attention to what has been termed the 'working alliance' in psychotherapy. Gelso and Carter (1985), in their extensive review of the literature on the therapy relationship, include the working alliance as one of three components of the relationship, the other two being the transference or the 'unreal' relationship, and the real relationship. In the working alliance are included the therapist's concern and compassion, empathy, genuineness and respect. The real relationship includes openness, honesty and genuineness.

It appears that there is general agreement that the relationship offered or provided by the therapist is a (the) basic common characteristic of all approaches to psychotherapy. There is disagreement, however, on how the elements in this relationship are viewed — as nonspecific or specific, and as necessary or as necessary and sufficient.

Specific versus nonspecific factors

The common elements have long been referred to as nonspecific factors. The term seems to derive from their wide variety, their general nature, and 'the lack of a clear and consistent meaning for what these factors are. *Nonspecific factors* has been used as a catch-all term for many variables inherent in one or more treatments . . . the researchers may view them as ancillary to therapeutic change but important to rule out explicitly . . .' (Kazdin, 1979, p. 846).

The number and variety of the common or nonspecific factors suggest that it might be useful to attempt to group them into categories. Nearly 30 years ago this writer suggested that there are two kinds of so-called nonspecific or common variables (Patterson, 1959, Chap. 13). One category includes factors such as the therapist's authority, status, expertise, prestige, attractiveness, credibility. It includes techniques such as persuasion, suggestion, encouragement, reassurance, guidance. The second category includes therapist acceptance, permissiveness, warmth, respect, nonjudgmentalism, honesty, genuineness, and empathy or empathic understanding.

There is little disagreement about the importance, even the necessity, of the second group of therapist variables in psychotherapy. Prioleau, Murdock, and Brody (1983) are among the many who recognize this: 'The importance of such qualities have [*sic*] ... been almost universally accepted by all psychotherapies, with varying levels of emphasis'. Lambert, Shapiro, and Bergin (1986) note that 'virtually all schools of psychotherapy accept the notion that these or related therapist variables are important for significant progress in psychotherapy, and in fact, fundamental in the formation of a working alliance' (p. 171). After recognizing the crucial nature of relationship factors, however, they state that this 'is not to say that techniques are irrelevant but that their power for change is limited when compared to personal influence' (p. 202). The belief that techniques are necessary dies hard, as will be noted later.

Lambert (1986), referring to a current review (Lambert, Shapiro, and Bergin, 1986), notes that client ratings of therapist understanding and acceptance have been found to be related to client-rated outcome 'across a wide variety of therapies' and such results, are quite common in the psychotherapy literature' (p. 189). He continues that this suggests that,

at least from the patients' point of view, effective treatment is due to factors associated with relationship variables and the personal qualities and attitudes of the therapist. That these personal qualities bear a striking resemblance to each other, across studies and methodologies, is evidence that they are important in psychotherapy outcome and are prominent ingredients of change in most if not all therapies (p. 189).

It is argued here that the variables in the first category above are truly nonspecific. They constitute, in effect, the placebo (Fish, 1973; Patterson, 1985b; Pentony, 1981; Shapiro, 1971; Shapiro and Morris, 1978). Critelli and Neumann (1984) note that 'the common factors of psychotherapy conform closely to traditional listings of placebo variables, including factors such as suggestion, persuasion, treatment credibility, therapist attention, expectancy of cure, and demand for improvement' (p. 35).

Many writers seem to consider the entire relationship, or the therapist's entire contribution to the relationship, as nonspecific. The behavior therapists appear to be among these. This view would imply that psychotherapy is (nothing but) a placebo. Shapiro (1971) stated that his chapter would be 'an examination of psychotherapy as a placebo' (p. 443). Shapiro and Morris (1978) refer to the study by Luborsky, Singer, and Luborsky (1975) that found in a comparison of the effectiveness of several types of psychotherapy that all were about equally effective, and that concluded that this improvement was related to the patient-therapist relationship shared by all types. Shapiro and Morris refer to this as a demonstration of the placebo effect.

Frank, viewing the relationship as nonspecific, at least implies that it is a placebo (1982). His common elements appear to be those included in the placebo category above. And later (Frank, 1983), in a response to an article on placebos, titles his response 'The placebo is psychotherapy'.

The variables in the second category of common elements, far from being nonspecific, are the specific elements in psychotherapy. They are the active ingredients in a healing or therapeutic relationship. Kazdin (1979, p. 850) notes that 'Some of the variables grouped together as part of nonspecific factors may constitute very active ingredients in many different techniques'. The three conditions enumerated by Rogers (1957) and Truax and Carkhuff (1967) have been the focus of a tremendous amount of research. The significance of this research has been questioned by a number of reviewers (Bergin and Suinn, 1975; Mitchell, Bozarth, and Krauft, 1977; Orlinsky and Howard, 1978; Parloff, Waskow, and Wolfe, 1978; Lambert, DeJulio and Stein, 1978; Watson, 1984). Any single study involves flaws and limitations. But the positive nature of the accumulative evidence is impressive (Patterson, 1984). Convincing evidence for the effectiveness of any of the variables in the first category is lacking.

The Vanderbilt psychotherapy project (Strupp and Hadley, 1979), published after the major critiques, is particularly impressive since it was conducted by a long-term skeptic about the effectiveness of the therapist's relationship conditions without the addition of specific techniques. In a well-designed experiment, five experienced male therapists and five untrained male college professors (selected for their ability to form an understanding, warm, empathic relationship) each treated three male college undergraduates, in twice-weekly sessions for up to a maximum of 25 sessions. There was no difference in the quality of the relationship provided by the trained and experienced therapists and the college professors. While all clients improved, compared to their initial status and compared to two control groups, 'patients undergoing psychotherapy with college professors showed, on the average, quantitatively as much improvement as patients treated by experienced professional therapists' (p. 1134) and 'The study, on the whole, lent no support to the major hypothesis that, given a benign human relationship, the technical skills of professional psychotherapists produce measurably greater therapeutic changes' (p. 1135). Imagine what the results might have been had the college professors had some training in providing a therapeutic relationship!

Common specific elements as the core of a systematic eclecticism

The thesis of this paper is simple, and should now be obvious. A systematic eclecticism must be based upon, if it does not consist of, those factors common to all the major theories, factors that are specific in their nature, and that have the support of more research than any other factors, methods, or techniques in psychotherapy. They are specific in that they provide a good or facilitative interpersonal relationship as a treatment for the lack of, or inadequate, interpersonal relationships in the past and/or the present lives of clients.

Current eclectic proposals attempt to build on the differences in methods or techniques in the major theories, resulting in a syncretism rather than an integrated systematic eclecticism. Theorists emphasize their differences from other theories rather than the commonalities, and attribute the effectiveness of their theories to the unique elements, usually those not included in the relationship, rather than to the commonalities. As Frank (1982) notes: 'Those features which distinguish them from each other . . . receive special emphasis in the pluralistic, competitive American society. Since the prestige and the financial security of the psychotherapists depend to a considerable extent on their being able to show that their particular theory and method is more successful than that of their rivals, they inevitably emphasize their differences; and each therapist attributes his or her success to those conceptual and procedural features that distinguish that theory and method from its competitor's rather than to the features that all share' (p. 10). Eclecticists, impressed by the claims for the distinctive elements of each theory, attempt to include them all.

Garfield (1982) has stated that 'one important step in the desired direction [toward integration in psychotherapy] is to delineate and operationalize clearly some of the common variables which seem to play a role in most psychotherapies, and, perhaps, to regard them as the basis for a clearer delineation of psychotherapeutic principles and procedures. This may not be popular, but I think it is well worth the effort' (p 620). This paper is such an effort.

Resistances to common elements as specific factors

There are a number of sources of resistance to the recognition of certain of the common elements as common specific factors in psychotherapy, and therefore a foundation for a systematic eclecticism. Foremost among them has been the reluctance, even the inability, to recognize that the relationship, and specifically the contribution of the therapist to the relationship, is not only the necessary but the sufficient therapist condition for effective psychotherapy.

Strupp has been one of the most persistent unbelievers (e.g. Strupp, 1982, 1986). He has repeatedly emphasized that although the therapist's contribution in the relationship is important, even necessary, there are, or must be, certain techniques or technical operations necessary for effective psychotherapy. Even after the findings of the Vanderbilt study reported earlier (Strupp and Hadley, 1979), Strupp persisted in his refusal to accept the implications of the results of this study. As Cornsweet (1983) notes, 'Strupp and Hadley do not interpret their results as evidence against the efficacy of technique' (p. 308).

Most recently, however (Butler and Strupp, 1986), he seems to recognize the inevitability of this conclusion. The 'interpersonal context', he recognizes, is primary, but still 'the procedures (techniques) and interpersonal factors are thoroughly intertwined and cannot be separated. Efforts to separate these aspects of therapy for the purpose of determining causal connections are suspect regardless of statistical or measurement sophistication' (p. 33). Later it is stated that *'psychotherapy is defined as the systematic use of a human relationship for therapeutic purposes'* (p. 36). In a footnote it is stated that 'in its strong version our hypothesis states that all psychotherapies are primarily interpersonal events and must be understood in this perspective' (p. 36). Parenthetically, it can be argued that specific techniques and therapist relationship factors can be separated for research purposes. In fact, much, or most of the research on the effectiveness of empathic understanding, warmth or respect, and genuineness, has evaluated these conditions apart from or in the absence of any specific techniques. Since these conditions have been found to lead to therapeutic changes in the absence of any other techniques, then it must be concluded that no other techniques are necessary for such change.

In fact, it can be argued that the presence of such techniques may impair the effectiveness of psychotherapy. Bergin (in Bergin and Suinn, 1975) made the interesting, though puzzling, statement, referring to these therapist variables, that 'in recent years, a number of studies have induced skepticism concerning the potency of these variables *except in highly specific client-centered type conditions'* (emphasis added). A possible conclusion might be that since these variables constitute or are the essence of client-centered therapy, and no other variables (or techniques) have been demonstrated to be effective, then only client-centered therapy is an effective therapy. Though these conditions may be present in other therapies, they can be nullified or counteracted by other conditions or therapist techniques. For example, Mintz, Luborsky and Auerbach (1972) found that therapists who were empathic, but also directive, were not effective. And Hoyt (1980) found that 'poor' sessions, in contrast to 'good' sessions, as rated by experts, were characterized by therapist efforts to extract factual information and to give advice.

A second source of resistance is that to view the essence of psychotherapy as the relationship is too simple: there must be more to psychotherapy! This may be behind the resistance of those who insist that additional techniques must be necessary. If there are no additional techniques, then the responsibility falls squarely upon the therapist as a person. For years many writers have been saying that the personality of the therapist is the most important factor in psychotherapy. But they have never specified just what the therapeutic personality is. Now it can be defined. The characteristics, attitudes, and behaviors of the therapeutic personality are represented in perceiving empathically, and communicating this empathy; showing warmth, respect and concern for the client; and being genuine, honest and authentic in the relationship.

The matter of techniques, or skills as they are frequently referred to, is not ignored. Although the common elements are personality characteristics or attitudes, they are manifested in specific behaviors. Techniques or skills are the behaviors which implement or communicate the attitudes. They operate through basic commonly recognized modalities of learning, including modeling, minimizing threat, reinforcement, and extinction, among others.

No doubt some of the resistance to the acceptance of these common elements is related to their identification with client-centered therapy. While it is true that they were first enunciated clearly by Rogers (1957), that they constitute the essence of client-centered therapy, and that most of the research on them has been done by researchers identified as client-centered, client-centered therapy has no monopoly or exclusive claim, or as Shlien puts it, a 'proprietary claim' (Shlien, 1984, p. 177) on them. And, as has been emphasized earlier, they are clearly implicit, if not explicit, in every major theory of psychotherapy and in the writings of many if not most therapists beginning with Freud (Truax and Carkhuff, 1967). Empathic listening and understanding, especially, is, as Strupp and Binder (1984, pp. 46–7) note 'perhaps the most fundamental principle rightfully shared by all forms of psychotherapy and by clinicians as divergent in their views as Rogers, Fromm-Reichmann, and Kohut'.

Many will resist accepting this basis for a systematic eclecticism because it is currently a minority point of view. The predominant view involves an active, interventionist approach to psychotherapy, with the therapist being an expert in behavior change. The approach emphasizing empathic understanding, respect, and therapeutic genuineness as the core of psychotherapy does not view the therapist as an expert in methods and techniques of changing behavior, but as an expert in providing the conditions under which the client engages in changing his/her own behavior.

The theory and philosophy behind this approach to psychotherapy are not generally or widely accepted. The position does not fit with the currently accepted paradigm for research in psychotherapy: to determine what treatment, by whom, for what problem in what kind of client produces what changes (Patterson, 1986, pp. 461–2). A paradigm shift will be necessary, toward the recognition of the concept of the unitary nature of psychological disturbances and a unitary concept of treatment.

Goldfried (1982, p. 991) has noted that 'although it has been possible to delineate commonalities across all theoretical persuasions, formidable pressures nevertheless exist that oppose such integration'. Therapists resist abandoning their habitual techniques, attributing their success to these techniques rather than to the relationship in which they are embedded.

Other elements
A basis, or a foundation, for a systematic eclectic psychotherapy has been suggested. What other elements — if any — might be added? To be incorporated into a systematic integration, any other elements must be consistent with the elements proposed here. Most of the specific elements or techniques common in psychotherapy are not consistent. They include active interventions from an external frame of reference rather than from the internal frame of reference of the client that is the basis for empathic understanding. The research indicating that the three elements considered here are sufficient for therapeutic personality change with a wide variety of clients and client problems, suggests that there may be no other necessary elements. To be sure, continued research is necessary to determine the limits, if any, of the effectiveness of these conditions.

But the therapeutic relationship is complex, and the three elements considered are themselves complex variables, or each a complex of variables. They need to be more carefully defined, analyzed, perhaps broken down into more specific elements, with the development of better measures, particularly of their perception by clients — a necessary condition in Rogers' (1957) proposal that has not been adequately studied (Watson, 1984).

In addition to the three basic factors considered here, Carkhuff and Berenson (1967) have proposed four others: concreteness or specificity, confrontation, therapist self-disclosure, and immediacy. These differ from the three basic factors; they are more properly techniques. Specificity, for example, would appear to be a way of implementing empathic understanding. The others are sometimes ways of implementing the other conditions (Patterson, 1986, pp. 75–90).

Empathic understanding, respect, and therapeutic genuineness account for from 25% to 40% of outcome variance (Patterson, 1984). Critics have emphasized that this leaves the major amount of variance unaccounted for. For example, an anonymous reviewer of an earlier form of this paper emphasizes that 'this means that other variables will account for more than half of the outcome variance'. But this assumes that therapist variables must contribute 100% of outcome variance. Bergin and Lambert (1978, p. 180), however, wrote: 'We believe . . . that the largest variation in therapy outcome is accounted for by pre-existing client factors such as motivation for change, and the like. Therapist personal factors account for the second largest proportion of change, with technique variables coming in a distant third.' Norcross (1986, p. 15) states that 'experts estimate that about one-third of treatment outcome is due to the therapist and two thirds to the client'. Thus the three core conditions account for most of the therapist variance. Techniques such as concreteness and confrontation as defined by Carkhuff (Patterson, 1985, pp. 76–8) may account for the remainder. In other words, these conditions and techniques are not only necessary but sufficient.

The elements considered here are all included in the nature of the relationship provided by the therapist. Are there any non-relationship variables that are candidates for inclusion in a systematic eclecticism? Some might suggest information, social skills training, assertiveness training, etc. These, however, properly fall under teaching or tutoring. In learning theory terms, psychotherapy may be considered a problem in performance (with the response being in the repertoire) rather than a problem in acquiring responses not in the repertoire. Thus, behavior therapy, as well as cognitive therapy, may be considered as essentially teaching or tutoring, or re-education. In teaching, the relationship is necessary but not usually sufficient; in psychotherapy it is necessary and sufficient.

It is concluded that currently there are no other clear candidates for inclusion in the therapist's contribution to the therapy relationship in addition to empathic understanding, respect, therapeutic genuineness, and concreteness.

Conclusion

Most attempts at integration and eclecticism in psychotherapy are limited to combining two approaches, or bringing together techniques from various approaches. What is needed is a comprehensive, all-encompassing system including an integrating philosophy, theory, and related principles as well as techniques. A starting point is the basic common therapist elements of the major recognized theories. Three of these elements have been identified: empathic understanding, respect and genuineness. It is contended that these elements define a therapeutic relationship that provides the specific treatment variables for psychological emotional disturbances. It is further suggested that they constitute the necessary and sufficient therapist conditions for therapeutic change.

There is a considerable literature on the theory and philosophy supporting these conditions, generally recognized as the client-centered approach. This philosophy and theory are not consistent with the current *zeitgeist* in psychotherapy. As a result, there is considerable resistance to the acceptance of this approach as the foundation for a single comprehensive eclecticism. It will require a change in the current paradigm for such acceptance, which is considered by the author as necessary for further progress in psychotherapy.

A proposal such as this will not be popular, as Garfield (1982, p. 620), noted, but nevertheless will be, as he suggested, 'worth the effort'.

References

Barrett-Lennard, G. T. (1962) Dimensions of the therapist response as causal factors in therapeutic personality change. *Psychological Monographs*, 76 (43), 562.

Bergin, A. E., and Lambert, M. J. (1978) The evaluation of therapeutic outcomes. In S. L. Garfield and A. E. Bergin (Eds.), *Handbook of psychotherapy and behavior change.* (2nd ed.) (Pp. 139–89.) New York: John Wiley.

Bergin, A. E., and Suinn, R. M. (1975) Individual psychotherapy and behavior therapy. *Annual Review of Psychology*, 26, 509–56.

Beutler, L. E. (1983) *Eclectic psychotherapy: A systematic approach.* Elmsford, New York: Pergamon Press.

Butler, S. F., and Strupp, H. H. (1986) Specific and nonspecific factors in psychotherapy: A problematic paradigm for psychotherapy research. *Psychotherapy*, 23, 30–40.

Carkhuff, R. R. (1969) *Helping and human relations. Volume I: Selection and training.* New York: Holt, Rinehart and Winston.

Carkhuff, R. R., and Berenson, B. G. (1967) *Beyond counseling and therapy.* New York: Holt, Rinehart and Winston.

Cornsweet, C. (1983) Nonspecific factors and theoretical choice. *Psychotherapy: Theory, Research and Practice*, 20, 307–13.

Critelli, J. W., and Neumann, K. F. (1984) The placebo: Conceptual analysis of a construct in transition. *American Psychologist*, 39, 32–9.

Dimond, R. E., Havens, R. A., and Jones. (1978) A conceptual framework for the practice of prescriptive eclecticism in psychotherapy. *American Psychologist*, 33, 239–48.

English, H. B., and English, A. C. (1958) *A comprehensive dictionary of psychological and psychoanalytic terms.* New York: McKay.

Fee, A. F., Elkins, G. R., and Boyd, L. (1982) Testing and counseling psychologists:

Current practices and implications for training. *Journal of Personality Assessment*, 46, 116–8.

Fish, J. M. (1973) *Placebo therapy*. San Francisco: Jossey-Bass.

Frank, J. D. (1961) *Persuasion and healing*. Baltimore: Johns Hopkins University Press.

Frank, J. D. (1982) Therapeutic components shared by all psychotherapies. In J. H. Harvey and M. M. Peeks (Eds.), *Psychotherapy research and behavior change* (Pp. 9-37) Washington, DC: American Psychological Association.

Frank, J. D. (1983) The placebo is psychotherapy. *The Behavioral and Brain Sciences*, 6, 291–2.

Garfield, S. L. (1980) *Psychotherapy: An eclectic approach*. New York: Wiley.

Garfield, S. L. (1982) Eclecticism and integration in psychotherapy. *Behavior Therapy*, 13, 610–23.

Garfield, S. L., and Bergin, A. E. (1986) Introduction and historical overview. In S. L. Garfield and A. E. Bergin (Eds.), *Handbook of psychotherapy and behavior change*. (3rd ed.)(Pp. 3–22.) New York: Wiley.

Garfield, S. L., and Kurtz, R. M. (1974) A survey of clinical psychologists: Characteristics, activities and orientation. *The Clinical Psychologist,* 28 (1), 7–10.

Garfield, S. L., and Kurtz, R. M. (1976) Clinical psychologists in the 1970s. *American Psychologist*, 31, 1–9.

Garfield, S. L., and Kurtz, R. M. (1977) A study of eclectic views. *Journal of Consulting and Clinical Psychology*, 45, 78–83.

Gelso, C. J., and Carter, J. A. (1985) The relationship in counseling and psychotherapy. *The Counseling Psychologist*, 13, 155–243.

Goldfried, M. R. (1980) Toward a delineation of therapeutic change principles. *American Psychologist*, 35, 991–9.

Goldfried, M. R. (1982a) *Converging themes in psychotherapy: Trends in psychodynamic, humanistic, and behavioral practice*. New York: Springer.

Goldfried, M. R. (1982b) On the history of therapeutic integration. *Behavior Therapy,* 13, 572–93.

Goldfried, M.R., and Newman, C. (1986) Psychotherapy integration: An historical perspective. In J. C. Norcross (Ed.), *Handbook of eclectic psychotherapy*. New York: Brunner/Mazel.

Hart, J. (1983) *Modern eclectic therapy: A functional orientation to counseling and psychotherapy*. New York: Plenum.

Held, B. S. (1984) Toward a strategic eclecticism: A proposal. *Psychotherapy,* 21, 232–41.

Hoyt, M. F. (1980) Therapist and patient actions in 'good' psychotherapy sessions. *Archives of General Psychiatry*, 37, 159–61.

Kazdin, A. E. (1979) Nonspecific treatment of factors in psychotherapy outcome research. *Journal of Consulting and Clinical Psychology,* 47, 846–51.

Kelly, E. L. (1961) Clinical psychology 1960. Report of survey findings. *Newsletter: Division of Clinical Psychology of The American Psychological Association,* 14, 1–11.

Lambert, M. J. (1986) Future directions for research in client-centered therapy. *Person-Centered Review*, 1, 185–200.

Lambert, M. J., DeJulio, S. S., and Stein, D. (1978) Therapist interpersonal skills. *Psychological Bulletin*, 85, 467–89.

Lambert, M. J., Shapiro, D. A., and Bergin, A. E. (1986) The effectiveness of psychotherapy. In S. L. Garfield and A. E. Bergin, Eds.): *Handbook of psychotherapy and behavior change.* (Pp. 157–211.) New York: Wiley.

Larson, D. (1980) Therapeutic schools, styles, and schoolism: A national survey. *Journal of Humanistic Psychology,* 20 (3), 1–20.

Lazarus, A. A. (1981) *Multimodal therapy.* New York: McGraw-Hill.

Luborsky, L., Singer, B., and Luborsky, L. (1975) Comparative studies of psychotherapy: Is it true that 'everybody has won and all must have prizes?' *Archives of General Psychiatry,* 32, 995–1008.

Mahoney, M. J., Norcross, J. C., Prochaska, J. 0., Nissar, C. D. (1986) *Human psychological development and psychotherapy: Convergence among American clinical psychologists.* Unpublished manuscript.

Mintz, J., Luborsky, L., and Auerbach, A. H. (1972) Dimensions of psychotherapy: A factor analytic study of ratings of psychotherapy sessions. *Journal of Consulting and Clinical Psychology*, 36, 106–120.

Mitchell, K. M., Bozarth, J. D., and Krauft, C. C. (1977) A reappraisal of the therapeutic effectiveness of accurate empathy, non-possessive warmth, and genuineness. In A. S. Gunman and A. M. Razrin (Eds.), *Effective psychotherapy.* (Pp. 482–502.) New York: Pergamon Press.

Norcross, J. C. (Ed.) (1986) *Handbook of eclectic psychotherapy.* New York: Brunner/Mazel.

Norcross, J. C. (1986b) History and overview. In J. C. Norcross (Ed.), *Handbook of eclectic psychotherapy.* (Pp. 3–24.) New York: Brunner/Mazel.

Norcross, J. C., and Prochaska, J. O. (1982) A national survey of clinical psychologists: Affiliations and orientations. *The Clinical Psychologist,* 35 (3), 1–6.

Orlinsky, D. E., and Howard, D. I. (1978) The relation of process to outcome in psychotherapy. In S. L. Garfield and A. E. Bergin (Eds.), *Handbook of psychotherapy and behavior change.* (2nd ed.) (Pp. 283–330.) New York: Wiley.

Palmer, S. (1979) *A primer of eclectic psychotherapy.* Monterey, CA: Brooks/Cole.

Parloff, M. B., Waskow, I. E., and Wolfe, B. E. (1978) Research on therapist variables. In S. L. Garfield, and A. E. Bergin (Eds.), *Handbook of psychotherapy and behavior change.* (2nd ed.) (Pp. 233–82.) New York: Wiley.

Patterson, C. H. (1959) *Counseling and psychotherapy: Theory and practice.* New York: Harper and Row.

Patterson, C. H. (1966) *Theories of counseling and psychotherapy.* New York: Harper and Row.

Patterson, C. H. (1973) *Theories of counseling and psychotherapy.* (2nd ed.) New York: Harper and Row.

Patterson, C. H. (1974) *Relationship counseling and psychotherapy.* New York: Harper and Row.

Patterson, C. H. (1980) *Theories of counseling and psychotherapy* (3rd ed.) New York: Harper and Row.

Patterson, C. H. (1984) Empathy, warmth, and genuineness in psychotherapy: A review of reviews. *Psychotherapy*, 21, 431–8.

Patterson, C. H. (1985a) *The therapeutic relationship: Foundations for an eclectic psychotherapy*. Pacific Grove, CA: Brooks/Cole.

Patterson, C. H. (1985b) What is the placebo in psychotherapy? *Psychotherapy*, 22, 163–9.

Patterson, C. H. (1986) *Theories of counseling and psychotherapy* (4th ed.) New York: Harper and Row.

Pentony, P. (1981) *Models of influence in psychotherapy*. New York: Free Press.

Prioleau, L., Murdock, M., and Brody, N. (1983) An analysis of psychotherapy versus placebo studies. *The Behavioral and Brain Sciences*, 6, 275–310.

Prochaska, J. O., and DiClementi, C. C. (1982) Transtheoretical therapy: Toward a more integrative model of change. *Psychotherapy: Theory, Research and Practice*, 19, 276–88.

Prochaska, J. O., and DiClementi, C. C. (1984) *The transtheoretical approach: Crossing traditional trends of therapy*. Chicago: Dorsey Press.

Prochaska, J. O., and Norcross, J. C. (1983) Contemporary psychotherapists: A national survey of characteristics, practices, orientations and attitudes. *Psychotherapy: Theory, Research,and Practice*, 20, 161–73.

Robertson, M. (1979) Some observations from an eclectic therapist. *Psychotherapy: Theory, Research and Practice*, 16, pp. 18–21.

Rogers, C. R. (1957) The necessary and sufficient conditions for therapeutic personality change. *Journal of Consulting Psychology*, 21, 95–103.

Rosenzweig, S. (1936) Some implicit common factors in diverse methods of psychotherapy. *American Journal of Orthopsychiatry*, 6, 412–5.

Shapiro, A. K. (1971) Placebo effects in medicine, psychotherapy and psychoanalysis. In A. E. Bergin and S. L. Garfield (Eds.), *Handbook of psychotherapy and behavior change*. (Pp. 439–73.) New York: Wiley.

Shapiro, A. K., and Morris, L. A. (1978) The placebo effect in medical and psychological therapies. In S. L. Garfield, and A. E. Bergin (Eds.), *Handbook of psychotherapy and behavior change*. (2nd ed.) (Pp. 369–410.) New York: Wiley.

Shlien, J. M. (1984) A counter-theory of transference. In R. F. Levant and J. M. Shlien (Eds.), *Client-centered therapy and the person-centered approach*. (Pp. 153–81.) New York: Praeger.

Smith, D. (1982) Trends in counseling and psychotherapy. *American Psychologist*, 37, 802–9.

Strupp, H. H. (1982) The outcome problem in psychotherapy: Contemporary perspectives. In J. H. Harvey, and M. M. Peeks (Eds.), *Psychotherapy research and behavior change*. (Pp. 39–71.) Washington, DC: American Psychological Association.

Strupp, H. H. (1986) Psychotherapy: Research, practice, and public policy. *American Psychologist*, 41, 120–30.

Strupp, H. H., and Binder, J. L. (1984) *Psychotherapy in a new key: A guide to time-limited dynamic psychotherapy*. New York: Basic Books.

Strupp, H. H., and Hadley, S. W. (1979) Specific versus nonspecific factors in psychotherapy: A controlled study of outcome. *Archives of General Psychiatry*, 36, 1125–36.

Swan, G. E., and MacDonald, M. L. (1978) Behavior therapists in practice: A national survey of behavior therapists. *Behavior Therapy*, 9, 799–807.

Truax, C. B., and Carkhuff, R. R. (1967) *Toward effective counseling and psychotherapy*. Chicago: Aldine.

Wachtel, P. L. (1977) *Psychoanalysis and behavior therapy: Toward an integration*. New York: Basic Books.

Watkins, C. E., Jr., Lopez, F. G., Campbell, V. L., and Himmell, C. D. (1986) Contemporary counseling psychology: Results of a national survey. *Journal of Counseling Psychology*, 33, 301–9.

Watson, N. (1984) The empirical status of Rogers' hypotheses of the necessary and sufficient conditions for effective psychotherapy. In R. F. Levant, and J. M. Shlien (Eds.), *Client-centered therapy and the person-centered approach: New directions* (Pp. 17–40) New York: Praeger.

WHAT IS THE PLACEBO IN PSYCHOTHERAPY?

10

Nearly 25 years ago I titled a chapter in *Counseling and Psychotherapy: Theory and Practice* (Patterson, 1959) 'Common Elements in Psychotherapy: Essence or Placebo?' At that time I suggested a division of the common elements in all psychotherapies into those which were essentially specific treatment variables and those which were essentially placebos. In the first edition of *Theories of Counseling and Psychotherapy* (Patterson, 1966) the suggestion was repeated. The suggestion has been ignored in the literature on psychotherapy and the placebo effect. In this paper I shall develop this suggestion further, in the light of more recent discussions of the psychotherapy relationship, particularly the attention to social psychological variables.

The placebo effect

The most extensive discussion of the placebo effect is that of Shapiro and Morris (1978) (28 pages and 523 references). A placebo is defined as: 'any therapy or component of therapy that is deliberately used for its nonspecific, psychological, or psychophysiological effect, or that is used for its presumed specific effect, but is without specific activity for the condition being treated. A placebo, when used as a control in experimental studies, is defined as a substance or procedure that is without specific activity for the condition being evaluated. The placebo effect is defined as the psychological or psychophysiological effect produced by placebos.'

These authors consider placebo effects in both medical treatment and psychotherapy. They note that 'the placebo effect may have greater implications for psychotherapy than any other form of treatment because both psychotherapy and the placebo effect function primarily through psychological mechanisms . . . The placebo effect is an important component and perhaps the entire basis for the existence, popularly, and effectiveness of numerous methods of psychotherapy.' It perhaps should be noted here that the placebo as an inert substance does not exist in psychotherapy. All the variables in the psychotherapy relationship are psychological and all are active, having some direct or specific effects on the client or patient. By the placebo in psychotherapy is meant nonspecific effects,

First published in *Psychotherapy*, 1985, 22, pp. 163–9. Reprinted by permission of the publisher that is, though the placebo may have some specific effects, these effects are not those which are the objectives the therapist is attempting to achieve. Placebo elements may promote such effects, but they presumably are not used *deliberately* to achieve such effects. The word 'deliberately' presumably is used because, as will be noted later, there are those who, viewing psychotherapy as nothing but the placebo, propose deliberately using the placebo.

In his earlier chapter in the first edition of the *Handbook of Psychotherapy and Behavior Change*, Shapiro (1971) stated that the chapter would be 'an examination of psychotherapy as a placebo effect', thus suggesting that psychotherapy is nothing more than a placebo. Shapiro and Morris don't go quite so far. However, they view the total psychotherapy relationship as a placebo. They refer to a review by Luborsky, Singer, and Luborsky (1975) which found, after a comparison of the effectiveness of several types of psychotherapy, that all were about equally effective, and which concluded that this improvement was related to the presence of the therapist-patient relationship in all forms of psychotherapy. Shapiro and Morris refer to this as a demonstration of the placebo effect.

Rosenthal and Frank (1956) much earlier came to much the same conclusion. Refering to the placebo effect as a nonspecific form of psychotherapy, they continue: 'The similarity of the forces operating in psychotherapy and the placebo effect may account for the high consistency of improvement rates found with various therapies, from that conducted by physicians to intensive psychoanalysis'. Most recently Pentony (1981), in his extensive analysis of the placebo as a model of psychotherapy, suggests that 'the placebo effect constitutes the most parsimonious explanation that would account for the apparently equal success achieved by each of the diverse collection of therapies practiced'.

There are many writers of diverse origin who view the total psychotherapeutic relationship as nonspecific, and therefore, at least by implication, a placebo. Frank (1961, 1973) has long maintained this position. Bergin (1978) and Strupp (1978) also have emphasized the nonspecific nature of the relationship. They repeatedly emphasize that specific techniques are necessary in addition to the nonspecific relationship, without being clear just what these techniques are. Bergin (Bergin and Lambert, 1978) however, perhaps unintentionally, implies that techniques themselves are placebos: 'Technique is crucial to the extent that It produces a believable rationale and congenial modus operandi for the change agent and the client'.

Behaviorists also view the therapeutic relationship as nonspecific, and the techniques of behavior therapy as specific. Wolpe, (1973, p. 9) for example, claims that his method of reciprocal inhibition, as well as other behavioristic techniques, increase the improvement rate over that of the relationship alone, stating that 'the procedures of behavior therapy have effects additional to those relational effects that are common to all forms of psychotherapy'. Such claims have been disputed, and do not seem to be supported; indeed, it appears that many, if not most, of the specific techniques in the various approaches to psychotherapy, including behavior therapy, operate through the placebo effect — that is they are themselves placebos.

It has been noted, for example, that systematic desensitization, which specifies certain conditions for its effectiveness, is effective when none of the conditions are present, which suggests that it is the placebo element in the persuasive ritual which gives the method its effectiveness.

Paraphrasing Pentony, we would say that the therapy relationship is the most parsimonious explanation of the relatively equal success of the diverse approaches to psychotherapy, since all approaches share the relationship. If the relationship is entirely a placebo, this statement and Pentony's are equivalent. But it is the thesis of this chapter that the complex therapy relationship may be separated into two major components, or classes of variables, the nonspecific and the specific. Moreover, in speaking of the relatively equal success of various therapies, we must be concerned about the definition of success, that is, the goal or goals of the treatment process. The success, or outcome, of those therapies that are mainly placebo may differ from the outcomes of therapy focusing on the specific variables in the therapy relationship.

Social psychology and psychotherapy

While recognizing the client's important contributions to the placebo effect, in the discussion to follow we will concentrate on the therapist's contribution, in effect hypothetically considering the client's contributions equivalent or constant across therapists and therapies.

In 1961 Jerome Frank suggested that psychotherapy is a process of persuasion. In 1966 Goldstein (1966) proposed that research in psychotherapy should be directed toward study of variables derived from research in social psychology, particularly the psychology of interpersonal attraction, and he, with Heller and Sechrest (1966), provided an analysis of relevant research in social psychology. There was a considerable literature on the process of persuasion in social psychology (Hovland, Janis and Kelley, 1953) which was drawn upon.

In 1968 Strong (1968) proposed applying the social psychological concept of cognitive dissonance to the interpersonal influence process in counseling or psychotherapy. He suggested that the greater the extent to which counselors are perceived as expert, attractive, and trustworthy, the greater would be their credibility, and thus their power to influence clients .

There are three main therapist variables in the concept of psychotherapy as a social influence process. The first is actually a loose cluster of variables designated as perceived expertness, or credibility. It also appears to include respect and perceived competence. Contributing to this perception by the client of expertness are indications of status (degrees, diplomas, office decor, and furnishings); prestige (reputation); power and authority. While trustworthiness is often considered a separate variable, it is also included with expertness in the concept of credibility.

The second variable is perceived attractiveness. Included in this are therapist-client similarities in opinions, attitudes, beliefs, values and background; therapist liking for the client; therapist likability, friendliness and warmth; and therapist self-disclosure.

The third variable is therapist expectancy. Therapist self-confidence in the methods and techniques used, leads to expectation of change or improvement in the client. This expectancy is communicated to the client through various subtle, unintentional ways an well as through direct expressions of optimism, suggestions, and reassurance.

Strong's article stimulated a series of research studies. The research has been reviewed by Beutler (1978), Strong (1978), and Corrigan, Dell, Lewis and Schmidt (1980). Almost all of the studies (68 out of the 70 reviewed by Corrigan, et al.) were analogue studies, involving the presentation of audiotapes or videotapes, or a single contrived interview with nonclients, usually college students, as subjects. Most of the studies were concerned with correlates of or cues for expertness and attractiveness. The measures or criteria used in outcome studies included subject reports or self-ratings of changes in attitudes or opinions, of improvement or satisfaction, or of likelihood of self-referral. The results of these studies have been varied, inconsistent within and between studies and even directly contradictory. Beutler (1978) concludes that 'it is not clear from these findings that credibility consistently produces attendant attitude change in psychotherapy . . . These persuader variables serve only as a basis for facilitating a therapeutic relationship and are not necessarily a direct contributor to therapeutic change.' In other words, they are nonspecific variables.

Strong (1978), in spite of the mixed results and the fact that the studies reviewed were analogue studies and did not include outcome studies, states that 'as a whole, these studies show that therapist credibility is an important variable in psychotherapy'. This would seem to be an unjustifiable conclusion. In regard to perceived therapist attractiveness, he concludes that 'studies of the effect of client attraction to the therapist on the ability of the therapist to influence the client have obtained mixed and generally pessimistic results'.

Corrigan et al (1980) conclude that 'The effects of expertness and attractiveness on counselors' ability to influence client are, at best, unclear . . . Those studies that successfully manipulated attractiveness failed to find differential effects on client change.' Yet these authors recommend further research on these social influence variables in counseling as 'interesting and reasonable,' though they admit that 'the question of the utility of considering counseling as a social influence process remains'.

These conclusions, as negative as they are, would appear to be too optimistic. It is difficult to understand the continued enthusiasm for this line of research. The reviewers have all been among the major researchers in the field, however, and this commitment and identification with the area probably influences their conclusions. A study published after these reviews were written should be noted.

This study, by LaCrosse (1980), was not an analogue study, but involved 36 clients in a drug counseling program whose counseling ranged from 4 to 31 sessions. Clients rated their counselors at the beginning and end of counseling on an instrument devised to measure client perceptions of expertness, attractiveness, and trustworthiness. They also rated themselves on change following counseling. There was a highly significant relationship between the clients' ratings of their counselors and their self-ratings of outcome. However, not only is there questionable validity of the self-ratings of outcome, there is the distinct possibility of a spurious element in the correlations, since both variables were ratings by clients. In addition, only two of the clients came to counseling voluntarily, so there is a real question about the relevance of the research for the usual situation in counseling or psychotherapy, where clients come voluntarily for help.

These mixed and inconsistent results are exactly what would be expected if the variables operating were placebos. Placebo effects are highly varied and unreliable — not all subjects respond to the placebo — and are usually temporary in nature. It is interesting that Shapiro and Morris discuss these variables, including expectancy, among others, as methods by which the placebo operates.

Related to or an element in the therapist's expectations of positive results are his/her belief and faith in himself/herself and in his/her methods or techniques, factors which Shapiro emphasizes as important elements in the placebo effect. These factors appear to be the same factors which Orne (1962) has called the 'demand characteristics' in psychological experiments. Rosenthal (1966) among others, has demonstrated the influence of the experimenter's beliefs, expectations and desires on the outcome of psychological experiments both in and outside the laboratory. In psychological research these are unwanted, or placebo, effects. It would seem that they should be regarded as such in psychotherapy, as indeed they are by Shapiro and Morris.

These variables appear to constitute the 'good guy' factor in psychotherapy (Muehlberg, Pierce and Drasgow, 1969). LaCrosse and Barak (1976) suggest that the common factor in expertness, attractiveness, and trustworthiness is the 'influence' of Strong, or the 'persuasiveness' of Frank and LaCrosse, or the 'power' of Strong and Matross, and Dell. They then note that 'these terms are also related to what might be described as "charisma" or "impressiveness"'. All of this suggests an image of the counselor or therapist as a person exuding or projecting self-confidence, self-assurance, competence, power and persuasiveness — a charismatic snake-oil salesman.

If psychotherapy is nothing but a placebo, then it would appear to be desirable to maximize the effect. As Krasner and Ullmann (1965, p. 230) note:

> Whereas the problem had previously been conceptualized in terms
> of eliminating 'placebo effects', it would seem desirable to maximize
> placebo effects in the treatment situation to increase the likelihood
> of client change. The evidence is growing that 'placebo effect' is a
> euphemism for examiner influence variables.

This is exactly what Fish (1973) attempts to do in his systematic development of what he calls placebo therapy.

In this approach, the therapist does everything possible to establish himself/herself as an expert and an authority in the eyes of the client. Then this is used as a power base to influence the client. Recognizing that 'the social influence process has been considered the active ingredient in the placebo,' Fish states that placebo therapy 'denotes a broad frame of reference for considering all forms of human interaction, especially psychotherapy, in terms of social influence process' (p. vi). It also refers to 'a method of conducting psychotherapy based on social influence principles' (pp. vi-vii). The therapist fosters the client's belief in the potency of the therapeutic intervention by an impressive and detailed interrogation and exploration of the client's history and current behaviors. This process itself sets the therapist up as an authority, using a thorough 'scientific' approach. It also assesses the client's susceptibility to influence and persuasion. The process implies to the patient that 'Once I know what is wrong with you I can cure you'. A treatment strategy is formulated and communicated to the client in a plausible manner, tailored to the individual client's belief system. The major techniques used are those of behavior modification, together with suggestion and hypnosis, 'Placebo therapy is a strategy for getting the maximum impact from such techniques regardless of their validity' (p. vii). The placebo formulation and communication 'is designed to activate one powerful set of the patient's beliefs (his faith) to change another set of beliefs (his problems). Placebo therapy can thus be seen as a form of spiritual judo in which the therapist uses the power of the patient's own faith to force him to have a therapeutic conversion experience' (p. 16). 'The patient must be persuaded that it is what he does, not what the therapist does, which results in his being cured . . . Thus a therapist must encourage his patient to believe that he is curing himself, whether or not the therapist believes it' (p. 17).

Placebo communications are used not because they are true but because of their effect. It is the patient's faith or belief in psychotherapy and in whatever methods or techniques the therapist uses that is the source of cure. Thus, the validity of the techniques, or the therapeutic ritual, to use Fish's term, is important only as it enhances the patient's faith — that is, how persuasive, believable, intriguing or impressive it is to the patient. 'The therapist's role in placebo therapy involves acting in ways which inspire faith because he believes that the patient's faith cures him' (p. 30).

The therapist 'says things for the effect they will have rather than for his belief that they are true. Thus, instead of speaking empathically because he believes that empathy cures, he does so because he sees that such statements add to his credibility in the patient's eyes' (p. 32).

The patient's expectations of help tend to result in some improvement, producing increasing pressure in him/her for further change. The knowledge — or belief — that he/she is receiving expert treatment is likely to increase this improvement. The patient has faith in the truth of 'high status sources, such as the therapist . . . One of the strong points in the therapist's role as a socially sanctioned healer is his status as an agent in psychotherapy' (pp. 45, 46).

Whether or not Fish's presentation is a tour de force is a question that might be raised. Someone has suggested that the author may have been writing with tongue in cheek. Yet the presentation seems to be sincere, though doubts may be raised by some statements such as that 'placebo therapy is a nonschool of persuasion whose therapeutic title is intended ironically' (p. vii). It may be viewed as carrying the social influence approach to an absurd extreme. For example, 'lying to a patient is desirable if the lie furthers the therapeutic goals, is unlikely to be discovered (and hence backfire), and is likely to be more effective than any other strategy' (p. 39).

A number of questions or objections may be raised about placebo therapy. First, of course, is the fact that there is little if any research support for it. Fish, who claims that it works, urges that the reasons need to be researched. The unreliability of the placebo effect — that not all subjects respond to the placebo, also is a limiting factor. Fish notes that many are called but few are chosen. It is not possible to predict who will respond — who are placebo reactors. Fish refers to the problem client who expects and desires a (different) relationship with the therapist. Pentony (1981) writes that 'it seems questionable whether a treatment procedure based on suggestion (persuasion) alone will be universally applicable', given the existence of strong resistance to change. 'The placebo model would seem to be most appropriate for clients who are disposed to accept the therapist's message. Such clients typically have relatively specific problems, often involving low self-esteem, lack of self-confidence, and anxiety. Their disabilities range from physical symptoms to inability to assert themselves in social contexts. Their life goals are relatively realistic and attainable once they gain confidence in themselves. But not all cases which come to the attention of therapists fall into such a category' (p. 8). Nor is it necessarily true that placebo therapy is the most appropriate therapy even for them.

And there are other objections that must be raised against placebo therapy. The placebo effect is often, if not usually, temporary. No studies of the social influence process in psychotherapy have gone beyond the evaluation of immediate or short-term effects.

Pentony raises three other questions about placebo therapy:

> 1. Is it ethical to mislead the client in regard to the therapeutic strategy? 2. Will the therapist be convincing when he is not a true believer in the ritual he is carrying through? 3. If placebo therapy becomes general and clients become aware of its nature, will they lose faith in the healing ritual and hence render these ineffective? (pp. 63–4.)

Fish's attempts to handle these questions are less than convincing.

Placebo therapy — and the social influence model of psychotherapy — assumes not only that psychotherapy is an influencing process, which few would deny, but that it is a process of influencing through persuasion. The therapist is concerned only with those actions or techniques which enhance his persuasibility. Having achieved a power base from which to operate, the therapist then uses whatever methods or techniques are necessary to influence the client toward goals chosen by the client and the therapist. It becomes a situation where the ends justify the means. Moreover, there is no consideration of unintended outcomes or side effects, such as increase in client dependency. Reading the procedures considered by Fish, one has a *deja vu* experience of being regressed to the practices of counselors and psychotherapists in the 1930s and 1940s, before the influence of Rogers began to be felt.

The therapeutic relationship

If perceived expertness, attractiveness, and trustworthiness are essentially placebos, that does not mean that the entire therapy relationship is a placebo. There is more to the therapeutic relationship than these three variables. Three other variables have been extensively studied: empathic understanding, warmth or respect, and genuineness, all in terms of client perceptions. These variables, or core conditions as they have become known, are defined and described in many places (e.g. Patterson, 1974). The evidence for the specific effects of these conditions has been accumulating for over 25 years. This research has been evaluated elsewhere (Patterson, 1984).

On the basis of this research, it is proposed that these variables are the specific conditions for certain client behaviors in the counseling or therapy process and for certain outcomes of the process. In the process, the client responds to these conditions with self-disclosure, self-exploration, and self-understanding. The client assumes responsibility for himself/herself in the process, engages in problem solving, and makes choices and decisions. The client becomes more understanding, respecting, and accepting of others, more honest and genuine in relationships with others. These behaviors continue outside and after the therapy process ends, and are thus also outcomes of the process. They constitute aspects of self-actualizing persons, which is the ultimate goal of counseling or psychotherapy.

These conditions and the social influence variables are probably not entirely independent. LaCrosse (1977) found significant correlations between the Counselor Rating Form, measuring client perceptions of counselor expertness, attractiveness, and trustworthiness, and the Barrett-Lennard Relationship Inventory, measuring client perceptions of counselor empathic understanding, congruence, level of regard, and unconditional positive regard. Observer ratings were also highly correlated, though ratings by the counselors themselves were not, raising some question about the presence of an artifact, such as the halo effect, in the client and observer ratings.

The presence of relationships between these two groups of relationship variables poses the question of which is primary, or which causes or leads to the others. That the core conditions are primary is suggested by the fact that they have been shown to be related to various therapy outcomes in numerous studies, while this has not been done for the social influence variables. Krumboltz (1979) has indicated the direction of the relationship when he suggests, after his review of the research, that 'counselors who want to be seen as attractive should be empathic, warm and active . . .' It also would appear, from LaCrosse's research, that counselors who want to appear to be experts should also be empathic, show respect and warmth, and be congruent or genuine. Similarly, it might be suggested that counselors who want to be perceived as trustworthy should show respect and warmth and be genuine or congruent. And if the therapist really respects clients, he/she will expect the best from them, and will probably find that clients respond in expected ways, that is, by assuming responsibility for the conduct of therapy, making choices and decisions, and solving problems.

It thus appears that the complex therapeutic relationship cannot be prevented from being 'contaminated' by placebo elements. The client perceives the therapist, to some extent at least, as an authority and an expert. He/she puts trust in the therapist. The therapist's belief in his/her methods or approach is inextricable from the methods or techniques used. If the therapist did not have confidence in them, he/she would use other methods or techniques. Similarly, if he/she did not have confidence in himself/herself as a therapist, he/she would not continue to practice.

But if the placebo elements cannot be eliminated from psychotherapy, they can be either minimized or maximized. If they are maximized, then the therapist is engaging in placebo therapy, with the possibility that results may be limited, superficial, or temporary. When the placebo elements are minimized, as in client-centered or relationship therapy, the therapist is focusing on those conditions which appear to be specific for the outcomes which are the goals of this approach to psychotherapy.

Summary
In this paper the question, 'What is the placebo in psychotherapy?' has been considered. Since in psychotherapy there is no inert substance comparable to the placebo in medicine, the discussion has concerned the specific versus the nonspecific elements in psychotherapy. Many, if not most, of the writers on psychotherapy, including the behaviorists, view the entire therapy relationship as nonspecific, and thus as essentially a placebo. The behaviorists have been almost the only ones who have been clear in proposing specific factors, claiming that the various techniques of behavior therapy are specific. However, this claim has been increasingly disputed. Not only does behavior therapy depend on the relationship between the therapist and the client, but the specific methods and techniques of behavior therapy may be essentially placebos.

During the last 15 years, increasing attention has been given to what has become known as the social influence model of psychotherapy, derived from the social psychological research on the nature of the persuasive process. The three variables which have been emphasized are perceived expertness, attractiveness, and trustworthiness. The research on these variables, almost entirely analogue research, is inconsistent and contradictory in its results. It is suggested that this is consistent with the hypothesis that these variables are essentially placebos. Fish (1973) has systematically developed an approach which includes these variables, particularly perceived expertness, as its central focus, which he calls Placebo Therapy.

There are other variables in the psychotherapy relationship which have received considerable support from extensive research not involving analogue situations. Three of these variables are empathic understanding, respect or warmth, and therapeutic genuineness. It is proposed that these are specific conditions for certain desirable outcomes in counseling or psychotherapy.

It appears to be impossible to separate out or to eliminate placebo elements from psychotherapy, since the client attributes a certain degree of expertness, authority, and attractiveness to the therapist, and the therapist's belief or confidence in himself and his methods lead to certain expectations for favorable response in the client, which are communicated to the client in various ways. The therapist, however, has the choice of maximizing or minimizing the placebo elements. It is suggested that maximizing the placebo elements, which is essentially placebo therapy, has the disadvantages of the placebo effect. That is, it is not reliable or consistent in that not all clients are strong placebo reactors, and its effects can be limited and temporary in nature.

References

Bergin, A. E., and Lambert, M.J. (1978) The evaluation of therapeutic outcomes. In S. L. Garfleld and A. E. Bergin (Eds.), *Handbook of psychotherapy and behavior change: An empirical analysis*. 2nd. Ed. New York: Wiley.

Beutler, L. E. (1978) Psychotherapy and persuasion. In L. E. Beutler and R. Greene (Eds.), *Special problems in child and adolescent behavior*. Westport, Conn.: Technomic Publishing Co.

Corrigan, J. D., Dell, D. M., Lewis, K. N., Schmidt, L. D. (1980) Counseling as a social influence process. *Journal of Counseling Psychology Monograph, 27,* 395–441.

Fish, J. M. (1973) *Placebo therapy*. San Francisco: Jossey-Bass.

Frank, J. D. (1961, 1973) *Persuasion and healing*. Baltimore. Johns Hopkins Press.

Goldstein, A. P. (1966) Psychotherapy research by extrapolation from social psychology. *Journal of Counseling Psychology*, 13, 38–45.

Goldstein, A. P., Heller, K., and Sechrest, L. B. (1966) *Psychotherapy and the psychology of behavior change*. New York: Wiley.

Hovland, C. L., Janis, I. L., and Kelley, H. H. (1953) *Communication and persuasion: Psychological studies of opinion*. New Haven: Yale University Press.

Krasner, L., and Ullmann, L. P. (Eds.) (1965) *Research in behavior modification*: New York: Holt, Rinehart and Winston.

Krumboltz, J. D., Becker-Haven, J. F., and Burnett, K. F. (1979) Counseling psychology. *Annual Review of Psychology, 30,* 555–602.

LaCrosse, M. B. (1971) Comparative perceptions of counselor behavior: A replication and an extension. *Journal of Counseling Psychology*, 24, 464–71.

LaCrosse, M. B. (1977) Comparative perceptions of counselor behavior: A replication and an extension. *Journal of Counseling Psychology.* 24, 464–71.

LaCrosse, M. B. (1980) Perceived counselor social influence and counseling outcomes: Validity of the Counselor Ratings Form. *Journal of Counseling Psychology, 27,* 320–7.

LaCrosse, M. B., and Barak, A. (1976) Differential perception of counselor behavior. *Journal of Counseling Psychology, 23,* 170–2.

Luborsky, L., Singer, B., and Luborsky, L. (1975) Comparative studies of psychotherapy. *Archives of General Psychiatry*, 32, 995–1008.[See also Smith, M.L., and Glass, G.V. (1977) Meta-analysis of psychotherapy outcome studies. *American Psychologist, 32,* 752–60, and Smith, M. L., Glass, G. V., Miller, J. (1980) *The benefits of psychotherapy*. Baltimore: Johns Hopkins Press.]

Muehlberg, N., Pierce, R., and Drasgow, J. (1969) A factor analysis of the therapeutically facilitative conditions. *Journal of Clinical Psychology*, 25, 93–5. (The authors note that this term was proposed by F. C. Thorne in a personal communication.)

Orne, M. E. (1962) On the social psychology of the psychological experiment:

With particular reference to demand characteristics and their implications. *American Psychologist*, 17, 776-783.

Patterson, C. H. (1959) *Counseling and psychotherapy: Theory and practice*. New York: Harper and Row.

Patterson, C. H. (1966) *Theories of counseling and psychotherapy*. New York: Harper and Row.

Patterson, C. H. (1974) *Relationship counseling and psychotherapy*. New York: Harper and Row.

Patterson, C. H. (1984) Empathy, warmth and genuiness in psychotherapy: A review of reviews. *Psychotherapy*, 21, 431–8.

Pentony, P. (1981) *Models of influence in psychotherapy*. New York: Free Press.

Rosenthal, R. (1966) *Experimental effects in behavioral research*. N. J.: Prentice-Hall.

Rosenthal, D., and Frank, J. D. (1956) Psychotherapy and the placebo effect. *Psychological Bulletin*, 53, 294–302.

Shapiro, A. K.(1971) Placebo effects in medicine, psychotherapy, and psychoanalysis. In A. E. Bergin and S. L. Garfield (Eds.). *Handbook of psychotherapy and behavior change: An empirical analysis*. New York: Wiley.

Shapiro, A. K., and Morris, L. A. (1978) The placebo effect in medical and psychological therapies. In S. L. Garfleld and A. E. Bergin, (Eds.), *Handbook of psychotherapy and behavior change: An empirical analysis*. 2nd Ed. New York: Wiley.

Strong, S. R. (1968) Counseling: An interpersonal process. *Journal of Counseling Psychology,* 15, 215–24.

Strong, S. R. (1978) Social psychological approach to psychotherapy research. In S. L. Garfield and A. E. Bergin (Eds.) *Handbook of psychotherapy and behavior change: An empirical analysis*. 2nd Ed. New York: Wiley.

Strong, S. R., and Matross, R. (1973) Change processes in psychotherapy. *Journal of Counseling Psychology,* 20, 25–37.

Strupp, H. H. (1978) Psychotherapy research and practice: An overview. In S. L. Garfield and A. E. Bergln (Eds.), *Handbook of psychotherapy and behavior change: An empirical analysis*. 2nd Ed. New York: Wiley.

Wolpe, J. (1973) *The practice of behavior therapy*. 2nd Ed. New York: Pergamon Press.

VALUES IN COUNSELING AND PSYCHOTHERAPY

11

Values are difficult to define even though everyone recognizes and uses the concept. The failure of writers to define values or attempt to delineate the nature of the concept has led to some confusion and fuzziness in discussions in the literature.

Kluckhohn, an anthropologist, noted that the concept of values involves the concept of:

> the desirable, which influences the selection, from available modes, means, and ends of action . . . Value implies a code or standard, which has some persistence through time, or put more broadly, which organizes a system of action. Values, conveniently and in accord with received usage, place things, acts, ways of behaving, goals of action, on the approval-disapproval continuum (Kluckhohn, et al., p. 395).

But values carry more than an approval-disapproval connotation. Smith's (1954) definition is more accurate. He stated that 'by values, I shall mean a person's implicit or explicit standards of choice, insofar as these are invested with obligation or requiredness' (p. 513). The words *society's* and *culture's* should be added to *person's* in the definition. It makes clear the oughtness or should nature of values. Thus, it avoids the frequent confusion of values with preferences — tastes, likes, and interests. The objects of such preferences may be said to be valued, but they do not constitute values. There is no obligatoriness or requiredness attached to them.

The relationship, or difference, between values and morals is not always clear. It seems that morals are a class of values, specifically relating to interpersonal relations. Grant (1985) noted that 'moral values are distinguished from values in general in that they encompass only attitudes towards other individuals and attitudes towards actions that affect them' (p. 143). Thus, morals are more specific than values. This article is concerned with values in a broader sense, even though the counselor's or therapist's attitudes toward the client that are implemented in the therapy relationship may be considered moral values, and even though the values

First published as an invited paper. *Counseling and Values,* 1989, 33, pp. 164–76.
© ACA. Reprinted with permission. No further reproduction authorized without written consent from the Association for Counseling and Development.

represented in other aspects of therapy may have moral implications (cf. Grant, 1985). Preferences vary widely among individuals and societies or cultures, but there are some values that seem to be universal. 'Thou shalt not kill' is, perhaps, the most widely recognized and accepted value. Honesty, the obligation to tell the truth, is another widely accepted value. Freedom is, perhaps, a third. These values seem to be based on requirements necessary for the survival of society. A society whose members kill each other will not survive. Neither will a society in which a basic minimum of honesty and truthfulness is not present. (At one time, some primitive societies that were organized on the basis of deceit may have existed, but they have not persisted.) History seems to indicate the prevalence of the value of freedom, as evidenced by resistance and revolution when freedom is restricted or denied.

Certain values are universal, but this does not mean that they are absolute. Killing may be permitted in certain circumstances — to get rid of a tyrant to obtain freedom, to execute a heinous criminal, to preserve one's life, or in war, to preserve the society. Lying may be permitted — to save a life, to mislead the enemy during wartime, to spare a terminally ill patient from further worry in certain cases, or to prevent a child from getting hurt in specific circumstances. But in each case, it is recognized as an exception to be justified, usually in terms of another value taking precedence. Some values are not absolute, but this does not mean that they are relative, except in the sense that they are relative to each other.

There are other lower order, limited values, or values that are elements of, or related to, more universal or higher values. One must be careful, however, that preferences or tastes are not elevated to the level of values and then propagated as desirable for all persons. There are several ways in which values are involved in counseling or psychotherapy.

The client's values in psychotherapy

There seems to be little, if any, disagreement that the counselor deals with value problems and issues brought to counseling by the client. The counselor need not accept or approve of the client's values. Disagreement with or nonacceptance of the client's values does not mean that the client is not accepted as a person. The way in which the client's values and value problems are dealt with does, however, constitute an issue in counseling. This process will be discussed in the following sections.

The counselor's values in psychotherapy

During the first half of this century, the position taken on the counselor's values in counseling or psychotherapy was that of orthodox psychoanalysis. The analyst, it was presumed, functioned as a blank screen upon which the client projected his or her beliefs, attitudes, and values. The therapist was neutral; his or her values were not involved.

Counselor imposition of values

Associated with the orthodox psychoanalytic view was the belief that the analyst ought to remain neutral. Wilder, commenting on an article by Ginsberg and Herma (1953), noted that 'it has been taken for granted that the analyst must not try to impose his [or her] value systems on the patient'. Deutsch and Murphy (1955) stated that 'the therapist should by all means avoid impressing his [or her] own philosophy on a patient' (p. 8). Although this position seems to be the prevailing one and counseling students are usually admonished not to impose their values or value system on clients, this position is not universally accepted. Wilder (Ginsberg and Herma, 1953) referred to 'rising voices to the effect that the analyst not only does but should transmit his [or her] value system to the patient'. He continued, 'A patient often says, "Doctor, after all, you seem to have found a measure of peace and stability; why don't you shorten therapy by simply telling me your philosophy?"' Weisskopf-Joelson (1953) proposed that the inculcation of a philosophy of life should be considered as one of the objectives of psychotherapy. Beutler (1979), viewing psychotherapy as a process of persuasion, seems to 'consider the therapy process as one which systematically induces the patient to develop alternative beliefs which approximate those of the therapist' (p. 432).

Some years ago, Murphy (1955), writing to counselors, asked, 'Shall personnel and guidance work . . . attempt to impart a philosophy of life?' Although Murphy conceded that 'no one knows enough to construct an adequate philosophy of life', he wrote that 'nevertheless, if he who offers guidance is a whole person, with real roots in human culture, he cannot help conveying directly or indirectly to every client what he himself sees and feels, and the perspective in which his own life is lived'. He suggested that 'it is not true that the wise man's sharing of a philosophy of life is an arrogant imposition upon a defenseless client'. He felt that the young need help and advice from those who have thought things through. But he warned counselors not to 'attempt the arrogant and self-defeating task of guiding men and women without a rich, flexible, and ever-growing system of values of your own' (p. 8).

Wrenn (1958) less strongly wrote that the counselor 'may or may not . . . assist the client in an understanding of life's purposes and meanings, and the alternate ways in which one may relate oneself to the Infinite' (p. 332). Counselors with a religious orientation seem to be more accepting of the appropriateness of directly influencing client values than are counselors without a strong religious orientation. But direct influence of client values and philosophy is not limited to counselors with a religious commitment. Several theorists support such an approach. Williamson's approach (Patterson, 1980) involves direct instruction. Ellis's rational-emotive therapy (Patterson, 1986) is, essentially, instruction in a philosophy of life. Victor Frankl (Patterson, 1986) also instructs clients in values and in an approach to living. In addition, Thorne (Patterson, 1986) included re-education in a philosophy of life as a method of counseling.

There are several reasons why it might be inappropriate for a counselor or therapist to indoctrinate clients or attempt to inculcate a system of values or a philosophy of life in them.

1. Though there are, no doubt, some generally and even universally accepted values, principles, or ethical standards, these do not constitute a philosophy of life. Each individual's philosophy is unique in some details, although it may have

much in common with the philosophies of others, particularly those in the same culture. No individual's philosophy is necessarily appropriate for another individual. Yet, a philosophy that does not include the basic universal values is not an acceptable or viable philosophy for existence in a society.

2. It is too much to expect all counselors or psychotherapists to have a fully developed, adequate, or ideal philosophy of life ready to be impressed on clients. Murphy, (1955) quoted above, referred to a wise man's sharing of a philosophy of life. But sharing is one thing, and instructing or guiding is another. Moreover, not all counselors are 'wise men'.

3. It may be questioned whether the counseling or therapy relationship is the appropriate place for instruction in ethics and a philosophy of life. Among many, there is an apparent confusion between counseling and tutoring or individual instruction. The home, the church, and the school are appropriate places for such instruction.

4. An individual usually does not adopt a system or code of ethics or a philosophy of life from one source at a particular time. (Religious conversion is an exception.) These are products of many influences over a long period of time.

5. It would seem to be best for each individual to develop his or her own unique philosophy of life from many sources and not to be deprived of the experience of doing so. Such a philosophy will probably be more useful and meaningful than one adopted ready-made from someone else, no matter how wise such a person may be. A viable philosophy cannot be impressed from outside of oneself but must be developed from within.

6. Finally, the imposition of values or a philosophy on clients is inconsistent with the values of some systems of psychotherapy. These systems accept the right of the client to refuse to accept or develop any system of values or ethics, and to endure the consequences of such choices.

The counselor or therapist should not impose his or her values on clients, but this does not mean that the therapist should refuse to discuss values, ethics, or philosophy. Nor does it mean that the therapist may not, at times, express his or her values. The therapist may do so at the request of the client. In addition, there may be times when the therapist thinks it is necessary or desirable for the client to be aware of these values, or times in which the client should know how the therapist stands on certain ethical or value issues. Being genuine or honest in the relationship sometimes means that the therapist should express his or her values. When therapists believe that the therapy relationship or process would be improved by explicitly acknowledging their values and beliefs, they can do so. Such values should be clearly labeled as their own (or possibly sometimes as society's in general). When values are openly expressed in this way, there is no coerciveness about them. In addition to the explicit imposition of the counselor's values in psychotherapy, there are several other ways in which the counselor's values enter the process of counseling or psychotherapy.

Implicit involvement of counselor values
The problem is not simply whether or not therapists should openly impose their

values on clients. Can therapists avoid influencing the values of their clients?

The attempt to define psychotherapy as a science or a technology would seem to remove values from the process (Margolis, 1966). Many years ago, Watson (1958) wrote that 'one of the falsehoods with which some therapists console themselves is that their form of treatment is purely technical, so they need take no stand on moral issues' (p. 575). More recently, Garfield and Bergin (1986) noted that 'progress in developing new and more effective techniques of psychotherapy' has obscured 'the fact that subjective value decisions underlie the choice of techniques, the goals of change, and the assessment of what is a "good" outcome' (p. 16).

Many psychoanalysts came to realize that the therapist could not remain a neutral figure to the client. The effort to remain a 'blank screen' was intended to allow the client to project his or her perceptions on the therapist — the creation of a transference. But the analyst was not, in fact, a blank screen, and the 'real person' of the therapist was involved in the relationship. As Wolberg noted (comment in Ginsburg and Herma, 1953):

> No matter how passive the therapist may believe himself [or herself] to be, and no matter how objective he [or she] remains in an attempt to allow the patient to develop his [or her] own sense of values, there is an inevitable incorporation within the patient of a new superego patterned after the character of the therapist as he [or she] is perceived by the patient. There is almost inevitably an acceptance by the patient of many of the values of the therapist as they are communicated in the interpretation or through direct suggestion, or as they are deduced by the patient from his [or her] association with the therapist.

Karl Menninger (1958) wrote the following:

> We cannot ignore the fact that what the psychoanalyst believes, what he [or she] lives for, what he [or she] loves, what he [or she] considers to be the purpose of life and the joy of life, what he [or she] considers to be good and what he [or she] considers to be evil, become known to the patient and influence him [or her] enormously, not as 'suggestion' but as inspiration . . . No matter how skillful the analyst in certain technical maneuvers, his [or her] ultimate product, like Galatea, will reflect not only his [or her] handicraft but his [or her] character (p. 91).

And Ingham and Love (1954) wrote the following:

> The existence of the therapeutic relationship puts the therapist in a position in which he [or she] does, without choice, influence values in the mind of the patient. It is almost impossible for the therapist to avoid giving some impression of whether he [or she] favors such things as general law and order, personal self-development, and emotional maturity . . . If they have discussed an issue that involves

> moral values for a period of time, it is evident that the patient will have a concept of what the therapist thinks. His [or her] attitudes about right and wrong, or good and bad, are likely to be particularly influential for the patient (pp. 75–6).

Because clients perceive the values of therapists as well as their interests and beliefs, even when these are not overtly expressed, clients focus on different things with different therapists or with therapists who operate from particular theoretical orientations. When therapists value dreams, clients dream and report their dreams; when therapists value sexual material or any other specific content material, clients produce it, thus 'validating' the theories of their therapists.

Several research studies provide evidence for the therapist's influence on client values, beginning with an early study by Rosenthal (1955). (See Beutler [1979] for other references.)

The recognition that the values of the counselor or therapist cannot be kept out of the therapy relationship makes it imperative that counselors be clearly aware of their values, and clear about how these values are and should be involved in their counseling. The current emphasis on techniques in therapy, and on skill training in the education of counselors, clouds this recognition. The concept of the therapist as a technician is kept to a minimum if it includes the consideration of the therapist's values. The awareness that the therapist is a person who is participating in a personal relationship with the client brings the importance of the therapist's values into focus.

Values in counseling philosophy and theory

Values, as Glad (1959) noted, are inherent in theories of counseling or psychotherapy. It is likely that students and therapists select a theoretical orientation (to the extent that they are aware of theories and are theory oriented) on the basis of the congruence of the philosophy and values of the theory with their own values and philosophy. Although most, if not all, theories profess to respect the autonomy of the client, there is considerable variation in the degree to which this respect is manifested. Some years ago, I suggested that there were two contrasting approaches to human relations, including psychotherapy (Patterson, 1958, 1959). One, labeled the manipulative or authoritarian approach, emphasized the authority, prestige, status, and expertise of the therapist. The other, labeled the understanding approach, emphasized empathic understanding, warmth, respect, and genuineness. Theories or approaches to counseling or psychotherapy can be roughly classified into these two categories, representing quite contrasting philosophies and values. Current support for this classification comes from the 1985 Phoenix Conference on the Evaluation of Psychotherapy, at which 7,000 people from 29 countries gathered to hear the world's greatest living therapists or theorists. Margo Adler (incidentally a granddaughter of Alfred Adler) reported on the conference for the National Public Radio program, *All Things Considered*. There were two kinds of therapists at the conference, she said — the manipulators and the enablers, or facilitators, and she illustrated the differences with quotations from speakers.

These two orientations represent two different value systems and two different views of clients. They have implications for the goals and methods of psychotherapy.

The therapist's goals as values

'Both the therapist's goals and the methods selected to achieve them can be viewed as reflecting distinct value orientations' (Madell, 1982, p. 52). A review of the many and varied goals of psychotherapy is not possible here. In an edited volume 20 years ago, (Mahrer, 1967) revealed the wide variety of goals advocated by various therapists. Taking a cue from Parloff (1967), I have organized goals into three levels: ultimate, mediate, and immediate (Patterson, 1970, 1985). The ultimate goal is a broad, general goal, incorporating many of the concepts of various theories and philosophies of therapy, and it represents an ideal. It is an attempt to answer the following questions: What do we want our clients to be like? What should people be like? What kind of person do we want or need in a desirable world? This involves the goal of life or living together as human beings. The term or concept that can incorporate this goal is self-actualization, as defined by the work of Maslow (1956). Rogers's concept of the fully functioning person is similar (Rogers, 1969). It is unfortunate that the concept of self-actualization has been misunderstood and misrepresented by several writers, including some prominent psychologists (Patterson, 1985). It has been presented as self-centered, selfish, antisocial, represented in the 'me' generation of the 1960s and in some of the activities of the human potential movement. But, in Maslow's description, it includes an acceptance of and empathy for others. Rogers's descriptions include concern for others; the self-actualizing person must live in a society of others (Rogers, 1959, 1969).

Self-actualization — or the self-actualizing process — is a goal common to all persons. As adequately defined, it is a goal that is not limited by time or culture. It might be considered the highest value for human beings. It is a goal that is not limited to psychotherapy — it is, or should be, the goal of society and of all its institutions. It is a goal that is not chosen by the therapist or the client, nor is it simply a religious or philosophical goal. It is derived from the nature of the human being, indeed, of all living organisms, whose nature is the actualization of potentials. The actualization of potentials is the basic, dominant nature of life. This derivation of a value from the nature of living organisms can be criticized for being what philosophers call the Naturalistic Fallacy (Margolis, 1966). But it seems only reasonable that values may be evaluated in terms of their relation to (supportive of or in disagreement with) the nature of human beings and their developments. Skinner (1953) suggested that science can provide a basis for values:

> If a science of behavior can discover those conditions of life [that] make for the strength of men, it may provide a set of 'moral values' which, because they are independent of the history and culture of any one group, may be generally adopted (p. 445).

It can be maintained that the ultimate 'strength of men' lies in the characteristics of self-actualizing persons, and unless there are enough individuals possessing the characteristics to a minimal degree, society cannot survive. Historically, self-actualizing men and women have been the major contributors to the development of civilization.

Therapists who disclaim any ultimate goal may, nevertheless, implicitly have such a goal and impose this goal on their clients while being unaware that they are doing so. The reluctance of counselors or therapists to adopt an ultimate goal is based on the difficulties of defining such a goal (such as 'mental health', for example). But self-actualization, properly defined, is a goal that more and more psychologists and psychotherapists are adopting, in one form or another or under one rubric or another.

The mediate goals of counseling or therapy are the more specific goals that are usually the concern of counselors. Although the ultimate goal is common to all persons, mediate goals vary with individuals. They include such things as educational and career goals, family and personal relationships, and the common objectives of symptom removal or alleviation, and reduction of psychological pain and suffering. These goals may be related to the ultimate goal in two ways: they are steps or means toward becoming a more self-actualizing person, or they may be by-products of the development of the more abstract qualities of becoming a more self-actualizing person. Besides integrating common and individual goals, the concept of an ultimate goal provides a criterion for the acceptability of individual goals. In addition, while the ultimate goal is, in effect, a given and is not chosen by either the therapist or the client, mediate goals are chosen by the client.

The immediate goal of counseling or psychotherapy is the initiation and continuation of the process of counseling or psychotherapy, the process by which the client achieves mediate goals and becomes a more self-actualizing person. The methods or techniques are chosen by the counselor or therapist. They represent the values of the therapist. They will differ radically depending on whether the therapist functions as a facilitator or enabler, or as a director or manipulator. The therapist as a facilitator is consistent with the ultimate goal of self-actualization. The self-actualizing person is autonomous, independent, and responsible (responsibly independent). The therapist's methods are consistent with these characteristics, providing a relationship in which the client is respected and given responsibility in and for the therapy process and is expected to make choices and decisions. These methods are presented in what Strupp (1980) referred to as essential therapeutic values: 'People have the right to personal freedom and independence'; as members of society, 'they have rights and privileges' and also 'responsibilities to others'; they should, 'to the greatest extent possible, be responsible for conducting their own affairs'; 'their individuality should be fully respected, and they should not be controlled, dominated, manipulated, coerced or indoctrinated'; 'people are entitled to make their own mistakes and to learn from their own life experiences' (pp. 397–8).

The essential condition for such a process is a relationship characterized by empathic understanding; respect, warmth or caring; and genuineness or honesty.

The therapist's communication of values

The therapist's values are, as Strupp noted, not communicated directly to the client. Yet, they are communicated in the following ways:

1. The methods the therapist uses, as noted, represent values. They communicate the essential therapeutic values listed above, or the lack of them.
2. The therapist's methods are not simply objective techniques but are part of the therapist as a person. The therapist as a person relates to the client as a person. The therapist becomes a model for the client. As the therapist shows empathic understanding, respect, and genuineness in a positive relationship, the client also becomes more empathic, respecting of others, and genuine.
3. The responses of the therapist reveal what the therapist values — they reinforce certain behaviors in the client. In these behaviors, the client proceeds from self-disclosure to the specific content of self-exploration. These responses also reveal whether the therapist considers himself or herself an expert by leading, questioning, interpreting, guiding, suggesting, advising, or whether the therapist places the responsibility on the client by listening, responding, and following the client.

A dilemma and its resolution

The therapist, it has been emphasized, should not impose his or her value beliefs, value system, or philosophy on clients. Yet, it has also been noted, the therapist cannot avoid communicating his or her values to the client through the acceptance of an ultimate goal — the kind of behavior or person toward which therapy is directed — and through the methods or procedures used to implement the therapeutic process. Thus, there is a conflict or dilemma. The ultimate goal requires freedom and autonomy for the client, yet the client does not choose the goal or methods, nor can he or she avoid being exposed to and influenced by the procedures of the therapist. The methods of the therapist, however, must be consistent with the ultimate goal of the therapy. (And this goal, although in a sense 'imposed' by the therapist, is not actually imposed because it is derived from the nature of the client and human beings — it is imposed by this nature.) These conditions lead to the goal of a self-actualizing person. As Rogers (1961) phrased it:

> We have established by external control conditions which we predict will be followed by internal control by the individual, in pursuit of internally chosen goals . . . the client will become more self-directing, less rigid, more open to the evidence of his [or her] senses, better organized and integrated, more similar to the ideal he [or she] has chosen for himself [or herself] (p. 397).

In other words, the client becomes more self-actualizing.

A postscript

There is a recent development that could have a significant effect on the relation of values to psychotherapy — in effect, 'devaluing' psychotherapy. This is the attempt to 'medicalize' psychotherapy. About two decades ago, the medical model of psychotherapy was rejected by clinical psychologists. More recently, however, it has been re-espoused. The basic reason for this is that if psychotherapy is to be covered by insurance, it must be a treatment for a medical condition — a disease or disorder. Health insurance does not — and, perhaps, could not be expected to — cover a social-psychological disorder — a problem in living. In addition to the threat to independent practitioners of psychotherapy by nonmedical therapists, there are other implications for the practice of psychotherapy and research. The medical model involves specific treatments for specific conditions. Insurers as well as 'clinicians and policy makers need to know the extent to which treatments achieve desired or optimal therapeutic outcomes with the least restrictive and costly effort' (Newman and Howard, 1986, p. 181; see also Howard, Kapka, Krause, and Orlinsky; 1986; Kisch and Kroll, 1980). This has led to attempts by some psychologists and psychiatrists to standardize treatment, to the extent of developing manuals that therapists are to follow. 'The proliferation of manuals for treating particular ills by particular methods reflects the confidence of increased rigor in controlled research and increasing acceptance of brief clinical psychotherapies' (Parloff, London, and Wolfe, 1986, p. 337–8). Although this seems to be desirable for controlled research, there is a question as to whether this should, or even can, be done. Goldfried (1982) wrote:

> Should psychotherapy be made more scientific? Can psychotherapy be made more scientific, i.e., can its activities be made more measurable and replicable? . . . The rigorous research design does not place sufficient value on the centrality of the therapeutic alliance — the depth, stability, and benignity of the relationship between therapist and patient . . .Can a psychological intervention ever be as fully specified and be made as 'pure' as a pharmacological one? (Pp. 342–3.)

Beyond this, the implications for values and ethical problems in psychotherapy are radical. At one extreme, clients with problems involving values, choices, and issues involved in living would not be eligible for or entitled to psychotherapy — because, indeed, they are not eligible now for insured treatment without a diagnosis of psychopathology. Goals and methods of treatment would be prescribed with the therapist having no choices to make, no value decisions. He or she would be simply a technician following a manual. The relationship would not be important, let alone the essence of psychotherapy. This would dispose of the value problems in psychotherapy; it would also dispose of psychotherapy.

Conclusion

Beutler, Crago, and Arizmendi (1986) recently noted that 'many authors are urging therapists both to attend to their own religious and attitudinal systems and to be aware of the potential value of those of their patients' (p. 274). It is interesting that this comment is in the present tense, suggesting that it is only recently that the importance of values in psychotherapy has been recognized. Yet, the citations in this article (and they are by no means complete) go back some 35 years. With the exception of discussions of cross-cultural psychotherapy, few textbooks give much consideration to the place of values in counseling and psychotherapy. Yet, the problem of values permeates the entire process, entering into the goals and methods of every theory or approach. In this article, I have presented and considered the issues and have suggested an approach to counseling and psychotherapy that recognizes and incorporates those values that are basic to a democratic philosophy and the goal of a democratic society — the development of self-actualizing persons.

References

Beutler, L.E. (1979) Values, beliefs, religion and the persuasive influence of psychotherapy. *Psychotherapy: Theory, Research and Practice*, 16, 432–40.

Beutler, L.E., Crago, M., and Arizmendi, T.G. (1986) Research on therapist variables in psychotherapy. In S.L. Garfield and A.E. Bergin (Eds.), *Handbook of psychotherapy and behavior change.* (Pp. 257–310.) New York: Wiley.

Deutsch, F., and Murphy, W.F. (1955) *The clinical interview.* New York: International Universities Press.

Garfield, S.L., and Bergin, A.E. (1986) Introduction and historical overview. In S.L. Garfield and A.E. Bergin (Eds.), *Handbook of psychotherapy and behavior change.* (Pp. 3–22.) New York: Wiley.

Ginsberg, S.W., and Herma, J.L. (1953) Values and their relationship to psychiatric principles and practice. *American Journal of Psychotherapy*, 7, 536–73.

Glad, D.D. (1959) *Operational values in psychotherapy.* New York: Oxford University Press.

Goldfried, M.R. (1982) *Converging themes in psychotherapy: Trends in psychodynamic, humanistic, and behavioral practice.* New York: Springer.

Grant, B. (1985) The moral nature of psychotherapy. *Counseling and Values*, 29, 141–50.

Howard, K.I., Kapka, S.M., Krause, M.S., and Orlinsky, D.E. (1986) The dose-effect relationship in psychotherapy. *American Psychologist*, 41, 159–64.

Ingham, H.V., and Love, O.R. (1954) *The process of psychotherapy.* New York: McGraw-Hill.

Kisch, J., and Kroll, J. (1980) Meaningfulness versus effectiveness: Paradoxical implication in the evaluation of psychotherapy. *Psychotherapy: Theory, Research and Practice*, 17, 401–13.

Kluckhohn, C., et al. (1952) Values and value orientation in the theory of action. In T. Parsons and E.A. Shils (Eds.), *Toward a general theory of action.* (Pp. 288–443.) Cambridge, MA: Harvard University Press.

Madell, T.O. (1982) The relationship between values and attitudes toward three therapy methods. *Counseling and Values*, 27, 52–60.

Mahrer, A.R. (Ed.) (1967) *The goals of psychotherapy.* New York: Appleton-Century-Crofts (Prentice-Hall).

Margolis, J. (1966) *Psychotherapy and morality: A study of two concepts.* New York: Random House.

Maslow, A.H. (1956) Self-actualizing people: A study of psychological health. In C.E. Moustakas (Ed.), *The self: Explorations in personal growth.* (Pp. 160–

94.) New York: Harper and Row.

Menninger, K. (1958) *Theory of psychoanalytic technique,* New York: Basic Books.

Murphy, G. (1955) The cultured context of guidance. *Personnel and Guidance Journal,* 34, 4–9.

Newman, F.L., and Howard, K. (1986) Therapeutic effect, treatment outcome, and national health policy. *American Psychologist,* 41, 181–7.

Parloff, N.B. (1967) Goals in psychotherapy: Mediating and ultimate. In A.R. Mahrer (Ed.), *The goals of psychotherapy.* (Pp. 5–19.) New York: Appleton-Century-Crofts (Prentice-Hall).

Parloff, M.B., London, P., and Wolfe, B. (1986) Individual psychotherapy and behavior change. *Annual Review of Psychology,* 37, 321–49.

Patterson, C.H. (1958) Two approaches to human relations. *American Journal of Psychotherapy,* 12, 691–708.

Patterson, C.H. (1959) *Counseling and psychotherapy: Theory and practice.* New York: Harper and Row.

Patterson, C.H. (1970) A model for counseling and other interpersonal relationships. In W.H. Van Hoose and J.J. Pietrofesa (Eds.), *Counseling and guidance in the twentieth century.* (Pp. 169–90.) Boston: Houghton Mifflin.

Patterson, C.H. (1980) *Theories of counseling and psychotherapy.* (3rd ed.) New York: Harper and Row.

Patterson, C.H. (1985) *The therapeutic relationship: Foundations for an eclectic psychotherapy.* Monterey, CA: Brooks/Cole.

Patterson, C.H. (1986) *Theories of counseling and psychotherapy.* (4th ed.) New York: Harper and Row.

Rosenthal, D. (1955) Changes in some values following psychotherapy. *Journal of Consulting Psychology,* 19, 431–6.

Rogers, C.R. (1959) A theory of therapy, personality and interpersonal relationship, as developed in the client-centered framework. In S. Koch (Ed.), *Psychology: A study of science.* (Vol. 3, pp. 184–256.) New York: McGraw-Hill.

Rogers, C.R. (1961) *On becoming a person.* Boston: Houghton Mifflin.

Rogers, C.R. (1969) *Freedom to learn.* Columbus, OH: Merrill.

Skinner, B.F. (1953) *Science and human behavior.* New York: Macmillan.

Smith, M.B. (1954) Toward scientific and professional responsibility. *American Psychologist,* 9, 513–6.

Strupp, H.H. (1980) Humanism and psychotherapy: A personal statement of the therapist's essential values. *Psychotherapy: Theory, Research and Practice,* 17, 396–400.

Watson, G. (1958) Moral issues in psychotherapy. *American Psychologist,* 13, 574–6.

Weisskopf-Joelson, E. (1953) Some suggestions concerning Weltanschauung and psychotherapy. *Journal of Abnormal and Social Psychology,* 48, 601–4.

Wrenn, C.G. (1958) Psychology, religion, and values for the counselor. *Personnel and Guidance Journal,* 36, 331–4.

A Universal System of Psychotherapy

12

Introduction

Over 20 years ago I began putting together what we know, from experience and experiment, about psychotherapy. I used the term 'model' to describe the result. It is not a model in the formal or mathematical sense, but a conceptual model. It has gone by different names in the process of development as I realized that it is not limited to psychotherapy. It is actually a model for all facilitative interpersonal relationships — family (parent-child, husband-wife), teacher-student, employer-employee, supervisor-supervisee. Recently I have also come to realize that it is a universal model, in that it is not time-bound nor culture-bound.

I am aware that to suggest that there is a universal system of psychotherapy flies in the face of almost everything that has been written about cross-cultural psychotherapy. Currently it is generally accepted that existing theories and approaches to psychotherapy, developed in the Western cultures, are not applicable to other cultures. The system developed here, while based on theoretical and research foundations in Western culture, also recognizes and derives from the universal motivation and goal of all human beings.

There are three major elements of psychotherapy: (1) goals or objectives; (2) the process in the client; and (3) the therapist conditions necessary for client progress.

Goals

There has been surprisingly little fundamental consideration of the goal or goals of psychotherapy. This is surprising in view of the tremendous amount of attention to methods and techniques; it would appear that a prior concern would be the determination of goals. Outcome studies have simply accepted and used any and all measures available, with little concern about their relevance to methods and techniques or to any desirable goals of the process.

Mahrer's (1967) edited book, *The Goals of Psychotherapy*, revealed the almost endless number and variety of goals considered by the contributors. Parloff's (1967) contribution suggested a way of dealing with the problem. He proposed two levels

First published in *The Person-Centered Journal,* 1995, 2, 1, pp. 54–62. Reprinted by permission.

of goals — mediating and ultimate. He notes that although there may be great differences in mediating goals, 'differences in the stated ultimate goals will in all likelihood be small' (p. 9).

Parloff's suggestion is the basis for the present discussion. Three, rather than two, levels of goals are considered, and the definitions of ultimate and mediating goals are different. The three levels are (1) the ultimate goal, (2) mediate or mediating goals, and (3) immediate goals. The last consists of the client's behavior in the process.

The ultimate goal

The ultimate goal in psychotherapy concerns the kind of person we want the client to become as a result of psychotherapy. It should be apparent that the kind of person we want the client to be is the kind of person we would like all persons to be. It relates to the question of what is the purpose of life, a question with which philosophers have been concerned since Aristotle.

There have been many suggested goals. Jahoda (1958) proposed the concept of positive mental health, but it has been impossible to clearly define it. Concepts of adjustment raise the question of adjustment to what? White's (1959) concept of competence raises the question of competence for what? Psychological effectiveness involves the same problem. All require a higher level criterion.

There are a number of terms or concepts that appear to transcend this question and to constitute an acceptable criterion. These include *self-realization, self-enhancement,* the *fully-functioning person* of Rogers, and *self-actualization*. This last term appears to be widely and commonly used, and is adopted here.

The definition of the self-actualizing person derives form the work of Maslow (1956). He formulated a general definition of self-actualizing people as being characterized by the full use and exploitation of talents, capacities, potentialities, etc. Such people seem to be fulfilling themselves and to be doing the best that they are capable of doing. They are people who have developed or are developing the full stature of which they are capable (pp. 161–2).

Selecting a group of people, living and dead, who seemed to represent self-actualizing people, Maslow attempted to find what these people had in common that differentiated them from ordinary people. Fourteen characteristics emerged:

1. More efficient perception of reality and more comfortable relations with it.
2. Acceptance of self, others, and nature.
3. Spontaneity; lack of rigid conformity.
4. Problem-centeredness: sense of duty, responsibility.
5. Detachment; need for privacy.
6. Autonomy, independence of culture and environment.
7. Continued freshness of appreciation.
8. Mystic experiences; oceanic feelings.
9. Gemeinschaftsgefuhl; empathy, sympathy, compassion for all human beings.
10. Deep interpersonal relations with others.
11. Democratic character structure; respect for others.
12. Discernment of means and ends.

13. Philosophical, unhostile sense of humor.
14. Creativeness. (For more detail, see Maslow [1956] and Patterson [1985].)

I pause to note some objections to the concept of self-actualization. These derive, in my opinion, from misconceptions or misunderstandings of the nature of self-actualization and of self-actualizing persons. One such objection is that *self-actualization* is inimical to individuality, since, it is claimed, self-actualization consists of a collection of traits that are the same for all persons, resulting in standard, identical behaviors. But what is actualized are varying individual potentials. As Maslow (1956, p. 192) notes, 'self-actualization is actualization of a self, and no two selves are altogether alike'.

A second, and opposite, misconception is that a self-actualizing person is antisocial, or at least, asocial. Maddi (1973a,1973b) has taken this position. Williamson (1950,1958,1963,1965) also makes this criticism. And even Smith (1973) appears to see self-actualization as including undesirable, or antisocial behaviors, and thus unacceptable. And White (1973) appears to view self-actualization as selfish: 'I ask readers,' he wrote, 'to observe carefully whether or not self-actualization, in its current use by psychological counselors and others, is being made to imply anything more than adolescent preoccupation with oneself and one's impulses' (White, 1973, p. 69). And Janet Spence, in her 1985 presidential address to the American Psychological Association (Spence, 1985), spoke as follows of the youth of the 1960s and early 1970s:

> Although some were led to careers that were expressions of idealism, others turned their backs on the work ethic or substituted as a goal for material success self-actualization and 'doing your own thing'. . . Although the pursuit of self-actualization was stimulated by rejection of materialistic goals, it represents another facet of unbridled materialism (pp. 1289–90).

These criticisms appear to confuse the concept of self-actualization with selfishness and self-centeredness, and identify it with the characteristics of the 'me' generation of the 1970s, the 'culture of narcissism' (cf. Amitai Etzioni [1982], Christopher Lasch [1979] and Tom Wolfe [1976]). It is also perhaps influenced by the human potential movement, which no doubt, in many of its manifestations, promoted extreme individualism and self-centeredness.

Rogers answered these criticisms when he noted that individuals live in a society of others, and can become actualized only in interaction with others. They need others, and the affiliation, communication and positive regard of others (Rogers, 1959, 1961).

Self-actualization as the goal of psychotherapy has some significant implications:
1. It constitutes a criterion in the sense that it is not vulnerable to the question: For what? Self-actualization avoids the problems of an adjustment model, which include (in addition to the question adjustment to what?) the questions of conformity and social control (Halleck, 1971).

2. Self-actualization as a goal avoids the problems of the medical model and its illness-health dilemma. The goal involves more than the elimination of pathology, and the achievement of some undefined (and undefinable) level of mental health or 'normality'. It is not a negative concept, such as the absence of disturbance, disorder, or 'mental illness'. It is a positive goal.

3. It eliminates the conflict or dichotomy between intrapersonal and interpersonal. It includes the whole person in a society of other persons.

4. The goal is a process, not a static condition to be achieved once and for all. It is the development of *self-actualizing persons*, a continuing process. An adequate goal for persons must be an ideal that is ever more closely approximated but never completely achieved.

5. Self-actualization as a goal is not limited to psychotherapy, or to the treatment of disturbed individuals. It is the goal of life, for all persons, all of whom are, to some degree, dissatisfied with themselves, unhappy, unfulfilled, and not fully utilizing their capabilities or potentials. Thus, self-actualization should be the goal of society and all of its institutions — education; marriage and the family; political, social and economic systems — all of which exist for the benefit of individuals. As a matter of fact, psychotherapy has come into existence as a way in which society provides special assistance to those whose progress toward self-actualization has been blocked, interrupted or impeded in some way, mainly by the lack of good human relationships.

6. There is another aspect of self-actualization that is particularly significant. Goals are related to — or are the adverse of — drives or motives. Thus when we talk about the goal of life, we become involved in purpose, needs, drives or motives, since goals are influenced by, indeed determined by, needs. Self-actualization is the basic motivation of all human beings, indeed of all living organisms. Goldstein (1939, p. 196), one of the earliest writers to adopt the term 'self-actualization', stated that 'an organism is governed by a tendency to actualize, as much as possible, its nature in the world'. The goal, then, is not an abstract, theoretical, philosophical, ethical or religious goal, but derives from the biological nature of the organism.

7. Since the drive toward self-actualization is biologically based, it is not time-bound nor culture-bound. It is thus a universal goal. And as a universal goal, not only for psychotherapy but for life, it provides a criterion for the evaluation of cultures. Maslow (1971, p. 213), influenced by the anthropologist Ruth Benedict, wrote: 'I proceed on the assumption that the good society, and therefore the immediate goal of any society which is trying to improve itself, is the self-actualization of all individuals'. (More extended discussion will be found in Patterson [1978, 1985].)

8. This formulation of the ultimate goal of psychotherapy resolves the problem of who selects the goal — the therapist or the client. Neither the therapist nor the client chooses this goal. It is a given; it is implicit in the nature of the individual as a living organism. It is the nature of the organism, a characteristic of Rogers's actualizing tendency, to grow, to develop, to strive to actualize its potentials, to become what it is capable of becoming — to be more self-actualizing.

9. Finally, the concept of self-actualization provides a solution to the problem of organizing needs in some hierarchy. All specific drives, including those in Maslow's (1970) hierarchy, are subservient to the drive toward self-actualization. All specific needs are organized and assume temporary priority in terms of their relevance to the basic drive toward self-actualization (Patterson, 1985).

Mediate goals

Mediate goals are the usual goals considered by counselors and psychotherapists. They include the specific and concrete goals of behavior therapists. Contributors to Mahrer's (1967) book focused upon this level of goals, such things as reduction of symptoms; reduction of anxiety, and of psychological pain and suffering, and of hostility; elimination of unadaptive habits, acquisition of adaptive habits.

Other mediate goals include good marital and family relationships; vocational and career success and satisfaction; educational achievement, including study skills and good study habits; development of potentials in art, music, athletics, etc.

The ultimate goal is a common goal, applicable to all individuals. Mediate goals provide for, or allow for, individual differences. People have differing, and multiple, potentials; they actualize themselves in differing ways.

A number of implications of the separation of goals into ultimate and mediate become apparent:

1. While the ultimate goal is universal, applying across time and cultures, mediate goals vary with individuals, time and cultures. It is here that client choices and decisions operate.
2. Mediate goals may be considered as mediating goals, between the immediate goal and the ultimate goal. That is, they are steps toward the ultimate goal. In some instances they may overlap with aspects of the ultimate goal — the development of self-understanding, self-esteem, or self-acceptance, for example.
3. The ultimate goal provides a criterion for the acceptability of mediate goals, something that is lacking, or implicit, in behavior therapy.
4. While mediate goals may be considered as sub-goals, or steps toward the ultimate goal, they may also be seen as by-products of the ultimate goal. Self-actualizing persons normally and naturally seek to achieve the mediate goals on their own, or seek and obtain the necessary assistance, such as tutoring, instruction, information, education and training, or re-education, to achieve them. As by-products, they are not necessarily goals to be directly achieved or specifically sought. Thus, in psychotherapy, mediate goals need not be determined or defined in advance, but are developed by the client during, or even following, the therapy process. It appears that it may be sufficient, in some cases, to provide the conditions leading to the development of self-actualizing persons; thus, as individuals become more self-actualizing, they develop, pursue and achieve their own more specific goals.
5. It is apparent that many of the mediate goals are the objectives of other helping processes, of education, re-education and skill training.

The immediate goal

The mediating goals of Parloff (1967) are aspects of the psychotherapy process, the initiating and continuing of which is the immediate goal in the present model or system. The therapy process and its elements have been described in many ways, in the various theories of psychotherapy. Parloff (1967) included the following specific goals: making the unconscious conscious; recall of the repressed; deconditioning; counterconditioning; strengthening or weakening of the superego; development and analysis of the transference neurosis; promoting increased insight; increasing self-acceptance. There is little, if any, evidence that many of these goals lead to desirable therapy outcomes, particularly to increased self-actualization.

An essential of the therapy process is client activity of some sort. Client activity involving self-exploration, or intrapersonal exploration, appears to be universally present in successful psychotherapy. It includes some of the mediating goals mentioned by Parloff, such as developing awareness of unconscious (or preconscious) material (self-awareness).

The process of self-exploration is complex, involving several aspects or stages:
1. *Self-disclosure.* Before clients can explore themselves, they must disclose, or reveal, themselves, including their negative thoughts, feelings, problems, failures, inadequacies, etc. These are the reasons clients come for therapy, their 'problems', and it is necessary to state the 'problem' before it can be dealt with. Self-disclosure, or self-exposure, requires that clients be open and honest, or genuine.
2. *Self-exploration.* This consists of clients working with the disclosed material, exploring what and who they as persons really are. The self-exploration process may be slow, and not smooth or continuous. There is resistance to looking at and facing up to one's undesirable aspects.
3. Self-exploration leads to client *self-discovery*, an awareness of what one is really like.
4. With self-discovery comes *self-understanding*. Clients become aware of failures to actualize themselves and their potentials. They see the discrepancies between their actual selves and their ideal selves. They begin to reduce the discrepancies, modifying their actual or ideal selves, or both. A realistic *self-concept* is developed, a self-concept more congruent with experience. Clients are able to accept themselves as they are, and to commit themselves to becoming more like they want to be (see Patterson [1985] and Rogers [1961], especially, for fuller discussions of the therapy process in the client).

Questions have been raised about self-disclosure and self-exploration by writers about cross-cultural counseling. Persons in other cultures (as well as the poor in our own culture [Goldstein, 1973]), it is said, cannot, or do not, engage in self-disclosure or self-exploration (or 'introspection'). Pedersen, for example, referring to American Indian clients, writes: 'A counselor who expects clients to verbalize their feelings is not likely to have much success with Native American clients' (Pedersen, 1976, p. 26). Sue (1981, p. 48) refers to 'certain groups' (Asian Americans, Native Americans, etc.) that dictate against self-disclosure to strangers.

He refers (p.38) to 'the belief in the desirability of self-disclosure by many mental health practitioners'. Yet, paradoxically, he also refers to self-disclosure as an 'essential' condition that is 'particularly crucial to the process and goals of counseling ... ' (Sue, 1981, p. 48).

That is the problem. If self-exploration is essential for progress in psychotherapy (and this is supported by the research), then it cannot be abandoned, as some suggest, with the therapist taking an active, directing, leading or structured approach.

But client reluctance to self-disclose or difficulty in self-disclosing is a social, not a purely cultural characteristic. People (in general, not only Asians) do not disclose to strangers, social superiors, experts, including professionals. Yet, paradoxically, people sometimes tell things to strangers (as well as to therapists) that they wouldn't tell to families or friends. Chinese with whom I have talked assure me that they self-disclose among their families and friends. The reluctance to self-disclose or difficulty in self-disclosing among certain clients is not a reason for abandoning psychotherapy (for which it is a necessary condition), but for providing the conditions which make client self-disclosure possible.

The conditions
How does the therapist make it possible for the client to engage in those activities necessary for therapeutic progress? He or she does so by providing certain conditions. Three major conditions have been identified and defined (Rogers,1957) and are now supported by considerable research (Patterson, 1984, 1985). The nature of these conditions is now well known, and they are simply enumerated here.
1. Empathic understanding, an understanding of the client from his or her frame of reference, and the communicating of this understanding.
2. Respect, unconditional positive regard, the manifestation of a deep interest, caring, concern, even compassion for the client.
3. Therapeutic genuineness, congruence in the therapist, an authenticity, transparency, honesty. It is necessary that the adjective 'therapeutic' be used, since the term 'genuineness' alone has led to therapists manifesting behaviors, under its guise, that are harmful to clients.
   There is another condition, that may be more a technique than a condition, that I believe has the status of a necessary element in the therapist's behavior:
4. Concreteness or specificity in responding to client productions. This is the opposite of abstractions, labels, generalizations or interpretations, all of which, rather than encouraging client self-exploration, stifle or extinguish it.

These four conditions may be summed up, I think, in the concept of love, in the sense of *agapé*. They are part of all the great world religions and philosophies. In 1986, Dr. Louis Thayer interviewed Carl Rogers. At one point in the interview, when Rogers commented on the presence of too much intervention, by parents, governments and policy makers (as well as by therapists), he stopped to take from his wallet a verse he carried with him, 'a little quotation I treasure,' he said. It is this poem by Lao Tzu, a Chinese philosopher of the fifth century BC that I have been using in my teaching for several years, substituting *therapist* for *leader*:

> **A Leader** [Therapist]
> A leader [therapist] is best when people [clients] hardly know he exists;
> Not so good when people [clients] obey and acclaim him;
> Worst when they despise him.
> But.of a good leader [therapist] who talks little,
> When his work is done, his aim fulfilled,
> They will say, 'We did it ourselves.'
>
> The less a leader [therapist] does and says,
> The happier his people [clients];
> The more he struts and brags,
> The sorrier his people [clients].
>
> [Therefore] a sensible man says:
> If I keep from meddling with people [clients], they take care of themselves.
> If I keep from commanding people [clients], they behave themselves.
> If I keep from preaching at people [clients], they improve themselves.
> If I keep from imposing on people [clients], they become themselves.

Client conditions

Psychotherapy is of course a two-way process, a relationship, and it takes two to form a relationship. There are two conditions that must be present in the client before the process of therapy can begin.

1. Therapy cannot be imposed on a passive, so-called involuntary client. The client must be 'motivated'. Rogers (1957, p. 96) states, as one of the conditions of therapeutic personality change, that the client 'is in a state of incongruence, being vulnerable or anxious'. That is, he or she 'must be someone who is feeling some concerns . . . some degree of conflict, some degree of inner difference, some expression of concern'. (Rogers, 1987, pp. 39,40).
2. The client must perceive the conditions offered by the therapist. 'The communication' to the client of 'the therapist's empathic understanding and unconditional positive regard is to a minimal degree achieved' (Rogers, 1957, p. 96).

Characteristics of the system

There are some characteristics of this system of psychotherapy that are worth noting:

I . Note the similarities in the Goals, the Process, and Conditions. All include empathy, respect, and genuineness or honesty. *The conditions are also the goal.*
2. The client, in becoming more self-actualizing becomes a therapeutic influence

on others, contributing to their self-actualizing progress.

3. The conditions operate in a number of ways, consistent with our understanding of the learning or change process.

    a. The conditions create a nonthreatening environment, in which the client can feel safe in self-disclosing and self-exploring. A high level of threat, as is well known, is inimical to learning. The warm, accepting atmosphere provided by the therapist contributes to desensitizing the client's anxieties and fears in human relating, and inhibitions about self-disclosure.

    b. The psychotherapeutic process is not a straight-line progression, but is like the typical learning process, with plateaus or even regressions. The client evidences the approach-avoidance conflict, progressing up to the point when internal threat or anxiety becomes too great, then retreating or 'resting' until the anxiety is reduced. Nor is the process one in which separate problems are worked on until each is resolved. All problems interrelate, and the client grapples with one for a while, then may move on to another, and another, then returning to each in an alternating or spiraling process.

    c. The conditions provide an environment for self-discovery learning. While discovery learning is not always possible or desirable in other areas, it is the most relevant and most effective method for learning about oneself.

    d. The conditions are the most effective reinforcers of the desired client behavior of self-exploration. More broadly, love is the most potent reinforcer of desirable human behavior.

    e. The conditions also operate through modeling. The client becomes more like the therapist in the therapy process. It follows that the therapist, to be a model, must be at a higher level of the conditions, and of the self-actualizing process, than the client.

    f. The conditions, when offered at a high level by the therapist, include the expectation by the therapist of change in the client. Expectations have a powerful effect on the behavior of others.

    g. The therapist conditions free the actualizing tendency in the client, so that he or she can become a more self-actualizing person.

4. The conditions are the specific treatment for the lack or inadequacy of the conditions in the past and/or present life of the client. This lack is the source of most functional emotional disturbances, and of failures in the self-actualizing of human beings.

5. The conditions constitute, or include, the major basic, general, enduring and universal values of life. They are necessary for the survival of a society or culture. Society could not exist if these conditions were not present in its members at a minimal level. They are the conditions necessary for human beings to live together and to survive as a society. Skinner (1953, p. 445) wrote: 'If a science of behavior can discover those conditions of life which make for the ultimate strength of men, it may provide a set of "moral values" which, because they are independent of the history and culture of any one group, may be generally accepted.' We have those values (Patterson, 1966).

6. Thus this system of psychotherapy, incorporating the goal of living, and the

conditions for achieving this goal, is a universal system, neither time- nor culture-bound (Patterson, 1996).

References

Etzioni, A. (1982) *An immodest agenda: Rebuilding America before the 21st century.* New York: McGraw-Hill.

Goldstein, A. P. (1973) *Structured learning therapy: Toward a psychotherapy for the poor.* New York: Wiley.

Goldstein, K. (1939) *The organism.* New York: Harcourt Brace Jovanovich.

Halleck, S. L. (1971) *The politics of therapy.* New York: Science House.

Jahoda, M. (1958) *Current concepts of mental health.* New York: Basic Books.

Lasch, C. (1979) *The culture of narcissism: American life in an age of diminishing expectations.* New York: Norton.

Maddi, S. (1973a) Ethics and psychotherapy: Remarks stimulated by White's paper. The *Counseling Psychologist*, 4 (2), 26–9.

Maddi, S. (1973b) Creativity is strenuous. *The University of Chicago Magazine*, September-October, 18–23.

Mahrer, A. R. (Ed.) (1967) *The goals of psychotherapy.* Englewood Cliffs, NJ: Prentice-Hall.

Maslow, A. H. (1956) Self-actualizing people: A study of psychological health. In C. E. Moustakas (Ed.), *The self: Explorations in personal growth.* (Pp. 160–94.) New York: Harper and Row.

Maslow, A. H. (1970) *Motivation and personality*, 2nd edition. New York: Harper and Row.

Maslow, A. H. (1971) *The farther reaches of human nature.* New York: Viking Press.

Parloff, M. B. (1967) Goals in psychotherapy: Mediating and ultimate. In A. R. Mahrer (Ed.), *The goals of psychotherapy.* (Pp. 5–19.) Englewood Cliffs, NJ: Prentice-Hall.

Patterson, C. H. (1966) Science, behavior control and values. *Insight*, 5 (2), 14–21.

Patterson, C. H. (1978) Cross cultural counseling or psychotherapy. *International Journal for the Advancement of Counseling,* 1, 231–47.

Patterson, C. H. (1984) Empathy, warmth and genuineness in psychotherapy: A review of reviews. *Psychotherapy, 21*, 431–8.

Patterson, C. H. (1985) *The therapeutic relationship.* Pacific Grove, CA: Brooks/Cole.

Patterson, C. H. (1996) Multicultural counseling: From diversity to universality, *Journal of Counseling and Development,*74, 227–31.

Pedersen, P. (1976) The field of multicultural counseling. In P. Pedersen, W. J. Lonner, and J. G. Draguns (Eds.), *Counseling across cultures.* Honolulu: University Press of Hawaii.

Rogers, C. R. (1957) The necessary and sufficient conditions of therapeutic personality change. *Journal of Consulting Psychology*, 21, 95–103.

Rogers, C. R. (1959) A theory of therapy, personality and interpersonal relationships, as developed in the client-centered framework. In S. Koch (Ed.), *Psychology: A study of a science. Vol. 3: Formulations of the person and the social context.* (Pp. 184–256.) New York: McGraw-Hill.

Rogers, C. R. (1961) *On becoming a person.* Boston: Houghton Mifflin.

Rogers, C. R. (1987) The underlying theory: Drawn from experience with individuals and groups. *Counseling and Values,* 32, 38–46.

Skinner, B. F. (1953) *Science and human behavior.* New York: MacMillan.

Smith, M. B. (1973) Comments on White's paper. *The Counseling Psychologist, 4* (2), 48–50.

Spence, J. T. (1985) Achievement American style: The rewards and costs of individualism. *American Psychologist,* 40, 1285–95.

Sue, D. W (1981) *Counseling the culturally different: Theory and Practice..* New York: Wiley.

Thayer, L. (1987) Excerpts from an interview with Dr. Carl Rogers. *Person-Centered Review,* 2, 434–6.

White, R. W. (1959) Motivation reconsidered: The concept of competence. *Psychological Review,* 66, 297–333.

White, R. W. (1973) The concept of healthy personality: What do we really mean? *The Counseling Psychologist, 4* (2), 3-12, 67–9.

Williamson, E. G. (1950) A concept of counseling. *Occupations,* 29, 182–9.

Williamson, E. G. (1958) Values orientation in counseling. *Personnel and Guidance .Journal,* 37, 520–8.

Williamson, E. G. (1963) The social responsibilities of counselors. *Illinois Guidance and Personnel Association Newsletter,* Winter, 5–13.

Williamson, E. G. (1965) *Vocational counseling.* New York: McGraw-Hill.

Wolfe, T. (August 23, 1976) The 'ME' decade. *New York Magazine,* 26–30.

The Current State and the Future of Psychotherapy

13

For most of my professional life I have found myself in disagreement with some of the contributions to the professional literature. I am comforted by a saying of Mark Twain: 'Whenever you find yourself on the side of the majority, it is time to pause and reflect'. One of my fantasies is to see myself standing beside a bandwagon, asking those who are scrambling to get on, 'Do you know where you are going?'

One of my earliest articles, published in the *American Psychologist* (Patterson, 1948), was entitled, 'Is Diagnosis Necessary for Psychotherapy?' It might not be accepted for publication today, although the argument is still valid. I became client-centered in 1947, after spending some time with Rogers at the University of Chicago. I have stated that I became inoculated against directive systems of psychotherapy, and I have continued to be protected without a booster shot. I have suggested that I have been to Carl Rogers as Paul was to Christ. I have preached one gospel, the gospel of Carl Rogers. I apparently have not been a very effective disciple. I sometimes feel more like John the Baptist — a voice crying in the wilderness. The name of Carl Rogers is revered, but few, if any, graduate students now read any of his writings. At the 1985 Phoenix Conference on the Evolution of Psychotherapy (Zeig, 1987), he was the only one honored with a standing ovation, lasting five minutes. Yet one searches in vain for signs of his influence on the other presenters. It is true that the importance of the therapist-client relationship is being recognized by many theorists, including the psychoanalysts (e.g. Lomas, 1993; Meissner, 1991; Rowe and Mac Isaac, 1991). Yet there is not a single reference to Rogers in the psychoanalytic literature I have perused. It appears to be a case of the reinvention of the wheel.

My focus of interest in the past several years has been psychotherapy. Over 30 years ago, Rogers (1963) wrote, 'The field of psychotherapy is in a state of chaos' (p. 5). Others have echoed that conclusion since, and it appears to describe the

First published in *The Counseling Psychologist*, 1996, 24, pp. 338–40. The Leona Tyler Award Address: 'Some Thoughts on Reaching the End of a Career' presented at the 1995 American Psychological Association annual convention. © Division of Counseling Psychology. Reprinted by permission of Sage Publications/Corwin Press, Inc.

field today. In 1985, Leo, reporting on the Phoenix Conference for *Time* magazine, reported one participant as saying that none of the experts present agreed. Joseph Wolpe (1987), in his presentation, called the conference 'a babble of conflicting voices' (p. 134). Prochaska (1988) titled his review of the report of the conference 'The Devolution of Psychotherapy' and quoted from Zeig's (1987) introduction: 'Here were the reigning experts on psychotherapy and I could see no way they could agree on defining the territory. Can anyone dispute, then, that the field is in disarray?' (p.305).

The implications of this situation are significant:

1. If there is no agreement on what psychotherapy is, how can we license or control its practice? How can it be packaged and sold to consumers? Yet it is being marketed through providers of cost-effective services of health care, who are monitored for quality control and accountability. Just what are consumers getting? If psychotherapy were a drug, it could not be approved by the Federal Drug Administration (see Patterson, 1994).

2. If there is no agreement on what psychotherapy is, how are psychotherapists educated? Every training program decides for itself how its students are educated. Every faculty member teaches his or her own approach to psychotherapy. Education in psychotherapy is where the education of physicians was before the Flexner report in 1910 (Flexner,1910/1960).

3. Psychotherapy is being reduced to a multitude of techniques — skills, or interventions, as they are now called. Psychotherapy is being moved from a profession to a trade, complete with manuals and handbooks. The specific treatments paradigm, following Paul's (1967) dictum, attempts to prescribe specific treatments for specific diagnoses, following the medical model (see Patterson and Watkins, 1996, Chap. 15, for a critique of this model). And the multicultural movement attempts to prescribe specific treatments for each culture, subculture, ethnic group, race, sex, etcetera, etcetera (see Patterson,1996 for a critique of this movement).

It is a paradox that as medicine has been moving away from invasive to noninvasive procedures, psychotherapy is moving toward more invasive procedures.

Of course, there have been those interested in integration in psychotherapy, going back to Dollard and Miller's (1950) classic joining of behavior theory and psychoanalysis. The current movement, however, does not have as its goal the development of a single, universal system. Rather, the movement has focused on the combination of methods and techniques in what I have called the eclectic solution. Numerous eclectic positions have been proposed. Paradoxically, eclecticism as an integrating force actually appears to be fostering divergence. Again, I must refer you to *Theories of Psychotherapy* (Patterson and Watkins, 1996, Chap. 15) for a fuller discussion.

I have proposed what I call the common elements solution to the problem of integration (see Patterson and Watkins, 1996, Chap. 16). It appears that any attempt at integration must be based on those elements present in all the major systems or theories. These factors are those involved in the relationship between the therapist and the client. The major elements were identified and defined by Rogers (1957) in his classic article, 'The Necessary and Sufficient Conditions of Therapeutic Personality Change.' They consist of the well-known therapist conditions of empathic understanding, respect or warmth, and therapeutic genuineness, as well as the client conditions of vulnerability, anxiousness, and perception of the therapist conditions. These are now widely recognized and accepted as common elements in psychotherapy.

There is all but universal agreement that the relationship — or the therapeutic alliance as some now prefer to call it — is a necessary condition for progress in psychotherapy. My position is that the relationship *is* psychotherapy and that the therapist conditions can be summed up as *agapé* — or love. A few years ago, I visited Changua University in Taiwan. In a group of undergraduate students in a counseling course, one student asked, 'What is the most important thing for a counselor to do?' After a few moments reflection I replied, 'Love your client.' So, if you ask me, 'Is that all there is to psychotherapy?' my answer is, 'Yes, my friends, that is all there is to psychotherapy.' Love is the most potent reinforcer of behavior change, or as Martin Luther King is reported to have said, 'Whom we wish to change we must first love.' Gordon Allport (1950), over 40 years ago, wrote, 'Love is incomparably the greatest psychotherapeutic agent' (p. 80). Almost 30 years ago, Burton (1967) said that 'after all research on psychotherapy is accounted for, psychotherapy still resolves itself into a relationship best subsumed by the word love' (pp. 102–3). This is the essence of my 'A Universal System of Psychotherapy'. It would have been an appropriate article for today, but when I was informed of the award, it had already been accepted for publication (Patterson, 1995). Earlier, it had been rejected by the *American Journal of Psychotherapy*, whose reviewers contended that there could be no such thing as a universal system. There are many who share this view.

References

Allport, G. W. (1950) *The individual and his religion.* New York: Macmillan.

Burton, A. (1967) *Modern humanistic psychotherapy.* San Francisco, CA: Jossey Bass.

Dollard, J., and Miller, N. E. (1950) *Personality and psychotherapy.* New York: McGraw-Hill.

Flexner, A. (1960) *Medical education in the United States and Canada: A report of the Carnegie Foundation for the advancement of teaching.* Washington: Author. (Original published in 1910.)

Leo, J. (1985) A therapist in every corner. *Time,* December 23, 59.

Lomas, P. (1993) *Cultivating intuition: An introduction to psychotherapy.* Northvale, NJ: Jason Aronson.

Meissner, W. W. (1991) *What is effective in psychoanalytic therapy: The move from interpretation to relation.* Northvale, NJ: Jason Aronson.

Patterson, C. H. (1948) Is diagnosis necessary for psychotherapy? *American Psychologist.* 3, 155–9.

Patterson, C. H. (1994) Are consumers of psychotherapy able to make an informed choice? Or do they have a choice? *Psychotherapy Bulletin*, 29 (4), 40–1.

Patterson, C. H. (1995) A universal system of psychotherapy. *Person-Centered Journal*. 2, 54–62.

Patterson, C. H. (1996) Multicultural counseling: From diversity to universality. *Journal of Counseling and Development*, 74, 2127–231.

Patterson, C. H., and Watkins, C. E., Jr. (1996) *Theories of psychotherapy* (5th ed.). New York: Harper Collins.

Paul, G. (1967) Outcome research in psychotherapy. *Journal of Consulting Psychology,* 31, 109–18.

Prochaska, J. O. (1988) The devolution of psychotherapy. Review of J. K. Zeig (Ed.), 'The evolution of psychotherapy'. *Contemporary Psychology*. 33. 305–6.

Rogers, C. R. (1963) Psychotherapy today or where do we go from here? *American Journal of Psychotherapy*, 17, 5–16.

Rogers, C. R. (1957) The necessary and sufficient conditions of therapeutic personality change. *Journal of Consulting Psychology*, 21, 95–103.

Rowe, C. E., and Mac Isaac, D. S. (1991) *Empathic attunement: The technique of psychoanalytic self-psychology.* Northvale, NJ: Jason Aronson.

Wolpe, J. (1987) The promotion of a scientific psychotherapy. In J. K. Zeig (Ed.), *The evolution of psychotherapy.* (Pp. 133–42.) New York: Brunner/Mazel.

Zeig, J. K. (1987) *The evolution of psychotherapy*. New York: Brunner/Mazel.

On Client-Centered Counseling and Psychotherapy

PHENOMENOLOGICAL PSYCHOLOGY

14

It is a basic tenet of so-called depth psychology or dynamic psychology that behavior is determined by deep unconscious motives, and that in order to understand, predict, or control behavior one must understand these motives. This is not a simple matter, since one cannot easily recognize motives. The apparent or obvious motives, or the motives reported by the subject, are not the real motives. Indeed, the so-called real motives are commonly the reverse of those reported by the subject. Thus nothing can be accepted at face value. Nothing is what it appears to be. Reports of subjects are not to be trusted. The widespread acceptance of this point of view, by lay as well as professional people, attests to the influence of Freud and psychoanalysis.

There is another point of view, which has not been widely accepted, but which is increasing its influence in psychology. This approach suggests that for the purpose of understanding and predicting behavior it is profitable to make the assumption that things are what they appear to be, that the significant determinants of behavior are not some mysterious unconscious motives nor some so-called reality, but the individual's perceptions of himself and his environment. 'There is more to seeing than meets the eyeball' (Hanson, 1958). 'We see things', to quote Gibson (1951, p. 98) 'not as *they* are but as *we* are'. Or to say it another way, it is not 'seeing is believing', but 'believing is seeing'. In more technical terms, the response defines the stimulus, rather than the stimulus defining the response. Gombrich, in a discussion of art and illusion (1960, p. 394), notes that ' . . .we can never neatly separate what we see from what we know.' 'The individual sees what he wants to see, not in the sense that he manufactures out of whole cloth, but in the sense that he appropriates to himself, from what is given, the 'pattern that he needs' (Murphy, Murphy, and Newcomb, 1937, p. 218).

This second point of view is phenomenology. It is not widely accepted. Snygg (1961), in reviewing a recent book, states: 'Phenomenology is not in this country an honored, going concern with a historical past. American phenomenologies therefore emerge rather suddenly, as workers in applied fields run into problems

First published in *Personnel and Guidance Journal*, 1965, 43, pp. 97–105. © ACA. Reprinted by permission. No further reproduction without written permission from the Association for Counseling and Development.

they cannot solve by the traditional objective approach, are forced to develop conceptual models better suited to their needs and then go on to apply them in wide fields.' It is interesting to list some of the names of those who have come to entertain a phenomenological approach. They include William James, John Dewey, George H. Mead, the Allports, Wertheimer, Koffka, Koehler, Kurt Lewin, Adelbert Ames, and Carl Rogers.

Phenomenology and introspection

A number of years ago a colleague declared that Rogers had set psychology back by 50 years. His basis for the statement was the identification of phenomenology with introspection. It is not necessarily undesirable that we go back 50 years, since it might be contended that psychology has been on the wrong track or in a blind alley during this time, and that it is necessary to go back and pick up a new fork in the road. Psychology has been dominated in the past 50 years by behaviorism and psychoanalysis. While these two approaches or systems are antithetical in many respects, they are similar in that they view the individual from an external position, as an object. Phenomenology, on the other hand, takes the internal frame of reference, and in this respect is related to introspection. However, there is a difference. Introspection was concerned only with the subject's report or description of his conscious sensations and feelings. Phenomenology is concerned with the individual's report, not only of his own sensations and feelings, but of his perceptions of the external world as well as of himself. While phenomenology is thus related to introspection, and to some extent grew out of it, phenomenology as represented by Gestalt psychology, as Boring (1953) points out, was a protest against classic introspection.

Phenomenology, using introspection in the form of verbal reports, produced extensive and significant experimental research in perception. In using verbal reports, phenomenological experiments are no different from psychophysical experiments, in which the subject reports physical sensations or judgments. In fact, much of current experimental psychology, including behavioristic psychology, depends upon verbal reports, so that phenomenology can't be condemned as unscientific because it also utilizes verbal report. It is true that there are problems involved in the use of self-reports, but as Bakan (1954) points out, in this respect the method is no different from any other method of science. And there is no other way in many instances to study certain significant problems, such as the self-concept, or to determine the perceptual field of the subject. Nevertheless, it must be recognized that the description of the perceptual field by a subject is not identical with the field itself.

It is interesting that stimulus-response psychology supports the phenomenological point of view. It has been noted that for phenomenology, the response defines the stimulus. Experimental psychologists have come to realize this in the recognition that the same objective or physical stimulus means different things to different subjects, and that if the stimulus situation is to be standardized, it must be in terms of the subjects' perceptions of the stimulus, not the stimulus as objectively defined, or as perceived by the experimenter. In this respect all stimuli are response-inferred (Jessor, 1956, Wylie, 1961, pp. 13–21).

Phenomenology defined

What is phenomenology? It is the purpose of this paper to attempt to describe briefly the phenomenological approach to behavior. English and English (1958, p. 387) define phenomenology as follows: 'A theoretical point of view which advocates the study of phenomena or direct experience taken naively at face value; the view that behavior is determined by the phenomena of experience rather than by external, objective, physically described reality'. Phenomenalism is defined as 'a philosophical doctrine teaching that human knowledge is limited to appearances, never reaching the true nature of reality' (English and English, 1958, pp.38ff). Phenomenology as a distinct philosophical point of view is a development mainly of the present century, usually being associated with the philosopher Husserl whose phenomenological writings date from the early years of the century (Spiegelberg, 1960). A brief description of philosophical phenomenology is impossible, in part because of differences among its exponents; there are phenomenologies rather than a school. But they agree in that they are all concerned with experience as the basic data of knowledge. Knowledge can come only from experience, whether sensory or nonsensory, or extrasensory. Whether there is some reality that gives rise to experiences, and if so what is the nature of this reality, is unimportant, since it can only be known through experience. Taking this experience, phenomenology attempts to study it, through observing, describing, and analyzing it, attempting to generalize from the particular experiences, determining relationships, studying the various appearances of phenomena and the development of perceptions and conceptions in the phenomenological field.

The position that we can never know the true nature of reality is resisted, both by those who feel that common sense indicates that there is a reality, as when we stub a toe on a brick, by those whose needs or desires require the certainty of some reality and by scientists who accept their objective measurements and operational definitions as reality. But it should be obvious, both to common sense and to objective observation and measurement, that 'reality' varies with different attitudes, motives, desires, or points of view, and with different operations. Whether or not these individual realities add up to a general, absolute, natural reality is a question that has little if any practical significance, for reasons that will become apparent. Philosophically, a phenomenologist may or may not be a realist. Phenomenology represents a 'neutralism with regard to reality rather than an outright commitment to realism' (Spiegelberg, 1960, p. 686).

Spiegelberg (1960), in his history of philosophical phenomenology, notes that 'Phenomenology is hardly one of the leading philosophical movements in the United States'. He later states that 'actually in the United States phenomenology has had a much bigger impact on extraphilosophical studies such as psychology and theology, though to be sure in forms which differ considerably from those stressed by the philosophical phenomenologists' (p. 637). In psychology, he continues,

> . . . the reaction against behaviorism takes more and more the form of developing a wider phenomenological approach, which tries to give introspection as objective and critical refinement as possible (pp. 643–4).

While, as has been indicated, the Gestaltists were essentially phenomenological, as well as a number of social psychologists identified with sociology, notably G. H. Mead, the first specific treatment of phenomenological psychology was the 1941 article by Snygg (1941). At the present time perhaps the most definitive statement of phenomenological psychology is that of Snygg and Combs, first published in 1949 and recently revised (Combs and Snygg, 1959).

A synthesis of phenomenological psychology

What is phenomenological psychology? What are its distinguishing features? Phenomenology in psychology did not develop from philosophical phenomenology, but arose almost independently, although psychologists such as James, Koehler, and Lewin had some contact with the latter. There is, as yet, no formal school of phenomenological psychology. It is thus not possible to present a statement of a formal or complete system. The outline of the characteristics of a phenomenological approach to human behavior that follows is an attempt to synthesize or integrate the ideas of those who have been identified as phenomenological in their psychological approach to behavior. The attempt rests most heavily, perhaps, on Combs and Snygg (1959):

1. *The individual is a living, and therefore active, organism engaged in the attempt to organize its world.* Two characteristics of this fact are important:
   a. The individual is not an empty organism, waiting to be prodded into action by external or even internal stimuli. The response seeks the stimulus, rather than waiting for the stimulus to evoke it.
   b. The interaction of the organism with its environment is the basis for experience. This experience constitutes the basic data of psychology. It consists of or underlies and gives meaning to, overt behavior. Phenomenological psychology is concerned with the study of the experiencing individual.
2. *The organization which the individual gives to the world is known as his perceptual or phenomenal field.* This is more than the area of sensory perception, including cognition, conceptions, and knowledge. The importance of phenomenology was first recognized by perceptual psychology, since the study of perception was the focus of early psychology and the lack of a constant relation of perception to the objective stimulus became apparent.

   The phenomenal field is the universe, including the individual himself, as it is perceived and experienced by him. It consists not of the so-called 'reality', but of the world as it appears to him, as he perceives it. He can only know the world through his perceptions, and there is no reality for the individual other than what constitutes his perceptual or phenomenal field. 'To each individual, his phenomenal field is reality; it is the only reality he can know' (Combs and Snygg, 1959, p. 21). The perceptual field of the individual is influenced by his needs and beliefs. 'What is perceived is not what exists, but what one believes exists, . . . what we have learned to perceive as a result of our past opportunities or experiences' (Combs and Snygg; 1959, pp. 81, 85).

   Perceptions are often referred to as accurate, true, veridical, or inaccurate, wrong, or distorted. It is probably better not to think of perceptions in these terms, since they involve an evaluation from an external frame of reference. All perceptions, from the point of view of the perceiver, are accurate and true, since there is no other experience, at the time of perceiving, with which they may be compared and evaluated. A perception may not agree with the perceptions of others under the same conditions, or with the perception of the same individual at another time or from another vantage point. All perceptions are thus true or accurate, as perceptions. In the case of so-called illusion, such as the Ames demonstrations, the illusion is a true perception. What is in error, what is wrong, is the inference from a perception regarding the nature of the stimulus. What is perceived, from one angle, as a chair, is found not to have the qualities of a chair from another angle and is not perceived as a chair from the changed position. Thus, inferences regarding the stimuli may be changed, or corrected, on further experience with a stimulus. The same point of view may be taken with regard to what have been called distorted perceptions resulting from the needs of the perceiver (Combs and Snygg, 1959, pp. 154–5). It is not the perceptions that are distorted — they are experienced as clear and unambiguous. It is the stimuli which are distorted.

3. *The individual can act only on the basis of his perceptions, his phenomenal field.* As Combs and Snygg state it, 'All behavior, without exception, is completely determined by, and pertinent to, the perceptual field of the behaving organism' (1959, p. 20). Appearances may be deceiving but we act on them, nevertheless. We can act on nothing else, of course. 'People can behave only in terms of what seems to them to be so' (Combs and Snygg, 1959, p. 5).

   Some confusion has arisen because of a lack of understanding of the nature of the phenomenal field. Two problems in particular may be mentioned.

   a. Combs and Snygg state that the perceptual field is 'each individual's personal and unique field of awareness' (1959, p. 20). This word 'awareness' has been equated with consciousness by some, and the phenomenological approach criticized for neglecting unconscious motivation (Smith, 1950). The concept of unconscious motivation cannot be dealt with here, other than to say that both the concept of the unconscious and of motivation are so fuzzy that when combined it is doubtful that the resulting construct has any real meaning or value. But the point to be made is that awareness is a matter of degree. As Combs and Snygg point out, 'Although the perceptual field includes all the universe of which we are aware, we are not aware of all parts with the same degree of clarity at any moment' (1959, p. 27). Much of the field is ground, rather than figure, in Gestalt terminology. But what is in the ground is not unconscious. The individual may not be able to label or to report all the elements of his perceptual field, but unreportability is not to be equated with the unconscious. (See Phillips, 1956, Chapter 3, for a consideration of this problem.)

   b. A second problem has arisen because of the apparent ahistorical nature of phenomenology. If all behavior is determined by the perceptual field at the moment of action, then are we not leaving out of consideration the important historical determinants of behavior? The answer to this is relatively simple. Snygg and Combs (1959) reply that 'certainly the events of an individual's life affect his behavior. But it is important for us to recognize that it is the perceptions of these events and not the events themselves which are the immediate causes of behavior.' Earlier events are part of the phenomenal field; as Lewin (1943) puts it: 'The behaver's field at any given instant contains all the views of the individual about his past and future . . .The psychological past and the psychological future are simultaneous parts of the psychological field existing at a given time'. It must also be recognized that it is not the event as it occurred objectively, nor even the individual's perception of it as it occurred at the time, but his present perception of it which is a determinant of behavior. This fact perhaps explains the lack of a strong relationship between early significant or presumably traumatic events and later behavior, and suggests a phenomenological approach to the study of the relation of childhood events to later behavior.

4. *The phenomenological field is an inference and thus a hypothetical construct.* It is an inference of the subject as well as of the observer. It is not open to direct observation. Inferences concerning the phenomenological fields of individuals may be developed in several ways.

a. The phenomenal field may be inferred from the observation of behavior. While this is an objective method, it is limited, and inferences can be dangerous. Sufficient observation may not be possible, the observer may project himself into the situation, and his inferences may be interpretations which force behavior to fit a preconceived theory or system of behavior analysis.

b. The individual may be asked to report on his phenomenal field. The ability of the human subject to verbalize his perceptions offers us an approach to his phenomenal field. However, there are limitations. First, the subject may not wish to communicate certain aspects of his experience or perceptions. Second, he may not be able to report accurately, because of the lack of clarity and low awareness level of much of the field. Third, the conscious concentration upon the field changes the field. While attention to the field may crystallize something for the first time, and bring into clearer focus or awareness parts of the field that were at a lower level of awareness, the field then changes and further report is influenced by the changed field. Fourth, some aspects of the field may not be capable of being expressed in words, or may not be represented adequately by verbalizations.

c. The phenomenal field may be studied by means of tests and inventories. The usefulness of this approach is limited, however, by the lack of data upon which to make inferences regarding the perceptual field. Tests and inventories have been studied almost entirely in terms of empirical relationships to external behavior, or, in the case of some projective techniques, external evidence of internal experience or hypothesized dynamic characteristics. A technique such as the Rorschach might be useful in understanding the phenomenal fields of individuals if we knew how to assess the meanings of the stimuli to the individual or convert the responses into information relevant to the subjects' perceptual fields. It is my hypothesis that insofar as the Rorschach is useful it is a result of its use in this way, and the generally negative results of its use are related to the fact that it is not usually employed in this manner.

d. Perhaps the most useful approach to inferring the phenomenal field of another is the use of the free, unstructured interview. The free interview method is less likely to impose the investigator's structure on the subject's field. It also minimizes some of the disadvantage of the self-report, in that the subject's attention or concentration is less consciously directed at analysis of the field. In other words, the report may be more clearly descriptive rather than interpretive. This approach leads us to a basic distinction between the so-called objective and the phenomenological approach to the study of behavior.

5. *Phenomenology, as should be apparent by now, takes the internal frame of reference rather than the external frame of reference in its study of behavior.* As Snygg (1941) points out, this is similar to the common-sense approach, when an observer, in attempting to understand 'Why did he do that?', asks 'Under what circumstances would I have done that?' This approach has been resisted, both because it is seen as subjective, and perhaps too close to common sense. The approach, however, is useful with animals as well as humans. Koehler (1931) pointed out long ago the common error of animal psychologists of structuring the test situation in terms of their own perceptual and conceptual field rather than in terms of the rat's. Tolman once said (1938), in response to a question or charge of anthropomorphism, that he would 'go ahead imagining how, if I were a rat, I would behave' because it gave him insight and understanding of his results. Snygg (see references in Snygg, 1941) has demonstrated the fruitfulness of this approach in developing hypotheses, which were confirmed, regarding the perceptual behavior of rats.

In using the internal frame of reference the investigator attempts to place himself, insofar as possible, in the subject's place in order to view the world and the subject as the subject does. This is the approach to the unstructured interview suggested above for the investigation of another person's phenomenal field. The investigator avoids as much as possible the influence of his own phenomenal field on the subject's report by refraining from structuring, probing or direct questioning, or interpreting or evaluating the productions of the subject.

6. *Since the phenomenal field of the individual determines his behavior, prediction for the individual becomes possible when one knows the behaver's phenomenal field, which is then projected into the future field.* Understanding of the inferred future field makes possible the prediction of future behavior. Such predictions for an individual should be more accurate than predictions based upon group characteristics and memberships. The process is complicated, not only by the difficulty of inferring the present field, but because some aspects of the future field, which will be affected by external conditions, cannot be known. Nevertheless, such an approach to prediction is promising. It is similar to the proposals of the Pepinskys (1954), Koester (1954), Parker (1958), McArthur (1954), and Soskin (1959), that suggest the development of a hypothetical

model of an individual. The application of this method, as in the studies by McArthur and Parker, have not been successful, however. These investigators suggest that the counselors were too hasty and premature in building their models of the clients. Another more important reason for the lack of success might be the failure to build the model on the basis of the phenomenal field of the subject.

7. We finally come to the matter of the self and the self-concept. *The self is part of the individual's phenomenal field.* It includes all the perceptions and conceptions he has about himself, his attitudes and beliefs about himself. Whether there is a real self apart from the perceptual or phenomenal self is a hypothetical philosophical question. The phenomenal self is the real self in terms of the individual's behavior. The perceptions which others have of an individual's self may influence the phenomenal self. But the perceptions of others, even though in agreement, are still phenomenal, and do not necessarily constitute any 'real' self.

The phenomenal self is a most significant part of the phenomenal field since it is the central or pivotal part of the field, about which perceptions are organized: it is the frame of reference for the individual. 'All perceptions . . . derive their meaning from their relation to the phenomenal self' (Combs and Snygg, 1959, p. 131). 'What a person thinks and how he behaves are largely determined by the concepts he holds about himself and his abilities' (Combs and Snygg, 1959, p. 122). Combs and Snygg (1959 pp. 126–7) distinguish between the phenomenal self and the self-concept, the latter being defined as 'those perceptions about self which seem most vital or important to the individual himself'. However, the difficulty of defining and applying criteria to make this differentiation would seem to give it little usefulness. It is no doubt true that some perceptions about the self are more central and vital than others, but it is doubtful that there is any dividing line that can be drawn between these and other less vital self-perceptions. We shall therefore make no distinction between the phenomenal self and the self-concept.

Since the self-concept is the crucial point about which the phenomenal field is organized, its importance in understanding the field and making inferences about it for predictive purposes is apparent. The centrality of the self in phenomenological psychology is indicated in the postulate that the single motive for behavior is the preservation and enhancement of the phenomenal self.

8. *We have indicated that since perceptions, particularly the perceptions of the self, determine behavior, in order to change behavior we must first change perceptions.* What are the conditions under which perceptions change? Essentially, perceptions change under those conditions that have relevance to the basic need for the preservation and enhancement of the self. Conditions that are not relevant to this need are not perceived. It appears, then, that the first condition for perceptual change is an experience which is relevant to the self or self-concept. But if the experience, even though relevant, is consistent with or reinforces the self-concept, it seems clear that change is not likely to occur. To lead to change, the experience must be inconsistent with the existing

self-perception in order to raise a question, or pose a problem. Since the existing self-concept is the object of the need for preservation, it is apparent that it is resistant to change, and that experiences that are inconsistent with the self-concept may not enter into or become the figure in the perceptual field. The so-called mechanisms of defense, the misinterpretation of stimuli or experiences, the failure to perceive which is represented by tunnel vision, and the denial of the experience, are ways in which the self resists perceiving experiences that are inconsistent with the self-concept. It would thus appear that the less important or more peripheral aspects of the self will change more readily than the central core.

This reaction of the organism to preserve its perceptual field, particularly the phenomenal self, is the characteristic reaction to threat. It would seem to be apparent, then, that an individual under threat does not easily change his perceptions, but instead becomes resistant to change. Stimuli or experiences that are perceived as threatening, tend to be relegated to the ground rather than being focused upon as figure. Now this does not mean that threat does not change behavior — it is obvious that threat results in withdrawal, resistance, aggression, or other kinds of obstructing behavior. It may also result in acquiescence, submission, etc. These are all the result of changes in perception of the individual, and the recognition of the threat, leading to attempts to cope with it by capitulation if this is felt to be necessary or desirable for the preservation or enhancement of the self. Thus, behavior, and perceptions, can be influenced and changed by threat, or by other forms of manipulation. The question is raised as to whether this is desirable, from an ethical and moral standpoint, and whether, even though the goal of the manipulator is claimed to be for the good of the person manipulated or influenced, the ends justify the means, or even whether the ends are acceptable under any circumstances, since they are imposed from the outside and thus deny the individual freedom of choice and independence of action. Thus, if voluntary changes of behavior are desired, behavior which is responsible and independent, it would appear that threat should be avoided. Combs and Snygg (1959, pp. 163–96 suggest that '. . . other things being equal, change in the self is most likely to occur in situations which do not force the individual to self-defense'.

It appears, then, that for the phenomenal field to change, there must be a clear experience that is relevant to but inconsistent with the existing field, yet not highly threatening to the self.

In summary

This paper has attempted to present the nature of phenomenological psychology. While this approach to human behavior begins with a common sense level, it goes beyond this to an analysis of the nature and conditions of behavior and its changes. The central nature of perception in behavior leads to the study of perception in all its aspects, including the perception of the self as the point about which the phenomenal field is organized.

There is evidence that psychology is turning to the study of experience, and to the phenomenological method. Koch, the editor of the monumental *Psychology:*

A study of Science, indicates the trend as follows: 'Behavioral epistemology is under stress; neobehaviorism is on the defensive, while neobehaviorism enfolds itself in a womb of its own manufacture. There is a strongly increased interest in perception and central process even on the part of the Stimulus-Response theories; in fact a tendency for the central area of psychological interest to shift from learning to perception. There is a marked, if as yet unfocused, disposition on the part of even fundamental psychologists to readdress human phenomena and to readmit questions having experiential reference' (Koch, 1961). In other words, psychology is becoming psychological, and is returning to a study of experience in its psychological aspects, after a half century of wandering in search of the objectivity of physics on the one hand, and the subjectivity of depth psychology on the other. From the extremes of the empty organism of the behaviorists .and the organism seething with unconscious desires and motives of the depth psychologists, we are striking the happy medium of the experiencing organism interacting with and being shaped by and shaping its environment. This approach promises to lead to a fruitful era in the understanding of human behavior.

References

Bakan, D. (1954) A reconsideration of the problem of introspection. *Psychological Bulletin,* 51, 105–18.

Boring, E. G. (1953) A history of introspection. *Psychological Bulletin*, 50,169–89.

Combs, A. W. (1949) A phenomenological approach to adjustment theory. *Journal of Abnormal and Social Psychology*, 44, 29–35.

Combs, A. W., and Snygg, D. (1959) *Individual behavior.* Rev. ed. New York: Harper.

English, H.B., and English, A. C. (1958) *A comprehensive dictionary of psychological and psychoanalytical terms*. New York: Longmans, Green.

Gibson, J. J. (1951) Theories of perception. In Dennis, W. (Ed.) *Current trends in psychological theory*. Pittsburgh: Univ. Pittsburgh Press.

Gombrich, E.E. (1960) *Art and Illusion.* New York: Pantheon Books.

Hanson, N. R. (1958) *Patterns of discovery: an inquiry into the conceptual foundations of science*. New York: Cambridge Univ. Press.

Ittelson, W. H. (1952) *The Ames demonstrations in perception.* Princeton, N. J.: Princeton Univ. Press.

Jessor, R. (1956) Phenomenological personality theories and the data language of psychology. *Psychological Review*, 63, 173–80.

Jessor, R. (1961) Issues in the phenomenological approach to personality. *Journal of Individual Psychology,* 17, 28–8.

Koch, S. (1961) Psychological science versus the science-humanism antinomy: intimation of a significant science of man. *American Psychologist*, 16, 629–39.

Koehler, W. (1931) *The mentality of apes.* London: Kegan Paul, Trench, Trubner Co.

Koester, G. A. (1954) A study of the diagnostic process. Educational and Psychological Measurement,1954, 475–86.

Kuenzli, A. E. (1959) (Ed.) *The phenomenological problem*. New York: Harper.

Landsman, T. (1958) Four phenomenologies. *Journal of Individual Psychology*, 14, 29–37.

Lewin, K. (1943) Defining the field at a given time. *Psychological* Review, 50, 292–10.

MacLeod, R. B. (1947) The phenomenological approach to social psychology. *Psychological Review* , 54, 193–210.

McArthur, C. (1954) Analyzing the clinical process. *Journal of Counseling Psychology*,1, 203–8.

Murphy, G., Murphy, L. B., and Newcomb, T. M. (1937) *Experimental social psychology*. Rev. ed. New York: Harper.

Parker, C. A. (1958) As a clinician thinks . . . *Journal of Counseling Psychology*, 5, 253–61.

Patterson, C. H. (1959) *Counseling and psychotherapy: Theory and practice*. New York: Harper.

Patterson, C. H. (1961) The self in recent Rogerian theory. *Journal of Individual Psychology* ,17, 5–11.

Pepinsky, H. B., and Pepinsky, P. (1954) *Counseling: theory and practice*. New York: Ronald.

Phillips, E. L. (1956) *Psychotherapy: a modern theory and practice*. Englewood Cliffs, N .J.: Prentice-Hall.

Smith, M. B. (1950) The phenomenological approach in personality theory: Some critical remarks. *Journal of Abnormal and Social Psychology*, 45, 510–22.

Snygg, D. (1941) The need for a phenomenological system of psychology. *Psychological Review*, 48, 404–24.

Snygg, D. (1961) Review of Kilpatrick, F. P. (Ed.) Explorations in transactional psychology. *Journal of Individual Psychology*, 17, 230.

Snygg, D. and Combs, A. W. (1959) The phenomenological approach and the problem of 'unconscious' behavior: a reply to Dr. Smith. *Journal of Abnormal and Social Psychology*, 45, 523–8. In Kuenzli, A. E. (Ed.) *The Phenomenological Problem*. New York: Harper.

Soskin, W. F. (1959) Influence of four types of data on diagnostic conceptualization in psychological testing. *Journal of Abnormal and Social Psychology*, 38, 69–78.

Spiegelberg, H. (1960) *The phenomenological movement: a historical introduction*. 2 vols. The Hague: Martimus Nijhoff.

Tolman, E. C. (1938) Determiners of behavior at a choice point. *Psychological Review*, 57, 243–59.

Wylie, R. C. (1959) *The self-concept: a critical survey of pertinent research literature*. Lincoln: Univ. Nebraska Press, 1961.

THE SELF IN RECENT ROGERIAN THEORY

15

When I agreed to participate in this symposium it was with the thought in mind that this would be an opportunity to clarify my own thinking about the nature of the self and its place in modern psychological theory. In carrying out the inquiry, I have formulated a number of questions about the client-centered framework which I hope others will find useful for purposes of further research and discussion.

Although William James in his *Principles of Psychology* devoted over 100 pages to a discussion of the self (James, 1890), the topic fell into disrepute as a concern of psychology and for over 50 years has been neglected by psychologists. The influence of Watsonian behaviorism upon American psychology may be credited with this neglect of the self, for to behaviorism the self was not capable of objective study and the self-concept was only an example of introspection. Consciousness was merely an epiphenomenon and self-consciousness was of little concern. Even psychoanalysis, although including the ego among its concepts, did not begin to develop a psychology of the ego until relatively recently.

Sociology, I think, anticipated psychology in reacting against behaviorism and recognizing the importance of the self. In the middle thirties, as an undergraduate in sociology at the University of Chicago, I was exposed to the writings of Cooley (1902) and Mead (1934), among others, on the self. This was where I took on the phenomenological approach to human behavior. It was not until several years later that the self and phenomenology were introduced, or reintroduced, into psychology. I say reintroduced because James, in addition to recognizing the importance of the self, was, it seems to me, a phenomenologist as well.

Now, not only psychoanalysis but most other theories of personality are converging upon the concept of the self as the central focus of personality. This development of attention to the self in contemporary psychology is perhaps evidence of the return of psychology to its major concern. Psychology was very early defined as the study of the soul; it might now be defined as the study of the self. To revise a common saying, psychology first lost its soul, then its consciousness, is now in the process of losing its mind, but is beginning to find its self.

The main objective of this paper is to sketch the place of the self in the current

First published in *Journal of Individual Psychology*, 1961, 17, pp. 5–11. Reprinted by permission.

client-centered approach to personality. While the self is, as indicated above, becoming of central importance in all theories of personality, it appears to constitute the core or essence of the Rogerian approach. Perhaps this is because client-centered theory is based upon the observations of individual clients in therapy. The emphasis on the self in client-centered theory has led to its designation by some writers (e.g. Pepinsky and Pepinsky, 1954; Hall and Lindzey, 1957) as 'self-theory'.

Client-centered therapy began as an art, a more or less pragmatic or empirical approach to helping disturbed individuals. To be sure, there were some theoretical elements present, but they were probably incidental. But as experience in therapy developed, both the need for a theoretical formulation and the materials for such a formulation developed. While a number of people have contributed to the theory, the most detailed and comprehensive formulations have been those of Rogers.

The earliest formulation was presented in 1947 as 'Some observations on the organization of personality' (Rogers, 1947). In this presentation, the dependence of behavior upon the perception of the self was illustrated. As the perception of self alters, behavior changes: '. . . the self is a basic factor in the formation of personality and in the determination of behavior'. The perception of the self — which is the self-concept — is an important determinant of behavior. The person's feeling of adequacy is thus basic to psychological adjustment. It was in this paper that Rogers pointed out the importance of the absence of threat for the development of an adequate self-concept and as a condition for changes in the self-concept.

The importance of perceptions, particularly the perception of oneself, is clear in this beginning formulation of a theory of personality. And the theory of perception adopted is a phenomenological one, both as regards perception of so-called 'reality', and of the self. The self-concept is, by definition, a phenomenological concept. It is the self as seen by the experiencing person.

In the chapter on 'A theory of personality and behavior' in *Client-Centered Therapy* (Rogers, 1951), Rogers amplified and extended his discussion of the self in nineteen propositions. The point of view underlying the propositions is perceptual and phenomenological; there is no reality for the individual other than that given by his perceptions. The self is the central concept of personality and behavior. While the general proposition is stated that the basic drive of the organism is the maintenance and enhancement of the organism, the psychological self may take precedence over the physiological organism. The self is part of the perceptual field of the individual, but may contain conflicting perceptions arising on the one hand from organismic experiences and on the other from introjected values and attitudes.

Once the self has developed, it becomes the center about which all experience is organized. Experiences are perceived and evaluated in terms of their relevance and significance to the self. Behavior is normally consistent with the self-concept, even at the expense of the organism. However, organic experiences or needs which are unsymbolized (because they are unacceptable) may at times lead to behavior inconsistent with the self-concept ('I was not myself'), or to psychological tension and maladjustment. Experiences which are inconsistent with the self-concept may be perceived as threatening, and may be rejected, denied, or distorted; the self-concept is defended.

Psychological adjustment or integration, on the other hand, exists when the concept of the self is congruent with all the experiences of the organism. Under conditions of absence of threat to the self, all experiences — including the organismic — may be examined and assimilated into the self-concept, leading to changes in the self-concept. This occurs in therapy.

This 1951 statement by Rogers is essentially a lengthier account of the 1947 paper. It does not analyze the nature of the self in detail nor delineate aspects of the self, even to the extent to which Snygg and Combs (1949) differentiated the self-concept from the phenomenal self. There is no mention of the concept of the ideal self in the 1951 formulation.

The most recent and most detailed of Rogers' theoretical discussions appeared in mimeographed form in 1955 and is included in Volume 3 of *'Psychology: A Study of a Science'* (Rogers, 1959). This is essentially a more systematic and extended formulation of earlier expressions of the theory. It is difficult to summarize adequately this lengthy statement. The self again occupies the central focus, although the theory encompasses the total organism. For example, the single motive for behavior which is postulated is the actualizing tendency, i.e., the 'inherent tendency of the organism to develop all its capacities in ways which serve to maintain or enhance the organism' (Rogers, 1959, p. 196). Self-actualization is an important aspect of the general actualizing tendency.

The self-concept is defined as 'the organized, consistent conceptual gestalt composed of characteristics of the "I" or "me" and the perceptions of the relationships of the "I" or "me" to others and to various aspects of life, together with the value attached to these perceptions' (Rogers, 1959, p. 200). The ideal self is introduced into the theory and is defined as 'the self-concept which the individual would most like to possess, upon which he places the highest value for himself' (Rogers, 1959, p. 200).

As in the earlier formulation, discrepancies between the self as perceived and actual experiences may develop. When this incongruence approaches awareness, anxiety results. Anxiety is the result of the threat involved in the perception of this incongruence. As seen by others, the individual is psychologically maladjusted. The threat to the self is reacted to with defensive behavior, including denial or distortion of the threatening experience.

In addition to the ideal self, the current statement includes several concepts having to do with regard. It is postulated that there is a basic, though secondary or learned, need for positive regard — that is for warmth, liking, respect, sympathy, and acceptance from others. There is also a similar need for positive self-regard, which is related to or dependent upon the positive regard for others.

Unconditional self-regard is a state of general positive self-regard, without regard to conditions. Positive self-regard may be conditional, however, when the individual 'values an experience positively or negatively solely because of . . . conditions of worth which he has taken over from others, not because the experience enhances or fails to enhance his organism' (Rogers, 1959, p. 209). This constitutes a situation in which the individual is vulnerable to threat and anxiety.

We may state the central ideas in the theory of self as follows:

1. The theory of the self as part of the general personality theory is phenomenological. The essence of phenomenology is that 'man lives essentially in his own personal and subjective world' (Rogers, 1959, p. 191).
2. The self becomes differentiated as part of the actualizing tendency, from the environment, through transactions with the environment — particularly the social environment. The process by which this occurs is not detailed by Rogers, but presumably is along the lines described by Cooley (1902) and Mead (1934).
3. The self-concept is the organization of the perceptions of the self. It is the self-concept, rather than any 'real' self, which is of significance in personality and behavior. As Combs and Snygg note, the existence of a 'real' self is a philosophical question, since it cannot be observed directly (1959, p. 123).
4. The self-concept becomes the most significant determinant of response to the environment. It governs the perceptions or meanings attributed to the environment.
5. Whether learned or inherent, a need for positive regard develops or emerges with the self-concept. While Rogers leans toward attributing the need to learning, I would include it as an element of the self-actualizing tendency.
6. Positive self-regard, or self-esteem, likewise is a need which, according to Rogers, is learned through internalization or introjection of experiences of positive regard by others, or, alternatively, may be an aspect of the self-actualizing tendency.
7. When positive self-regard depends on evaluations of behaviors by others, discrepancies may develop between the needs of the organism and the needs of the self-concept for positive self-regard. There is thus incongruence between the self and experience, or psychological maladjustment. Maladjustment is thus the result of attempting to preserve the existing self-concept from the threat of experiences which are inconsistent with it, leading to selective perception and distortion or denial of experience.

This is a highly condensed summary and does not include the vicissitudes of the self through the processes of disorganization or the processes of reorganization which take place in therapy. The summary is based entirely upon Rogers' formulations, since his is the most complete. A number of persons have contributed to the development of the theory, including Raimy (1948), Snygg and Combs (1949), and many others who have been associated with Rogers. There has been no other comparable exposition of the theory nor are there any adequately stated alternatives or variations of the theory. The terminology differs in some respects from that used by other client-centered writers, but the basic concepts are similar if not identical. For example, some theorists, including myself (1959), have used the term self-esteem to refer to what Rogers designates as positive self-regard.

The theory appears to be complete and self-sufficient, at least in its detailed statement. The recent additions, such as the concept of the ideal self, have rounded it out. But is it actually self-contained? What about some of the views of the self that have been proposed by other writers?

Several theorists have emphasized two aspects of the self, using different terms, but essentially distinguishing between the *self as object*, the 'me', and the *self as subject*, the 'I'. The first is often referred to as the self-concept, the second as the ego although, as Hall and Lindzey (1957, p. 468) point out, there is no general agreement upon terms. James called the 'me' the empirical self and the 'I' the pure ego — the sense of personal identity or the judging thought. This personal identity, he suggests, may not exist as a fact, 'but it would exist as a *feeling* all the same; the consciousness of it would be there, and the psychologist would still have to analyze that . . .' (James, 1890, p. 333). The ego would appear to be self-consciousness. Mead's conceptions of the 'I' and the 'me' appear to be similar, although his discussion is difficult to follow. The 'I' appears to be the awareness of the self as of the moment of action (1934, pp. 173–8, 192).

These concepts, while preferable to the idea of the 'I' as an executive, which lends itself to reification, are vague and difficult to pin down. At least, I am not able to do so — to differentiate actually, practically, or operationally between the executive aspects of the self and the self as an object to the self. Rogers avoids the problem by omitting any concept of the 'I'. The self of Snygg and Combs is both an object and doer. Others, including Allport (1943) and Sherif and Cantril (1947), appear to adopt this point of view. Hilgard (1949) suggests that the concept of the self as a doer is an error into which psychologists have been led by the common-sense or lay view that behavior seems to be self-determined.

Although in Rogers' theory the self-concept is an important determiner of behavior, it is not an executive or doer. There is no need for positing such an executive. The organism is by nature continually active, seeking its goal of actualization, and the self as part of the organism is also seeking self-actualization through its constant activity. The self-concept thus influences the direction of activity, rather than initiating it and directing it entirely. Thus it appears that the theory avoids the problem of reification and the ambiguousness of the concept of the 'I' or the ego as an executive. James' sense of personal identity might be considered a part of the self-concept, and the ego or 'I' as the awareness of the self-concept. However, I am not sure that this solution is entirely satisfactory.

Again, the recent formulation of Rogers includes the concept of the ideal self. However, after defining the concept, there is little further specific reference to it in the theory. It is indicated in the statement of the outcomes of therapy in personality and behavior that the perception of the ideal self is more realistic, and that the self is more congruent with the ideal self. This suggests that personality disturbance and disorganization would be characterized by an unrealistic self-ideal, and/or incongruence between the self or self-concept and the self-ideal. Although this formulation has been the basis of some research by the client-centered school (e.g. Butler and Haigh, 1954), it is not incorporated in the statement of the theory. The theory apparently does not recognize conflict between the self-concept and the self-ideal as a source of disturbance, but emphasizes the conflict between the self-concept and organismic experiences as its source. In some other theories the self-ideal is a central concept and an important factor in psychological adjustment or maladjustment (e.g. Horney, 1950).

The notion of the self, or the self-structure, is broader than the self-concept. It includes the self-concept and the ideal self. What else it includes is not clear. Combs and Snygg speak of the phenomenal self, defined as the 'organization of all the ways an individual has of seeing himself' (1959, p. 126). The self-concept includes 'only those perceptions about self which seem most vital or important to the individual himself' (1959, p. 127). How these are to be differentiated is not indicated. Rogers appears to include in the self-concept the person's view of himself, which is thus presumably in awareness, whereas the self may include aspects not in awareness.

In concluding, I would like to comment upon a point regarding research which has been made by Rogers. This is the fact that an effort has been made to keep the constructs and concepts such that they can be operationally defined. The phenomenological approach, it seems to me, fosters this effort. One is not concerned about the 'real' self, the 'real' environment, etc., but with the perceptions of particular individuals. The self-concept is thus the perceptions of an individual of himself, and so with the self-ideal. These perceptions can be studied and objectified by instruments such as the Q-sort or tests of the 'Who Am I?' variety. The latter type of test, though it would appear to be an ideal one for use with client-centered theory, has not, however, to my knowledge, been used in connection with the theory.

A problem develops, as Rogers points out, in operationally defining the organismic experiences which, it is assumed, conflict with the self-concept. The aspects of the self, other than the self-concept and the self-ideal, are also not operationally defined. It might be suggested that we do not need these concepts which have not been operationally defined. I see no need for unconscious elements of the self, for example. Aspects of the self which are not in awareness but which can be brought into awareness, can be tapped by instructions such as 'Sort these statements in terms of your concept of yourself as a father'. The self, insofar as it is behaviorally effective, may consist only of the various self-perceptions — thus resolving the problem posed above about the area of the self apart from the self-concept and the self-ideal.

The organismic experiences, on the other hand, are an essential aspect of the theory, and must be brought within the realm of measurement. The approach of Chodorkoff (1954), using Q-sorts of self-referent items by clinicians as an 'objective description' of the total experience of the individual, though operational, may be questioned as to its validity.

Finally, there is an additional problem, pointed out by Combs and Soper (1957). This is that although the self-concept may be operationally defined as the individual's statements about himself, this is not necessarily his perception of himself. For as these writers point out, his statements constitute a self-description or self-report, which may be inaccurate for a number of reasons — including inability or unwillingness of the individual to give an accurate report. Yet there is no other approach to determining the self-concept, since by definition it is the perception of the self by the individual, and no one else can report upon it or describe it.

These are then, as I see it, the major points and problems that characterize Rogerian theory today .

References

Allport, G. W. (1943) The ego in contemporary psychology. *Psychological Review*, 50, 451–78.

Butler, J. M., and Haigh, G.V. (1954) Changes in the relation between self-concepts and ideal concepts consequent upon client-centered counseling. In C. R. Rogers and R. F. Dymond (Eds.), *Psychotherapy and personality change*. Chicago: Univer. Chicago Press. Pp. 55–6.

Chodorkoff, B. (1954) Self-perception, perceptual defense, and adjustment. *Journal of Abnormal and Social Psychology*, 49, 508–12.

Combs, A. W. and Soper, D.W. (1957) The self, its derivative terms, and research. *Journal of Individual Psychology*, 1957, 13,134–45. In A.E. Kuenzli (Ed.) (1959) *The phenomenological problem*. New York: Harper . Pp. 31–48.

Combs, A. W. and Snygg, D. (1959) *Individual behavior*. Rev.Ed. New York: Harper.

Cooley, C .H. (1902) *Human nature and the social order*. New York: Scribner's.

Hall, C. S., and Lindzey, G. (1957) *Theories of personality*. New York: Wiley.

Hilgard, E. R. (1949) Human motives and the concept of the self. *American Psychologist*, 4, 374–82.

Horney, K. (1950) *Neurosis and human growth*. New York: Norton.

James,W. (1890) *The principles of psychology*. Vol. I. New York: Holt.

Mead, G. H. (1934) *Mind, self and society*. Chicago: Univer. Chicago Press.

Patterson, C.H. (1959) *Counseling and psychotherapy: theory and practice*. New York: Harper.

Pepinsky, H. B., and Pepinsky, P. N. (1954) *Counseling: theory and practice*. New York: Ronald.

Raimy, V. C. (1948) Self-reference in counseling interviews. *Journal of Consulting Psychology*, 12, 153–63. In A. E. Kuenzli (Ed.) (1959) *The phenomenological problem*. New York: Harper. Pp. 76–95.

Rogers, C. R. (1947) Some observations on the organization of personality. *American Psychologist*, 2, 358–68. In A.E. Kuenzli (Ed.) (1959) *The phenomenological problem*. New York: Harper. Pp. 49–75.

Rogers, C. R. (1951) *Client-centered therapy*. Boston: Houghton Mifflin.

Rogers, C. R. (1959) A theory of therapy, personality, and interpersonal relationships, as developed in the client-centered framework. In S. Koch (Ed.), *Psychology: a study of a science*. Vol. 3. New York: McGraw-Hill. Pp. 184–256.

Sherif, M., and Cantril, H. (1947) *The psychology of ego involvements*. New York: Wiley.

Snygg, D., and Combs, A.W. (1949) *Individual behavior*. New York: Harper.

Empathy, Warmth and Genuineness in Psychotherapy: A Review of Reviews

16

Several reviews of therapist variables in relation to therapy outcome appear to be biased and to underestimate the effects of empathy, warmth (or respect) and genuineness. These reviews are analyzed and evaluated, and reviewer biases are noted. In spite of the generally negative, or, at best, equivocal conclusions of these reviews, the evidence is actually supportive for the necessity, if not the sufficiency, of these therapist conditions. Considering the statistical factors militating against the obtaining of significant positive results, it is concluded that the evidence for the effectiveness of the therapist variables is far greater than is recognized by many reviewers.

Research on empathy, warmth and genuineness, known as the core conditions of the counseling and psychotherapy relationship, is voluminous. It constitutes a body of research which is among the largest for any topic of similar size in the field of psychology. In the 1967 review of Truax and Carkhuff (1967), 439 references were listed. In the 1971 review of Truax and Mitchell (1971) there were 92 references. Most recent reviews contain many additional references.

It is manifestly impossible in the limits of this article to review all these studies. Moreover, it is not necessary to do so, since there are several recent reviews. The second edition of the *Handbook of Psychotherapy and Behavior Change* (Garfield and Bergin, 1978) includes four chapters which review research related to this topic.

This article presents a critical analysis and evaluation of several recent reviews. The conclusions of the reviewers in many cases do not appear to follow from their own summaries of the research studies. Since these conclusions are likely to be accepted as valid by most students, and others who do not have the time or opportunity to read the original studies, it is important that their deficiencies be revealed.

Reviewer bias

It probably goes without saying that all reviewers are biased. Reviewers do not identify their biases, however, even when they are aware of them. Many of the recent reviewers are biased against recognition or acceptance of the effectiveness

First published in *Psychotherapy*, 1984, 21, pp. 431–8. Reprinted by permission of the publisher.

of the core conditions in counseling or psychotherapy, perhaps, in part at least, for some of the reasons noted earlier (Patterson, 1980). The evidence for these biases becomes clear when one examines their analyses of, and conclusions from their analyses of, the individual research studies. Consider the following points:

1. Reviewers are biased in the selection of the studies which they review. Criteria for selection often seem to vary depending on the conclusions of the studies. Strict criteria are applied to reject inclusion of those studies whose conclusions disagree with the bias of the reviewer, while lesser criteria are applied to select those studies which support the reviewer's bias. Thus, the conclusions of the review are biased, even though they seem justified by the studies selected for review.

2. Similarly, of those studies admitted to the review, whether bias has entered into the selection or not, standards applied in the critiques of methodology and procedures and analysis of the data vary according to the reviewer's bias. Strict standards are applied to those studies inconsistent with the reviewer's bias, leading to rejection or minimizing of the results, while less strict standards are applied to other studies, leading to acceptance of the results.

3. Sometimes results of a single study, or two or three studies which are in accordance with a reviewer's bias, are emphasized or given great weight in conclusions. If two or three studies agree with the reviewer's bias, strong statements are made. Yet if, as noted later, 14 out of 21 studies yield results against the reviewer's bias, little emphasis is placed on 'only' two-thirds agreement.

4. When results are positive on some outcome measures, and negative on others, a reviewer may fail to mention or may de-emphasize the positive results, or may reject the measures yielding the positive results unacceptable to the reviewer. Yet, if in another study such measures yield results acceptable to the reviewer, these measures will be accepted.

These kinds of biases become evident in many of the reviews to be considered here. In addition, other evidences of bias were apparent. The language and phrasing frequently indicates bias, as will be seen in some of the statements of reviewers as we evaluate their reviews. Bias leads to misunderstanding, misinterpretation, or even misrepresentation of the findings of the original studies. It also leads to inconsistencies or discrepancies among statements — the stated results of studies reviewed are not consistent with the reviewer's conclusions. The existence of bias is also indicated by the differing evaluations and conclusions by different reviewers of the same studies.

Major reviews

Mitchell et al.'s (1977) review is particularly interesting since the earlier review by Truax and Mitchell (1971) was highly positive. Its conclusion reads as follows:

> Therapists and counselors who are accurately empathic, non-possessively warm in attitude and genuine are indeed effective. Also, these findings seem to hold with a wide variety of therapists and

counselors, regardless of their training or theoretic orientation, and with a wide variety of clients or patients, including college underachievers, juvenile delinquents, hospitalized schizophrenics, college counselees, mild to severe outpatient neurotics, and a mixed variety of hospitalized patients. Further, the evidence suggests that these findings hold in a variety of therapeutic contexts and in both individual and group psychotherapy or counseling (p. 310).

Mitchell et al. question, but do not refute, these conclusions, in their negatively toned review. Their evaluation rests heavily upon the Arkansas study by Mitchell et al. (1973). They performed various statistical analyses and state that:

in no instance was either empathy or warmth found to be related to client change. Genuineness was found to be related to client change in a sufficient number of analyses to allow us to say that minimal levels of genuineness were related modestly to outcome (p. 485).

There are, however, several flaws in this study. The 75 therapists included represented only five percent of those invited to participate in the study. Moreover, in this highly (self-) selected sample of therapists, 'the interpersonal interaction levels of the therapists with their clients were relatively superficial. Almost all the therapists in this sample were below minimal levels and, as a group, were not facilitative' (p. 485). The low levels and restricted ranges of the facilitative conditions would operate against obtaining any significant relationships with outcome variables. The authors recognize this problem when they note that 'a reasonable proportion of therapists in any particular study must provide at least minimally facilitative levels before the study can be seen as even testing the central hypothesis' that 'high level of skills lead to client improvement' (p. 486).

Fifteen studies conducted between 1970 and 1975 are reviewed, even though the authors estimate that none of them actually tested the central hypothesis. They summarize their evaluation as follows:

Perhaps seven (47 percent) offer at least minimal support for the hypothesis of *higher* levels of empathy (whether truly facilitative or not) and positive client outcome. Similarly, perhaps four (27 percent) offer such support for *higher* levels of warmth, and perhaps three studies (20 percent) offer such support for higher levels of genuineness (p. 488).

It would seem to be difficult to argue that such high levels of the conditions are not facilitative in the face of positive relationships with outcome. However, the authors state that:

our conclusion must be that the relationship between the interpersonal skills and client outcome has not been investigated adequately and, consequently, nothing definitive can be said about the relative efficacy of high and low levels of empathy, warmth, and genuineness (p. 488) (italics in original).

On the basis of these fifteen studies, and the Arkansas study, the authors offer the following equivocal conclusion:

> It seems to us to be increasingly clear that *the mass of data neither supports nor rejects the overriding influence of such variables as empathy, warmth, and genuineness in all cases* . . . *The recent evidence, although equivocal, does seem to suggest that empathy. warmth, and genuineness are related in some way to client change, but that their potency and generalizability are not as great as some thought* (p. 483) (italics in original).

Parloff et al. (1978) are perhaps the most negative in their evaluation of the research on therapist variables. While noting that 'all schools of psychotherapy appear to be in accord that a positive relationship between patient and therapist is a necessary precondition for any form of psychotherapy' (p. 243), they add that 'relevant clinical observations have . . . cast doubt on the universal applicability of the principle that the greater the degree of genuineness, empathy, and warmth, the greater the benefit to all patients' (p. 244). The validity of clinical observations is not questioned; moreover, no one claims that all patients benefit.

Parloff et al. criticize and reject the favorable conclusion of the Truax and Mitchell (1971) review, and quote approvingly from the more negative review of Mitchell et al. (1977). They recognize that there are positive findings, but emphasize the negative, failing to note that there are more positive than negative studies, or to note that the negative studies are not without serious problems or flaws. They make the important point that Rogers' (1957) statement included as a necessary condition the client's perception of the therapist's empathy, warmth, and genuineness, and note that most studies do not involve measures of client perceptions of the conditions, but rather use observer's ratings of the conditions. They fail, however, to recognize that this would lead to attenuation of the relationship between the conditions and outcomes, or to negative results in some cases where client ratings might produce positive results. Thus it is significant that positive results are obtained where the conditions are measured from an observer's rather than from the client's viewpoint.

These reviewers end by stating that 'it must be concluded that the unqualified claim that "high" levels (absolute or relative) of accurate empathy, warmth, and genuineness (independent of the source of rating or the nature of the instrument) represent "the necessary and sufficient" conditions for effective therapy (independent of the outcome measures or conditions) is not supported' (p. 249). This is an equivocating and essentially meaningless statement. No one makes such an unqualified claim. No one claims that the case has been absolutely proven. Parloff et al. do not, on the other hand, disprove it.

Orlinsky and Howard (1978) review much of the same research as do Mitchell et al. and Parloff et al., but with somewhat different conclusions. They state that 'approximately two-thirds of the 23 studies of warmth and a similar percentage of the 35 studies of empathy show a significant positive relationship between the externally rated aspects of therapist interpersonal behavior and therapeutic outcome' (p. 293). Of 20 studies of therapist congruence or genuineness, a similar proportion, two-thirds or 14, show a significantly positive relationship with outcome. They state that 'the studies done thus far suggest that the positive quality of the relational bond, as exemplified in the reciprocal interpersonal relationship behaviors of the participants, is more clearly related to patient improvement than are any of the particular treatment techniques used by therapists' (p. 296). This is a strong statement, in view of the emphasis on techniques by most therapists and current therapies. They go on to say that 'cumulatively these studies [of congruence] seem to warrant the conclusion that therapist genuineness is at least innocuous, is generally predictive of good outcome, and at most may be a causal element in promoting client improvement. Beyond a reasonable minimum, however, it is probably neither a necessary nor a sufficient condition of therapeutic benefit' (p. 307). This is a rather innocuous, if not negative, statement and one that cannot be drawn directly from the research they review. It seems to be inconsistent with the statements quoted above.

Orlinsky and Howard (1978) also review studies using measures of client perception of the therapist conditions. Fifteen studies of client perception of empathy vary some in results, but 'generally these studies support the notion that the sense of being understood by one's therapist is a fairly consistent feature of beneficial therapy as experienced by patients' (p. 299). Again, regarding respect (or warmth): 'The evidence of 13 studies . . . is unanimous in indicating that the patient's perception of the therapist's manner as affirming the patient's value is positively and significantly associated with good therapeutic outcome . . . It would seem foolish to discount the patient's sense of affirmation by the therapist as one probable ingredient of productive therapeutic experience' (p. 298). This is rather a weak conclusion for unanimous evidence.

Orlinsky and Howard (1978) reviewed other studies of client perceptions of their therapists and of themselves which support the importance of the relationship established in client-centered or relationship psychotherapy. These studies indicate that patients who saw their therapists as 'independence encouraging' had better outcomes than those who viewed their therapists as 'authoritarian'. Patients' perception of their therapists as being personally involved was also related to positive outcome. Other variables related to positive outcome were the patients' view of the relationship as warm, close, and intimate, rather than cold, domineering, or confrontative.

Gurman's (1977) earlier review of research on client perception of the therapeutic relationship agrees with Orlinsky and Howard (1978), stating the strong conclusion that 'there exists substantial, if not overwhelming, evidence in support of the hypothesized relationship between patient-perceived therapeutic conditions and outcome in individual psychotherapy and counseling' (p. 523).

Lambert et al.'s (1978) review is not actually a comprehensive review of the research on interpersonal skills. Eighteen studies done up to 1977 were selected as 'the best this area has to offer'. The authors conclude: 'Despite more than 20 years of research and some improvements in methodology, only a modest relationship between the so-called facilitative conditions and therapeutic outcomes has been found.

Contrary to frequent claims for the potency of these therapist-offered relationship variables, experimental evidence suggests that neither a clear test nor unequivocal support for the Rogerian hypothesis has appeared' (p. 486). Of course, if there has not been a clear test, one could not expect to find unequivocal support.

Most of the review is concerned with methodological issues. These include consideration of the following issues or questions: (1) Who should rate the conditions — clients, therapists, or outside raters? Relationships among these ratings are low. (2) The limits of audiotapes as the basis of ratings. Nonverbal behaviors are thus not observable. (3) Should the raters be experienced therapists or naive observers? (4) Should raters be trained or not? (5) Does the sex of the raters influence the ratings? (6) There are problems of sampling, both of interviews during the course of therapy, and within interviews. (7) Are the facilitative conditions independent, constituting three dimensions, or are they aspects of a single dimension, such as the 'good guy' therapist?

These are all sources of 'confounding variables that must be taken into account when carrying out research in this area', and the low relationships found are probably a function of these variables. 'Improvements in methodology may yet lead to a significant revision of the client-centered hypothesis and an increase in its ability to specify conditions leading to therapeutic change.'

These authors also mention some of the problems to be discussed below, including inadequate sampling of therapy excerpts, the low levels of ratings of the conditions, and their restricted range. Referring to the negative results of two major studies, they note that 'it would be a shame to see researchers discontinue the examination of the facilitative conditions because of these negative results'.

The *Annual Review of Psychology* includes reviews of psychotherapy at three-year intervals. These reviews cover much more than the research in which we are interested here, and only the material relevant to our interests will be discussed.

The review by Bergin and Suinn (1975) covers the years 1971 through 1973. Bergin, the author of the individual psychotherapy section of the review, puts much emphasis on three studies: The Temple University study (Sloane et al., 1975), the DiLoreto study (1971), and the Mitchell et al. (1973) Arkansas study. The first two studies were comparative studies, and they found little or no difference in the effects of a wide variety of techniques. Bergin fails to recognize that this is evidence for the importance of a common element (the relationship). He also is uncritical in his acceptance of the results of the second two studies as not supporting the effectiveness of the core conditions. Lambert et al. (1978) pointed out several deficiencies in the Temple University study, some similar to those in the Arkansas study: the restricted range of the ratings of the therapist conditions (though the levels were relatively high); ratings based on one sample from one interview; the ratings of the behaviorists were on samples selected when they 'were acting like therapists'. In addition, there were only three psychoanalytic and three behavioristic therapists involved in this study. Bergin concludes that 'it is clearer now that these variables are not as prepotent as once believed; but their presence and influence is ubiquitous, even showing up strongly in behavior therapies'.

Bergin makes the interesting statement that 'in recent years, a number of studies have induced skepticism concerning the potency of these variables except in highly specific, client-centered type conditions.' It is not clear just what Bergin means or could mean by this statement. But there is an interesting implication. Since the conditions constitute or are the essence of client-centered therapy, then only client-centered therapy is an effective therapy. Though these conditions may be present in other therapies, they can be nullified or counteracted by other conditions or therapist variables. Support for this conclusion is provided by the fact that there is no good evidence for the effectiveness of any other variables or techniques — or for the effectiveness of other approaches in the absence of these conditions.

The review by Gomes-Schwartz et al. (1978), three years later, devotes one paragraph to the research on warmth, empathy and genuineness, citing eight studies. Only one of these studies, Sloane et al. (1975), related the conditions to outcome; this study was considered in the earlier review by Bergin. The other studies were of interrelationships among the conditions and problems in their measurement by ratings. Nevertheless, the author (Gomes-Schwartz, who authored this part of the review) perpetuates the negative evaluation: 'Earlier assertions of strong empirical support for the relationship between therapist's facilitative "conditions" and therapy outcome [by Truax and Mitchell] have been challenged by recent findings' [citing Bergin's review]. Yet she also equivocates: 'This does not imply that the quality of the therapeutic relationship is not of major importance in determining the effectiveness of psychotherapy'.

It is very interesting that in a later section on the therapeutic relationship it is stated that 'in a relationship marked by warmth, closeness, and a sense that the therapist was involved and cared about the patient, patients were more likely to remain in therapy than terminate [4 studies cited], to be satisfied with the ongoing therapy process [2 studies], and to show greater improvement [3 studies]. The therapeutic relationship characterized by relaxed rapport and open communication was likely to promote continuation in therapy [2 studies] and better outcome [2 studies].' It is curious that these studies are separated from the section on warmth, empathy, and genuineness — they certainly are relevant supporting studies, making the negative conclusion questionable at least.

Hadley, in his section on behavioral interventions, noting that 'in the past, relationship variables have often been subsumed under "nonspecific effects,"' continues:

> Recently there has been increased attention to the importance of a good patient-therapist relationship, in effecting positive change. The thrust of most of these discussions is that the relationship, while not sufficient for change, is vital for *substantial improvement*. Furthermore, there is a growing consensus that an empirical, learning-based approach to clinical practice is not antithetical to recognition of the importance of 'relationship' factors (italics added).

Here, as in most of the previous reviews, one notes the inconsistencies and contradictions among the various statements and conclusions regarding relationship variables.

The 1979 volume of the *Annual Review* includes a chapter on Counseling Psychology (Krumboltz et al., 1979). A brief section on genuineness, warmth, and empathy notes an 'apparent substantiation of Rogers' triad of therapist genuineness, warmth, and empathy', but the reference is to the 1971 review of Truax and Mitchell. Further references are to studies of the reliability of ratings of the variables. In 1981 the chapter reviewing psychotherapy (Phillips and Bierman, 1981) makes no mention of studies on empathy, warmth, or genuineness. It is inconceivable that there were no such studies during the period covered (1976–1980). The review simply does not cover research on the therapy process or relationship. The review of counseling psychology in this issue of the Annual Review of Psychology (Holland et al., 1981) concerns itself only with career interventions, research, and theory.

Evaluation

If one reads these reviews of research — often by biased reviewers — one cannot help being impressed with the direction of the evidence. Yet the conclusions of the reviews do not adequately or accurately reflect the reviews' own reports of the studies reviewed. The reviewers are more than cautious in their conclusions — they are often inconsistent, ambivalent, and unable to accept the results of their own reviews. Allen Bergin and Hans Strupp, who have produced earlier biased reviews, show the same inconsistency and ambivalence in their overview chapters in Garfield and Bergin. Bergin and Lambert (1978) write, presumably after reading the other chapters considered above: 'Our hope that the study of specific treatments with specific problems would result in practically useful information has not been realized, with but few exceptions' (p. 180). This is true as regards the case of behavior therapy, to which they are referring in this statement. But they do not go on to note that this is not true regarding the conditions of client-centered or relationship therapy. They continue:

> Interpersonal and nonspecific or nontechnical factors still loom large as stimulators of patient improvement. It should come as no surprise that helping people . . . can be greatly facilitated in an interpersonal relationship that is characterized by trust, warmth, acceptance, and human wisdom. It appears that these personal factors are crucial ingredients even in the more technical [behavioral] therapies. This is not to say that techniques are irrelevant but that their power for change pales when compared to personal influence. Technique is crucial to the extent that it provides a believable rationale and congenial modus operandi for the change agent and the client (p. 180).

Bergin and Strupp have been writing for years about the 'crucial' importance of techniques in addition to the relationship. But neither they nor anyone else have clearly identified or specified these techniques or produced any evidence for the effectiveness of techniques. It is interesting that Gomes-Schwartz (1978), a colleague of Strupp, states that 'it remains to be demonstrated that what the therapist does has an impact over and above the effects of a supportive relationship'. If techniques 'provide a believable rationale and congenial modus operandi' they are not specific — in fact they are part of the placebo.

Bergin and Lambert state that 'although it was once felt that this hypothesis [that a positive relationship exists between therapist interpersonal skills and therapy outcomes] had been confirmed [an apparent reference to the 1971 review of Truax and Mitchell], it now appears that the relationship between these variables and outcome is more ambiguous than was once believed' (p. 167). Complex, perhaps, but hardly ambiguous. This statement is a misleading evaluation of the reviews which follow. They continue: 'We assume that as interpersonal dimensions of therapy interactions are more carefully examined, . . . it will become possible to define more clearly what kinds of persons help which kinds of clients most effectively' (p. 180). This is inconsistent with the research evidence to date, which indicates that the relationship variables are positively related to outcome with a wide variety of clients with a wide variety of problems.

Strupp (1978), in his opening chapter to Bergin and Garfield's *Handbook*, takes a similar position — again after presumably having read the other chapters. He says: 'Although the hypothesis of nonspecific factors [i.e., relationship variables or common elements] may be correct, it is still possible that some technical operations may be superior to others with particular patients, particular problems, and under particular circumstances' (p. 12). This is pure speculation — he does not even suggest what these particular techniques, patients, problems, and circumstances might be. It is interesting that in the face of the evidence for the effectiveness of the relationship variables over many kinds of clients with many kinds of problems, Bergin and Strupp, along with all other writers, persist in labeling them as nonspecific variables. This approach classifies them with placebo factors, to be eliminated or controlled for in research on psychotherapy as placebo variables are in medical research. But to do this would be to dismiss or eliminate the very active ingredients we are looking for.

Bergin and Strupp have been particularly persistent in relegating the relationship variables to the nonspecific or noncausal class of factors — noncausal in contrast to specific causal techniques, which, as has been noted, they never clearly specify — while at the same time they acknowledge the necessity and importance of the relationship in all therapies. In an otherwise excellent article, 'The Therapist's Theoretical Orientation: An Overrated Variable', Strupp (1978) ends by saying: 'The best therapists, in my view, are those whose empathic capacity and technical skills have become thoroughly blended in such a way that they interact flexibly with the unique constellation presented by each patient's personality'. Nowhere in the article are the technical skills identified. In another article by Strupp (1980), 'Humanism and Psychotherapy: A Personal Statement of the Therapist's Essential Values', there is only one use of the word technique. In discussing Freud as representing an extreme position, now considered superseded, he says that Freud:

> likened psychotherapy to a set of technical operations, analogous to
> surgery, in which the therapist, as a person, plays a negligible role.
> [The other extreme is] the view of psychotherapy as a unique human
> encounter, exemplified by client-centered, humanistic, existential

> writers, in which the therapist's personality is of the utmost
> importance.

He continues:

> In my view, the therapist's personality, including his or her values,
> is inextricably intertwined with the technical operations brought to
> bear on the dyadic interaction. Accordingly, it is meaningless to speak
> of techniques in the abstract, just as it is meaningless to speak of the
> therapist's personality in the abstract.

Yet this is exactly what he does — no further mention is made of any concrete techniques. In the case of personality he does essentially the same thing, with no reference to specific characteristics of the therapist other than his or her value commitments.

Strupp opens this paper by saying that 'most therapists and students of psychotherapy now seem to agree that the therapist's personality plays an important role in the formation of the patient-therapist relationship which in turn has a critical bearing on therapeutic outcomes'. It is curious, however, that those who accept this view, including Strupp, seldom go on to identify the characteristics of the therapeutic personality. Are they blind to the fact that the relationship variables provide a definition of the therapeutic personality?

There are a number of factors which militate against the obtaining of significant positive relationships between the therapist variables and the therapeutic outcomes. These include problems in the design and analysis of research studies. Some of these factors are recognized by reviewers (e.g., Lambert et al. 1978) in their critiques of the research. However, reviewers use these problems to reject or minimize the results of studies with positive outcomes, failing to recognize that the obtaining of positive results against such handicaps is an indication of the strength of the relationships. The following factors are in addition to the methodological problems enumerated by Lambert et al. (1978).

1. Not all therapists are therapeutic. Much of the research involves inexperienced therapists, therapists in training, or interns. The averaging of studies including such therapists with those involving experienced therapists attenuates relationships. As some reviewers have noted, most of the studies have included therapists offering low levels of the therapeutic conditions, often borderline or below — below level 3 on the 5-point scale. Furthermore, the ranges of scores on the measures are usually restricted; the resulting reduced variability attenuates relationships between the variables and outcome measures.

2. Critics have pointed to the small numbers of therapists and clients in most studies. Yet they do not recognize that the probability of obtaining significant results is directly related to the size of the sample.

3. Critics have complained about the small amount or percentage of variance in the outcome criteria accounted for by the therapist variables. Correlations between .50 and .65, the highest obtained, account for between 25 and 40 percent of the variance. There are several factors that must be considered,

however. No one expects perfect correlations in studies of human behavior. And the correlations are attenuated by (a) the relatively low reliabilities of measures of the therapeutic conditions; (b) similar low reliabilities of the outcome measures; (c) the less than perfect validities of the outcome measures, and (d) restricted ranges of scores on the predictor variables. Statistical corrections for unreliability of the therapist and outcome measures would increase the obtained correlations significantly. No one appears to have considered this. Smith et al. (1980) did not apply such corrections in their meta-analysis of the effectiveness of psychotherapy.

4. Outcome measures used in the various studies vary widely. The various measures show low intercorrelations. It appears that there is no single outcome measure, or group of highly related measures which is generally accepted. This problem of an appropriate criterion influences all outcome studies.

5. No one seems to have applied, or suggested the use of, probability statistics to estimate the probability of obtaining by chance the proportions of positive results in a series of studies.

All studies, as the critics have pointed out, are flawed, but the critics do not seem to be aware that these flaws, in almost all cases, militate against, not for, the obtaining of significant positive results.

Conclusion

Considering the obstacles to research on the relationship between therapist variables and therapy outcomes, the magnitude of the evidence is nothing short of amazing. There are few things in the field of psychology for which the evidence is so strong. The evidence for the necessity, if not the sufficiency, of the therapist conditions of accurate empathy, respect, or warmth, and therapeutic genuineness is incontrovertible.

As Orlinsky and Howard (1978) conclude: 'If study after flawed study seemed to point in the same general direction, we could not help believing that somewhere in all that variance there must be a reliable effect' (pp. 288–9). And a powerful effect! There is certainly more than meets the eyes of most reviewers.

The effectiveness of all methods of counseling or psychotherapy may be due to the presence of a therapeutic relationship. The crucial study to determine if this is so by eliminating the relationship is difficult, if not impossible, to conduct. It could be possible to vary the therapeutic level of the relationship; this is, in effect, what is done in comparing studies in which the levels of therapeutic conditions vary. The fact that therapeutic change occurs in a therapeutic relationship without the addition of so-called specific techniques, such as interpretation, suggestion, instruction, etc., is also evidence of the sufficiency of the relationship by itself.

The consistent positive findings regarding the elements of the therapeutic relationship are encouraging. This is particularly so in view of the lack of consistent findings in the area of (developmental) psychopathology in the search for specific causal factors. Thus there is no basis for specific interventions related to specific causal factors of psychopathology. The research on the effectiveness of the relationship over a wide range of client conditions or problems provides a basis for a therapy which does not depend on identifying specific causal pathological factors. This suggests either that the specific content of the client's disturbance is unimportant, or that the cause of much, if not most, psychological disturbance is related to the absence of good human relationships, or deficiencies in such relationships. It is also possible that improvement in the client's relationships springing from the therapeutic relationship leads to improvement in other areas of the client's life.

References

Bergin, A. E., and Lambert, M. J. (1978) The evaluation of therapeutic outcomes. In S. L. Garfield and A. E. Bergin (Eds.), *Handbook of Psychotherapy and Behavior Change.* (2nd ed.) New York: John Wiley, pp. 139–89.

Bergin, A. E., and Suinn, R. M. (1975) Individual psychotherapy and behavior therapy. *Annual Review of Psychology*, 26, 509–56.

DiLoreto, A. O. (1971) *Comparative Psychotherapy, An Experimental Analysis.* Chicago: Aldine-Atherton.

Garfield, S. L., and Bergin, A. E. (Eds.) (1978) *Handbook of Psychotherapy and Behavior Change.* (2nd ed.) New York: John Wiley.

Gurman, A. S. (1977) The patient's perception of the therapeutic relationship. In A. S. Gurman and A. M. Razing (Eds.), *Effective Psychotherapy.* New York: Pergamon Press, pp. 503—43.

Gomes-Schwartz, B., Hadley, S. W. and Strupp, H. H. (1978) Individual psychotherapy and behavior therapy. *Annual Review of Psychology*, 29, 435–47.

Holland, J. L., Magoon, T. M. and Spokane, A. R. (1981) Counseling psychology: career interventions, research, and theory. *Annual Review of Psychology*, 32, 279–305.

Krumboltz, J. D., Becker-Haven, J. E., and Burnett, K. F. (1979) Counseling psychology. *Annual Review of Psychology*, 30, 555–602.

Lambert, M. J., DeJulio, S. S. and Stein, D. (1978) Therapist interpersonal skills. *Psychological Bulletin*, 83, 467–89.

Mitchell, K. M., Bozarth, J. D., and Krauft, C. C. (1977) A reappraisal of the therapeutic effectiveness of accurate empathy, non-possessive warmth, and genuineness. In A. S. Gurman and A. M. Razin (Eds.), *Effective Psychotherapy.* New York: Pergamon Press, pp. 482–502.

Mitchell, K. M., Truax, C. B., Bozarth, J. D. and Krauft, C. C. (1973) *Antecedents to Psychotherapeutic Outcome.* NIMH Grant Report (12306), Arkansas Rehabilitation Services, Hot Springs, Arkansas.

Orlinsky, D. E., and Howard, K. I. (1978) The relation of process to outcome in psychotherapy. In S. L. Garfield and A. E. Bergin (Eds.), *Handbook of Psychotherapy and Behavior Change.* (2nd ed.) New York: John Wiley, pp. 283–330.

Parloff, M. B., Waskow, I. E., and Wolfe, B. E. (1978) Research on therapist variables in relation to process and outcomes. In S. L. Garfield and A. E. Bergin (Eds.), *Handbook of Psychotherapy and Behavior Change.* (2nd ed.) New York:

John Wiley, pp. 233–82.

Patterson, C. H. (1980) *Theories of Counseling and Psychotherapy.* (3rd ed.) New York: Harper and Row.

Phillips, J. S., and Bierman, K. L. (1981) Clinical psychology: Individual methods. *Annual Review of Psychology*, 32, 405–38.

Rogers, C. R. (1957) The necessary and sufficient conditions of therapeutic personality change. *Journal of Consulting Psychology*, 21, 95–103.

Sloane, R. B., Staples, E. R., Cristol, A. H., Yorkston, A. H., and Whipple, K. (1975) *Short-Term Analytically Oriented Psychotherapy vs. Behavior Therapy.* Cambridge, Mass: Harvard University Press.

Smith, M. L., Glass, G. V., and Miller, T. I. (1980) *The Benefits of Psychotherapy.* Baltimore: Johns Hopkins University Press.

Strupp, H. H. (1978) The therapist's orientation: An overrated variable. *Psychotherapy: Theory, Research and Practice*, 15, 314–7.

Strupp, H. H. (1978) Psychotherapy research and practice: An overview. In S. L. Garfield and A. E. Bergin (Eds.), *Handbook of Psychotherapy and Behavior Change.* (2nd ed.) New York: John Wiley.

Strupp, H. H. (1980) Humanism and psychotherapy: A personal statement of the therapist's essential values. *Psychotherapy: Theory, Research and Practice*, 17, 396–400.

Truax, C. B., and Carkhuff, R. R. (1967) *Toward Effective Counseling and Psychotherapy.* Chicago: Aldine.

Truax, C. B., and Mitchell, K. M. (1971) Research on certain therapist interpersonal skills in relation to process and outcome. In A. E. Bergin and S. L. Garfield (Eds.), *Handbook of Psychotherapy and Behavior Change.* New York: John Wiley, pp. 299–344.

On Being Client-Centered

17

The purpose of this paper is to consider the trend toward expanding or extending client-centered therapy, introducing new or 'innovative' methods and techniques, going beyond the necessary and sufficient conditions postulated by Rogers (1957). Attempts have also been made to integrate client-centered therapy with other approaches, such as Jungian therapy (Purton, 1989). The question is raised about the consistency of these additions, extensions, and integrations with the basic philosophy and assumptions of client-centered therapy.

The problem

As I have met, listened to, and talked with persons who profess to be client-centered, and as I have read the writings of others who profess to be client-centered, I confess to some puzzlement and concern. It seems to me that they have departed from the basic philosophy and principles of client-centered therapy.

Wood says that 'some of Rogers' closest colleagues use hypnosis, guided fantasies, paradoxical statements, dream analysis, exercises, give homework assignments and generally follow the latest fads' (1986, p. 351). Natiello says that 'many therapists who call themselves person-centered now direct their clients by using procedures such as hypnosis, relaxation, psychodrama, and so on' (1987b, p. 246). She herself proposes adding therapist power as a fourth condition to Rogers's three (1987a).

This leads me to wonder if it is clear just what the client-centered position is — what are its philosophy, beliefs, and assumptions? Rogers and others have written extensively about this, of course. And recently Combs (1986a) and Bozarth and Brodley (1986) have explicated the position. Yet its implications do not seem to have been recognized or understood. The three therapist conditions postulated by Rogers (1957) are given almost universal lip-service as necessary, though Wood says that 'Most people [and he seems to be including those who call themselves client-centered] repeat vacuously the cliche: "I believe that Rogers' conditions are necessary, but not sufficient"' (1986, p. 351). It would seem that with the considerable evidence that the conditions are sufficient (e.g. Patterson, 1985, pp.

First published in *Person-Centered Review*, 1990, 5, pp. 428–32. Reprinted with permission.

217–20, chap. 13), to be client-centered would require acceptance of their sufficiency until evidence to the contrary existed.

That it is not clear what is client-centered, and also what is not client-centered, is shown by Jennings's person-centered approach to dream analysis. Jennings illustrates this in his analysis of a client's dream. Stating that his objective is to have the client make her own interpretation of the dream, he directs the analysis following his system of dream analysis. The means is inconsistent with the end; he assumes the responsibility for the analysis. Purton (1989) also refers to 'exploring dreams in a person-centered way' (p. 415) but does not explain how this is done. He also suggests a fourth necessary condition, 'an attitude that could be called "openness to the unconscious"' (p .412).

There are numerous other examples of writers suggesting that we should break from 'traditional' client-centered therapy. According to Bozarth and Brodley, Gendlin (1974) and Rice (1974) 'suggested that the therapist at times knows the best direction for the client' (1986, p. 267). Combs suggests that since 'counseling is essentially a learning process', counselors 'ought to acknowledge the teaching role and use it, purposefully, for positive ends', though 'the concept of teaching, for many therapists, is practically an epithet, synonymous with autocrat or dictator. I think these attitudes are unnecessarily inhibiting' (1988, p. 268). He does not discuss just how the client-centered counselor teaches, or how this is consistent with client-centered principles.

Warner (1989) attempts to integrate strategic family systems theory into client-centered family therapy. However, it is not clear just how the therapist functions, but the use of terms such as 'urging', 'interpret', 'very few [but presumably some] demands or suggestions', 'address incongruence', and 'raising possibilities' does not appear to be consistent with client-centered therapy.

And Snyder (1989), attempting to integrate Rogers and Bateson in couple therapy, does not appear to function in consistency with the principles of client-centered therapy. She refers to her relationship enhancement model as therapy. She also refers to it as 'a skill training model' (p. 376). It is actually teaching, not therapy.

At least one other client-centered therapist shares my concern (J. M. Shlien, [1986] personal communication, and Shlien,1986). Referring to 'new directions', and to 'innovations' that make 'novelty a virtue in itself', Shlien notes that 'the question is not "what's new?", but "what's good?"' (1986, p. 347). He goes on to say that

> one reads that client-centered therapists include in their practice hypnosis, scream therapy, behavior modification, Gestalt psychodrama, relaxation, etc. How some of these can be considered client-centered is beyond me . . . The person-centered approach invites extensions that sometimes outreach the theory of client-centered therapy (pp. 347–8).

And Raskin (1987), in his review of Levant and Shlien (1984), refers to chapters by Gendlin, Rice, and Guerney, and by others, which are aimed at

> broadening both the theory and practice of client-centered therapy . . . practices designed to make more efficient the client's problem solving

and experiencing endeavors . . . On the one hand, such divergent approaches . . . are consonant with Rogers' hope that his students would not turn out to be little Rogerians, but would develop their own ways of working . . . On the other hand, each of these neo-Rogerian methods takes something away from the thoroughgoing belief in the self-directive capacities of clients so central to client-centered philosophy (p.460).

Are there no limits to what can be called client-centered? Is anything that is done by a therapist claiming to be client-centered actually client-centered? Did Rogers, in his modesty and openness to new ideas, issue a license for client-centered therapists to do whatever they feel like doing and still claim to be client-centered?

Perhaps we need a more specific analysis of what client-centered therapy is and what it is not. There are some things that are inconsistent with the philosophy and beliefs or assumptions of client-centered therapy. There are limits to what a therapist can do and yet remain client-centered. As Shlien says, 'It is essential to find a set of criteria to define the meaning of client-centered' (1986, p. 348).

Basic philosophy and assumptions of client-centered therapy

1. Every organism is motivated by one basic drive, the drive to actualize its potentials, at the biological and psychological levels (Patterson,1964). Combs and Snygg explain that 'from birth to death the maintenance of the phenomenal self is the most pressing, the most crucial, if not the only task of existence . . . Man seeks both to maintain and enhance his perceived self' (1959, p. 45).

   Rogers has stated this assumption in various ways, speaking of a growth tendency: 'The organism has one basic tendency and striving — to actualize, maintain, and enhance the experiencing organism' (1951, p. 247). Later, he refers to

   man's tendency to actualize himself, to become his potentialities.
   By this I mean the directional trend which is evident in all organic
   and human life — the urge to expand, extend, develop, mature, the
   tendency to express and activate all the capacities of the organism,
   or the self . . . it exists in every individual, and awaits only the proper
   conditions to be released and expressed (1961, p. 351).

   Later, Rogers talks of 'an underlying flow of movement toward constructive fulfillment of its [the organism's] inherent possibilities' (198, p. 117). 'It is clear that the actualizing tendency is selective and directional — a constructive tendency, if you will' (p. 121); the actualizing tendency and 'a formative tendency in the universe as a whole . . . are the foundation blocks of the person-centered approach' (p. 114); and 'the person-centered approach rests on a basic trust in human beings, and in all organisms' (p. 117).

2. Certain environmental conditions must be present for the actualizing tendency to operate. The biological organism needs air, water, food, and often clothing and shelter to survive. But biological survival requires another condition —

nurturing, caring, and loving by another person (Spitz, 1945; Lynch, 1977). In addition, certain information, knowledge, and skills are necessary. At the psychosocial level, a caring, loving environment is necessary for the social-emotional development of the individual. These are the conditions provided in client-centered therapy, which have been identified as empathic understanding, unconditional positive regard (respect, caring), and therapeutic genuineness.

3. Persons come to psychotherapy not because they lack biological necessities or information or skills (though some may lack these things). They come because of social-psychological needs — emotional and interpersonal deficiencies. Therapists do not provide the biological necessities; some, however, perhaps mistakenly, feel that they should provide the information, knowledge, and skill deficiencies — that they should be teachers.

   The three conditions postulated by Rogers are necessary and sufficient where there are no physical or information or skill deficiencies.

4. The goal of psychotherapy is to promote the self-actualization of the client. The conditions provided by the therapist in the therapeutic relationship are the specific conditions for the lack or insufficiency of these conditions in the past and/or present interpersonal environment of the client (Patterson, 1985).

5. The presence of the actualizing tendency in the client makes it possible for the client to control and direct the therapy process. Each client has multiple potentials and chooses those that will be actualized, and the ways or manner of actualization.

   In the process the client takes responsibility for him- or herself; engages in the self-disclosure and self-exploration necessary for therapeutic progress; engages in problem solving, and makes decisions and choices. The actualizing tendency as manifested in these characteristics means that the therapist need not engage in active interventions; provide or suggest alternatives; suggest solutions to problems; question or probe; offer interpretations or insights; or offer praise, encouragement, or reassurance. The therapist is not a director or even a guide; the specific path to self-actualization is not known to the therapist. The therapist trusts the actualizing tendency in the client, has faith that the tendency will manifest itself under the conditions offered by the therapist, and has the patience to allow the client the responsibility to direct the process and to progress at his or her own rate. The therapist is always responding to, or is responsive to, the client in the process.

   For any particular client, it is assumed that the client has the necessary drive toward growth and self-actualization. The actualizing tendency may be minimal, or even lacking because of organic damage or past and/or present deprivation or mistreatment. Rogers, however, believed that though 'the actualizing tendency can, of course, be thwarted or warped . . . it cannot be destroyed without destroying the organism' (1984, p. 118).

6. While the three therapist conditions of empathic understanding, unconditional positive regard or respect, and therapeutic genuineness may be sufficient, the question remains whether they are efficient. Are there other conditions, not necessary, that can improve the efficiency of the process, or facilitate or expedite it? This, it seems to me, is what many practitioners, such as those cited earlier,

are looking for. It is possible, for example, that relaxation processes and hypnosis could be used in a manner consistent with client-centered principles (Moore and Patterson, 'Client-Centered Therapy and Hypnosis', paper in preparation). The essential requirement of any of these processes is that they be consistent with the theory and philosophy of client-centered therapy — that is, that they do not take away the client's autonomy and responsibility, the client's opportunity to 'do it for him/herself'. Anything that deprives the client of this experience fosters dependence and detracts from the self-actualizing process in the client.

7. The three basic therapist conditions are present in all the major therapies. But client-centered therapy is unique in its position that these conditions are sufficient, and in its consistent adherence to these conditions.

    a. Client-centered therapy remains in the internal frame of reference of the client through the entire process. It neither limits the practice of empathic understanding to the development of so-called rapport, nor uses the understanding as a power base to intervene, direct, and influence the client through interpretation or other means.

    b. The client-centered therapist respects and trusts the client to the extent that the client is given control of the nature and rate of development of the therapeutic process. The therapist's trust in the client is not limited or restricted: It is complete.

    c. The therapist remains constantly in the responsive mode, never leaving it to initiate, direct, or control the process through interventions.

       No other approach to psychotherapy operates in this manner. Thus, it is not possible to integrate client-centered therapy with any other approach, nor to take or use methods or techniques from other approaches, which are usually direct interventions inconsistent with the client-centered philosophy and theory.

Apparently many seem to feel that the position taken here is narrow, rigid, and dogmatic. Yet it is logically necessary if one accepts the philosophy and assumptions of client-centered therapy. Some appear to feel that if one has the attitudes (represented in the conditions), one can do anything one feels like in therapy and still be client-centered. Rogers (1975) appears to have fostered this attitude: 'I've come to realize that techniques are definitely secondary to attitudes, that if a therapist has the attitudes we've come to regard as essential probably he or she can use a variety of techniques'. Cain writes that 'certainly being person-centered must mean more than possessing these qualities, as nice as these qualities are' (1986, p. 251). He notes also that

> although being client-centered has some boundaries regarding our beliefs and the manner in which we implement them, it seems that the qualities or attitudes that derive from our philosophy also free us to define ourselves in our own unique manner of being client-centered . . . Somehow I like the idea that person-centeredness offers more freedom than limits (p. 255).

The client-centered conditions can be implemented in different ways by different therapists with different clients. However, these ways must always be consistent with the basic philosophy and the nature of the conditions themselves. There is some freedom. But there are limits. The freedom of the therapist stops when it infringes on the freedom of the client to be responsible for and direct his or her own life.

References

Bozarth, J. A., and Brodley, B. T. (1986) Client-centered psychotherapy: A statement. *Person-Centered Review*, 1, 262–71.

Cain, D. J. (1986) What does it mean to be person-centered? *Person-Centered Review*, 1, 251–6.

Combs, A. W. (1986a) Person-centered assumptions for counselor education. *Person-Centered Review*, 1, 72–82.

Combs, A. W. (1986b) On methods, conditions, and goals. *Person-Centered Review*, 1, 378–88.

Combs, A. W. (1988) Some current issues for person-centered therapy. *Person-Centered Review*, 3, 263–76.

Combs, A. W., and Snygg, D. (1959) *Individual behavior.* (rev. ed.) New York: Harper and Row.

Gendlin, E. T. (1974) Client-centered and experiential psychotherapy. In D. A. Wexler and L. N. Rice (Eds.), *Innovations in client-centered therapy.* (pp. 211–26) New York: Wiley.

Jennings, J. L. (1986) The dream is the dream is the dream: A person-centered approach to dream analysis. *Person-Centered Review*, 1, 310–33.

Lynch, J. J. (1977) *The broken heart: The medical consequences of loneliness.* New York: Basic Books.

Natiello, P. (1987a) The person-centered approach: From theory to practice. *Person-Centered Review*, 2, 203–16.

Natiello, P. (1987b) Roundtable discussion. *Person-Centered Review*, 2, 245–6.

Patterson, C. H. (1964) A unitary theory of motivation and its counseling implications. *Journal of Individual Psychology,* 4, 17–31.

Patterson, C. H. (1985) *The therapeutic relationship.* Pacific Grove, CA: Brooks/Cole.

Purton, C. (1989) The person-centered Jungian. *Person-Centered Review*, 4, 403–19.

Raskin, N. J. (1987) From spyglass to kaleidoscope [Review of R. F. Levant and J. M. Shlien (Eds.), Client-centered therapy and the person-centered approach: New directions in theory, research and practice]. *Contemporary Psychology,* 32, 460–1.

Rice, L. N. (1974) The evocative function of the therapist. In D. A. Wexler and L. N. Rice (Eds.), *Innovations in client-centered therapy.* (pp. 289–311) New York: Wiley.

Rogers, C. R. (1951) *Client-centered therapy.* Boston: Houghton Mifflin.

Rogers, C. R. (1957) The necessary and sufficient conditions of therapeutic personality change. *Journal of Consulting Psychology,* 21, 95–103.

Rogers, C. R. (1961) *On becoming a person.* Boston: Houghton Mifflin.

Rogers, C. R. (Speaker) (1975) *Client-centered therapy.* (Cassette Recording.) Brooklyn, NY: Psychology Today.

Rogers, C. R. (1980) *A way of being.* Boston: Houghton Mifflin.

Shlien, J. M. (1986) Roundtable discussion. *Person-Centered Review*, 1, 347–8.

Snyder, M. (1989) The relationship enhancement model of couple therapy: An integration of Rogers and Bateson. *Person-Centered Review*, 4, 358–83.

Spitz, R. (1945) Hospitalism. In R. S. Eissler (Ed.), *The psychoanalytic study of the child.* (Vol. 1, pp. 53–74) New York: International Universities Press.

Warner, M. S. (1989) Empathy and strategy in the family system. *Person-Centered Review*, 4, 324–43.

Wood, J. K. (1986) Roundtable discussion. *Person-Centered Review*, 1, 350–1.

ON BEING NON-DIRECTIVE   18

I have been following the discussions of directiveness-nondirectiveness (Cain, 1989, 1990; Sebastian, 1989; Grant, 1990) with interest, and also with a sense of frustration and irritation. This is because the papers seem to constitute an exercise in sophistry. Each writer gives his own meaning to the terms, without clearly defining them. Moreover, the terms are used by each writer with different implicit meanings. Grant (1990), like Humpty Dumpty in Alice in Wonderland (Dodgson, 1931), creates out of whole cloth two kinds, or definitions, of nondirective.

Cain (1989) opens the discussion. He begins by discussing individual differences in learning styles. He fails to note that they apply to cognitive learning. He suggests that some clients need some direction from the therapist. Thus complete nondirectiveness is not always possible. But personal learnings, learning about oneself, in therapy is achieved best, and perhaps only, through self-discovery learning. It is doubtful if different learning styles are relevant to this kind of learning.

Grant (1990) appears to say that 'pragmatic concerns for promoting growth and "meeting needs"', and 'respect for persons' are incompatible, leading to his proposing two kinds of nondirectiveness — 'instrumental nondirectiveness' and 'principled nondirectiveness'. He says that in principled nondirectiveness there is 'an absence of the intention to make anything in particular happen' (p. 82). 'Client-centered therapists do not intend to free or constrain their clients' (p. 84). This is ridiculous, patent nonsense. Respect for clients is important because it leads to changes in the client. Principled nondirectiveness is involved with ends, as is instrumental directiveness. But in instrumental nondirectiveness the means are inconsistent with the ends.

Both Grant and Cain suggest that the therapist may offer activities, exercises, techniques, direction, advice, interpretations, etc., to clients who request them; Grant goes farther, saying that therapist offering of unsolicited opinions, suggestions and the like, can be consistent with 'principled' nondirectiveness. Clients, they say, can choose or reject these offerings. It is, however, naive to believe that clients are really completely free to reject such offerings from one who is perceived, to some extent at least, as an expert. Moreover, these offerings are inconsistent with respect and with the end of client-centered therapy — a

Previously unpublished paper.

responsible, independent, self-actualizing client.

Cain (1990), in his response to Grant, accurately represents Rogers' position on nondirectiveness. But he departs from this position when he argues against nondirectiveness because some clients do not like it or respond immediately to it, and sometimes leave therapy. So he abandons nondirectiveness; but in doing so he is also abandoning the belief and trust in the client's capability to take responsibility for him/herself, in the therapy process, as well as outside it — that is the basic assumption of Rogers' position. The resulting activities of the therapist, while pleasing to the client, are inconsistent with the goal of client-centered therapy. (It may be of interest to note here that 'to please' is the definition of placebo.)

Cain emphasizes individual differences among clients, and says that client-centered therapy does not recognize this fact in its practice. To the contrary, client-centered therapy is attuned to individual differences to a greater extent than any other therapy. The conditions of empathy, respect and genuineness make possible the expression of the uniqueness of each client. The conditions are the same for all clients, but the content and substance of the resulting process are unique to each client.

Sebastian's discussion (1989) is not directed to the directive-nondirective debate, but he does enter into it, nevertheless. He tries to avoid the conflict by posing both theoretical and metatheoretical levels, though the distinction is not entirely clear. At a metatheoretical level the therapist is an expert, a guide, and even a manipulator, apparently simply because the therapist knows where the process will lead. (Parenthetically, the use of the term 'manipulator' is not quite right, since manipulation includes an element of deviousness, with the manipulator attempting to achieve his or her ends without the knowledge of the person being manipulated.) His statement that 'if the person-centered therapist's goal is to help persons to develop as fully as possible their organismic selves, who cares whether the means are more or less directive' is simply unacceptable. Directive means are inconsistent with such a goal, which includes autonomy, responsibility and self-determination.

At the risk of stating the obvious, let me clearly and simply, without elaboration, state the nature of client-centered therapy.

1. Therapy is an influencing process. The intent of the therapist is to influence the client. If this were not so, the therapist would not be practicing. The issue is not directiveness-nondirectiveness. Rogers recognized the irrelevance of this as an issue when, as Cain (1989) notes, he abandoned consideration of the issue. The relevant issue is the nature and extent of this influence that is consistent with the philosophy and assumptions of client-centered therapy.

2. The goal of this influence is to free and foster the process of self-actualization in the client. This is a goal that is not chosen by either the therapist or the client — it is given by the nature of the client as a living organism. The actualizing tendency, as Rogers recognized, is a characteristic of all living organisms. (Parenthetically, this is the basis for a universal system of psychotherapy [Patterson, 1995]). In clients, this process of self-actualization is disturbed or impeded in some way.

3. The goal of therapy is fostered by the therapist through the providing of three conditions: empathic understanding, respect (unconditional positive regard), and therapeutic genuineness. These are the necessary and sufficient therapist conditions for therapeutic personality change (Rogers, 1957). If they are sufficient, then no other conditions are necessary. I am not aware that any definitions of these conditions include therapist direction or influencing by suggestions, advice, guiding, leading, etc. The only means of influencing the client are through these conditions. Any other active intervention by the therapist is inconsistent with the basic assumption of the existence of the drive toward self-actualization. The three conditions offered by the therapist frees the operation of this drive in the client.

4. The perception of these conditions by the client results in client self-disclosure, self-exploration, self-directed and self-discovery learning leading to changes in client perceptions and attitudes that result in changes in behavior. These changes are elements of the self-actualizing process. They are unique for each client (though there are some common elements). As Maslow (1962, p. 196) notes, 'Self-actualization is the actualization of a self, and no two selves are altogether alike'.

5. The conditions provided by the therapist constitute the highest values of the therapist in the area of interpersonal relations. Sebastian (1989, p. 496) says that 'person-centered therapists do not impose their values, attitudes and behaviors on their clients'. This is patently false. Through the implementation of the conditions, client-centered therapists (as do all therapists) impose their values on their clients (Patterson, 1989). Rogers' (1961, pp. 397, 398) comment is relevant here:

> . . . We have established by external control, conditions which we predict will be followed by internal control by the individual, in pursuit of internally chosen goals . . . the client will become more self-directing, less rigid, more open to the evidence of his senses, better organized and integrated, more similar to the ideal he has chosen for himself. . . The conditions . . . predict behavior that is essentially free.

In short, the client becomes a more self-actualizing person.

Rogers has elaborated on most of these points many times. Yet there appear to be many who call themselves client-centered who seem to be unaware of their implications for practice. Such therapists appear to have little faith in the actualization tendency in their clients.

References

Cain, D. J. (1989) The paradox of nondirectiveness in the person-centered approach. *Person-Centered Review*, 4, 123–30.

Cain, D. J. (1990) Further thoughts about nondirectiveness and client-centered therapy. *Person-Centered Review*, 5, 89–99.

Dodgson, C. L. (1931) *The Lewis Carroll book*. New York: Dial Press.

Grant, B. (1990) Principled and instrumental nondirectiveness in person-centered and client-centered therapy. *Person-Centered Review*, 5, 77–88.

Maslow, A. H. (1962) *Toward a psychology of being*. Princeton, NJ: Van Nostrand.

Patterson, C. H. (1989) Values in counseling and psychotherapy. *Counseling and Values*, 33, 164–76.

Patterson, C. H. (1995) A universal system of psychotherapy. *The Person-Centered Journal*, 2 (1), 81–8.

Rogers, C. R. (1957) The necessary and sufficient conditions of therapeutic personality change. *Journal of Consulting Psychology*, 21, 95–103.

Rogers, C. R. (1961) *On becoming a person*. Boston: Houghton Mifflin.

Sebastian, J. (1989) Metatheoretical response to the person-centered versus client-centered debate. *Person-Centered Review*, 4, 493–6.

Resistance in Therapy: A Person-Centered View   19

The purpose of this paper is to consider client resistance from a client-centered view of psychotherapy.

Client or patient resistance in psychotherapy has been the concern of therapists since the time of Freud. Freud identified several kinds of resistance. These included the patient's resistance to uncovering repressed material; resistance to the insights provided by the therapist's interpretations; resistance to the therapist as the provider of these insights — the negative transference; resistance to giving up symptoms, which provide certain gains; the resistance of the id to being deprived of its satisfactions; and the resistance of the superego to giving up the need for punishment to assuage its guilt.

While Freud at first saw resistance only as an obstacle to uncovering the unconscious, he later recognized it as something not simply to be overcome, but as an important element in psychotherapy along with patient psychodynamics and transference, and, like them, something to be interpreted.

The origin or source of these resistances were, and are still, seen by many therapists as residing in the client. The therapist bears little, if any, responsibility for client or patient resistance. Or, if any responsibility is accepted by the therapist, resistance is considered to be the client's nontherapeutic response to the good therapist's necessary and desirable methods of therapy. Resistance is thus inevitable, a universal and unavoidable element in psychotherapy. It is something to be overcome, and not something to be avoided.

The question arises as to whether psychotherapy, to be successful, must necessarily operate to lead to resistance in the client, or whether therapy can be practiced so as to eliminate, or minimize, client resistance. Resistance is a defense; defense is a response to threat. Therapist interventions can be, and often are, threatening to the client. Interpretations are often threatening to the client. Attempts to persuade the client through reasoning and argumentation, as in cognitive therapy and rational emotive therapy, as well as behavior therapy, can be threatening. Even less overt and obvious therapist behavior can be threatening to the client. Rogers (1961, pp. 44, 54) cites research by Dittes which found that 'whenever the therapist's attitudes changed even slightly in the direction of a lesser degree of

Previously unpublished paper.

acceptance, the number of abrupt GSR [Galvanic Skin Response]deviations significantly increased' (p. 44). And '. . . the psychogalvanic reflex . . . takes a sharp dip when the therapist responds with some word which is just a little stronger than the client's feelings'. (p. 54). There is thus physiological evidence that therapist judgmentalism, evaluation, and interpretation are threatening.

Now, it is well known that threat is inimical to learning and (voluntary) behavior change. Under threat people resist, cling to what they have and are, become more fixed in their ideas and feelings. Perception is narrowed, as in tunnel vision, so that there is failure to perceive all the elements in a person's experience and environment (Combs & Snygg, 1959, pp. 171–88).

But can threat be eliminated from psychotherapy, or at least be minimized? Rogers (1942) dealt extensively with resistance and its source in therapist's statements. (Curiously, resistance does not appear in the index to *Client-Centered Therapy* [Rogers, 1951]. The hypothesis, he wrote,

> . . . is that resistance to counseling and to the counselor is not an inevitable part of psychotherapy, nor a desirable part, but it grows primarily out of poor techniques of handling the client's expression of his problems and feelings . . . out of unwise attempts on the part of the counselor to short-cut the therapeutic process by bringing into discussion emotionalized attitudes which the client is not yet ready to face (p. 151).

'Insight', he wrote, 'is an experience which is achieved, not an experience which can be imposed' (p. 196).

Anything that is really helpful, that leads to real and lasting learning, is not the result of imposition. The only effective learning in psychotherapy is self-discovered learning. '*I have come to feel that the only learning which significantly influences behavior is self-discovered, self-appropriated learning*' (Rogers, 1961, p. 276. Italics in original).

Trying to speed up therapy or client progress by interpreting, or bestowing on clients the therapist's insights, does not facilitate therapy but retards it. Learning can occur only at the rate the client is able to progress on his/her own.

There is discussion in the literature about the need for the client to experience an 'optimum' level of anxiety if he/she is to be motivated to make progress. For example, Strupp and Binder (1984, pp. 191–2) write about the therapist as 'someone who evokes anxiety. . . . As always in therapy, the trick is to steer a course which on the one hand maintains sufficient tension, thereby keeping the patient motivated, and on the other, prevents the experience of too much anxiety.' What is 'optimum', 'sufficient' or 'too much' are not specified; Strupp and Binder do not tell us how to perform the trick.

Client-centered therapy, on the other hand, provides a simple, clear and valid method for maintaining optimum anxiety in the client. Rogers states it succinctly: '[I]f I can free him (the client) as completely as possible from external threat, then he can begin to experience and to deal with the internal feelings and conflicts which he finds within himself' (Rogers, 1961, p. 54).

There are sources of resistance in the client that are not caused by threatening aspects of the therapist's behavior. There are resistances to change, resistance to facing negative and painful aspects of the self and ones behaviors. Clients may have difficulty in trusting the therapist, and in self-disclosure. There is resistance against giving up old habits, or symptoms.

Such resistances cannot be avoided or eliminated. They are accepted and responded to as any other statements or behaviors of the client. Therapy is accompanied by a certain amount of client anxiety. Learning is to some extent accompanied by anxiety; in fact, low levels of anxiety may facilitate learning.

Conclusion

Client resistance has received little attention in the literature on client-centered therapy. This is probably for the same reason that transference has also apparently been neglected: 'In client-centered therapy, this involved and persistent dependency relationship does not tend to develop' (Rogers, 1951, p. 201). Client-centered therapy minimizes resistance by minimizing threat to the client. The therapist conditions of client-centered therapy — empathic understanding, respect and warmth, and therapeutic genuineness — provide an atmosphere and relationship that minimizes threat. A relationship between the therapist and client characterized by these conditions provides the optimum conditions for meaningful voluntary learning and progress on the part of the client.

References

Combs, A. W., and Snygg, D. (1959) *Individual behavior: A perceptual approach to behavior*. New York: Harper & Row.

Rogers, C. R. (1942)*Counseling and psychotherapy: Newer concepts in practice*. Boston: Houghton Mifflin.

Rogers, C. R. (1951) *Client-centered therapy: Its current practice, implementation and theory*. Boston: Houghton Mifflin.

Rogers, C. R. (1961) *On becoming a Person: A therapist's view of psychotherapy*. Boston: Houghton Mifflin.

Strupp, H. H., and Binder, J. L. (1984) *Psychotherapy in a new key: A guide to time-limited dynamic psychotherapy*. New York: Basic Books.

Involuntary Clients: A Person-Centered View

20

The purpose of this paper is to consider the problem posed by so-called involuntary clients in client-centered therapy.

Actually, there is no such thing as an involuntary client. Psychotherapy is a relationship entered into for the purpose of client change. It takes two to form a relationship. A person becomes a client when he or she voluntarily enters a relationship with a therapist. The term 'involuntary client' refers to persons who, in the view of others (family members, teachers, associates, the courts), have a problem and are referred to, or are required to present themselves to, a therapist. However, they do not see themselves as having problems, or as in need of psychotherapy. Rogers (1957) states as one of the conditions of psychotherapy that the client is incongruent, vulnerable, and anxious. That is, he or she 'must be someone who is feeling some concerns . . . some degree of conflict, some degree of inner difference, some expression of concern' (Rogers, 1987, pp. 39, 40).

Therapy is not something that can be imposed on someone, or given or administered, like a shot of penicillin. A person does not become a client until he or she decides to become one. So-called involuntary clients are persons who reject or decline psychotherapy and refuse to become clients.

Such persons, because they present themselves, or are brought, to a therapist, constitute a problem for the therapist. They are often considered to be unmotivated. But as there is no such thing as an involuntary client, there is no such thing as an unmotivated client (Patterson, 1964). They are unmotivated for psychotherapy, but they are motivated to avoid participating in psychotherapy. They are not motivated as we would like them to be motivated.

Rogers (Rogers and Stevens, 1967), writing of his experience with unmotivated clients, notes that

> the absence of conscious motivation constitutes a really profound problem in psychotherapy . . . There is a great difference between working with the consciously motivated client, whether neurotic or psychotic, and working with the person who has no such conscious motivation, whether that person is normal, neurotic, or psychotic (p.183).

First published in *Person-Centered Review*, 1990, 5, pp. 316–20. Reprinted by permission.

Here, the term *unmotivated client* refers to the client who has no conscious desire for help, that is, the involuntary client. He continues: 'For working with the person who has no conscious desire for help we need, I believe, a new term . . . It is my present conviction that working with a lack of conscious motivation in the individual is more difficult than working with the problem of psychosis' (pp. 183, 184). Referring also to working with unmotivated normal people of low socioeconomic status, Rogers says: 'I believe the absence of conscious desire for help presents a greater challenge to the therapist than the presence of psychosis' (p.184). Then, significantly, he continues:

> In any event, I have come to believe that we will make more progress in this area if we recognize that dealing with the person who does not wish help is a clearly different undertaking from psychotherapy, and if we build up the concepts, theories, and practices appropriate to it we should not be misled by the fact that *a relationship with such an individual may become psychotherapy when he chooses to seek help* (p.184, italics added).

Rogers does not go on to suggest any such concepts, theories, and practices. Nor has anyone else done so, to my knowledge. Thorne (1968) suggested that the therapist attempt to create or induce a conflict in the client by bringing into consciousness inconsistent and conflicting attitudes. When the client becomes aware of the inconsistency, he or she will be motivated to resolve it. But he noted that 'the use of induced conflict . . . must be handled with great caution . . . efficacy of the technique depends upon the clinical sagacity of the case handler, who must be able to guide the therapeutic process in positive directions' (p. 453). I am very skeptical about the success of this method. At the very least it will induce or provoke resistance. But then any method of intervention is likely to provoke resistance in persons who are not voluntarily present with a therapist. No doubt therapists have tried many kinds of interventions — questioning; probing; offering suggestions, advice, and guidance; moralizing; admonishing; even threatening — undoubtedly with little effect. In fact, such methods may reduce the possibility that the person will enter a therapy relationship and become a client.

But what about the growth tendency, the drive toward self-actualization, assumed to be present in every person? It is 'the tendency upon which all psychotherapy depends' (Rogers, 1961, p. 35). But it is only a tendency, even though universal and often strong. 'This tendency may become deeply buried under layer after layer of encrusted psychological defenses; it may be hidden behind elaborate facades which deny its existence' (p. 35). And it may have been suppressed by destructive or inhumane treatment by others. But it is Rogers' belief that 'it exists in every individual, and awaits only the proper conditions to be released and expressed' (p. 35).

What are these conditions? They are the well-known conditions of client-centered therapy — empathic understanding, respect or warmth, and therapeutic genuineness. But the problem inheres in the fact that these conditions must not only be provided by the therapist; they also must be perceived by the person to whom they are offered. As Rogers (1957, p. 96) puts it, 'The communication to the client of the therapist's empathic understanding and unconditional positive regard is to a minimal degree achieved'. So-called involuntary clients will not, or cannot, recognize and accept the understanding, interest, and concern of the therapist. They will not or cannot trust the therapist.

Yet if, as Rogers has stated it, these therapist and client conditions are the necessary and sufficient conditions for therapeutic personality change (Rogers, 1957), there is no other way to achieve such change. Behavior can be changed in other ways — by threat, coercion, brain surgery, drugs. But lasting change through self-discovered learning does not follow such changes.

The only solution to the problem appears to be through persistent offering of the conditions until, in some cases at least, they are perceived and accepted by the person to whom they are offered, who then becomes a client. Gendlin (1962) has described his work with hospitalized schizophrenic patients, some of whom were reached. Rogers, Gendlin, Kiesler, and Truax (1967) also report some success with hospitalized schizophrenic patients. Therapists who work with persons in the criminal justice system achieve some success. Three of my former students at the University of Illinois have been working for almost 15 years with adolescents on probation, with some success. The success rate with both these groups (psychotics and delinquents) is low, and anyone working with such persons should not require a high success rate for personal or professional satisfaction. But such persons should not be rejected. Working with them could be a long, slow process. But the persistent offering of a relationship — communicating interest, concern, caring, respect, and understanding — can succeed in some cases, making the effort worthwhile. Resistance, antagonism, rejection, lack of interest are to be expected; they are met with acceptance and patience — without questioning, probing, confrontation, or pressure.

Some therapists may not believe that such an approach is effective. They do not have the patience or do not want to invest the time and effort necessary to finally establish a relationship. So they abandon the necessary and sufficient conditions for psychotherapeutic change and attempt to effect change through confrontation, argument, persuasion, coercion, and other methods. They are not likely to be successful in achieving lasting change.

Conclusion

The problem of reluctant or so-called involuntary clients is a difficult one. It is becoming more common as therapists are expected to work with people who do not voluntarily come for help, such as substance abusers. Directive and educational approaches can have a place in group work with such persons, but there is no substitute for the necessary and sufficient conditions for therapeutic personality change.

References

Gendlin, E. T. (1962) Client-centered development in work with schizophrenics. *Journal of Counseling Psychology*, 9, 203–311.

Patterson, C. H. (1964) A unitary theory of motivation and its counseling implications. *Journal of Individual Psychology*, 20, 17–31.

Rogers, C. R. (1957) The necessary and sufficient conditions of therapeutic personality change. *Journal of Consulting Psychology*, 21, 95–103.

Rogers, C. R. (1961) *On becoming a person: A therapist's view of psychotherapy.* Boston: Houghton Mifflin.

Rogers, C. R. (1987) The underlying theory: Drawn from experience with individuals and groups. *Counseling and Values*, 32, 38–46.

Rogers, C. R., Gendlin, E. T., Kiesler, C. A., and Truax, C. B. (1967) *The therapeutic relationship and its impact: A study of psychotherapy with schizophrenics.* Madison: University of Wisconsin Press.

Rogers, C. R., and Stevens, B. (1967) *Person to person: The problem of being human.* Lafayette, CA: Real People's Press.

Thorne, F. C. (1968) *Psychological case handling. Vol. 2. Specialized methods of counseling and psychotherapy.* Brandon, VT.: Journal of Clinical Psychology.

CLIENT-CENTERED SUPERVISION 21

Bernard and Goodyear (1992) group methods of supervision into two classes. The first includes those methods that derive from or are grounded in a theory or system of psychotherapy. The earliest, and still the major, such approach is that of psychoanalysis and its offshoots: 'The psychotherapy-based supervisor is one whose supervision is based totally and consistently on the supervisor's theory of psychotherapy or counseling' (Bernard and Goodyear, 1992, p. 12). These authors include client-centered supervision in this category. They note that 'there are fewer purely psychotherapy-based supervisors than one might think' (p. 13). Although these authors' eclectic supervision is theory-based, they say that 'it must be noted, however, that the theoretical underpinning of these two theories [humanistic and behavior theories] are contradictory' (p. 19). It appears that eclectic supervision was included here because it does not fit into their second category.

The second major category of supervision includes the so-called developmental approaches. The recent and current literature consists almost entirely of discussions of these approaches. It is curious that the developmental approaches ignore the fact that both therapy and supervision are interpersonal relationships.

The developmental approaches to supervision also ignore the theoretical orientations of both the supervisee and the supervisor. Yet each has an approach, or some idea about how therapy should be done, whether or not it is a conscious or recognized theory. The developmental approaches thus fail to consider how the supervisor and supervisee are to reconcile differences or reach agreement on what is expected of the supervisee — what the criteria for the supervisee's practice and performance are.

The client-centered approach to supervision, first described by Patterson (1964), is the focus of this chapter. It is a theory-based approach deriving from client-centered therapy.

The current state of supervision
In actual practice, most supervision does not appear to follow either a theory-based or developmental approach, being atheoretical or eclectic. The reason is that most

First published in C. Edward Watkins, Jr. Editor, *Handbook of Psychotherapy Supervision*. New York: John Wiley & Sons, 1997, pp.134–46. © John Wiley & sons Inc 1997. Reprinted by permission of John Wiley & Sons, Inc.

supervisors do not subscribe to or follow a particular theory of psychotherapy or of supervision and consider themselves to be eclectic. This situation creates problems for supervisees.

There is little, if any, agreement on the preparation of the student for supervised practice. Courses on theory and practice may be taken from different instructors with differing theoretical orientations or with no theoretical orientation. Instructors may or may not have a commitment to a particular theory. They may have been discouraged from making a commitment to any particular theory, or they may have been encouraged to develop their own theory. Supervisors also may or may not be committed to a consistent philosophy or theory. If both student and supervisor claim to be eclectic, there may be little agreement on what this means in actual practice.

The current situation has led this author (Patterson, 1992) to suggest a change in the programs for the education of psychotherapists. Each program would commit itself to two or three theoretical orientations depending on the competence and expertise of its faculty. Each student would enroll in a theories course that covers the major theories in some depth, using a text such as Patterson and Watkins (1996) or Ford and Urban (1963). Students would then select the theory they prefer and enroll in an advanced course covering that theory, with an instructor who is an expert in it. Students would then continue in supervision with that instructor. If a student desires training in a theory that is not a specialty of a faculty member in that institution, he or she would be facilitated in transferring to an institution offering such training. This approach is considered an interim one, pending the time when there would be agreement on one system of psychotherapy — a universal system (Patterson, 1995; Patterson and Hidore, 1996).

This writer has attempted a similar approach to the education of psychotherapists. Early on (at the University of Illinois, 1956–1977) students in the supervised practicum had an introductory course with exposure to the major theories. In the supervised practicum, a seminar (four hours per week) was conducted in which the students were exposed to a client-centered approach, reading Porter (1950), then later Patterson (1959, 1974).

More recently (at the University of North Carolina at Greensboro, 1984–1994), I accepted for supervision only those students who had had my course on client-centered therapy, requiring that they had read *The Therapeutic Relationship* (Patterson, 1985), among others.

In most programs preparing students for the practice of psychotherapy, students are assigned to supervisors without regard to the theoretical orientation of the student or the supervisor. The student may or may not have had a basic theory course with the supervisor. As a result, mismatches are common. This means that the early stages of supervision are taken up with (a) the supervisee trying to learn where his or her supervisor is coming from and (b) the supervisor engaging in teaching or informing the student about his or her approach. The process of supervision is thus slowed considerably.

My approach to supervision
The desirability and advantages of the supervisor and supervisee sharing the same

theoretical basis for psychotherapy have not been adequately recognized. Matarazzo and Patterson (1986) are the only ones to address this issue. They write: 'It appears important for supervisor and supervisee to have a similar theoretical orientation' (p. 838).

My position on this is clear. It is not simply desirable or important, but necessary that the supervisor and supervisee be committed to a theory — and the same theory:

> The supervisor has a commitment to a theory, and the supervisee must
> have at least a tentative commitment to a theory; it should be obvious
> that if learning is to occur, they must be committed to the same
> theory.(Patterson, 1983, p. 22).

The supervisory process
Orientation of the supervisee. Supervisees meet in a group prior to the first individual supervision session. Most recently (1990-1994), a videotape of a published interview (Freeman, 1992) with me on client-centered supervision was shown. This interview provides an orientation to the supervisory process and is followed by discussion with the supervisees. The points made in the interview and the following discussion include the following:
1. As a result of the course, supervisees are familiar with the client-centered therapist conditions of empathic understanding, respect, therapeutic genuineness, and concreteness (Patterson, 1985). Students recognize and accept that these conditions are necessary for therapeutic personality change (Rogers, 1957). The emphasis is that therapy is not a matter of skills, but of basic attitudes; nevertheless, it is necessary that therapists be able to implement these attitudes with clients. Three simple rules for the beginning therapist are emphasized:
   a. The therapist listens, the client talks. Therefore, keep your mouth shut. You can't listen to the client while you are talking.
   b. Never ask a question — unless you don't understand what the client is saying.
   c. Remain in the responsive mode. The client initiates, the therapist follows.
2. It is not expected that supervisees should accept that the therapist conditions are sufficient as well as necessary for therapeutic personality change. It is emphasized that supervisees are expected to test the assumption that they are sufficient. This means that the supervisees are not to depart from these conditions, thus abandoning the assumption, and try other techniques. Although theoretically it may be that the assumption is not correct, supervisees are not prepared to go beyond them. Engaging in other practices would involve the supervisees being irresponsible. As a corollary to this requirement, it is emphasized that the supervisor is responsible for the supervisee's clients, and supervisees are not permitted to experiment on their clients.

   Parenthetically, in my experience during some 35 years of supervision, supervisees have been universally successful in working with clients without going beyond these conditions, often to their surprise when they realize this at the end of the semester.
3. Supervisees are told the criteria by which they will be evaluated. These consist of effectiveness in providing the therapeutic conditions. Knowing these criteria,

supervisees are able to evaluate themselves. Earlier at the University of Illinois, I gave supervisees the option of being evaluated on the basis of an audiotape of a therapy session they submitted at the end of the semester. The tape would be rated by trained raters. No supervisee chose this option to my evaluation.

4. Supervisees were expected to audiotape their sessions, provided their clients agreed to be taped. Clients seldom refused to be taped.

5. In preparation for supervision, supervisees are expected to review their tapes and make notes during the review, including questions they wish to bring into supervision. It is impossible for the supervisor to listen to all of the tape recordings; therefore, supervisees are expected to select tapes and sections of tapes that they wish to work on during supervision. Although it might be expected that supervisees would present their best tapes, this is not the case. They select those tapes and sections of tapes in which they realize they did poorly or were confused about their performance and on which they want help.

These practices allow for the development of a supervisory atmosphere that minimizes threat and anxiety for the supervisee. They provide a structure that facilitates supervisee learning (Freeman, 1993). Because the supervisee knows where the supervisor is coming from — they share the same theoretical system — and has the criteria by which he or she is being evaluated, evaluative comments or statements by the supervisor are practically nonexistent. Supervisees make their own evaluative comments. Similarly, the need for and the amount of feedback from the supervisor are minimized: The supervisee gives him/herself feedback. The stage is set for a relationship that is immediately productive. So-called stages in the process are not present. There is a smooth progression, or supervisee progress.

The actual process
The supervisor provides a client-centered — or supervisee-centered — relationship. He or she is genuine in the process, respects the supervisee, and empathizes with the supervisee's relationship with the client, putting her/himself in the place of the supervisee in the relationship. The supervisee has the responsibility for the supervision process — selecting the taped material to be considered and raising questions, problems or issues.

1. Because the supervisor bears the responsibility for the supervisee's clients and not every tape, or a tape for each client, can be included in the supervisory session, each session begins with the supervisee reviewing each of his or her clients. This may be more, or less, detailed, depending on the client. Also, it is considered important that at least one continuing client is followed in some detail by the supervisor.

2. There is little concern with diagnosing or labeling clients and little if any discussion of personality dynamics. Such an approach views the client as an object to be analyzed and evaluated rather than as a person to be accepted and understood. Supervisees are, however, helped to be sensitive to evidence of severe disturbances or organic problems, as well as indications of conditions that would warrant referral. Such conditions become apparent in the course of a therapy that focuses

on the client's frame of reference and perceptions.

3. The supervisor does not engage in didactic instruction to any great extent because the supervisee has had a course in the theory being practiced. When a question or problem involving an element of the theory or its application arises and it is considered by the supervisor to be an issue of interest or concern to other supervisees, it is brought up for discussion in a group meeting.

4. Supervision is not therapy. Nevertheless, both are interpersonal relationships, and they have some commonalities, as already noted: empathic understanding, respect, and genuineness. But these conditions are implemented somewhat differently. The focus is not on the supervisee's personality or problems, but upon his or her relationship with his or her clients. The supervisee's personality becomes of concern only if it detrimentally affects the therapy. Then it is dealt with only in terms of this situation, that is, the supervisor responds to the difficulty in the supervisee's relationships with his or her clients. Yet because of the overlap in supervision and therapy, 'one should not be surprised to find at times the line between supervision and therapy becomes difficult to determine' (Bonney, 1994, p. 35).

If it becomes apparent that the supervisee's personal adjustment is pervasive and interferes with his or her ability to function as a therapist, psychotherapy should be recommended. In extreme cases, when clients could be hurt, the supervisee should be discontinued from the practicum or internship.

Group meetings. Supervisees meet regularly in a group with the supervisor. Problems, questions, and issues arising in individual sessions are discussed. With the supervisee's permission, sections of tapes may be played. Professional and ethical issues are considered, including record keeping, privileged communication, confidentiality, duty to warn, referrals (e.g., because of suspicion of physiological or neurological conditions or indications of the desirability of medication), and other topics.

Example

The following excerpts are from a supervisory session with a supervisee who was interning at a family service agency. This session took place near the end of the third month of his internship. At the beginning of the semester, he reported that he was to see his first family group (one of those discussed later) that evening and that he was concerned about how to approach it, because he had not had a course in family therapy. I recalled for him what I had said in a brief discussion of family therapy in one of the class sessions in the course he had had with me: The function of the therapist in family therapy (and in group therapy also) is (a) as in individual therapy to listen and respond with empathic understanding and (b) to facilitate each person's understanding of the others in the family or group. If there is evidence that one participant fails to understand, or misunderstands, what another participant has said, respond with 'It seems to me that what he or she was saying was . . .' or 'I heard her or him saying . . .' or a similar response, to help participants to more accurately hear and understand one another. In the group session the next day, he reported with satisfaction that the meeting had gone very well.

In the following excerpt, the supervisee begins immediately without the supervisor (this author) saying anything. He proceeds as usual by reviewing his clients, here in more detail than is often the case, as they are clients that we have followed closely in previous sessions. SEE is the supervisee; SOR is the supervisor. The family consists of mother, father, son, and daughter.

SEE: Well, I had a hard time — as I sat in group yesterday — I was having a hard time sort of recapturing all that's happened in the last week. Let me go through the clients and maybe that will spark fresh memories. [SOR: uhuh] Ahh — I can't remember — did I tell you that the family with the boy who had been running off and making all those disruptive phone calls to his mother at work and at school — he — I guess two weeks ago tomorrow — that would have been after I last saw you — they took him down to the Baptist Adventure Camp.

SOR: Yeah — they were going to do that.

SEE: And that was hard. I talked to the mother that morning. The supervisor of the nursing program she is in had wanted some confirmation that the family was in counseling — she wanted some reassurance before the mother re-enrolled for the spring quarter [SOR: uhuh] and — ah — so I called the mother, as I wasn't going to talk to this woman — she had left a message on the machine — until I had permission from the mother, and in the course of talking to her about that it became apparent that she was pretty emotional about — understandably — about having to take her son off and leaving him somewhere. This was a significant milestone for the family in terms of the family development . . . And I talked to her again on Monday, I guess, and they had taken him down again [to the camp] on Friday, and I'm not sure whether it was Saturday or Sunday that he had run away and — oh — but they had found him and taken him back — and she was going to call that day to find out how he was doing — you know — he had no access to the telephone there. I haven't heard anything more from them. Again I invited her to be in touch if there was a need.

    So — let me get it all straight — the nine-year-old boy I have been seeing where the sexual abuse by his cousin came to light recently. I had a good session with him a week ago . . . [continues reviewing this case, including a meeting with the parents]. You know, it seems to me that ongoing couple's work, or some individual work for the father would be helpful for the boy. I guess I'm not real sure where my role is in broaching all of that. I guess it's still very much a gray area for me as to what my role is, as to sharing my perception — my thoughts about what might be useful. At this point I suspect the father — it seemed early to me to talk with the father about individual work . . .

SOR: Now you're going to continue seeing him twice [a week], then once.

SEE: I think so.

[SEE continues talking about the idea that the boy has an attention-deficit disorder.

There have been no apparent results of treatment with Ritalin.]

SEE: But the mother did report that there had been some significant changes at home in his behavior, especially with homework.

SOR: But you're thinking that at some point you feel that he [the father] could benefit from individual therapy.

SEE: I think so. He described his own depression. Do you have any thought on that, on . . .

SOR: Well, uh, I'm thinking probably that at some point he may focus on himself when they are both there and you might just suggest that he might want to talk about these things without his wife present — then the problem would be whether you could do it. [SEE: uhuh] It's been a kind of a pattern of parent education and it might not be easy to shift for both of you.

SEE: [Goes on to suggest the possibility of the father joining a parent group for male survivors of child abuse, at the agency — the father is such a survivor.] So I think if it came to that I would certainly refer him, rather than trying to do that myself — OK, that feels better. So it appears that things are moving in a positive direction.

[The SEE goes on to review other cases for a considerable period of time. Several families were involved. Then]:

SEE: The 38-year-old woman who is on the tape called me and wanted to know if I could see her that morning. She went to work and was unable to stay, and — ah — said she was feeling like she was going to hurt herself. I was supposed to go to a workshop, but I hesitantly agreed to see her, and did. I think it was the right thing to do — hindsight, the powerful tool that it is, tells me that she probably could have made it without it [the appointment]. But — I didn't know that at the time. [SOR: Yeah.] What I've learned since told me that. She brought her 200 Valium with her, poured them all out on the table during our session. We met for about an hour and a half during which she — ahh — well, it's amazing — I listened to the tape — I listened to part of the tape right after that session. She talked in the session about how up and down she felt. She — the night before — she takes Elavil daily and was prescribed Tranxen to help her sleep. [A psychiatrist monitors her drug treatment.] She had taken four instead of two the night before — said she had taken the four hoping she wouldn't wake up, but had. When she talked about the rapid cycling up and down I wondered if that was a product of the medication [SOR: uhuh] and suggested that we try to get in touch with her psychiatrist to find out whether that might be the case or not. So we did track him down and I talked to him a bit and told him what was going on and then he talked to her briefly, and she told him as she told me that she didn't want to be hospitalized. She had been hospitalized twice — once involuntarily — and she said, she had told me on the phone and she told me before and she told me in the session that she had a gun and that if either of us tried to have the police come and commit her involuntarily that she would have the gun out and she would force the police to kill her — that she wouldn't hurt them, that she would lead them to think that she might and force them to blow her away — to use her term. So she was pretty distraught, certainly. [SOR: uhuh] And by the end of the hour and a half I felt fairly certain that she wouldn't do anything to hurt herself. She called me later in the day — she called me several times during the day. I guess in the session I had talked to her about hospitalization in terms of it being a way for people who — ahh, felt like they might hurt themselves but still had some desire to live, to get help. Well, when she talked to me on the phone in the afternoon, I had an interesting, or what for me was a very illuminating misunderstanding. She almost always speaks in the third person and she said: 'You don't do anything but sit there.' (I had broached the topic of hospitalization again.) And I took that to be a criticism of me — that I didn't do anything in sessions but just sit there — so I responded — as clearly as I can remember — I wrote it down last night when I was listening to the tape, something like 'so you're trying to provoke a different response from me.' And then — I don't think she really understood that — she said: 'No — up there at the hospital you just sit there and watch TV.' So that was very interesting to me. What she was saying was that in the hospital all you do is just sit there — how is that going to help me? But because of where I was coming from I read that [SOR: Yeah, right] as 'you just sit there.'

SOR: She was picturing the hospital and herself.

SEE: So that was very interesting and instructive. And I think my response was a very appropriate one and it did in fact clarify what it was she was talking about. But it was telling me that I was somehow feeling at least mildly attacked or questioned or criticized [SOR: Yeah] and that's the way I read her comment. So she made it through the day. [The SEE then talks for a time about the client calling him frequently on the telephone, sometimes at his home, and discusses the possibility of seeing her twice a week to reduce the phone contacts. Then]:

SOR: Let me express a feeling I have: What about the possibility you're doing something to create a dependency relationship with her?

SEE: Well, I think that has happened.

SOR: Yeah, but whether it is something you have contributed to . . .

SEE: [Pause] Well, I don't know. I mean, I wouldn't rule it out. I don't — I mean she's obviously a very needy woman who has very little [SOR: Yeah] support coming from anywhere else. I guess I would ask you, did you hear specific things [SOR:Well] that made you wonder about that or worry about that?

SOR: I listened to the tape from where you set it on to the end. You're presenting her with two different roles. Part of the time you're responding to her but then part of the time because of your concern about suicide you're taking over and questioning and probing. And these are inconsistent. You're showing this concern about possible suicide — getting a contract. [The SEE had picked this up from another course or his reading.] At one point she said she wouldn't do it — at one point you say: 'Have you been feeling that way lately, that you might use them?' And when she said 'No,' you said 'Good' — showing your own feeling. And I think you may be communicating to her that you're really worried about her — what she might do, what might happen. And I don't say she's manipulating you. But this is a possible reason why people — they talk about a suicide gesture — that she's using these things, talking about — a kind of gesture to get your concern, to get you involved in some way. So that she's becoming dependent rather than independent. I think she's getting two kinds of messages from you.

SEE: Yeah. Yeah. I see that. Uhuh. Well, it's interesting, because in thinking about that now I have felt that and I've — I think in the phone contacts since I haven't seen her since last Tuesday I've been — I've been more limited in my responses.

SOR: Yeah. Not more reassuring, maybe?

SEE: No. I think consciously — because I think the history of all these phone calls has told me as long as I offer that to her she's going to continue to seek it. And if I throw her back on her own resources that she's got more ability to do it than she would want me to think. An example of that being that her husband, from whom she is separated, was arrested for nonpayment of child support — from a previous marriage and she called me and was all teary about — she couldn't get anyone to cosign the bail bond — she was obviously, I think, wanting me to say I would. But I didn't even think of biting on that one — I guess the thing that you're raising the question makes me think more about is, should I have said I would see her today, you know. [SOR: Yeah] Do I need to, from here on out, say there are our scheduled appointment times [SOR: Yeah] particularly if there is a true emergency, there is a crisis response and assessment team at_____ hospital. I think that's what's going to be necessary. I think — I see what you're saying here. I guess what's still unclear to me in a situation where you have someone who is talking about suicide is — uh — morally, ethically, is it sufficient to respond? Is there a responsibility to do more?

SOR: But when you do that you're damaging your relationship.

SEE: Yeah. Then I guess the response is then to know what the potential hazards are if you see a need to do that and make the choice.

SOR: I think people in general — and the current literature and everything — overemphasize the danger. Everybody who talks about suicide isn't going to do it. People who are vulnerable — like you — have got to protect yourselves and I think too easily panic and lose confidence in the client and take over.

SEE: Well, it's certainly been a good experience, working with her — very different than anybody I've ever worked with before, certainly. And has raised this whole realm of boundary questions in a way I haven't had to deal with before. But I think it's caused me to think about what was the cost of intervening in that way at this point, and — ah — I can see in this session too — of this tape — which was a long session with her last Tuesday, that I skated between different roles at that time too.

[There is a period of listening with the supervisee to a portion of a tape with the client. In addition to the difficulty of listening to a tape recording of a tape recording, the client's voice has a childish pitch as a result of a recent experimental treatment for her stuttering, consisting of injection of a substance into her voice box.]

SEE: This tape is very hard to hear. [Tape not audible for a while. SEE then responds to the client.] Therapist is the supervisee: *Therapist: There may be a part of you that wants to open up in the same way but it's been so tight for so long it's hard to accept that change.*

SEE: A little bit of interpretation?

SOR: Yeah. [Client speaks inaudibly.]

SEE: She didn't really respond to it. I couldn't hear what that little bit was. I think she said 'I'm just so tired.' I was seeing it metaphorically, and she just didn't get it.

SOR: Yeah. Well, it seems to me that you have this hypothesis of a multiple personality and you're trying to find something.

SEE: Well, that was it. I was smuggling it in there as [my teaching assistant] would say — to see whether it would turn anything up.

[We continue to listen to the tape though it wasn't possible for the supervisor to hear clearly what the client was saying, partly because of her voice quality. The supervisee's statements were audible, and some of these were commented on by the supervisor.]

Therapist: [to client]: With your voice being different now, do you sound more to yourself like you did when you were little? Younger?

Client: I never thought of that.

SEE: See, hindsight tells me that I could have phrased that — I could have commented on her voice [SOR: Yeah] instead of questioning her about it — towards the same — the same end, or by saying 'Your voice has a childlike quality to it.'

SOR: Yeah, right.

SEE: Even though I'm getting to be a more experienced counselor, I still feel — I guess I feel a lack of an experience base to help me temper expectations — especially with a very different client like this. [SOR: Yeah] I think that uncertainty — I don't know if it's impatience — I guess it is uncertainty as much as anything. [SOR: Yeah] It's part of what has led to my shifting gears and roles.

SOR: Yeah. It's difficult to get in and stay in her field of reference.

SEE: Yeah. At one point during this session she — she was saying 'You can't know what my life has been like.' And I simply said: 'Yes, you're right. I cannot know.' And that's really true. I can be with her, but . . .

SOR: You can try, as far as you can.

SEE: But there's an obvious limit to that.

SOR: There's a limit with everybody, but with some much more than with others.

SEE: I don't have anything else pressing. Do you — any threads that you . . .

SOR: I think this is an interesting case and I see a — I think I have some concern that — uh — the best way to help her is to give her all the responsibility — and yet — you feel you have some responsibility about the pills and the gun and those kind of things. And yet when you show your concern about it — it bothers you — it just communicates to her that this must be serious, and it can lead her without manipulating you, bringing up things like this when she wants your attention, and something from you. And yet in the long run that's not going to help her independence. She's got to take responsibility for everything all the time.

SEE: Yeah.

SOR: I think of _____ 's [a former student] case where for 30 years therapists took responsibility for her — she was hospitalized much of the time — and _____ is giving it all back to her, consistently and completely — with a miraculous change.

SEE: Yeah. Well, I've seen that and what you're noting on this tape really fits with what I've experienced in the past week in dealing with her — and — not seeking to be reassuring.

SOR: Right.

SEE: And I'm seeing more how she can do it for herself.

SOR: Yeah. If you really let her, she can.

SEE: But what's become clear to me in the course of my time here talking about this is that — uh — my seeking to reassure her is probably going to only increase the likelihood that she will lose her job, for example. Now I can't say, as things go on, that she may not lose her ability to — uh — function well enough to hold her job. But neither can I take responsibility for that — but I think what you've pointed out and what I've experienced in the last weeks suggests that — well, to use the codependency lingo, the more I enable her to be irresponsible the more she will be.

SOR: Yeah. As you say, you're setting limits more, and in a real emergency she goes somewhere else. You'll see her twice a week and that's going to be it.

SEE: Because I think what I've seen is the real emergencies — is going to be a crisis that is going to require a response that I am not going to be able to provide anyway.

Well, it's interesting — I don't remember when it was — I remember — saying at some point — and I'd be interested in your response to this — that borderline personalities can eat up a client-centered therapist, and I've been mulling that over. And I guess what I've made of it is that there's an assumption there that — uh — because a client-centered therapist seeks to be responsive you're more apt to be manipulated. And may not set the kind of limits that are necessary — uh . . .

SOR: Yeah. The concept of borderline personality is very popular now — but it's very vague.

SEE: It's a catch-all. [The session closes with a discussion of borderline personalities, or psychopathic personalities as clients.]

Little comment on this excerpt appears to be necessary. It is clear that the supervisee takes responsibility for the session, explores issues and problems, and comes to his own insights and decisions. The supervisor listens, responds, and follows the lead of the supervisee.

The supervisee's perception
The supervisee was interviewed briefly on videotape by Suzanne Freeman, following his viewing of the videotape of her interview with the supervisor (Freeman, 1992). IOR designates the interviewer and IEE the interviewee.

IOR: Can you give us a little information about what your thinking and expectations were before supervision?

IEE: Well, I'd had Dr Patterson for his advanced theories course, so I had developed something of a personal relation with him through that. I think I was intrigued by the notion of being supervised by someone of his experience and background so there was a sense of excitement and anticipation — a little bit of anxiety because I wasn't sure whether his approach would be one which was doctrinaire or whether he would have expectations that I didn't feel able to meet. But I thought of it as an opportunity that I didn't want to pass up, certainly.

IOR: Can you speak to how you felt — did he clarify for you the roles and responsibilities of you as a supervisee and him as a supervisor?

IEE: Yeah. That was really the first thing that he did. I think he refers to that as structuring the relationship. And that was done very clearly and overtly at the start of the semester. It was the only time he did anything of that sort, letting me know what the minimal expectation — letting me know it would be primarily my role to bring things to our supervision and for me to be responsible to determine what these sessions would consist of.

IOR: And, how did that occur — you taking responsibility for the sessions?

IEE: Well, it took the form of me having listened to audiotapes of my sessions, and bringing those, or segments of those, to the actual supervisory sessions. And — uh — making choices about what portions I wanted him to hear. How he was intent on developing an in-depth understanding of at least one of my clients, so that was something that could be built on, session to session. But it also included my bringing questions that I had that came up either in the context of a session [with a client] or about some aspect of counseling that then provided the focus for discussion that came out of that.

IOR: Uhuh. Comment on this idea: If a student is being evaluated in supervision, and a student has the responsibility for what the student brings into the session, then likely the student is going to bring in their very best work. How did that work for you? How did you experience that kind of freedom?

IEE: Well, certainly there is the temptation to want to put a good face on things, but I think it became clear to me very quickly that I wasn't going to learn very much if that was all I did. And my motivation to be the best I could for the clients I was working with ultimately led me to wanting to use Dr Patterson for a time in supervision to figure things out that were posing difficulties or things that represented hard spots for me. So I think I fairly quickly went beyond the urge to present things that would make me look or sound good.

IOR: Can you think of a specific time when you were struggling with a case and you brought the difficulty into the discussion? How was it handled? Did Dr Patterson give you what you should have said, did he ask questions? How did he help you with the specific problem that you brought in?

IEE: Well, I can think of one particular instance where I was — uh — approaching termination with one of my clients and was concerned that I should have been more active in the session than I was, and I was seeking some clarification from Dr Patterson about my perceptions of that, and as he listened to the tape to know of my question around that, for the most part he reflected what it was I was raising and in a sense guided me as I thought about what I was concerned about and why and — uh — he helped me become clearer about what I had done in the session and whether that had been an appropriate response to what the client brought to the session or not.

IOR: Were you aware of the core conditions being present in that supervisory relationship? Empathy, respect . . .

IEE: Uhuh. Very definitely, and I commented to Dr Patterson at the end of the semester that one of the things I found most impressive about the process — and about him as an individual — was the fact that I experienced a high level of congruence between the things that I had heard about in his course and understand about a relationship-based approach to counseling and seeing those things being demonstrated by him in his relationship with me.

IOR: O.K. Now, he says that he divides the didactic role — the teaching role — in one session, and the facilitative role in another session. How did that work for you?

IEE: Well, I think there was very definitely a distinction about how he functioned in those two roles. We had a group process at the same time under way with several of us graduate students and that tended to be more of a — well, to be the time in which didactic processes happened. Dr Patterson would sometimes bring a specific topic to that group or he would respond to one that came out of a question or difficulty that one of us was having. But the time in individual supervision was much more — ahh — responding to what I brought rather than coming with an agenda of his own that he felt I needed to hear about or be part of.

IOR: Uhuh. In those individual sessions would you say that there was therapy going on for you, or would you say that it was therapeutic in some way within the session?

IEE: I think — it was therapeutic for me at different points — ahh — I worked at different things that were issues for me as a becoming counselor. I certainly did not feel that the process was therapy, or conceived as such. That was not my goal or was it his goal — that it be therapy for me. The focus was my clients and me in the process of being helpful to those people.

IOR: Over the semester do you feel that you changed as a counselor because of what went on in supervision?

IEE: Very definitely. I think that really for the first time in the program I felt both an invitation and an expectation to — ahh — submit to a discipline which was represented by the core conditions and the invitation to test the hypothesis whether the conditions were necessary and sufficient in doing psychotherapy with an individual client and — ahh — that discipline was not one that I submitted to easily but I'm grateful to have had the chance to do that, and I see real value in having had that experience, certainly.

IOR: OK Are there any other comments that you would like to make about the experience? Anything that . . .

IEE: Only to say that it really was a very productive experience. Qualitatively different than a previous supervisory experience, to the extent that I did feel a different responsibility placed with me for what the nature and the content of the individual sessions would be — ahh — and that was scary sometimes in the sense that it would have been easier to have been lazy and — ahh — let that revert to Dr Patterson as the supervisor. But I think, especially coming to a point of conclusion in a program, it was important to feel that responsibility and decide what I was going to do with it.

IOR: Thank you very much.

Conclusion

The approach to supervision described here has several advantages:

1. The supervisor and supervisee have a common or shared philosophy and theory of psychotherapy, namely, client-centered theory.
2. The supervisor follows the principles of this system in the supervisory process.
3. The result is a climate or atmosphere in which threat and anxiety are minimized, thus providing an optimum learning situation.
4. The supervisor, in respecting the supervisee, allows the supervisee to direct the sessions by selecting and presenting the materials to be considered by the supervisor.
5. The supervisee knows the criteria by which he or she is being evaluated, thus allowing him or her to apply these criteria in evaluating him- or herself.
6. Supervision begins at a high level, precluding a slow process in which the supervisee must attempt to understand and adapt to the system and criteria of the supervisor. There is no long, drawn-out process of so-called stages in supervision.
7. Although this approach has been designated as client-centered, it is a basic, generic approach. The focus is on elements or conditions commonly recognized as client-

centered, but that are actually elements common to all the major theories. Client-centered therapy does not have a monopoly on these conditions. Students or supervisees are informed that whether or not they eventually decide to continue as client-centered therapists, these elements are necessary in any system they might choose. Other elements can be added from their preferred theory. However, any additions can be, and usually are, inconsistent with client-centered philosophy, and the result is not client-centered therapy.

References

Bernard, J. M., and Goodyear, R. K. (1992) *Fundamentals of clinical supervision*. Boston: Allyn and Bacon.

Bonney, W. (1994) Teaching supervision: Some practical issues for beginning supervisors. *The Psychotherapy Bulletin*, 29 (2), 31–6.

Ford, D. H., and Urban, H. B. (1963) *Systems of psychotherapy*. New York: Wiley.

Freeman, S. (1992) C. H. Patterson on client-centered supervision: An interview. *Counselor Education and Supervision*, 31, 219–26.

Freeman, S. C. (1993) Structure in counseling supervision. *The Clinical Supervisor*, 11 (1), 245–52.

Matarazzo, R. G., and Patterson, D. R. (1986) Methods of teaching therapeutic skill. In S. L. Garfield and A. E. Bergin (Eds.), *Handbook of psychotherapy and behavior change*. (3rd ed., pp. 821–43.) New York: Wiley.

Patterson, C. H. (1959) *Counseling and psychotherapy: Theory and practice*. New York: HarperCollins.

Patterson, C. H. (1964) Supervising students in the counseling practicum. *Journal of Counseling Psychology*, 11, 47–53.

Patterson, C. H. (1974) *Relationship counseling and psychotherapy*. New York: Harper Collins.

Patterson, C. H. (1983) A client-centered approach to supervision. *The Counseling Psychologist*, 11 (1), 21–5.

Patterson, C. H. (1985) T*he therapeutic relationship*. Pacific Grove, CA: Brooks/Cole.

Patterson, C. H. (1992) The education of counselors and psychotherapists: A proposal. *Asian Journal of Counseling*, 2 (1), 81–8.

Patterson, C. H. (1995) A universal system of psychotherapy. *The Person-Centered Journal*, 2 (1), 54–62.

Patterson, C. H., and Hidore, S. (1996) *Successful psychotherapy: A caring, loving relationship*. Northvale, NJ: Jason Aronson.

Patterson, C. H., and Watkins, C. E., Jr. (1996) *Theories of psychotherapy*. (5th ed.) New York: HarperCollins.

Porter, E. H., Jr. (1950) *An introduction to therapeutic counseling*. Boston: Houghton Mifflin.

Rogers, C. R. (1957) The necessary and sufficient conditions of therapeutic personality change. *Journal of Consulting Psychology*, 21, 95–103.

Outcomes in Counselor Education 22

Counselor education involves more than the imparting of facts and information. Counsellors must develop a philosophy and a system of beliefs. Natiello (1986, p. 342), in discussing the continued development of the theory and application of client-centered therapy, cited the need for 'more effective training programs, integrating theoretical and experiential learning'. Combs (1986, pp. 74–7) emphasizes the importance of counsellor beliefs in counsellor education. Again, in another place, Combs (1988, p. 267) writes: 'If counsellors, like their clients, behave in terms of their belief systems, the acquisition of trustworthy belief systems must become a prime objective of educational programs. The task of training must be seen as a problem in personal becoming rather than the traditional "how to" concept.' Thayer (1987) has presented a detailed statement of an introductory course in counsellor education touching on this problem.

For the past six years I have been teaching a course titled 'Advanced Theories of Counselling/Phenomenological'. There are two texts for the course (Patterson, 1985, 1986), with an assignment in Rogers' *On Becoming a Person* (Rogers, 1961, Part II). I meet with the students for three hours every other week (a total of 24 hours). A doctoral student meets with them in alternate weeks, providing paper-and-pencil exercises, tapes and films and discussion. There is no experiential group or skill training components, as in Thayer's (1987) course. For the first three years, Nil Moore was the co-instructor; currently it is Suzanne Freeman.

Cain (1986, p. 373) suggests that if we are to learn from our student 'teachers', we must encourage our students to disclose their learnings to us. At the end of the semester, our students are asked (as a 'take home' examination) to respond to two questions: 'What, if anything, have you learned from this course? Will it make any difference in your personal or professional life?' Several unedited responses follow, with the permission of the students.

Karen C. Havens
I do not know whether adults naturally grow psychologically and spiritually the way a child grows physically, but four years ago I began a journey that has turned

First published in the *Asian Journal of Counselling*, 2, 1, pp. 81–7. Reprinted with permission.

out to be one of the most intense and significant growing spurts of my life. It began, seemingly, unintentionally. It is difficult to pinpoint the exact time that my mind began to expand; slowly at first, and then accelerating; turning inward and outward all in the same breath in an effort to explore new territory. This growth is psychological and spiritual, which are two aspects of my being that seem inseparable. Psychological development, as I perceive it, implies a spiritual evolution as well. I slowly began to search for a better, broader way of seeing things; towards a way of being and thinking that would provide more fertile ground for my psychological and social development. I searched for an approach to life that would maximize the quality of my existence and interactions with others. I am not sure what precipitated this journey but I remember a gnawing at my spirit about attitudes, behaviors, and social interactions that I both personally experienced and observed in other people. I began to experience a dawning awareness of incongruity between how I felt living should be approached and conducted and what I perceived was actually happening in my life and the lives of others. Perhaps wanderlust triggered the journey; wanderlust for the age-old quest for goodness, rightness, and abundant living. Then again, maybe I had an urge for what is referred to as self-actualization. I am not sure. But apparently, just below conscious awareness, I knew something was not right. Something was out there wanting me to discover it. This 'something' involved me and other people, and I meant to find it.

Feelings of restlessness accompanied this journey because of my awareness that certain attitudes, behaviors, and social interactions tended to bind human spirits and cause needless trouble, anxiety, and confusion in social interactions. Furthermore, I felt that there existed an approach to life guided by principles which freed human spirits; an approach girded by attitudes and philosophies that created arable environments for maximum human functioning and happiness. The restlessness was compounded by my inability to identify and define misalignments I continued to experience in my own life and observe in the lives of others. I could point out attitudes, behaviours, specifically identify why I did not like them or what was wrong about them. I felt the need to specifically identify these dislikes and flaws. I wanted to start intentionally steering myself away from damaging and suppressive attitudes, behaviors, and interactions. I felt that my navigation was, and would continue to be, a hit-and-miss proposition until I could discern harmful characteristics in social and psychological functioning. Oddly enough, what I needed, as I discovered later, were words. Words, and their respective definitions, which clarify and distinguish harmful and beneficial elements in attitudes, behaviors, and social interactions.

It has often seemed strange and interesting to me — and sometimes rather spooky — how and when answers come; and even what form they take. The words and definitions that I needed to identify and define the misalignments I had sensed came to me — unexpectedly and timely — in this course. They explained the incongruity I felt between how I thought living should be approached and conducted and what I perceived was actually happening. They created a clear distinction in my mind between harmful and beneficial elements in psychological and social functioning. They calmed my restlessness.

Those words and definitions represent the concepts and principles of Rogerian theory. They describe three core conditions — empathic understanding, respect, and genuineness — which I believe are necessary conditions for an approach to life that frees human spirits and creates arable environments for maximum human functioning, happiness, and actualized human potential. I also believe that these core conditions can eliminate much psychological and social pathology.

I can now *intentionally* navigate psychologically and socially to change what I want to change in myself. I can provide what I want to provide to others more effectively. I can also go where I want to go more expediently; without it being a hit-and-miss proposition. There are, of course, many aspects of empathic understanding, respect, and genuiness that I will continue to define throughout my life. At least I now know *what to refine*. I know what to work toward to provide the best possible psychological world for myself and others. I can continue my journey; but with a compass.

Significant learnings — Kathy Gramley
As I consider the way this course has changed my life, it may be the counseling relationship which is the critical issue and how I feel about its importance for the success of therapy. Carl Rogers expressed my feelings and fears perfectly in *On Becoming A Person*, when he said in his early professional years, he was asking the question, 'How can I treat, or cure, or change this person?' Those are the same questions which have been going over and over in my mind as I have been doing my internship and approaching the completion of my degree and actually 'doing' counselling. After years of experience Rogers said a better question is, 'How can I provide a relationship which this person may use for his or her own personal growth?' This same question is one we could ask concerning all human relationships, not just counselling relationships. This type of relationship which enables the other person to discover within herself or himself the capacity to grow, change and develop is effective in marriage, parenting, friendship, the work environment and in organizational work. This approach can be useful in international understanding and conflict resolution, as Carl Rogers demonstrated. Now I know counselling isn't anything I do, it is something I am, or hope to be — caring, empathic and congruent.

When writing about the significant learnings I have acquired in this course, I am taking the freedom to define 'significant learnings' as those learnings which I feel will be significant for me — those learnings which I feel will influence my counselling.

In the theories course which I took two semesters ago, it was the client-centered approach which seemed to say all those things about people and counseling which I believed. Among the things I like about the client-centered approach is that self-actualization, a common goal of all people, is the ultimate goal of counselling. An individual has within himself or herself the capacity and the tendency, latent if not evident, to move toward that self-actualization. I selected this course in order to gain a better understand of Carl Rogers' way of counselling. My most significant learnings are things I have learned about the client-centered approach.

• I have learned that providing the core conditions for a facilitative interpersonal relationship can be difficult.

• I have learned that diagnosis is necessary when using the client-centered approach only to determine whether the client's emotional disturbance is psychological and if it can be helped by psychotherapy.

• I have learned that assessment in the client-centered approach should benefit the client and not focus on what the counsellor can do to the client.

• I have learned that the client-centered approach can be used for cross-cultural counselling.

• I have learned that a facilitative interpersonal relationship is not only necessary, but is the sufficient condition for positive personality and behavior change.

• I have learned that not only change, but the amount of personality or behavior change, is dependent on the degree to which the counsellor is able to provide the core conditions (empathy, respect and genuineness) for the therapeutic relationship.

In conclusion, I think learning about 'The Therapeutic Relationship: Formulations for an Eclectic Psychotherapy', was significant because I have a feeling it will be my 'handbook' for counselling. Thank you, Dr Patterson.

This semester I 'sat at the feet' of the renowned and client-centered professor and writer, Dr C. H. Patterson, who has been described as more Rogerian than Carl Rogers. This was my reason for taking the course. I entered this path in my life too late to hear Carl Rogers in person, and am grateful for this opportunity to experience the next best thing!

Changes and insights — Rudell A. Lawrence
In thinking about some of the changes that have taken place in me over the duration of this course and as a result of this course, they have not been dramatic nor earthshaking, but subtle, gentle and comfortable.

This course was a beautiful experience to have, especially since it was not expected. The course has helped me become less didactic, less fearful, and more trusting in my dealings with my grown children. I am not yet at a place where I am doing internships in the program, but I find that the philosophical basis of the phenomenological approach embraced by our professor can be used almost like a blueprint for living one's everyday life, and given a true change, the rewards can be very satisfactory. Before, I found it difficult not to rush into situations my children were dealing with, and try to make it better. Now, I restrain myself and let them handle their own lives, as I can now allow myself to trust that they can. This is not an easy thing for me at all because I have a strong nurturing personality. The nurturing part of me has gone through a change also. It is evolving from the sympathetic to the empathetic which will allow me to be a more beneficial counsellor. This course has helped me to understand that entering another's frame of reference and listening to them is much more helpful than saying, 'I know how you feel,' and trying to do something about a situation myself. By listening, this enables another to take actions to come to their own resolutions. I now believe the only lasting real fix comes from within the person themselves, and cannot be accomplished from without. The kind of counsellor I would have become without this course would have been an entirely different one. So I can honestly say that this has not only changed me in the present but will have lasting effects on the way I conduct myself professionally in the future. Sort of a future change. I probably would have been more of the teaching, directing kind of counsellor without having taken this course. My future clients thank you.

Besides the beneficial changes in me and my relationships, I feel it has been a pleasure and an honor to have been a part of this class. I know we have been fortunate in having Dr C.H. Patterson for our professor, and I will always count myself fortunate to have been present to hear what he had to say and to tape a great deal of it to listen to later.

I have learned, most importantly, that if in one's relationships and dealing with other people we treat them as capable, valuable, responsible, and trustworthy, that the majority of the time our beliefs will be confirmed. I have also learned what a personally freeing philosophy the person-centered counselling approach really is. One of the things that kind of put me off from the profession was that I thought I must take responsibility for the lives or problems of clients; now that I believe they must take responsibility for their own lives, choices, and actions, I believe I will be of far greater service and help to them without carrying an unbearable burden.

I can truly say the most significant thing that I have learned in this course is that a warm, accepting, and caring relationship is the most helpful, curative, beneficial and healing thing of all. I think it took a while for this to really sink in, and I think it is truly remarkable that this is true. I will always wonder at it, it was a wonderful discovery. Thank you for the rest of my life.

These may not be the kinds of significant learnings you might have been asking about, for they are not necessarily book learnings. We have surely been exposed to many different theories. But, these were the most important learnings to me because they were truly personalized internally, they are the kind of learnings that last. That was one of the significant things about this course. We really acquired something special, a philosophy to guide our lives.

*What I have learned and how it affects my personal and professional life —
Darlene Hopkins*
The learning that took place, for me, in C.H. Patterson's course in counselling theories was phenomenal. I am not exaggerating when I say that I cannot remember a single course where I learned more. I learned about several counselling theories. I learned names and approaches to associate with them. I feel that I can converse about various theories with confidence in my familiarity with them. This learning took place from my reading, from the discussions and films in the class, and from the lectures.

I learned the differences between the various theories. I learned that some methods of psychotherapy focus on cognition, some on behavior, and some on affect. I learned about the disagreements in the profession over the best way to work with a client. Of much more importance than the differences between the theories is what I learned about their similarities.

I believe that, in this course, I learned what makes psychotherapy work. I gained a real understanding of what Carl Rogers' core conditions are and why they are the foundation of every psychotherapy that helps people function better. I now understand the theory behind client-centered counselling and I am now familiar with the research that supports it.

I wrote a paper for the class, in which I explored the similarities between Jungian psychotherapy and Rogerian psychotherapy. I didn't start out looking for similarities when reading *A Way of Being* by Rogers and *Memories, Dreams and Reflections* by Jung. I read the writings of both therapists just to be familiar with them, but I was struck again and again by how Jung practiced the core conditions in his therapy. Since then, in reading about other approaches, I see the similarity. It seems to me that psychotherapy is effective to the extent that it incorporates the core conditions. This learning, that the core conditions are what makes psychotherapy work, is of immense value to me as a counsellor. I want to be the best counsellor I can be and I now know that to the extent that I develop my ability to be empathetic, warm, accepting, and genuine, my ability to enter the perceptual world of the client — I will be effective. I want to learn as much about human behavior as I possibly can, I want to know what other therapists have done with other clients that seemed to help. But, I know that such knowledge is not what will make my therapy helpful; it is my capacity to form therapeutic relationships that will be effective.

This philosophy of counselling says three important things: that people grow and heal when they have unconditional acceptance, that you can trust the actualizing tendency in people to draw them toward health, and that each individual's perception of the world is unique and totally valid for that person. If I accept those things for my counselling practice, and I do, then I have to realize that they are no less true in my personal life. Embracing this philosophy, changes the way I relate to other people. I am the mother of teenaged daughters. Relating to them as if I believed that their perceptions and feelings are valid, and that they can be trusted to develop into healthy adults, and treating them with unconditional positive regard, is a challenge which I face on a daily basis. I know that I will be an effective mother to the extent that I am able to treat them this way.

My experience in this course has been extremely valuable to me, both professionally and personally. I have gained academic knowledge and I have gained knowledge that enriches my personal life, as well.

Personal learnings — David John Bergen
I have a personal belief that true learning does not really involve facts and theories at all, but symbolizes a way of living. Certainly one must acquire information about the world and oneself, yet true learning is how we process this information and what we do with it. It is also my belief that there are two types of classes. One type of class is a means to an end, such as credit towards a degree. In the other type of class the means is the end. Our class is this second type and has been full of true learning for me. I could write down all the bits of information I got from

the books, but then what would that tell you? I have enjoyed the readings and am looking forward to spending more time with the eclectic psychotherapy book over Christmas. I want to include within this paper the process I have gained from the stimulations I received in both classes, yours and Suzanne's. Process is difficult to objectify and put on paper, but I will try.

I leave our time together with a greater sense of who I am as a counsellor. During my Master's program I was inundated with theoretical foundations that offer tremendous cognitive appeal, but did little in my work with clients. In fact, I rejected all schools of therapy and did what I felt was the most facilitative with the client. It was through this process that I came to consider myself client-centered in approach. This is also my approach to life. Life to me is relationships with others and it has taken me a long time to begin to be able to develop these connections. Counselling has facilitated my process toward full functioning while I was able to enable someone else. We learn together. I have gained a new clarity in my observations of myself in working with clients. It is through this process that I am able to develop and grow and become more effective as a facilitator.

I am very aware of the rare moments when I leave a class with things to reflect upon and to process with myself. This class has offered me these rare and valued gifts which I take hungrily. I felt as though each week built upon the previous one and that the road of discovery travels in all directions with no ends that are beyond choice. We do control our destiny and are able to face the forks in the road. Sometimes we need support as we travel along the path and in time we are not only able to walk alone, but can support someone else. It is a gift that you can give to others while also keeping it for yourself.

The philosophies that we discussed in class represent a lifestyle that I continually work to achieve, both personally and professionally. The issue of responsibility has been the most difficult for me to process. As I move through life, I catch myself assuming responsibility for those who are able to assume this by themselves. I work toward allowing them to be who they are, as I do for myself. It is not easy, but I am more able to let go both of them and myself. And as I am able to let go, I get even closer.

I want to express so much, but the words get in the way. I take much from the class and am truly sad it is over. I do not say this about my other classes! You both carry messages that a lot of people are not ready for or are unable to hear. I am sure that I have missed many. My point here is that I have heard quite a few and thank you for them, the others will come to me later. You have given me the gift that keeps on giving as the value you have for it increases. Thanks again.

References

Cain, D. (1986) On learning from our 'teachers'. *Person-Centered Review,* 3, 371–4.

Combs, A.W. (1986) Person-centered assumptions for counsellor education. *Person-Centered Review*, 1, 72–82.

Combs, A.W. (1988) Some current issues for person-centered therapy. *Person-Centered Review,* 3, 263–76.

Natiello, P. (1986) Roundtable discussion. *Person-Centered Review,* 1, 342.

Nelson-Jones, R., and Patterson, C.H. (1976) Effects of counselor training: Further findings. *British Journal of Guidance and Counselling,* 4, 66–3.

Patterson, C.H. (1969) Effects of counsellor education on personality. *Journal of Counselling Psychology,* 14, 444–8.

Patterson, C.H. (1985) *The therapeutic relationship.* Pacific Grove, CA: Brooks/ Cole.

Patterson, C.H. (1986) *Theories of counselling and psychotherapy* (4th ed.). New York: Harper and Row.

Rogers, C.R. (1961) *On becoming a person.* Boston: Houghton Mifflin.

STILL RELEVANT – STILL REVOLUTIONARY [SPECIAL INVITED RETROSPECTIVE REVIEW]

23

Carl R. Rogers
Counseling and Psychotherapy: Newer Concepts in Practice
Boston: Houghton Mifflin, 1942. 450 pp.

Carl R. Rogers
Client-Centered Therapy: Its Current Practice,
Implications, and Theory
Boston: Houghton Mifflin, 1951. 560 pp.

Carl R. Rogers
On Becoming a Person: A Therapist's View of Psychotherapy
Boston: Houghton Mifflin, 1961. 429 pp.

This review will consist of four parts. The first three will each consider one of the books under review. The fourth will be a concluding statement.

Counseling and Psychotherapy

I first saw this book in 1942 or 1943 when I was a psychological assistant in the Air Force. I remember a psychoanalytically oriented colleague remarking that Rogers was nothing but a country hick. I did not read the book until 1946, just before a short course with Rogers and his staff at the University of Chicago, in preparation for a position with the Veterans Administration as a Personal Counselor, a title which later became Counseling Psychologist.

The book grew out of Rogers's experience in Rochester and his first year at Ohio State. Although Rogers claimed no credit for the 'newer concepts', his systematization and his experiential and research support of them constitutes a revolution in counseling and psychotherapy (the terms are used interchangeably). It turned upside down the concept of the therapist as an expert, solving the client's problems, or leading the client to (the therapist's) solutions, while the client remained a passive participant. The term *nondirective* specifies the role of the

First published in *Contemporary Psychology,* 1996, 11, pp. 759–62. Reprinted by permission of the American Psychological Association.

therapist. The client was responsible for the process, as well as its goal or outcomes. This reversal was responsible for jokes and stories, particularly among instructors in undergraduate psychology courses — some of which still persist. An apocryphal story circulated in the late 1940s as a parody of nondirective counseling. Rogers, it was said, was counseling a client high-up in an office building.

> Client: I feel terrible.
> Rogers:You feel terrible.
> Client: I really feel terrible.
> Rogers: You really feel terrible.
> Client: For two cents I'd jump out that window.
> Rogers: For two cents you'd jump out that window.
> Client: (getting up and going to the window) Here I go!
> Rogers: (getting up and going to the window): There you go!
> [Another line was apparently added later. The client hits the ground with a 'plop' sound.]
> Rogers: Plop.

This story includes a basic hypothesis or assumption of non-directive counseling, along with a misconception of its practice. This hypothesis states that human beings have within themselves the potential and capability to challenge and grow; therapy frees the individual for normal growth and development. The misconception is that the therapist does nothing but repeat what the client says, or, as it is usually stated, *reflects* the client's statements. Nondirective therapy is characterized by the technique of reflection. But nowhere does Rogers use the word; it is not indexed in the book. The terms Rogers uses are acceptance, recognition, response to and *clarification* of feelings. The objective is to encourage expression of feelings and attitudes by the client. Thus, though the book is usually thought to focus on techniques, they are secondary to, and implementations of, counselor permissiveness, warmth, and understanding, designed to enable the client to release and express feelings.

The book was unique in its time in the recognition of the need for research and the introduction of research findings in support of the practices it described. Early in the book Rogers refers to the need for 'hypothetical formulations' derived from experience, to be put to test (p. 16). The book, he states,

> endeavors to formulate a definite and understandable series of hypotheses . . . which may be tested and explored (pp. 16–7).

This theme pervades all of Rogers's writings. The basic hypothesis or definition of counseling is that a free and permissive relationship allows the client to develop an understanding and acceptance of self and to take self-initiated positive actions. The book is also unique in the use of many examples taken from recorded interviews and the inclusion of the first complete transcription of an actual therapy case. The case of Herbert Bryan consists of 176 pages of eight complete interviews, with comments by Rogers. The therapist is anonymous. but it was most certainly Rogers himself.

Counseling and Psychotherapy was not enthusiastically received. Psychotherapy and counseling were dominated by psychoanalysis or the Minnesota (directive) point of view. It is amazing how current and relevant the book is today. Yet there is currently an increase in directive methods of psychotherapy, while paradoxically, medicine is moving toward less invasive procedures. The book could well be used as an introductory text today.

Client-Centered Therapy

This book represents an advance over *Counseling and Psychotherapy* in several respects. It replaces the term *nondirective* with *client-centered*, a term that occurs some dozen times in the earlier book as an alternative to nondirective. The latter still occurs occasionally in *Client-Centered Therapy*. There is no discussion of the reasons for this change, which was present in articles during the 1940s (e.g. Rogers, 1946).

The focus of the approach is changed from techniques to attitudes, a term used occasionally in the earlier book. The basic attitude is a philosophical orientation characterized by a deep respect for the individual and his or her right to and capacity for self-direction. Techniques are implementations of this attitude. The core implementation is empathy, by which the therapist enters the client's frame of reference — the client's world as it were. Empathy is a manifestation of acceptance, respect, and trust and confidence in the client, developing a relationship that is the essence of therapy.

Rogers emphasizes that this relationship is a hypothesis that is tested with each client. It is posed as an 'if-then' statement: If certain therapist attitudes are present and perceived by the client, then certain client responses and behaviors result.

The movement away from techniques is seen in the differences between the case of Bryan and excerpts in *Client-Centered Therapy*. Rogers quotes from his 1946 article recognizing 'the subtle directiveness' in the case of Bryan.

A long chapter on the process of therapy, with excerpts from therapy sessions and references to research, culminates in a brief statement of a theory of the therapy process. The process is essentially one of changes in the client's perception of and attitudes toward the self, or the self-concept, leading to a reorganization of the self. Changes in perception lead to changes in behavior. A nonthreatening relationship makes these changes possible.

There is a brief consideration of transference, diagnosis, and the applicability of client-centered therapy. Simply stated,

> transference as a problem doesn't arise; diagnosis is regarded as
> unnecessary, and client-centered therapy is applicable to all cases
> (p. 198).

Countertransference is not mentioned. However, in the earlier discussion of the therapist's functioning it is stated that where the therapist is nonevaluative and operates from the frame of reference of the client, where the therapist endeavors to keep himself out, as a separate person, and where his whole endeavor is to understand the other so completely that he becomes almost an alter ego of the client, personal distortions and maladjustments are much less likely to occur (p. 42).

A chapter on the training of counselors and therapists describes a short-term program for the Veterans Administration and the then current doctoral program at the University of Chicago. Today's instructors might profit from this chapter.

The book ends with a 50-page chapter on 'A Theory of Personality and Behavior'. Nineteen propositions are stated as assumptions or hypotheses. It is a phenomenological theory. The self and the self-concept are central; the theory has been designated as self-theory. A more extended and formal statement of a theory of personality, interpersonal relationships, and of therapy and personality change appears in Koch's *Psychology: A Study of a Science* (Rogers, 1959).

Three chapters on applications of client-centered therapy beyond individual psychotherapy are included: a chapter on play therapy by Elaine Dorfman, on group therapy by Nicholas Hobbs, and on leadership and administration by Thomas Gordon. There is also a chapter on student-centered teaching by Rogers. Rogers later published books on education (Rogers, 1969, 1983) and groups (1970).

As in *Counseling and Psychotherapy,* material from recorded interviews is interspersed throughout, as well as comments on their therapy by clients, including the comments of one client following each of eight interviews. The excerpts and the comments on them provide an understanding of the therapy not possible from a didactic exposition. Although there are no reports of actual research, research evidence is repeatedly referred to. And as in the earlier book, Rogers repeatedly emphasizes that his statements and conclusions are tentative. As was stated about the earlier book, *Client-Centered Therapy* is relevant for psychotherapy today.

On Becoming a Person

Unlike the other two books, this is a collection of 21 papers, published and unpublished, written between 1951 and 1961. The papers go beyond psychotherapy and include teaching, family life, interpersonal relationships, persons and science, and the place of the person in the behavioral sciences.

The book opens with a piece titled, 'This Is Me', that is a brief autobiographical statement of Rogers's personal and professional development, in which it becomes clear that his interpersonal relationships replicated or mirrored his professional relationships with his clients.

The chapter dealing with psychotherapy reiterates the conditions of a good therapeutic relationship. Though considered in various chapters, they do not become repetitive: There are nuances in each. They fill out in considerable detail the therapist attitudes and the process and outcomes of client-centered therapy. The attitudes are not only effective in psychotherapy but in all human relationships, including marriage, parenting, teaching, and administration. Excerpts from therapy sessions are frequent. Research evidence is referred to or cited, with cautions about the tentative nature of the findings.

The if-then nature of the therapy process is stated in various forms. For example:
> When I hold in myself the kind of attitudes I have described, and
> when the other person can to some degree experience the attitudes,
> then I believe that change and constructive personal development
> will invariably occur — and I include the word 'invariably' only
> after long and careful consideration (p. 35).

The excerpts and comments focus on the therapy process and the client's experience of it. But the therapist is also there and emerges as an awesome person.

Concluding remarks

Rereading the three books made me think about Rogers as a person and his place, and that of client-centered therapy, in psychology and psychotherapy today and in the future.

Rogers was a very modest person. He not only would not impose any beliefs, values, or solutions on his clients, but also not on his students, readers, and colleagues. His statements were cautious, tentative, proposed as hypotheses. He wrote that: 'there can be no closed system of beliefs, no unchanging set of principles which I hold . . . There is no closed system of beliefs or set of principles which I would encourage others to have or hold' (1961, p. 2). In the education of therapists he stated: 'The first step in training client-centered therapists is to drop all concern as to the orientation with which the student will emerge' (1961, p. 432).

Yet it is clear that Rogers did have a philosophy, convictions, and beliefs that, although not closed or unchanging, did guide his life and his practice of psychotherapy. His emphasis always was that it was his way of doing therapy. But he was deeply concerned about the effects of his therapy on his clients. At a workshop in a Wisconsin state hospital, three psychotherapists interviewed the same patient. Following the third interview, by Rogers, he commented in the discussion:
> Most of the time, especially in a discussion during a workshop of
> this sort, I can really let other people have their own way of working
> with people and realize, 'Sure, they're working in their own way'.
> Then it's surprising how deeply I feel in an actual specific situation
> how much of a partisan I have become (Rogers, 1958).

Then, after commenting critically on the approach of the other two interviewers, he said, 'And my feeling is, there's an in-between kind of way. And curiously enough, it happens to be the way I work' (Rogers, 1958).

Rogers was unusual, if not unique, in the extent to which he combined being a therapist with being a researcher. His experience as a therapist led to hypotheses that were the bases for the great amount of research conducted by himself, his students, and his colleagues. In the chapter 'Persons or Science' (1961, p. 200), he refers to his ' "double life" of subjectivity and objectivity' and explores these dual roles, attempting to integrate them.

The if-then relationship between the therapist-provided conditions and therapy outcomes recurs several times in Rogers's books. One statement reads as follows: 'We have established by external control, conditions which we predict will be followed by internal control by the individual' (1961, p. 397). This sounds like a statement by a behaviorist. It occurs in a chapter based on Rogers's statement in a debate with Skinner at the American Psychological Association Convention in 1956. Implicit in it is the basis for reconciling behavioral psychology with humanistic psychology. The difference is in goals. The conditions are stimuli for 'behavior which is essentially free' (1961, p. 398). They are also reinforcers for the in-therapy behaviors of the client.

There is a paradox in the esteem in which Rogers is held and his current influence in the field of psychotherapy. Kirschenbaum and Henderson (1989) make the following statements:

> A pioneering psychotherapist . . . the most influential psychologist in American history . . . he carried out and encouraged more scientific research in counseling and psychotherapy than had ever been undertaken anywhere . . . more than any individual he was responsible for the spread of counseling and psychotherapy beyond psychiatry and psychoanalysis to all the helping professions — psychology, social work, education, ministry, lay therapy and others (p. xi).

Client-Centered Therapy and *On Becoming A Person* are still in print and widely read. Rogers was listed (no. 54) among the 75 authors who must be read (Writer's Digest, 1995). His books are read by nonprofessionals and have been translated into a dozen languages, yet they are no longer required reading in programs in clinical and counseling psychology. Kirschenbaum and Henderson (1989, p. xiii) note that Rogers's work 'is not held in high esteem in academic settings'. A student desiring to learn to practice client-centered therapy would be unable to find a program where it would be possible, though there are a few places where a course is available. There is more interest in client-centered therapy in other countries — Europe, South America, Japan — than in the United States.

In the 1985 Phoenix Conference on the Evolution of Psychotherapy (Zeig, 1987), Rogers received a five-minute standing ovation, the only person so honored. Yet there is no evidence of his influence in the presentations of the other participants. In the *History of Psychotherapy* edited by Freedheim (1993), there is a chapter on client-centered therapy (by Zimring and Raskin), but only 17 references to Rogers. In a special issue of the *Journal of Psychotherapy* on 'The Future of Psychotherapy' (Norcross, 1992), consisting of 21 papers, there is not a single reference to Rogers.

When one reads — or rereads — these books it becomes clear that the system of therapy they present is revolutionary. It is directly opposed to the current approaches to psychotherapy. The statement of a graduate student in a meeting at which Rogers spoke is still relevant:

> I spent three years in graduate school learning to be an expert in clinical psychology. I learned to make diagnostic judgments. I learned the various techniques of altering the subjects' attitudes and behavior. I learned subtle modes of manipulation, under the labels of

interpretation and guidance. Then I began to read your material, which upset everything I had learned. You were saying that the power rests not in my mind but in his organism. You completely reversed the relationship of power and control which had been built up in me over three years (Rogers, 1977, p. 3).

Yet its philosophy, theory, clinical evidence, and research evidence are compelling. The research evidence accumulated over a period of some 50 years has been resisted, even rejected. There is some evidence that this negative evaluation is changing. The most recent review (Beutler, Machado, and Neufeldt, 1994, p. 259) concluded that:

consistent evidence exists to support the assertion (now almost a 'truism') that a warm, supportive therapeutic relationship facilitates therapeutic success . . . Research in this area continues to be strong.

In his classic article on the necessary and sufficient conditions of therapeutic personality change, Rogers (1957) wrote:

It is not stated that these six conditions are the essentials of client-centered therapy, and that other conditions are essential for other types of psychotherapy . . . My aim in stating this theory is to state the conditions which apply to any situation in which constructive change occurs, whether we are thinking of classical psychoanalysis, or any of its modern offshoots, or Adlerian therapy, or any other (p. 101).

Beutler, Machado, and Neufeldt (1994, p. 244) wrote: 'Collectively the quality of the therapeutic relationship, by its various terms, has consistently been found to be a central contributor to therapeutic progress. Its significance traverses theoretical schools, theory-specific concepts, and diversity of measurement procedures.' The necessary and sufficient conditions of Rogers are the common elements in all approaches to psychotherapy. Immersing oneself in the work of Rogers leads to the conviction that this system of psychotherapy must eventually become the treatment for psychosocial disturbances. Rogers was — and still is — beyond the times.

The rereading of these books after some 35–50 years was a humbling experience. I discovered that some of my ideas that I had thought were original were present in Rogers's writings. This led to the realization that other writers, including myself, have added little of significance to these classics.

References

Beutler, L. E., Machado, P. P. P., and Neufeldt, S. A. (1994) Therapist variables. In A. E. Bergin and S. L. Garfield (Eds.), *Handbook of psychotherapy and behavior change* (4th ed., pp. 229–69). New York: Wiley.

Freedheim, D. K. (Ed.) (1993) *History of psychotherapy*. Washington, DC: American Psychological Association.

Kirschenbaum, H., and Henderson, V. M. (Eds.) (1989) *The Carl Rogers reader*. Boston, MA: Houghton Mifflin.

Norcross, J. C. (Ed.) (1992) *The future of psychotherapy* (Special issue). Psychotherapy, 29 (1), 1–158.

Rogers, C. R. (1946) Significant aspects of client-centered therapy. *American Psychologist*, 1, 415–22.

Rogers, C. R. (1957) The necessary and sufficient conditions of therapeutic personality change. *Journal of Consulting Psychology*, 21, 95–103.

Rogers, C. R. (Speaker) (1958) Interview with Loretta (Tape No. 1). American Academy of Psychotherapists Tape Library.

Rogers, C. R. (1959) A theory of therapy, personality and interpersonal relationships, as developed in the client-centered framework. In S. Koch (Ed.), *Psychology: A study of a science. Study 1: Conceptual and systematic. Vol. 3: Formulations of the person and the social context.* (Pp. 184–256.) New York: McGraw-Hill.

Rogers, C. R. (1969) *Freedom to learn: A view of what education might become.* Columbus, OH: Charles Merrill.

Rogers, C. R. (1970) *Carl Rogers on encounter groups.* New York: Harper and Row.

Rogers, C. R. (1977) *On personal power: Inner strength and its revolutionary impact.* New York: Delacorte Press.

Rogers, C. R. (1983) *Freedom to learn for the 80s.* Columbus, OH: Charles Merrill.

Zeig, J. K. (Ed.) (1987) *The evolution of psychotherapy.* New York: Brunner/Mazel.

WINDS OF CHANGE FOR CLIENT-CENTERED COUNSELING

24

The winds of change they are a-blowing. Client-centered counseling should be growing.

The winds of change are blowing on client-centered counseling (among others, Cain, 1986, 1989a, 1989b, 1989c, 1990; Combs, 1988; Sachse, 1989; Sebastian, 1989). In the three years following the death of Carl Rogers, many were expressing dissatisfaction with 'traditional' or 'pure'client-centered counseling and were engaged in trying to supplement it, extend it, and modify it. The basic complaint seems to be that the counselor conditions specified by Rogers (1957) are not sufficient. Tausch, at the International Conference on Client-Centered and Experiential Psychotherapy in Belgium in 1988, is quoted by Cain (1989c) as stating that client-centered therapy, in its pure form, is not effective for some clients and insufficient for others.

Cain (1989c) commented on Gendlin's (1988) plenary address at the Belgium conference, noting that 'some consider Gendlin's work a creative extension of client-centered therapy, while others contend that experiential therapy is simply incompatible with the theory and practice of client-centered therapy' (pp. 5–6). Brodley (1988) belongs to the latter group, judging from her paper at the same conference 'Client-Centered and Experiential — Two Different Therapies.' Cain (1989c) reported that Gendlin said he 'goes with the clients' approach as long as that works', but goes with focusing 'when what the client is doing doesn't work.' This statement represents the problem posed by many who feel that they are supported in going beyond the client-centered approach because what they do 'works'.

How does one know what works? That requires research; however, those who justify what they do on this basis are not referring to research, but to their clinical impression — usually the impression that it pleased the client and thus, the counselor, suggesting that it is usually the placebo that is operating.

I will not discuss all the innovations to client-centered therapy that have been

First published in *Humanistic Education and Development*, 1993, 31, pp. 130–3. Reprinted by permission. No further reproduction permitted without written authorization from the American Counseling Association.

proposed. Wood (1986) noted that 'some of Rogers' closest colleagues use hypnosis, guided fantasies, paradoxical statements, dream analysis, exercises, give homework assignments and generally follow the latest fads to supply their [Rogers' necessary and sufficient conditions] missing deficiencies' (p. 351). Shlien (1986) wrote that 'one reads that client-centered therapists include in their practice hypnosis, scream therapy, behavior modification, Gestalt, psychodrama, relaxation, etc.' (p. 347). My purpose here is to propose some requirements for accepting such innovations, as follows:

1. Any new methods or techniques should be consistent with the philosophy and theory of the client-centered approach. Currently, I am unaware of any that meet this criterion (Patterson, 1989).
2. New methods would require some evidence that the conditions proposed by Rogers (1957) as necessary and sufficient are in fact not sufficient. There is considerable research evidence demonstrating that they are sufficient for a wide variety of clients, even though the levels at which the conditions are provided are not particularly high (Patterson, 1984).
3. The traditional or pure client-centered approach should not be rejected as inadequate simply because it is not effective with all clients: (a) no approach is expected to be effective with all clients, and (b) Rogers proposed two necessary conditions in clients (that they are experiencing psychological disturbance of some kind and that they perceive the conditions offered by the therapist). Other conditions can also prevent success.
4. Research evidence must exist to support the effectiveness of any new approach that meets the preceding requirements.
5. Thorne's (1989) statement at the Belgium conference should be taken to heart before rejecting the traditional or pure approach:

> I believe that the limitations of the approach are a reflection of the personal limitations of the therapist . . . We should not, I believe, be seeking to supplement the core conditions . . . Instead, we should be asking ourselves what would it mean to offer the core conditions more deeply, more intensely, more consistently (pp. 25–6).

What would happen if we were more patient with our clients?

Cain (1989c), in his paper on the conference, reported that he overheard one participant 'gently chide another for being "more Catholic than the pope"' (p. 5). It was Bozarth, I believe, who once said that I was more client-centered than Rogers. I aspire to nothing more than to approach being as client-centered as Rogers. Although he was very open to change during his 50 years of practice, Rogers never found it necessary to change his basic philosophy and theory. His changes in practice were directed to bringing practice more in line with the philosophy and theory.

There seems to be some confusion or disagreement about the use of the terms 'person-centered therapy' and 'client-centered therapy'. Person-centered therapy refers to the extension of the person-centered relationship epitomized in client-centered therapy to nontherapy relationships — encounter groups with 'normal' individuals, international relations, education (although student-centered may be used here) and parenting (although child-centered may be used here). Therapy involves clients, and the term client-centered therapy would be used here. This usage is consistent with that of Rogers (1986,) who wrote about the 'person-centered approach' and 'client-centered therapy'.

I am not alone in my concern about some of the new directions being taken by some who call themselves client-centered. Shlien (personal communication, September 6, 1987), referring to the 1987 Forum on Client-Centered Therapy at LaJolla, said, 'I had to separate myself from the "person-centered" position because I am only client-centered, and believe that the extensions go carelessly and mindlessly beyond the present theory.' And in the aforementioned reference, Shlien (1986) said that 'the person-centered approach invites extensions that sometimes outreach the theory of client-centered therapy' (p. 348). Raskin also (1987) said that 'each of the neo-Rogerian methods takes something away from the thorough-going belief in the self-directive capacities that is so central to client-centered philosophy' (p. 460).

If it ain't broke don't fix it.

References

Brodley, B. (1988) *Client-centered and experiential therapy: Two different therapies.* Paper given at International Conference on Client-Centered and Experiential Psychotherapy. Leuven, Belgium.

Cain, D. J. (1986) What does it mean to be 'person-centered'? *Person-Centered Review*, 3, 252–6.

Cain, D. J. (1989a)The paradox of nondirectiveness in the person-centered approach. *Person-Centered Review*, 4, 123–31.

Cain, D. J. (1989b) Proposals for the future of client-centered and experiential psychotherapy. *Person-Centered Review*, 4, 11–15.

Cain, D. J. (1989c) A report on the International Conference on Client-Centered and Experiential Therapy. *Person-Centered Review,* 4, 3–9.

Cain, D. J. (1990) Further thoughts about nondirectiveness in person-centered and client-centered therapy. *Person-Centered Review*, 5, 89–99.

Combs, A. W. (1988) Some current issues for person-centered therapy. *Person-Centered Review*, 3, 263–76.

Gendlin, E. (1988) *The small steps of the therapy process; How they came and how to help them come.* Plenary address, International Conference on Client-Centered and Experiential Psychotherapy, Leuven, Belgium.

Patterson, C. H. (1984) Empathy, warmth, and genuineness in psychotherapy: A review of reviews. *Psychotherapy*, 21, 431–8.

Patterson, C. H. (1989) Foundations for a systematic eclectic psychotherapy. *Psychotherapy*, 26, 427–35.

Raskin, N. (1987) Review of R. Levant and J. Shlien (Eds.), Client-centered therapy and the person-centered approach: New directions in theory, research, and practice. *Contemporary Psychology*, 32, 460–1.

Rogers, C. R. (1957) The necessary and sufficient conditions of therapeutic personality change. *Journal of Consulting Psychology*, 21, 95–103.

Rogers, C. R. (1986) Carl Rogers on the development of the person-centered approach. *Person-Centered Review*, 1, 257–9.

Sachse, R. (1989) Proposals for the future of client-centered and experiential psychotherapy. *Person-Centered Review*, 4, 20–4.

Sebastian, J. (1989) Metatheoretical response to the person-centered versus client-centered debate. *Person-Centered Review*, 4, 493–6.

Shlien, J. M. (1986) What is most essential to the continual development of the theory and application of the client-centered approach? *Person-Centered Review*, 1, 347–8.

Thorne, B. (1989) Proposals for the future of client-centered and experiential psychotherapy. *Person-Centered Review*, 4, 24–6.

Wood, J. K. (1986) What is most essential to the continued development of the theory and application of the client-centered approach? *Person-Centered Review*, 1, 350–1.

THE EDUCATION OF COUNSELORS AND PSYCHOTHERAPISTS: A PROPOSAL

25

With the concern for integration in counselling and psychotherapy in the 90s, there is an opportunity for change in the education of counselors and psychotherapists. Although integration has not proceeded very far, and the focus is upon techniques rather than philosophy and theory, there is the beginning of hope for a single unifying theory. The basis for this theory is the acceptance of the common elements in all the major theories of counselling or psychotherapy. They should be made the focus of the education of counselors and psychotherapists.

Medical education in the first decade of this century was in a confused state. Each medical school had its own program. A study of the situation by the Flexner Commission led to the standardization of medical education. The present situation in the education of counselors and psychotherapists appears to be similar to that of the education of physicians at that time. While APA accreditation has led to some standardization of the various foundation areas to be included in programs in counselling and clinical psychology, preparation in the function of counselling and psychotherapy itself varies widely. Some programs may focus on a particular approach, such as behavior therapy, while others attempt to cover a variety of approaches or techniques, labeled (or mislabeled [Patterson 1989a, 1989b]) eclecticism.

The current situation

In most programs, students are exposed, though often superficially, to the major theories of counselling or psychotherapy. But following this, there is little further attention to philosophies or theories. Emphasis is on techniques, or skills, as they are now commonly called, or more recently, interventions. While there is much talk (or writing) about basing practice on research, there is in fact very little research support for what students are taught. The model of specific techniques for specific clients with specific problems is widely espoused. But there is virtually no research indicating what technique is appropriate for what clients with what problems. Courses in research are separated from practice and seldom do the twain meet.

First published in the *Asian Journal of Counselling*, 1, 1, pp. 1–4. Reprinted by permission.

In practice and internships, students are taught to apply or use a variety of techniques, according to the particular preferences of their supervisors, who often do not agree with each other, leaving the student puzzled about just what to do at the end of his/her training program. Mahoney (1986, p. l69) expresses it well:

> During my internship experience I often found myself wondering how my clinical mentors seemed to know what to do at each moment in therapy (while I, of course was privately struggling to understand) . . . The textbooks — both elementary and advanced — simply did not capture the complexity of what I encountered in real-life attempts to be helpful. I slowly began to appreciate that my expert clinical mentors were themselves operating according to abstract and tacit 'rules' rather than concrete and explicit guidelines.

The current system appears to be producing technicians rather than professionals. Technicians apply a hodge-podge of techniques, justified (without evidence) as being empirically derived, but lacking in any philosophical or theoretical bases as to why they are effective — if indeed they are effective. 'What works' is based on idiosyncratic, unevaluated experience rather than reasons and research.

This approach is often justified by claiming that there is no one best way to practice counselling or psychotherapy. Practitioners are therefore free to do what seems to be required in the particular situation, free of any limiting philosophy and theory. This approach is also described as eclectic. But it lacks the systematic integration that is necessary for a true eclecticism (Patterson, 1989a, 1989b).

If it is true that there is no agreed upon single or best way to practice counselling or psychotherapy, then counselling or psychotherapy is not a profession, and should not be taught at all. Those teachers who profess not to know what counselling or psychotherapy is (Grater, 1988) should not be teaching.

The teaching of counselling or psychotherapy appears to be in the state of medical education in 1900–1910. There is little agreement on the nature of psychotherapy and therefore on the education of counselors or psychotherapists. Numerous schools of psychotherapy still exist. There is no generally accepted theory or system.

Insisting that students not commit themselves to a systematic theoretical approach, but instead use a smattering of unintegrated techniques is not acceptable. It does not produce competent professional practitioners.

Alternative programs of education
In the current state of the field there are two alternative approaches to the education of counselors or psychotherapists. Under the first alternative, the existence of differing, perhaps incompatible, theoretical systems is accepted. Each educational institution would offer its students professional preparation in a few, probably no more than three, systems. These would be selected on the basis of the interests and expertise of the faculty. Prospective students would be informed of the systems in which training is offered, and would select the schools or universities to which they would apply for admission on the basis of their (tentative) interests. In any

case, all schools would offer — and require students to take — a basic, in-depth course covering the major extent theories. (Texts such as Patterson [1986], Ford and Urban [1963] and/or Corsini [1989] would be used.) Students would then confirm their selection, or make a new selection, of the system in which they desire intensive training. In the event that a student decides upon a system not offered by the school in which he/she has enrolled, the student could transfer to a school where such a system is offered.

The program of training for each system would consist of (a) an intensive study of that system, its philosophy and theory; (2) supervised practicum experiences in that system; and (3) an internship in that system. All these phases would be taught by an experienced expert or experts in the system. This is, of course, the model that has been followed in the preparation of psychoanalysts. It is a consistent, progressive program including philosophy, theory, and application or practice.

There is a second, and to me a preferred, approach to education in counselling or psychotherapy. The objective of science is to arrive at a common theory or consensus — an agreement on the best theory and practice in terms of present knowledge. I believe psychotherapy is (slowly) approaching this stage. If we cannot agree on a single approach in all its aspects, it is nevertheless the case that there is agreement (at least implicit) on some fundamentals of psychotherapy, on some necessary, if not sufficient, conditions for effective psychotherapy. These therapist conditions, or common elements, are well known. They were first identified and described by Rogers (1957). He called them empathic understanding, unconditional positive regard, and congruence. The second and third conditions are more often called respect or warmth, and therapeutic genuineness. Rogers (1957, p. l01) states that he was not proposing that these conditions applied only to client-centered therapy. He wrote: 'My aim in stating this theory is to state the conditions which apply to any situation in which constructive personality change occurs, whether we are thinking of classical psychoanalysis, or any of its modern offshoots, or Adlerian psychotherapy or any other'. In 1967 Truax and Carkhuff (1967), in a chapter titled, *Central Therapeutic Ingredients: Theoretic Convergence*, reviewed the major theoretical approaches and found that these three conditions are 'aspects of the therapist's behavior that cut across virtually all theories of psychotherapy and counselling' (p.25). Moreover, there is considerable research evidence for the effectiveness of these conditions (Patterson, 1984).

Yet, while there is general acceptance of the importance or necessity of these conditions, they are not widely taught. It appears to be assumed that students are capable of offering or providing these conditions without being taught. In many counselor education programs it is true that there is an effort to teach them as skills, or techniques. But they are not techniques, to be learned and applied apart from the philosophy or beliefs of the therapist. They are attitudes, and as such they are part of the personal characteristics and beliefs of the therapist. To teach them as simply skills does not lead to effective counselors or psychotherapists, but to technicians. It is inconsistent with the widely accepted assumption that it is the person of the therapist that is of basic importance in psychotherapy.

As in the preceding program, in this alternative all students would have a basic theories course. Following this, rather than an in-depth course in one of the theories, would be a course in the basic conditions, or common elements, covering philosophy, theory and implementation. Since it is true that these conditions have been developed and explicated best by writers with a client-centered point of view, the work of these writers (including Rogers and Patterson) would be the basis for such a course. Practicum and internship experiences, with supervision by instructors committed to and expert in the core conditions would follow. The emphasis in the program would not be on skills or techniques, but upon philosophy, theory and attitudes. Attitudes, it may be objected, cannot be taught. To some extent this is true. Students must have the potential for empathy, and possess a respect and concern for others. That attitudes can be cultivated and enhanced has been demonstrated to me in some 35 years of teaching. Most recently it has occurred in a course taught at the University of North Carolina at Greensboro. (See, for example, Patterson, C.H. Outcomes in Counsellor Education. *Asian Journal of Counselling*, 1993, 2 (1), 81–97.)

Rogers (1957) proposed that these conditions are not only necessary but sufficient. There is considerable research showing that they are indeed sufficient in many cases. But it is not necessary that they be regarded as sufficient before accepting them as the basis for any education in counselling or psychotherapy.

Conclusion

The education of counselors and psychotherapists appears to be in the state of medical education in the first decade of this century. The current interest in integration in counselling or psychotherapy offers hope for the development of a common focus in the preparation of professional counselors or psychotherapists. This focus, it is suggested, should be on the common elements of all the major theories of counselling or psychotherapy. These common elements are known and are accepted by proponents of all the major theories, but they are not specifically included in programs of education. A program focusing on these elements is proposed.

References

Corsini, R.J. (Ed.) (1989) *Current psychotherapies* (4th ed.). Itasca, IL: Peacock.

Ford, D.H., and Urban, H.B. (1963) *Systems of psychotherapy*. New York: Wiley.

Grater, H. (1988) I still don't know how to do therapy. *Journal of Counseling and Development, 67*, 129.

Mahoney, M.J. (1986) The tyranny of techniques. *Counseling and Values, 30*, 169–74.

Patterson, C.H. (1984) Empathy, warmth, and genuineness in psychotherapy: A review of reviews. *Psychotherapy, 21*, 431–8.

Patterson, C.H. (1986) *Theories of counseling and psychotherapy* (4th ed.). New York: Harper/Collins.

Patterson, C.H. (1989a) Eclecticism in psychotherapy: Is integration possible?

Psychotherapy, 26,157–61.

Patterson, C. H. (1989b) Foundations for a systematic eclectic psychotherapy. *Psychotherapy*, 26, 427–35.

Patterson, C. H. (1993) Outcomes in counselor education. *Asian Journal of Counselling,* 1993, 2 (1) 81–7.

Rogers, C. R. (1957) The necessary and sufficient conditions of therapeutic personality change. *Journal of Consulting Psychology*, 21, 95–103.

Truax, C. B., and Carkhuff, R.A. (1967) *Toward effective counseling and psychotherapy*. Chicago: Aldine.

SOME SOCIAL ISSUES
AND CONCERNS

TWO APPROACHES TO HUMAN RELATIONS

26

Within the last generation there has been evidence of a change in various fields of human relations from a relatively authoritarian approach to a more egalitarian one. This change has reflected a general cultural change in attitudes toward the individual. Family relationships have become more democratic, as has education, and to some extent industry also.

Nevertheless, this change has not been complete in any area, even in the field of psychotherapy. Methods of dealing with people, of human relations, appear to be divisible into two major types which are in conflict with each other. This division and conflict seem to exist in each field of human relations. Gordon (1955, chap. 2) analyzes the two approaches in terms of two conflicting views of the nature of man. One reflects a positive, optimistic, encouraging view, while the other is based on a negative, pessimistic, discouraging view.

Understanding

The first point of view is associated with respect for the individual and his autonomy. His right to freedom of choice, for self-determination of his behavior, for living his own life is recognized. On the other hand, the second point of view sees the individual as one who cannot take responsibility for himself, who cannot be trusted to make his own decisions. Rather he needs to be controlled from the outside. He cannot be given freedom to make his own decisions to live his life as he sees fit.

To be sure, these are descriptions of extremes, and there is a broad area in between. Nevertheless, the extremes must be recognized; they do exist in some instances, and they are the end results of two opposed attitudes toward human beings. Politically, the two approaches are represented by the democratic and authoritarian or totalitarian philosophies of government. But the conflict extends throughout all areas of human relations.

The first approach to human relations appears to be based on an understanding of the individual as a distinct, unique, self-autonomous human person or self.

First published in the *American Journal of Psychotherapy*, 1958, 7, pp. 691–708. Reprinted in C. H. Patterson (1959) *Counseling and Psychotherapy: Theory and Practice*, pp. 111–35. New York: Harper. © C. H. Patterson 1959. Published here with permission of the Association for the Advancement of Psychotherapy.

There is an attempt to understand the feelings, needs, desires, motives, attitudes, etc., of the individual, and to respect them rather than to attempt to influence or to control them. We shall therefore designate this as the *understanding approach* to human relations.

Manipulation

The second approach to human behavior appears to be characterized by attempts to influence or control it. This control may be direct or indirect. There is relatively little respect for the individual, although there may be claims that the influence or control is for the presumed good of the individual being influenced or controlled. Whether this claim is sincere or not is immaterial; it is the fact of external control or influence which is the essence of this approach. There may be attempts to understand the individual's feelings, needs, and attitudes; but this is done for the purpose of influencing or changing them. Because of this aspect of manipulation, we shall designate this as the *manipulative approach* to human relations.

This latter point of view, while it may in some respects be designated as authoritarian, is not therefore to be considered as necessarily inimical to the American tradition and philosophy. In fact, it is actually an expression of the American philosophy of efficiency. It represents an expression of the desire to get results in the shortest time, in the easiest and most direct way. In psychotherapy it represents a dissatisfaction with the length and complex involvements of orthodox psychoanalysis. It is perhaps an expression of American optimism about being able to achieve results ever more quickly and efficiently (Adelson, 1956). Weinberg (1952, p. 325) suggests that brief psychotherapy, in the manner of Alexander and French (1946), with its manipulation of the process and the client by the therapist, is a manifestation of the influence of American society upon the social and psychological sciences. Ruesch writes: 'Things have to be done fast in America, and therefore therapy has to be brief' (Ruesch and Bateson, 1951, p. 148).

In addition to the American desire for efficiency and speed of results, there is another factor which supports the manipulative approach to human behavior. This is the influence of the scientific point of view. The objectives of science are commonly listed as understanding, prediction, and control. The physical sciences have set an example of the extent to which control of the physical environment is possible. The social sciences, in emulation, appear to be seeking to control human behavior to the same extent. When we go from understanding and prediction to control, we face certain problems. This is true in the physical sciences, where the uses to which such discoveries as atomic energy is put, raise questions which involve values and ethics. These questions include those of control by whom, for whom, and for what purposes. In the social and psychological fields there is the additional question of who controls whom. By what right does one individual control others? We shall consider this problem later.

In government

In the field of government, the implications of the need of the individual to have a sense of personal value are being recognized. Mayo (1933, chap. 7) called attention to this need in connection with his work in industry, suggesting that the sense of personal futility is not limited to the work situation. That the understanding of and respect for the individual is basic to democratic government would not be questioned. There is impressive evidence of the concern of government for the individual and his rights, from the development and expansion of social security programs, not as relief but as human rights provided as social insurance, to the recent recognition of the Fourteenth Amendment by the Supreme Court in the field of educational integration.

Nevertheless, it is also true that government, even democratic government, in its administration tends to become bureaucratic, and to disregard the individual as a person. Gellhorn points out areas in which such a tendency seems to have been developing in recent years. He says that, 'to a degree not remotely approached in the past, American citizens are the objects of suspicion of administrators rather than the object of their services' (1956, p. 38).

Leighton, in a study of the administration of a Japanese relocation camp during World War II, states some principles and recommendations for the governing of men. He concludes that

> the problem which faces the administration of a community under stress is the problem of introducing remedial change . . . this does not mean that great change is always necessary, but only that great understanding is . . . not infrequently the natural reactions of self-healing in the community are adequate (1944, pp. 355–6).

In government, therefore, we see both of these trends. There are those who desire to manipulate the governed, either for their own purposes, or because of lack of trust in the governed to be responsible for themselves. 'Society needs,' says Gordon, 'to evolve a kind of leadership that puts human values first, a leadership that facilitates man's realization of his creative capacities, man's free expression of his individuality, man's actualization of his own uniqueness' (1955, p. 3), free from the oppressive control of external authority.

In industry

In industry, perhaps the beginning of the recognition of the importance of understanding was in the Hawthorne experiment at Western Electric (Mayo, 1933; Roethlisberger and Dickson, 1939), conducted between 1927 and 1932. In this study, five operators, engaged in relay assembly, were set off by themselves, and subjected to varying external conditions of work, including the introduction and then the elimination of rest pauses and midmorning food, changes in working hours, etc. It was found that regardless of changing conditions, including reversion to less favorable conditions, production increased continuously over the entire period. The women expressed an increased satisfaction in work, and there was a decrease in absences. They attributed their better production to a greater freedom in the work situation, with opportunity to vary the pace at will, and to less strict supervision. However, supervision and company policy had been good prior to the experiment and no simple 'error' of supervision could be uncovered. Interviews with about 20,000 other workers did not reveal any reliable or flagrant instances of poor supervision. There did emerge, however, some evidence of an experience of personal futility, related to feelings of constraint and interference in their work. While a background of out-of-work personal problems seemed to be involved in this feeling, there also appeared to be a lack of understanding of the work situation, involving poor communication between the working group, the supervisor, and company policies, resulting in conflicts of loyalties.

There was clearly a need for improved understanding of the workers' situation. This understanding was the effective factor in the experimental situation, and in the conduct of the interviews with other employees. Both the experimental situation and the interviews indicated interest in the individual, respect for the worker as an individual and for his opinions. A report made during the study is quoted by Mayo as follows: 'Much can be gained industrially by carrying greater personal consideration to the lowest levels of employment' (Mayo, 1933, p. 69).

The increase in wages — real as well as absolute; shorter working hours; holidays; vacations with pay; and fringe benefits, which now can be numbered by the dozen, have not satisfied the worker in an industrial society. Studies of what the worker desires in a job indicate that these material rewards are not at the top of the list. There are variations in different studies and, where the economic returns are low, the material aspects rank high. Surveys indicate, however, that workers are interested in intangible or psychological satisfactions in their work — security, freedom, responsibility, independence and responsibility in doing one's work, good supervisory relationships, knowledge of one's status, interesting work, recognition and approval for achievements, fair treatment, and opportunity for self-expression (Thomas, 1956, chap. 9). These represent a need and a desire to be recognized and treated as human individuals, a need to be accepted, understood, and informed. Morale in industry is largely a matter of such factors, rather than of wages and hours.

These human elements in the work situation are being recognized in industrial and personnel psychology, and by employers. A recent book in this field is concerned with 'overcoming communication barriers, preventing misunderstandings, and developing the constructive side of man's nature' (Maier, 1952, p. vii). Industry's interest in employee morale and satisfaction is not, of course, entirely altruistic, since it has been clearly demonstrated that the psychological state and attitudes of employees affect production, absenteeism, and labor turnover. There is also a genuine interest of progressive management, and of unions, in the welfare and satisfaction of the employee. It might be held that unless there is genuine interest, a basic attitude of consideration and respect for the individual worker, satisfactory results will not be achieved, since employees will recognize the discrepancy between attitudes and actions. Good supervision requires attitudes of respect, understanding, and consideration for the individual worker. A study by Ghiselli (1956) concludes that 'The most outstanding self-perception of the "poor" supervisor is his sales approach to human relations', while 'the good supervisor . . . sees himself as respecting the rights and dignity of others'. Bass (1956) found that those who believed in consideration for subordinates were later rated as successful supervisors, while there was no relation between later rated success and opinions favoring initiation of structure.

While in the area of supervision the understanding point of view has been increasingly accepted, in other areas of industry and industrial management the manipulative approach is more in evidence. In selection and placement, in grooming executives for promotion and advancement, management seeks to control and mold the lives of its employees, even extending its influence into their social and family lives. The nature and extent of this attempted influence is portrayed in a recent book by Whyte (1956).

Shartle's study of leadership in administration (1956) clearly illustrates the simultaneous operation of these two approaches to dealing with subordinates. A factor analysis of nine dimensions of leadership resulted in two major factors, which Shartle labels 'initiating structure' and 'consideration'. They seem to reflect the manipulative and the understanding approaches, respectively. He identifies these two dimensions of leadership with the 'get the work out' approach and the 'human relations' approach. He points out their similarity to dimensions appearing in the classroom and in parent-child relationships (pp. 120–1). While the two dimensions may be viewed as complementary, with administrators using both in an integrated fashion, they are often in conflict.

Shartle writes that

> Anyone who has been in a position of high leadership potential has experienced a conflict between the two dimensions. An executive knows that his superior and other persons of high influence expect them to produce. But he may regard his staff highly and may be reluctant to put the pressure on them. This conflict may become so intense that he may even seek another position (p. 125).

Shartle also recognizes that this conflict exists in our society:

> There seems to be a basic conflict in our ideology of leaders. We want persons in leadership roles, and yet we do not want to place limitations upon ourselves to submit to leadership (p. 119).

Shartle aligns himself with the consideration dimension, stating that it is his 'point of view that manipulation runs counter to the ideals of a democratic society' (p. 111).

In advertising and public relations

The greatest source of manipulation in our contemporary society is in the field of advertising and public relations. In recent years, changes have begun which raise some serious questions about the uses to which the understanding of people is being put. In the past, research and practice in marketing and public opinion has tended to be concerned with discovering the attitudes and opinions of the public as bases for advertising and sales campaigns. True, there has always been some attempt to create or change attitudes, desires, and wants. Recently this aspect of influencing consumers has been receiving increased emphasis. The fact that people are often moved to action more on the basis of emotion than reason has been known, and exploited, for a long time. The fact that these emotions operate without the awareness of the individual, and that they can be influenced without such awareness, has become the basis for much of the current attempt to influence consumers and public opinion.

Advertising has often been justified as a service to the consumer, in educating him to the availability, qualities, and usefulness of commodities for the satisfaction of his needs and wants. Appeals have been considered to be based upon the relative qualities of competing products, or the relative desirability of satisfying competing wants. The newer trend, however, doesn't appeal to the rational bases of decisions or choices, but to the irrational impulses which have no relationship to the qualities or utility of the product being advertised. Psychology is thus used not to understand people and their needs, in order to satisfy those needs, but to apply this understanding to control the behavior of people without their conscious or rational consent. In other words, knowledge of the motivations and desires of human beings is used to manipulate them in conformity with the will and desires of the manipulators. This movement has been designated as motivation research, or MR. A recent popular survey of this field is given by Packard (1957). He details the

> large scale efforts . . . being made, often with impressive success, to
> channel our nonthinking habits, our purchasing decisions, and our
> thought processes by the use of insights gleaned from psychiatry
> and the social sciences' (p. 3) .

He points out that 'nothing is immune or sacred' (p. 5); the baser motives, anxieties, and weaknesses of people are played upon. So-called 'social engineers' are using psychological knowledge and understanding to manipulate people into conforming to what the 'engineers' consider desirable — ignoring the real needs of the individual — and calling the process 'human engineering'.

There is probably no doubt that the effectiveness of the techniques used is overrated, and that motivational research has been oversold. There is little, if any, research evidence of the validity of the claims of successful appeal to motivations. Much of the effort and activity is based on subjective or intuitive interpretations of results of so-called depth interviews or projective testing of small samples. And admittedly there are various reasons, some of them rational, for human behavior such as buying a particular product. But the methods used appear to be effective, even though the reasons may be wrong. Without research, advertising can easily and successfully appeal to emotional elements outside the consumer's awareness.

The most recent development in this field is the use of subliminal stimuli in movie and TV advertising. While there is again no experimental evidence of its effectiveness, there is sufficient research in the psychology of perception to indicate its potential effectiveness (McConnell, Cutler, and McNeil, 1958).

Ethical implications
The ethical and moral implications of such manipulation must therefore be considered. The potentiality of the methods in public relations and politics,

suggested by Packard, are great, and of considerable significance. Packard quotes Kenneth Boulding as saying that 'a world of unseen dictatorship is conceivable, still using the forms of democratic government' (1957, p. 181). Some of those engaged in the activity have some qualms about it. Packard quotes one as saying that 'It may be said that to take advantage of a man's credulity, to exploit his misapprehensions, to capitalize on his ignorance, is morally reprehensible — and this may well be the case . . . I do not know' (pp.258–9). Packard raises some of the ethical questions, such as 'When you are manipulating, when do you stop? Who is to fix the point at which manipulation becomes socially undesirable?' (p. 240). He suggests the need for a code of ethics in advertising and public relations to control manipulative efforts.

Some have sought to defend manipulation on the grounds that it is justified by the results. In the advertising field, the reasoning seems to be that increased consumption leads to increased production, with full employment and further increased consumption, resulting in prosperity, rising standards of living, and thus general happiness. But the results are not necessarily greater happiness psychologically, nor in some cases even materially. Particularly in the political field might this not be the case (Sargent, 1957). Moreover, one might question whether the ends justify the means. The means involve the manipulation of human personality, and this manifests a disrespect for the individual, his rights, and his worth. Packard writes that

> the most serious offense many of the depth manipulators commit, it seems to me is that they try to invade the privacy of our minds. It is this right to the privacy of our minds — privacy to be either rational or irrational — that I believe we must strive to protect (p. 266).

It would seem to be appropriate for those psychologists, sociologists, anthropologists, and other social scientists, who have given their support and services to these manipulators, to consider the consequences of their abetting the trend toward manipulation, and to examine their consciences regarding the desirability and morality of such activity. The frightful situation of thought control so vividly described by Orwell (1949) doesn't appear to be too fantastic in the light of the activities and goals of these manipulators of our attitudes and behavior in the fields of advertising, public relations, and particularly political campaigning.

Manifestations in psychology and psychiatry

Rogers (1948) feels that the major trend in clinical psychology and psychiatry has been toward the manipulative point of view. Suggesting that it leads to a philosophy of social control by the few, he feels, however, that few psychologists or psychiatrists would agree with this end, though he quotes Skinner as one psychologist who does advocate a frank facing of the possibility and desirability of controlling human behavior. Skinner apparently believes that such control by psychologists is better than leaving it to 'those who grasp it for selfish purposes: to advertisers, propagandists, demagogues, and the like' (1947, p. 25). Rogers points up the implications of control even by psychologists or experts, in terms of the loss of independence by the individual.

Currently in the field of counseling and psychotherapy, the trend toward manipulation does not appear to the writer to be as strong as the trend toward the understanding approach. Gordon (1955), however, seems to feel that at the present time the balance is still toward the manipulative approach. Bateson describes the changing conception of psychotherapy as follows:

> The change toward larger Gestalten and the necessity of this change for both humanistic and formal reasons can be illustrated by considering Sullivan's emphasis upon the phenomenon of interaction. This emphasis is very clearly part of a defense of man against the older, more mechanistic thinking which saw him so heavily determined by his internal psychological structure that he could easily be manipulated by pressing the appropriate buttons — a doctrine which made the therapeutic interview into a one-way process, with the patient in a relatively passive role. The Sullivanian doctrine places the therapeutic interview on a human level, defining it as a significant meeting between two human beings. The role of the therapist is no longer to be dehumanized in terms of definable purpose which he can plan, and the role of the patient is no longer dehumanized into that of an object of manipulation (Ruesch and Bateson, 1951, p. 263).

Bateson feels that 'by and large, psychiatrists have a permissive understanding' (p. 127). Sutich wrote in 1944 (Sutich, 1944): 'It is evident that modern therapeutic and analytical principles have their roots in democratic principles throughout the entire range of human behavior'. A recent volume on psychotherapy to which a number of outstanding contemporary psychotherapists contributed (Fromm-Reichmann and Moreno, 1956) seems to reflect a growing acceptance of the understanding approach; this appears to be the major theme of the contributions to the book.

Nevertheless, the manipulative approach is still much in evidence in counseling and psychotherapy. It is manifested by a lack of trust or confidence in the client to solve his own problems, to take responsibility for himself in the therapeutic process. It is characterized by activity on the part of the therapist, who takes responsibility for the treatment process, diagnosing and analyzing the client's problems and advancing solutions. There may be direct attempts to mold the client's attitudes, values, and behavior. There is an apparent assumption that the client is incapable of understanding himself and the complex psychological dynamics of his behavior. Rather, he needs an expert to explain, interpret, advise, teach, direct, persuade, even to exhort, inspire and preach. The client is helpless, and dependent on the therapist, who is strong and wise and who knows best what is good for him

In a recent series of addresses dedicating a new hospital in St Louis, Saslow (Saslow, 1956) detected as one of the major themes the question of control of behavior, although only one speaker (Cobb) explicitly mentioned it. Saslow raises a question about the values of those who control behavior even in a therapeutic community setting, or of any professional persons who have within their power some means of modification and control of the behavior of persons they wish to influence. In the case of the use of tranquilizing drugs, for example, he asks: 'Who will tranquilize whom? Under what circumstances? And for what purposes?' (p. 106).

It thus appears that we must question the use of methods of manipulation even in the hands of professional persons who presumably would use them for the good of those whom they manipulate. There is a question regarding the goals of such manipulation, even in the hands of professional persons. Essentially, it is this: is it desirable, or ethical, to manipulate anyone, for any purpose, or is this inimical to self-responsibility and self-determination, which appear to be increasingly recognized and accepted as desirable goals or values in our society?

Freud appears to have had a basic concept of the individual which would lead to a manipulative or controlling type of therapy (Bruner, 1956; Gordon, 1955; Rogers and Skinner, 1956; Walker, 1956). Freud viewed man as basically bad, accepting essentially the doctrine of original sin, as Mayo (1933, p. 158) points out. Life was viewed as a strenuous fight to control or to subdue perversion or pathological impulses. The individual was in constant conflict with society, and Freud identified himself with society. The therapist then would tend to be a controlling element. Nevertheless, though Freud was apparently rather authoritative in therapy, many other analysts in practice have not been particularly manipulative.

Attempts to shorten the traditional lengthy analysis have resulted in more activity and manipulation on the part of the therapist, as exemplified by Alexander and French (1946). A few other therapists have advocated active manipulation, e.g. Salter (1949) and Herzberg (1945). De Grazia (1952) also would appear to sanction considerable manipulation on the part of the therapist, and the sector or limited therapy of Deutsch and Murphy (1955) is relatively therapist controlled.

In the understanding approach in psychotherapy, emphasis is placed upon the capacity of the client for taking responsibility for himself, beginning with the therapeutic process itself. There is confidence that the client will make the best, or 'right', choices for himself, without coercion, direction, or pressure of any kind. He can be trusted to make his own decisions. Dependence is placed upon the natural or inherent growth forces in the individual. The therapeutic situation is one in which an atmosphere is created in which these growth forces can be released and allowed to operate. Maslow (1954) expresses it well as follows:

> The key concepts in the newer dynamic psychology are spontaneity, release, naturalness, self-acceptance, impulse awareness, gratification. They *used* to be control, inhibition, discipline, training, shaping, on the principle that the depths of human nature were dangerous, evil, predatory, and ravenous (24; p. 352).

One might question whether the understanding approach is not basically manipulative. The object of any therapy is to change behavior, and thus to control it. But there is a difference in the meaning of control here. In the understanding relationship the nature and the extent of the change is under the complete control of the client. The therapist provides only the atmosphere, or the conditions, under which the client can change if he chooses to do so. In the understanding approach, the objective is to facilitate self-determined change.

Institutional care of the mentally ill has been characterized by the manipulative attitude. Custodial care has had as its objective the control of patients; drugs, physiotherapy, hydrotherapy, and shock, as well as conventional restraints, have been used as methods of control. Recently, however, there has been progress toward the understanding approach (Bass, 1956; Greeenblatt, York and Brown (1955); Jones, 1953; Stanton and Schwartz, 1954). Gilbert and Levinson (1956) use the term 'humanistic' to apply to the newly developing viewpoint. In this conception, the hospital is 'a community of citizens rather than a rigidly codified institutional mold', and 'the hospital members (are) persons rather than mere objects and agents of treatment'. The hospital is conceived of as a therapeutic community, or a therapeutic social environment, existing for the patients rather than, as in many custodial institutions, for the staff. Gilbert and Levinson see the custodial orientation as autocratic with a rigid status hierarchy and a minimizing of communication. The humanistic orientation, on the other hand, attempts to democratize the hospital, increasing patient self-determination and opening channels of communication.

The fears of those who felt that giving patients freedom, treating them as persons rather than as objects, would result in a return of bedlam have not been realized. Instead, when patients have been given freedom and self-government or a voice in institutional management, they have shown themselves capable of accepting responsibilities. Rather than becoming agitated and violent, they have become less troublesome, less regressive. Stanton and Schwartz (1954) report that incontinence and soiling practically disappeared from the hospital. The results of the humanistic or understanding approach, where it has been tried, have been little less than spectacular and probably no less effective than the tranquilizing drugs.

Evidence of effectiveness of understanding

While questions regarding the effectiveness of the understanding approach might be raised, there is evidence of its value where it has been used. The effectiveness of the manipulative approach seems to be clear — in certain situations and for certain purposes. It is effective in influencing behavior in directions desired by the manipulator, such as in advertising. We can, of course, raise questions regarding the desirability of such manipulation, both as regards its purposes and its means.

The understanding approach may be questioned as a technique for controlling or influencing people toward behavior desired by someone else. This, however, is not the purpose of the approach. As indicated above in the discussion of psychotherapy, its purpose is to make possible self-desired change in the individual. Actually, such changes, as in psychotherapy, are usually in directions desired by society as a whole.

One might question whether this approach is economical or efficient in initiating change in behavior; one is reminded of the old problem of the efficiency of democracy relative to an authoritarian government. Which is desirable depend on one's goals and values. Democracy is slow and inefficient in situations where immediate, specific action is required. So may be the understanding approach. It is difficult to think of an army being led in battle on this basis, for example. Yet, even in the military situation, this approach may be the most effective in building up an organization with high morale prior to action. To achieve its purpose, which is self-responsible behavior, no other method appears to be as effective.

We have already referred to some situations in which this approach has been effective in developing satisfaction and adjustment in the individual as well as socially-desired behavior. The Western Electric study (Mayo, 1933; Roethlisberger and Dickson, 1939) indicates its effectiveness in industry. Maier (1952, pp. 7–10) refers to a number of studies which indicate that when groups participate in decision-making, with the point of view of each individual being recognized, understood, and considered, acceptance and satisfaction with the results is greater than where the decision is made outside the group. James Richards reports the effective use of group-centered leadership in an industrial situation in Gordon (1955, chap. 12).

Morse and Reimer (1956) report the results of two programs of decision-making in industry, one autonomous, the other hierarchically controlled. Worker satisfaction increased under the first, and decreased under the second. Productivity increased under both, though more under the second than under the first. Lewin (1947) reports a study in which it was found that group discussion and decision resulted in greater changes in food habits than did a lecture. The experiments of Lewin and his students (Lewin, Lippitt and White,1939; Lippitt, 1940; Lippitt and White, 1947) on democratic and autocratic atmospheres indicate that groups function more constructively in a democratic situation. Similar results were found in a study of teachers' classroom behavior (Anderson and Brewer, 1945); and in the area of parent-child relationships a democratic family environment was found to be related to child adjustment (Baldwin, Kalhorn and Breese, 1945). In the field of medicine and public health there is evidence for the effectiveness of this approach in helping the individual seek and accept treatment. The Peckham Experiment in London found that while direct medical advice is not usually followed, when the facts and their implications were simply presented without advice, action was taken in the overwhelming majority of cases (Pearse and Williams, 1938; discussed in Rogers [1951, pp. 59–60] and in Gordon [1955, p. 35]). In psychotherapy there are no adequate data regarding the relative effectiveness of various approaches. But it appears that the understanding approach, as represented by client-centered therapy, is at least as effective as any other approach. The general opinion of therapists seems to be that an understanding approach leading to self-initiated change yields greater and more permanent changes in personality and behavior than does the manipulative approach.

Rogers (1951), speaking of the understanding relationship, says:

> if the administrator, or military or industrial leader, creates such a climate within his organization, then his staff will become more self-responsible, more creative, better able to adapt to new problems, more basically cooperative. It appears possible to me that we are seeing the emergence of a new field of human relationships, in which we may specify that if certain attitudinal conditions exist, then certain

definable changes will occur.

The problem of control

Skinner (1953), an experimental psychologist, raises some serious questions which deserve attention. Pointing out that control is the result of science, he states that

> we have no guarantee that the power thus generated will be used for
> what appear to be the best interests of mankind . . . A science doesn't
> contain within itself any means of controlling the use to which its
> contributions will be put . . . Are we to continue to develop a science
> of behavior without regard to the use which will be made of it? If
> not, to whom is the control which it generates to be delegated? . . .
> There is good reason to fear those who are most apt to seize control
> (pp. 437–8).

He points out that to proclaim that man is a free agent is impossible — 'we all control, and we are all controlled' (p. 438). Moreover, 'to refuse to accept control . . . is merely to leave control in other hands' (p. 439). In psychotherapy, for example, the individual may be able to reach his own solution in a 'good' society, but what if he is subject to all kinds of controls outside of therapy? The advantage of democracy over totalitarianism is that control is diversified in the former. 'It is the inefficiency of diversified agencies which offers some guarantee against despotic use of power' (p. 440). Different sources of control cancel each other out, as it were. While the government may be assigned superior power, the problem of preventing its misuse remains. Skinner hopes, however, that 'science may lead us to the design of a government, in the broadest possible sense, which will necessarily promote the well-being of those who are governed' (p. 443). He suggests freedom, security, happiness, and knowledge as conditions of a strong society. These conditions, he recognizes, involve moral or ethical issues. Yet, he continues,

> If a science of behavior can discover those conditions of life which
> make for the ultimate strength of men, it may provide a set of 'moral
> values' which, because they are independent of the history and culture
> of any one group, may be generally accepted (p. 445).

By the 'strength of men' he appears to mean survival of the group or culture, but since the conditions for this survival cannot be predicted, we cannot discover the values that make for the 'ultimate strength of men'. Nor does Skinner answer the question of who should control. Who should control is determined by who will, in the group which survives.

Skinner, therefore, has no solution to the problem of control. He does not propose that scientists should control. But control exists. 'Western thought has emphasized the importance of the individual. The use of such concepts as individual freedom, initiative, and responsibility has . . . been well reinforced' (pp. 446–7). But:

> The hypothesis that man is not free is essential to the application of
> the scientific method to the study of human behavior. The free inner

man who is held responsible for the behavior of the external biological organism is only a prescientific substitute for the kinds of causes which are discovered in the course of scientific analysis. All these alternative causes lie outside the individual' (pp. 446–8).

As Ruesch and Bateson (1951, p. 216) put it, '. . . in regard to the Pavlovian subject we may now state that he will learn to expect a world in which he has no control over the good and evil which may befall him'. Thus behavior theory, as well as Freudian psychology, with their mechanistic concept of determinism, leave no place for individual choice and therefore responsibility. Mowrer (1957), disturbed by this lack of responsibility, appears to be repudiating behavioral psychology.

So we have no solution to the problem of control, says Skinner. Man is not a free agent, and has no control over his own behavior, which is determined from without. Skinner has returned to the stimulus response behaviorism of Watson. He describes three links in the chain of behavior: (1) an operation performed upon the organism from without; (2) an inner condition; and (3) a kind of behavior. The second link is not essential for the control of behavior.

> The objection to inner states is not that they do not exist, but that they are not relevant in a functional analysis . . . Unless there is a weak spot in our causal chain so that the second link is not lawfully determined by the first, or the third by the second, then the first and third must be lawfully related (p. 35).

Indeed, there is a weak spot in the chain; the second link is not determined solely by the first, but is influenced by other factors and conditions within the organism which affect the perception, definition, and interpretation of the stimulus, except perhaps in simple reflex acts. This factor accounts for what is referred to as the freedom of the individual, or free will. While it is true that all behavior is determined, the individual often experiences the sense of choice. This experience is a fact, which must be considered because of its influence on the individual's attitudes and behavior. Skinner states that 'science is a willingness to accept facts even when they are opposed to wishes' (p. 13). But what are 'facts'? What is truth, or knowledge? Behavior is not determined by objective stimuli, but by the perceptions of the world by the individual.

> Man lives essentially in his own personal and subjective world . . . though there may well be such a thing as objective truth, I can never know it; all I can know is that some statements appear to me subjectively to have the qualifications of objective truth. Thus there is no such thing as scientific knowledge; there are only individual perceptions of what appears to each person to be such knowledge (Rogers, 1956, pp. 10–11).

Bateson presents a similar statement, with the added concept that belief in one's perceptions (or values) constitutes validity.

> The definition of a relationship depends not merely upon the skeleton

of events which make up the interaction but also upon the way the individuals concerned see and interpret these events. Thus seeing or interpreting can be regarded as the application of a set of propositions about the world or the self whose validity depends upon the subject's belief in them. The individuals are partially free to interpret their world according to the premises of their respective character structure, and their freedom to do this is still further increased by the phenomena of selective awareness and by the fact that the perceiving individual plays a part in creating the appropriate sequences of action by contributing his own action to the sequence (Ruesch and Bateson, 1951, pp. 220–1).

Thus, the concepts of individual freedom, initiative, and responsibility are experienced, and are therefore facts; moreover, they are held to be values by a large part, if not the majority, of mankind. If accepted as such, then we are justified in attempting to preserve them, and in resisting the encroachment of control from the outside, whether or not it is for the presumed good of the individual.

The concept of control, as used by Skinner, covers several different things. He appears to include the determination or influencing of behavior by physical factors of the environment, by other individuals, by groups of individuals, and by agencies such as the government. Used in this sense, control is inevitable. Some control is no doubt necessary and desirable in order to prevent anarchy. For, although man may be fundamentally good, many men have been corrupted by the imperfect society in which we live; and even in a more perfect society, some men would no doubt have some antisocial impulses. Such control as is necessary or desirable is only for the purpose of protecting the legitimate freedom of the individual from being infringed upon by the unwarranted freedom of others. The control is of the environment, to assure that it makes possible the maximum freedom and initiative of individuals. As to who should exercise this control, it would seem that we have no better alternative than to vest it in the elected representatives of a free people, whether their choices are, in essence, determined in the sense that they are not capricious.

If we accept as values or goals of life the independence, freedom, initiative, and spontaneity of the individual, then we must prevent encroachment on these by the manipulative activities of others. If these concepts be illusory, we are still justified in preserving them, as long as they are values. And it might well be that these are the moral values which are independent of history and culture, and which constitute the 'strength of men' which will assure the survival of our society.

In this paper we have distinguished two major, and opposed, approaches to human relations — designated as the understanding and the manipulative approaches. Both are present, in varying degrees, in every field of human relations. Each is dominant in one or more fields, e.g. understanding in counseling and psychotherapy, manipulation in advertising and public relations. The manipulative approach creates certain problems in terms of the ethics of controlling human behavior. The apparent snowballing of the manipulative approach in advertising and public relations, and its entrance into politics, raise some real concern about the future, with specters of the horrors of Orwell's *1984*. The implications should be considered seriously by all students of human behavior who are concerned about the freedom of the individual. Some control apparently is necessary, and we have indicated its place in society. We do not pretend to have dealt with the problems of control at all adequately, however. Rogers and Skinner (1956) present a stimulating discussion of this problem.

Our main concern here is with counseling and psychotherapy. Understanding, rather than control, should characterize counseling and psychotherapy; and the understanding approach seems to be well entrenched in this field, though not universally applied or carried to its logical extreme. It is consistent with, and indeed the expression of, the ethical principles and philosophy of counseling . The ultimate expression of this approach is client-centered therapy.

References

Adelson, J. (1956) Freud in America: some observations. *American Psychologist*, 11, 467–70.

Alexander, F., and French, T. M. (1946) *Psychoanalytic therapy.* New York: Ronald Press.

Anderson, H. H., and Brewer, J. (1945) Studies of teachers' classroom personalities. *Journal of Applied Psychology Monograph*, No. 16.

Baldwin, A. L., Kalhorn, Joan, and Breese, Fay. (1945) Patterns of parent behavior. *Psychological Monograph*, 54, No. 3.

Bass, B. M. (1956) Leadership opinions as forecasts of supervisory success. *Journal of Applied Psychology*, 40, pp. 343–6.

Belknap, I. (1956) *Human problems of a state mental hospital.* New York: McGraw-Hill.

Bruner, J. S. (1956) Freud and the image of man. *American Psychologist*, 11, pp. 463–6.

De Grazia, S. (1952) *Errors of psychotherapy.* Garden City, New York: Doubleday.

Deutsch, F., and Murphy, W. F. (1955) *The clinical interview. Vol. Two: Therapy.* New York: International Universities Press.

Fromm-Reichmann, F., and Moreno, J. L. (1956) (Eds.) *Progress in psychotherapy: 1956.* New York: Grune and Stratton.

Gellhorn, W. (1956) *Individual freedom and governmental restraints.* Baton Rouge: Louisiana State University Press.

Ghiselli, E. E. (1956) Role perceptions of successful and unsuccessful supervisors. *Journal of Applied Psychology*, 40, pp. 241–4.

Gilbert, D. C., and Levinson, D. J. (1956) Ideology, personality, and institutional policy. *Journal of Abnormal and Social Psychology*, 53, pp. 263–71.

Gordon, T. (1955). *Group-centered leadership.* Boston: Houghton Mifflin.

Greenblatt, M., York, R. H., and Brown, E. L. (1955) *From custodial to therapeutic patient care in mental hospitals.* New York: Russell Sage Foundation.

Herzberg, A. (1945) *Active psychotherapy.* New York: Grune and Stratton.

Jones, M. (1953) *The therapeutic community.* New York: Basic Books.

Leighton, A. H. (1944) *The governing of men*. Princeton: Princeton University Press.

Lewin, K. (1947) Group decision and social change. In T. M. Newcomb and E. L. Hartley (Eds.) *Readings in social psychology*. New York: Holt.

Lewin, K., Lippitt, R., and White, R. K. (1939) Patterns of aggressive behavior in experimentally created social climates. *Journal of Social Psychology*, 271–99.

Lippitt, R. (1940) An experimental study of the effect of democratic and authoritarian group atmospheres. *University of Iowa Studies in Child Welfare*, 6, pp. 43–195.

Lippitt R., and White, R. K. (1947) An experimental study of leadership and group life. In T. M. Newcomb and E. L. Hartley (Eds.), *Readings in social psychology*. New York: Holt.

Maier, N. R. F. (1952) *Principles of human relations: Applications to management*. New York: Wiley.

Maslow, A. H. (1954) *Motivation and personality*. New York: Harper, 1954.

Mayo, E. (1933) *The human problems of an industrial civilization*. New York: Macmillan.

McConnell, J. V., Cutler, R. L., and McNeil, E. B. (1958) Subliminal stimulation: an overview. *American Psychologist*, 13, pp. 229–42.

Morse, N. C., and Reimer, E. (1956) The experimental change of a major organizational variable. *Journal of Abnormal and Social Psychology*, 52, pp. 120–9.

Mowrer, O. H. (1957) Some philosophical problems in psychological counseling. *Journal of Counseling Psychology*, 4, pp. 103–111.

Orwell, G. (1949) *Nineteen eighty-four*. New York: Harcourt, Brace.

Packard, V. (1957) *The hidden persuaders*. New York: David McKay.

Pearse, I. H., and Williams G. S. (1938) *Biologists in search of material*. London: Faber and Faber.

Roethlisberger, F. J., and Dickson, W. J. (1939) *Management and the worker*. Cambridge, Mass.: Harvard University Press.

Rogers, C. R. (1948). Divergent trends in methods of improving adjustment. *Harvard Educational Review*, 18, pp. 209–19.

Rogers, C. R. (1951) *Client-centered therapy*. Boston: Houghton Mifflin,.

Rogers, C. R. (1956) *Becoming a person*. Austin: The Hogg Foundation for Mental Hygiene, University of Texas.

Rogers, C. R. (1956) A *theory of therapy, personality, and interpersonal relationships as developed in the client-centered framework*. Chicago. (Mimeographed.)

Rogers, C. R. (1956) Implications of recent advances in prediction and control. *Teachers College Record*, 57, pp. 316–22.

Rogers, C. R. (1957) A note on 'The nature of man'. *Journal of Counseling Psychology*, 4, pp. 199–203.

Rogers, C. R., and Skinner, B. F. (1956) Some issues concerning the control of human behavior. A symposium. *Science*, 124, pp. 1057–66.

Ruesch, J., and Bateson, G. (1951) *Communication: the social matrix of psychiatry*. New York: Norton.

Salter, A. (1949) *Conditioned reflex therapy*. New York: Creative Age Press.

Sargent, W. (1957) *Battle for the mind*. Garden City, New York: Doubleday.

Saslow, G. (1956) Major themes. In *Theory and treatment of the psychoses: Some newer aspects*. Paper presented at the dedication of the Renard Hospital, St Louis, October, 1955. St Louis: Washington University Press.

Skinner, B. F. (1947) Experimental psychology. In W. Dennis (Ed.), *Current trends in psychology*. Pittsburgh: University of Pittsburgh Press.

Skinner, B. F. (1953) *Science and human behavior*. New York: Macmillan.

Shartle, C. L.(1956) *Executive performance and leadership*. Englewood Cliffs, N.J.: Prentice-Hall.

Stanton, A. H., and Schwartz, M. S. (1954). *The mental hospital*. New York: Basic Books.

Sutich, A. (1944) Toward a professional code of ethics for counseling psychologists. *Journal of Abnormal and Social Psychology*, 39, pp. 329–50.

Thomas, L. G. (1956). *The occupational structure and education*. Englewood Cliffs, N.J.: Prentice-Hall.

Walker, D. E. (1956) Carl Rogers and the nature of man. *Journal of Counseling Psychology*, 3, pp. 89–92.

Weinberg, S. K. (1952) *Society and personality disorders*. New York: Prentice-Hall.

Whyte, W. H., Jr. (1956) *The organization man*. Garden City, New York: Doubleday.

SCIENCE, BEHAVIOR CONTROL AND VALUES

27

Over 30 years ago John B Watson, the father of psychological behaviorism, wrote as follows:

> Give me a dozen healthy infants, well-formed, and my own specified world to bring them up in and I'll guarantee to take any one at random and train him to become any type of specialist I might select — doctor, lawyer, artist, merchant-chief and, yes, even beggerman and thief regardless of his talents, penchants, tendencies, abilities, vocation, and race of his ancestors (Watson, 1930, p. 104).

At the time this boast was made, Watson recognized that it was premature. Even at the present time such a claim cannot be fulfilled. But the science of psychology has made considerable progress in the last 30 years, and the ability to control human behavior has increased. On the one hand, there is developing evidence for the environmentalist point of view, indicating that man is more pliable and less limited by hereditary factors than has popularly been believed. Education in Russia, operating upon this assumption, has achieved some remarkable results (Chauncey, 1959). In this country, research by Passamanick and his associates on intelligence points to the limited influence of heredity on intelligence.

Passamanick and Knobloch (1960) state that

> it is now possible to entertain a new *tabula rasa* theory which hypothecates that at conception individuals are quite alike in intellectual endowment except for the few quite rare hereditary neurologic defects. It appears to be life experience and the sociocultural milieu influencing biological and physiological function which, in the absence of organic brain damage, make human beings significantly different behaviorally from each other.

On the other hand, there have been advances in the development of techniques for the control of human behavior. The influencing of behavior through the administrating of reward and punishment has been possible to some extent for a long time (Schlosberg, Skinner, Miller and Hebb, 1958). Learning, which is

---

First published in *Insight*, 1966, 5, 2, 14–21. Reprinted by permission.

behavioral change, has been studied by psychologists for a long time, and methods and techniques have been developed to facilitate the learning process. While there is no general agreement on a single theory of learning, there has been progress at the technical and applied levels. Rewards or reinforcement or drive reduction, while apparently not necessary or sufficient conditions of learning or behavior change, do result in, or at least precede, learning in many instances.

Also, although behavior is influenced by other factors than external stimulation, such stimulation does influence behavior.

One of the recent developments in the study of behavior is operant conditioning (Skinner, 1958; Sidman, 1962; Michael and Meyerson, 1962). This method of controlling behavior makes use of the principle of reinforcement. Behavior which is desired is rewarded when it occurs spontaneously. But since a response must occur before it can be rewarded, it might be questioned how new behavior can be developed. This is accomplished by what is called shaping. Shaping involves the reinforcement of behavior which is similar to, or approaches, the desired response, with selective reinforcement of behavior which approximates more and more closely the desired response. Skinner (1958) states that:

> It is dangerous to assert that an organism of a given species or age cannot solve a given problem. As a result of careful scheduling, pigeons, rats, and monkeys have done things in the last five years which members of their species have never done before. It is not that their forbears were incapable of such behavior; nature had simply never arranged effective sequences of schedules.

The subject is said to perform such behavior to achieve the reward or reinforcement, so that the behavior is said to operate on the environment rather than being a response to a stimulus in the environment. Nevertheless it is controlled by the stimuli, since behavior which is rewarded, or reinforced, tends to recur, and behavior which is not rewarded drops out. Skinner and his associates discovered that intermittent reinforcement is more effective than uninterrupted reinforcement.

This approach to the study and control of behavior has been applied to various kinds of verbal behavior, including behavior similar to that in a psychotherapeutic interview (Krasner, 1958, 1962b, 1963). It appears that the client learns by operant conditioning, through the expression in various ways of approval or pleasure by the psychotherapist, to talk about what the therapist wants him to talk about and in the way the therapist wants him to. We can understand now why and how Freud's patients talked about sex so much, and supported his theories.

While considerable progress has been made in this approach to behavior control, the techniques may be said to be still in the experimental stage. The effectiveness of the procedures in terms of the extent and duration of the changes produced is not known. Motor and verbal behavior can be controlled, but to what extent can attitudes, beliefs, emotions, values be controlled? To the strict behaviorist, of course these do not exist; only observable behavior is important or real, and if this can be controlled there is no need to be concerned with 'unobservable hypothetical inner determining agents' (Michael and Meyerson, 1962). But most people recognize the existence and importance of attitudes, values and beliefs and are concerned about them. We do not know the extent to which changes in verbal behavior results in change in attitudes, beliefs, values, or in other types of overt behavior. This is the problem of generalization. The persistence of behavior induced by operant conditioning is also a question. It appears that in every known conditioning situation, the behavior will cease, or extinguish, to use the technical term, if reinforcement is not continued.

Operant conditioning, moreover, doesn't always work. It appears that there are complex factors in the experimenter and the subject, and their relationship, particularly in the case of human beings, which affect the results. Conditioning of animals can be done by machines, but it does not appear that the mechanical approach is sufficient with human beings, except possibly in the case of very simple, limited kinds of behavior.

Nevertheless, although it has not been perfected, this approach to the control of human behavior is effective, and can be expected to become more effective as it is perfected. Klaw (1963) says in reference to Skinner's work: 'Human behavior can, in principle, be predicted and controlled just as certainly as the progress of a chemical reaction . . . he has cleared the way for the subjection of human behavior to scientific control that will eventually make all men happy and good'. Skinner (1948) presents the possibilities of operant conditioning in his utopian community. In this utopia everyone is well behaved, productive and happy. They are controlled, but they are not aware that they are controlled. The method of control is not one which depends on force or the threat of force. Skinner notes that 'if it's in our power to create any of the situations which a person likes or to remove any situation he doesn't like, we can control his behavior. When he behaves as we want him to behave, we simply create a situation he likes, or remove one he doesn't like. As a result, the probability that he will behave that way again goes up, which is what we want' (1948, p. 216). And he continues: 'We can achieve a sort of control under which the controlled, though they are following a code much more scrupulously than was ever the case under the old system, nevertheless *feel free*. They are doing what they want to do . . . there's no restraint and no revolt. By a careful design, we control not the final behavior, but the inclination to behave — the motives, the desires, the wishes' (1948, p. 218). He presents the possibility of molding personality: 'What do you say to the design of personalities ? . . . The control of temperament? Give me the specifications, and I'll give you the man!' (1948, p. 243). We are back again to J. B. Watson, but here we have more evidence to back up the boast.

The possibility, the probability, of direct manipulation and control of human behavior poses a problem for philosophy and ethics. As the advances of the physical sciences have posed problems of the uses of the discoveries of science, so now does the development of the behavioral sciences. There has been some concern expressed about the control of behavior through the use of drugs and electrical or surgical intervention in the brain. These methods are limited in use, or controlled, and thus have not aroused great controversy. Now we must face the problem of psychological methods of control, raising specters of brainwashing, and thought control. The implications of this power must be faced. We must be concerned about who controls whom, when and to what extent, and for what purposes or towards what goals. This brings us to philosophical problems about the nature of man, the desirable goals of man, and the ethics of behavior control. These problems are beyond science. The *uses* of the tools and techniques of science involve philosophy and ethics.

First, the question of who is in control. Just as in the case of nuclear energy, it will be impossible to limit the means or methods of control. Techniques of control may be, and are to some extent, used in politics, propaganda and indoctrination, advertising and brainwashing. Skinner recognized that 'There is good reason to fear those who are most apt to seize control' (1953, p. 438). Again, 'The possibility of the misuse of scientific knowledge must always be faced' (Rogers and Skinner, 1956). Others (Tillich, 1961; Krutch, 1953) are also concerned about who is in control. Control tends to be used for the selfish purposes of the controller.

Skinner (Rogers and Skinner, 1956) points out that control exists in our present society. Individuals control each other, and society controls the individual through social rewards and punishments for acceptable or unacceptable behavior, and through education and government. He admits that the new technique must be subject to countercontrol, and points out that this has always been the case with political control. Thus he states:

> A similar countercontrol of scientific knowledge in the interests of the group is a feasible and promising possibility Although we cannot say how devious the course of its evolution may be, a cultural pattern of control and countercontrol will presumably emerge which will be most widely supported because it is most widely reinforcing (Rogers and Skinner, 1956).

But this may be an oversimplification which overlooks the power of control when it is centered in the hands of a few. Once control has become complete, as in Skinner's utopia, who is to resist it, who is to develop a system of countercontrol? In Skinner's Walden there is none. Whereas in methods of control which utilize aversive, or punishing methods, brute force, deception, or the threat of force, etc., there is always awareness of the fact of control and resistance to it, in the control which is exerted by positive rewards, there is, as Skinner emphasizes, no resistance, indeed, no awareness of control. The controller in Skinner's Walden is a benevolent despot. Skinner's response to the charge of despotism is: 'I don't think anyone should worry about it. The despot must wield his power for the good of others. If he takes any step which reduces the sum total of human happiness, his power is reduced by a like amount. What better check against malevolent despotism could you ask for?' (Skinner, 1948). But benevolent despotism is nevertheless despotism, and the satisfaction of needs through rewards may not be acceptable as adequate for human life, a point to which we shall return.

The solution to the problem may relate to the flaw in Skinner's utopia. It concerns who is to succeed the despot Frazier when he dies. Someone will have to be let in on the secret, and trained in the method of control, in order to prevent chaos or the dissolution of the society. Here lies the possibility of countercontrol, in the differences of opinion among those who control. Even psychologists, whom Skinner would feel might be the most appropriate controllers, might disagree among themselves, and so might philosophers, who should also be included among the controllers. But in any event, the controller, or controllers, exercise the prerogatives of decision making and the selection of goals. They are, as Frazier admits, more omnipotent than God. This raises the question as to what are acceptable goals for Man.

Goals and values, it is repeatedly pointed out, are relative and change with the times. It is therefore apparent that there will be differences of opinion as to what are adequate and acceptable goals for man. Skinner chooses happiness, productivity, security, creativeness. Are these adequate goals? Would Skinner's Walden actually be a utopia? Some would feel that those are restricted, static goals. Rogers (Rogers and Skinner, 1956) notes being 'well behaved', productive, happy may be stultifying. Others would select goals such as maximum freedom of choice, self-determination, responsible independence, self-realization or self-actualization. These goals reflect values which emphasize respect for the individual, recognition of his worth, and the desirability of freedom of choice. While it may be claimed that these have not always existed as values, and are not presently universal, it does appear that they have been accepted by a large part of the world for the past two thousand years. Another way of looking at it is perhaps to say that since there are no universals, no absolutes, then we accept as the highest value freedom of the individual, within limits, to choose his own goals or values. This then, makes freedom an absolute. There appears to be evidence in history that man does strive for freedom, wherever he is aware that his freedom is being restricted (Wolfe, 1955).

Now these two sets of goals or values are different. They reflect two different assumptions about human beings and human behavior.

Allport (1961, 1962) delineates these two points of view or models. Actually, he describes three, but it appears that the first two constitute a single model. The first assumption sees man as a reactive being. He is a bundle of reflexes, reactions, responses, reacting to the stimuli and reinforcements of the environment. Or he is a reactive being in depth, to use Allport's term, reacting by means of repression, regression, resistance, reaction formations, etc., to inner stimuli, drives, motives, etc. The second model sees man as a being in the process of becoming. This concept sees man, in Rogers' terms, as

> a process of achieving worth and dignity through the development
> of his potentialities; the individual human being as a self-actualizing
> process, moving on to more challenging and enriching experiences,
> the process by which the individual creatively adapts to an ever new
> and changing world . . . (Rogers and Skinner, 1956).

A model of man in which freedom of choice is an element, is not acceptable to those who feel that determinism is a necessary basis for science. To Skinner, freedom does not exist. There is no such thing as choice. All behavior is determined, completely and irrevocably. The dilemma of determinism and free will has never been, and may never be, completely resolved. It may possibly be a pseudo-problem created by differing perceptions or points of view, including the current perception of science. The paradox of free will versus determinism is illustrated in the choice of Skinner to believe that free will does not exist, and at the same time choosing goals for mankind — goals which deny freedom of choice to the individual, goals which are not accepted by others While denying freedom of choice to others, he exercises it himself (Rogers, 1961b).

From a psychological point of view, the experience of freedom, of ability to choose, is a fact to be recognized, and a potential value to be considered as a goal. Possibly it *is* an illusion, as it is in Skinner's utopia, where people feel free without being free. However, we must recognize that there are differing *degrees* and *kinds* of control. Society's controls are variable, often inconsistent, often left to chance, and not very effective. Some would prefer that they remain this way, that control be minimized, while others, like Skinner, would like to organize and systematize the controls of society. It appears that in terms of the goals which we desire and the degree of control to which the individual is subjected, we do have a choice. Otherwise, neither Skinner nor anyone else would have any reason to write about or to recommend or be concerned about the future. We can, however, choose to give up our right or freedom to choose, to psychologists, philosophers, or benevolent despots who will determine the goals of society.

There appear, then, to be two conceptions of man and of the values or goals of society. One is of man as a reactive being, the subject, or victim of stimuli from within and without, for whom the goals of life are chosen by others and imposed on him by methods of control which do not make him aware of the fact that he is controlled, but which, because positive reinforcement, or rewards, are used, leave him feeling satisfied, happy, content — like a trained seal, or bear, or monkey in a circus.

The other conception views man as a being in process of becoming, who is to be provided the opportunity to develop his potential, realize his potential, realize his self, assume responsibility for his behavior, which requires the freedom to choose.

This difference in conceptions and goals appears to be dividing behavioral scientists into two groups. These two groups represent two approaches to human behavior and human relationships (Patterson, 1958). If ends determine means, then it would appear that the different goals for human behavior would imply different methods and techniques. What methods are there for influencing, or changing human behavior toward the goals of responsibility, freedom to develop potentials, etc.?

It would appear that if we are interested in developing responsible individuals who can make decisions and choices, then we must allow them the freedom to do so, in the present. Therefore an alternative approach to human behavior is one of respecting the individual as a person of worth, one who is capable of making the best decisions and choices for himself, and one who, moreover, has the right to determine his own behavior. These are some of the conditions which it has been found tend to lead to the goals which we desire. These conditions consist of certain qualities of interpersonal relationships, rather than the automatic or mechanical administering or withholding of reinforcement or rewards. They include genuine interest in and concern for another, acceptance of another as a person, understanding of him as an individual, and the communication of these to another. These are the basic principles of good human relationships whether in psychotherapy or in any other relationship. In the attempt to provide a way of identifying and distinguishing this method or approach and the method of direct control through operant conditioning, I have used the terms *understanding* and *manipulation* (Patterson, 1958), although they are perhaps not the best or ideal terms for the purpose.

What, then, of the fact of behavior control through operant conditioning? It cannot be denied that such techniques exist and are effective. What are we to do about them? Are we to outlaw them? Such a course would be impossible, even if it might be considered desirable. These methods are used in many areas of everyday behavior, as Skinner has pointed out. Rogers (1961b) suggests that these two currents in present-day American psychology 'seem irreconcilable because we have not yet developed the larger frame of reference that would contain them both'. Such methods are not, however, necessarily irreconcilable.

These two approaches are not necessarily mutually exclusive. We have already suggested that, for effectiveness with human beings, operant conditioning must be more than a mechanical application of reinforcements or rewards. Interest, attention, or concern on the part of the experimenter appear to be important. These factors seem to be generalized reinforcers (Krasner, 1962a) and may even be considered to be the most powerful reinforcers of human beings. On the other hand, in the understanding approach, conditioning and reinforcements do enter, naturally, into the relationship. There is thus an overlapping of methods and techniques for the effective use of both approaches.

The *essential difference* is the difference in *goals*, the purpose for which the techniques are used. In the case of the manipulative approach, techniques are used to determine the specific behavior of the individual, denying him freedom of choice. In the understanding approach, techniques are used to establish the conditions where the individual is free to determine his own specific behavior. Control is present here also, but it is control of the *situation*, the environment, or the relationship *for the purpose of increasing the freedom of the individual*. The individual is freed for self-direction, self-actualization. As Rogers (1961a) phrases it, referring to psychotherapy,

> We have established by external control conditions which we predict will be followed by internal control by the individual, in pursuit of internally chosen goals . . . by less dependence upon others, an increase of expressiveness as a person, an increase in variability, flexibility, and effectiveness of adaptation, an increase in self-responsibility and self-direction.

To the charge that this will lead to a self-centered, selfish, antisocial or asocial individual, it is pointed out that man is a social being, and in order to exist needs the group. To actualize himself he needs others, not only their presence but their acceptance and respect. In the long run, as Rogers notes (1951, p. 150), self-actualization or enhancement of the self 'inevitably involves the enhancement of others selves as well . . . The self-actualization of the organism appears to be in the direction of socialization, broadly conceived.'

If the fostering of freedom is the goal of behavior, then it would appear that there must be some controls placed upon the use of conditioning techniques by those who would use them in a way to deprive others of their freedom. This is, of course, a restriction upon the freedom of those who would use such techniques in this way, but it is based on the same principle of protecting society, or the individual, from those who would enslave others or impinge upon their rights and freedom. As the method of operant conditioning might be used to control others, so too might the understanding approach be used, or misused. This approach is a powerful method, and may be used to influence others in ways which would abrogate their freedom. Brainwashing may be most successful where this approach is used, where the person conducting the 'rehabilitation or re-education' of the subject genuinely believes in the system being indoctrinated and is genuinely interested in helping the subject accept the system. This is beautifully portrayed by Orwell in his novel *1984* (1949; see Patterson, 1959, pp. 149–50, 171).

Skinner says (Rogers and Skinner, 1956) that if control is relinquished by the experts, it then passes to others, who are not going to behave therapeutically or helpfully. While this may be true at the present time, it is the goal of the understanding approach to extend these kinds of human relationships throughout society. Then the locus of control would be in a society which would be therapeutic for the individual and provide the atmosphere and settings for his achieving the goals which we have suggested, which are the characteristics of good mental health. There would then be no need of an individual or group to operate a system of operant conditioning. Society would not be planless or without control, since the principles and conditions of good human relationships would need to be taught, and, at least for some time, there would need to be controls for those who would not or could not accept and practice the principles. But in the long run, a society which consisted of people who practiced the principles would need no controls or controllers.

This of course assumes that man has the potential for living together in harmony, that man is innately good rather than evil. It assumes that aggression and hostility are not innate, but are the results of environmental conditions or provocations. There is increasing evidence leading to the conclusion that aggression is not innate, but a response to threat or frustration. Montagu (1962) writes:

> My own interpretation of the evidence, strictly within the domain of science, leads me to the conclusion that man is born good, and is organized in such a manner from birth as to need to continue to grow and develop in his potentialities for goodness. . . [The view that aggressiveness is inherited] is not scientifically corroborated. In fact, all the available evidence gathered by competent investigators indicates that man is born without a trace of aggressiveness.

He cites Lauretta Bender as finding that hostility in the child is a symptom complex resulting from deprivations in development. Charlotte Buhler in her studies of infants found that

> they give evidence of a primarily positive orientation toward 'reality'

into which the baby moves with a positive anticipation of good things to be found. Only when this reality appears to be hurtful or overwhelming does the reaction become one of withdrawal or defense (Buhler, 1961, p. 71).

Maslow (1949) also declares that impulses of hate, jealousy, hostility, etc., are acquired: 'more and more,' he writes, 'aggression is coming to be regarded as a technique or mode of compelling attention to a satisfaction of ones needs' which have been frustrated. A recent novel purporting to depict the horrible results of the innate aggressiveness of man actually supports the view that aggression is a result of threat, since it developed under conditions of threat and fear (Golding, 1956).

The operant conditioning approach actually makes the same assumption, since it is based on the pliability of behavior, which responds to rewards. The difference between the two approaches in terms of long-term effectiveness is that while the understanding approach has the potentiality of perpetuating itself, the conditioning approach could not continue without a permanent system of external control.

We have taken the position that science does not determine values, but that values are ends chosen by society, and that science can provide us with means to these ends. Bronowski (1956), however, proposes that values grow out of science. Science is the pursuit of truth. The pursuit of truth requires independence, which leads to originality, and freedom, which allows for dissent. These imply a democracy, which provides tolerance and respect for the views of others. Thus, 'the values of science turn out to be the recognizably human values' (p. 32) .

However, there is, in the opinion of the writer, another way of looking at the relation of science to human values. Instead of saying, as does Bronowski, that the values of science derive from its methods (p. 86), it would appear to be more logical and more in line with the facts, to say that these values are necessary for its methods. These values did not, as Bronowski claims, arise following the development of science. Although it is true that they were not always observed, particularly during the dark ages, they existed before that time, going back to the golden age of Greece, as Bronowski recognizes, and also being a part of early Christianity. Thus, historically, it cannot be claimed that these values originated with the development of modern science. Furthermore, in addition to being essential for science, or the existence of a community of scholars or scientists, they are necessary for the existence of any community or society. They hold society together.

Now Skinner appears to accept survival of the group or culture as the ultimate goal. He says 'If a science of behavior can discover those conditions of life which make for the ultimate strength of men, it may provide a set of "moral values"[!] which, because they are independent of the history and culture of any one group, may be generally accepted' (1953, p. 445). Again (Skinner, 1955), he says: 'Eventually the practices which make for the greatest biological and psychological strength of the group will survive'. It would appear that we have some evidence as to the values which 'make for the ultimate strength of men'. These are the values which are necessary for the pursuit of truth in science, which are necessary for the survival of a society of men. They are independence, freedom, responsibility, respect for the individual. Bronowski (1956, p. 83), in saying that 'A true society is sustained by the sense of human dignity', seems to sum up these values. For the survival of science, for the survival of society, there must exist basic trust and integrity.

The science of history appears to indicate that where these values do not exist, where they are corrupted, society disintegrates and disappears. Science itself would disappear without them. It is relevant here to note that when and where these values have been violated in Russia, science has deteriorated, and that implicit recognition of this has tended to preserve these values in the scientific area in Russia while they have been destroyed in other areas. We face the dilemma of whether the lack of these values in communist society may lead to the use of the results of science to destroy society. There is thus no built-in control to guarantee the preservation of society without these values. Science may be fostered, but its results used to deny or destroy these values in the rest of society.

Summary
The behavioral sciences are advancing rapidly (Rogers, 1961c), and are approaching the stage where they promise the eventual power to control human behavior effectively and on a broad scale. As has been the case in the physical sciences, this power raises problems regarding its use. Traditionally the objectives of science have been asserted to be understanding, prediction, and control. Actually, the objective of science is understanding. Prediction is but a test or proof of understanding. Understanding provides the possibility of and the basis for control. But control itself is a technical and social problem, not a scientific problem or goal. Science provides the means, but does not determine the ends. Thus we must face the philosophical and ethical problems involved in the use of the power which science gives us.

The developments in the behavioral sciences thus raise questions about the use of the power to control. Who is to control? How are they selected and perpetuated? What is to be the goal of control? What kind of behavior do we want to develop in man? These questions involve values related to the nature of man, the meaning of life, and the goals of mankind.

Essentially two different approaches to human behavior and its control have been developing. One approach sees man's behavior as being determined by stimuli, from within and without, to which he reacts. It has been demonstrated that man can be influenced and controlled by the manipulation of stimuli, by rewarding or withholding rewards. This approach to the control of behavior involves the determination of what behavior is desired, and a controller who administers the rewards.

Another approach to human behavior sees man not as a reactive being, but as a person in the process of becoming. Its methods and procedures are directed to enabling the individual to develop his potentials, to actualize himself, to become a responsible, independent human being able to make his own choices or decisions.

These two approaches have usually been seen as antithetical. In the reaction against the concept of control, the first approach has been attacked as being antithetical to man's freedom. However, the second method also in a broad sense involves control. The important question is control for what purpose or toward what goal? The methods of control by conditioning or the use of rewards does not specify what behavior should be fostered. It is true that those most concerned with this method have been interested in limited and specific types of behavior.

But this approach is an effective method of controlling behavior, and it must be recognized and used in ways, or to achieve the kinds of behavior, which are most desirable. Thus it poses clearly the problem of the goals of behavior control. The second method faces this problem and clearly specifies its goals as well as its methods. This goal is essentially the freeing of man as much as possible to choose and control his own specific behavior. Its methods are consistent with its goal — the interest in, acceptance of, and understanding of other persons as autonomous individuals capable, under these conditions, of making adequate choices leading to self-realization and the development of their human potentials.

The first approach, as a method, is not independent of or inconsistent with the second approach. First, it appears that to be most effective with human beings, conditioning must be accompanied by human interest, concern, and understanding. Second, it may be that the most effective reinforcers, or rewards, are interest, concern, and understanding. Third, the technique of conditioning can be used to achieve the goal of freedom, responsibility, etc. Such behavior is rewarded, rather than more specific aspects of behavior.

The first method is therefore not to be rejected or discounted. It has been demonstrated to exist, it is effective, and it must be considered in any approach to human behavior. Its effectiveness is one of its problems, because it can be used for goals which may not be socially or ethically desirable. It does not depend upon the awareness, or understanding, of the individual, so that he may be manipulated, influenced and molded without being aware of it. It also appears that as a method of control in society it would require the determination of specific goals of behavior by an individual or group, and continuous control through reinforcement by elaborate and complicated methods.

This approach is thus considered to be a limited, or partial approach, requiring more than the mechanical providing of reinforcements and rewards in directions determined by someone else. It sees man as a potentially responsible autonomous individual capable of utilizing freedom and developing his potentialities as a human being. Its methods, including the use of conditioning, are directed toward this goal.

The acceptance of a narrow concept of control, with the denial of freedom and independence to man denies the values which are essential for the existence of science. Thus the behavioral sciences face the prospect of destroying society if, as appears to be the case, independence, freedom, mutual respect and trust, in short the existence of human dignity, is a condition for the existence of society.

The problem which the developments in the behavioral sciences poses is, then, essentially a philosophical or ethical one. We have, it appears, to make a choice of values or goals for man. The question is, do we want persons or automatons?

References

Allport, G. W. (1961) *Pattern and growth in personality*. New York: Holt, Rinehart and Winston.

Allport, G.W. (1962) Psychological models for guidance. *Harvard Educational Review*, 32, pp. 373–81.

Bronowski, J. (1956) *Science and human values*. New York: Julian Messmer, 1956. (Harper Torchbooks. New York: Harper and Row, 1959.)

Buhler, C. (1961) *Values in psychotherapy*. New York: Free Press of Glencoe.

Chauncey, H. (1959) Some notes on education and psychology in the Soviet Union. *American Psychologist*, 14, pp. 307–12.

Golding, W. (1955) *Lord of the flies*. New York: Coward-McCann.

Klaw, S. (1963) Harvard's Skinner: The last of the Utopians. *Harper's Magazine*, 226, pp. 45–1.

Krasner, L. (1958) Studies of the operant conditioning of verbal behavior. *Psychological Bulletin*, 55, pp. 148–70.

Krasner, L. (1962a) The therapist as a social reinforcement machine. In H. Strupp and L. Luborsky (Eds.) *Research in Psychotherapy. Vol. II*. Washington, D.C.: American Psychological Association, pp. 61–94.

Krasner, L. (1962b) Behavior control and social responsibility. *American Psychologist*, 17, pp. 199–204.

Krasner, L. (1963) Reinforcement, verbal behavior, and psychotherapy. *American Journal of Orthopsychiatry*, 33, pp.601–13.

Krutch, J. W. (1953) *The measure of man*. Indianapolis: Bobbs-Merrill.

Maslow, A. (1949) Our maligned animal nature. *Journal of Psychology*, 28, pp. 273–8.

Michael, J., and Meyerson, L. A. (1962) A behavioral approach to counseling and guidance. *Harvard Educational Review*, 32, pp. 382–402.

Montagu, A. (1962) *The humanization of man*. Cleveland, Ohio: World Publishing Co.

Orwell. G. (1949) *1984*. New York: Harcourt, Brace and World.

Passamanick, B., and Knobloch, H. (1960) Epidemiological studies on the complications of pregnancy and the birth process which have implications for the primary prevention of mental disorders in childhood. Paper presented at a meeting of the International Preparatory Commission for Child Psychiatry and Allied Professions, Cambridge, Mass.

Patterson, C. H. (1958) Two approaches to human relations. *American Journal of Psychotherapy*, 12, pp. 691–708.

Patterson, C. H. (1959) *Counseling and psychotherapy: Theory and practice*. New York: Harper and Row.

Rogers, C. R. (1951) *Client-centered therapy*. Boston: Houghton Mifflin.

Rogers, C. R. (1955) Persons or science? A philosophical question. *American Psychologist*, 10, pp. 261–78. Reprinted in C. R. Rogers, *On becoming a Person*. Boston: Houghton Mifflin, 1961.

Rogers, C. R. (1961a) The place of the person in the new world of the behavioral sciences. *Personnel and Guidance Journal,* 39, pp. 442–51. In C. R. Rogers.

On becoming a person. Boston: Houghton Mifflin, 1961.

Rogers, C. R. (1961b) Two divergent trends. In R. May (Ed.) *Existential psychology.* New York: Random House, pp. 85–93.

Rogers, C. R. (1961c) The growing power of the behavioral sciences. In C. R. Rogers, *On becoming a person.* Boston: Houghton Mifflin.

Rogers, C. R., and Skinner, B. F. (1956) Some issues concerning the control of human behavior: A symposium. *Science,* 124, 1057–66.

Schlosberg, H., Skinner, B. F., Miller, N. E. and Hebb, D. O. (1958) Control of behavior through motivation and reward. *American Psychologist,* 13, pp. 93–113

Sidman, M. (1962) Operant techniques. In A. J. Bachrach (Ed.) *Experimental foundations of clinical psychology.* New York: Basic Books.

Skinner, B. F. (1948) *Walden two.* New York: Macmillan.

Skinner, B. F. (1953) *Science and human behavior.* New York: Macmillan.

Skinner, B. F. (1955) The control of human behavior. *Transactions of the New York Academy of Sciences,* 17, pp. 547–51.

Skinner, B. F. (1958) Reinforcement today. *American Psychologist,* 14, pp. 94–9.

Tillich, P. (1961) Report of a speech given at Massachusetts Institute of Technology, in *Time,* April 21, 1961, p. 57.

Watson, J. B. (1930) *Behaviorism.* Rev. ed. New York: Norton.

Wolfe, J. B. (1955) Man's struggle for freedom against authority. In *Social science and freedom: A report to the people.* Minneapolis: University of Minnesota.

Humanistic Concerns and Behavior Modification

28

Introduction

We seem to be moving into a new social era in regard to moral and ethical behavior. Before I am misunderstood to be referring to the morality of Watergate and the apparent loosening of sexual morals, let me state that these represent the end of an era. It is the reaction against the political morality of Watergate which represents the new era. Other elements of the new ethic include the concern about the invasion of privacy by Government agencies, the movement to recognize the consumer in business and credit agencies, the Buckley amendment giving individuals the right to information in their academic records, and concern about the administration of the Freedom of Information Act. Closer to psychology are the court cases involving the right to treatment of patients in institutions for the emotionally disturbed and the mentally retarded, and the furor over the use of behavior modification in correctional institutions. Within psychology itself we see the new ethics manifested in the Ethical Principles in the Conduct of Research with Human Participants.

This social change has come none too soon, if Watergate is any indication of the state of morality in the nation's politics. It has been said by historians that a civilization or a nation in which corruption becomes widespread is doomed to destruction either from within or without.

It would of course be interesting to know the sources or social antecedents of this change. Not being a sociologist or even a social psychologist, I am not competent to deal with this question. However, it appears that professionals in the behavioral sciences, including psychologists, have not been in the forefront. Journalists, the traditional muck-rakers, have been involved in uncovering the corruption of morals in public life. Lawyers concerned about civil liberties and civil rights have been involved with many of the legal challenges to individual rights and freedom. But there seems to be an underlying wave of public concern, indignation, and demand for higher standards of ethics and morality. Where or how did this originate and develop?

First published in E. Beutler and R. Greene (Eds.) (1978) *Special Problems in Child and Adolescent Behavior*. Pp. 187–205. Westport, CT.: Technomic Publishing Co. Reprinted by permission. (Prepared for the conference on 'Moral and Ethical Implications of Behavior Modification,' University of Wisconsin-Madison, March 20–21, 1975.)

I think it is important to point out that the ethical and moral standards being demanded are not new. No new system of ethics has been developed or proposed. What is being demanded is that the long accepted principles of ethical and moral conduct be practiced. These principles are part of our culture. They are promulgated and taught in our religious and educational institutions.

Henry Steele Commager (1975), the historian, in a recent article entitled *The School as Surrogate Conscience*, writes that

> increasingly, schools are required to take on the function of a moral safety valve. The more virtuous the sentiments and standards of conduct they inculcate, the more effectively they perform the function of a surrogate conscience permitting society to follow its own bent while consoling itself with the assurance that they are training up a generation that will do better . . . Thus society rejoices when schools teach that all men are created equal and entitled to life, liberty and happiness, but has no intention of applying that noble principle to the ordinary affairs of business and government. Thus society applauds the principle of racial equality but does not itself provide the young an example of such equality — knowing instinctively that the example is more dangerous than the admonition. Thus society rewards pupils who can recite the Bill of Rights but has no serious interest in the application of these rights to the tiresome minority groups who clamor for them.

Commager then states that this method is ineffective:

> Rarely, if ever in the history of education have so many been exposed to so much with results so meager. To judge by results — the results of the past 40 years or so — this whole enterprise of relying on schools to reform society by direct teaching has been an unmitigated failure.

I suggest that this may be a premature judgment. Perhaps the schools have been more successful than we realize. It just may be that the public concern about social ethics and morality is, at least in part, an outcome of the teachings of our educational system.

Is behavior modification effective?

But our concern here is not with the sociological analysis of the developing public concern with ethics. Nor is it with the public concern about governmental and political morality. Our focus is upon the ethical implications of the control of behavior, specifically with the methods of control collectively designated by the term 'behavior modification'. It has been pointed out that the current interest in the ethics of behavior modification and in regulation or control of the controllers is an indication that psychology has become important and relevant because it is actually able to control human behavior (e.g. Robinson, 1973). If one reads the recent research on behavior modification, however, there is certainly room for questioning the ability of the behaviorists to control human behavior. The situation seems to be much more complicated, involving many more variables, than is suggested by the optimism of behaviorists a few years ago. The control of the behavior of pigeons and rats, and even of human beings, in the laboratory is a far cry from the control of human behavior in social situations (Reppucci and Saunders, 1974). The extent, and particularly the persistence, of the control achieved by behavior modification are questioned by research which involves longer time periods than the earlier studies.

If the behaviorists are subject to the influence of reinforcement, or the consequences of their own behavior, one can predict a precipitous decline in the application of techniques of behavior modification. It appears that much of the short-term effect may be due to variables which relate to the social psychology or the demand characteristics of the experiments, the Hawthorne and placebo effects (Davison, 1968), or to the genuine interest and concern of experimenters for their subjects. The APA Monitor (November, 1974) headline for its report of Professor Bandura's presidential address (Bandura, 1974) states the situation succinctly: 'Psychology's power exaggerated, says Bandura'.

At least one behavior therapist has modified his approach almost to the point of abandoning behavior modification, as a result of his follow-up of his patients (Lazarus, 1971). Lazarus obtained a 95 % return to a questionnaire sent to a random sample of his clients, and interviewed personally or by telephone additional members of the random sample which totaled 112 cases. Forty-one had relapsed in from one week to six years after treatment, usually because of new stress-producing situations, according to Lazarus. Successful cases suggested that improvements were related to adoption of a different outlook and increased self-esteem. On an adjective checklist, the words most frequently used to describe him (sensitive, gentle, honest) refer to humanistic characteristics rather than to behavioristic techniques.

In my opinion there are other methods of behavior control more dangerous than behavior modification. The methods employed by some of those involved in groups are highly manipulating. The transactional analysts are, in my opinion, particularly pernicious, since they disdain any responsibility for their clients. While the extreme behaviorists (e.g. Skinner) state that behavior is completely determined by the environment, the transactional analysts deny that the environment — or other people, including themselves — has any influence on their clients. Yet at the same time they engage in the most blatant manipulation of their clients.

Behavior can be influenced

But whether the methods of behavior modification are effective, and thus potentially dangerous or subject to abuse, it is the issue of the control of some persons by others, by whatever methods, which is of concern. There is no question that behavior is influenced, or, in some instances controlled, by others, and it is the general recognition and resistance to such influence and control which has raised, or is raising, questions about the ethics which are involved. The fact of influence and control has of course always been present. The nature and sources of political power have been continuing issues in society. The difference between the present and the past lies in the fact that now psychology is beginning to develop some understanding of how influence and control operates, thus making it possible to more effectively influence and control behavior. As indicated above, the extent of this knowledge is exaggerated, not only in the minds of the public but in the minds of some psychologists. But it is clear that knowledge and understanding of human behavior, and consequently the possibility of prediction and control, will increase. The issue of the objectives of such control, with its value and ethical implications, will become increasingly important. As we become better able to control human behavior, we cannot avoid facing the question of what kind of person we want to develop. Do we want to attempt to create the kind of persons who inhabit *Walden Two* (Skinner 1948), people who, although they are completely controlled, are unaware of it, but who feel free, and are productive and happy? While I do not believe that it will be possible to create such a society — this is one of the exaggerations of psychologists which has led to the public having an exaggerated idea of the power of psychology — it is a possible goal to be worked toward. If this is not an acceptable goal, what would be? What are the criteria for the acceptance of a goal for human behavior? Most practicing behaviorists have not considered this question. They have been satisfied with rather simple, concrete, immediate goals — reducing disruptive behavior in classrooms, reducing anxiety and eliminating phobias in college students or clients, etc., etc. It is assumed that these are desirable ends in themselves. But on what bases are they considered desirable? What is the criterion for accepting or rejecting specific objectives or goals of behavior modification?

Ethics of behavior modification

Until recently, the behaviorists in general have been little concerned about the ethical implications of their activities. (Leonard Krasner [1962] has been a notable exception.) They have avoided discussion of values as related to their goals. The general position has been that they are technicians. As such they have not been concerned about ethical or value aspects of their objectives, failing to recognize that, as Bandura (1969) has noted, the specification of objectives or goals involves a value system, implicitly if not explicitly. Technology is always related to goals, and exists in a situation where ethics are of concern.

Other behaviorists have accepted the goals and values of their clients, or of society in general. Thus, Michael and Meyerson wrote in 1962 that:

> In schools, no one questions that it is better for children to learn school subject matter than not to learn it; it is desirable to get along with other children and with adults without excessive conflicts; more is to be gained by staying in school than by dropping out; very early marriage of school children is unwise; law-abiding behavior is better than delinquent behavior . . .If the drop-out problem is a serious one; if we really believe that our society and economy require an educated population; and if the monetary and social costs of large numbers of uneducated and undereducated persons are great; there should be no hesitation in taking advantage of scientific principles of learning to

apply effective extrinsic reinforcers to help shape desirable behavior. Some problems of juvenile delinquency and its behavioral treatment can be considered in the same way (Michael and Meyerson, 1962).

A similar approach has been taken to the treatment of patients in mental hospitals, represented by the statement of Leonard Ullmann in a class lecture to the effect that no one in our society has a right to be a patient in a mental hospital, and therefore anything necessary to get him out is justified. James V. McConnell is quoted from *Psychology Today* in the APA Monitor (Trotter and Warren, 1974) as saying: 'I don't believe the Constitution of the United States gives you the right to commit a crime if you want to; therefore, the Constitution does not guarantee you the right to maintain inviolable the personality it forced on you in the first place — if and when the personality manifests strongly antisocial behavior.'

Beit-Hallahmi (1974), referring to this group, writes:

> We should commend our colleagues who practice behavior modification for their honesty in stating their value preferences. Most of them are quite open about the fact that they work to enforce social norms and prevent deviance . . . Their starting point is always what is socially desirable and socially acceptable.

This approach to the ethics of behavior modification assumes that the ends justify the means. It furthermore assumes that there is really no problem of values or goals, since society has already agreed upon these. It is an approach which puts society before the individual. As such it is more in keeping with an authoritarian society such as Russia than with a democracy. Moreover, it has become apparent that society, as represented by individuals subjected to such arbitrary treatment and their representatives — the lawyers and journalists concerned with human rights — is not in agreement about these goals or the ethics implicit in the means to them.

It is impossible for those who influence the behavior of others to abdicate responsibility for the ethical and moral aspects of their methods. Anyone who is in a position of influencing others has a responsibility to be aware of, and to be ready to defend or justify, the ethical bases or principles on which he operates. If one can influence or control behavior, an ethical problem is involved in deciding whether or not to do so and in what way or to what ends. What is 'good' or desirable behavior? It is not sufficient to claim that one is a technician in the service of society; that is what the professionals in Germany became during the Nazi regime with no support from world opinion and the postwar Nuremberg trials. Neither is it adequate to claim that one is a scientist, and that science is only concerned with empirical relationships between methods of influence and outcomes, and that values or ethics are not involved. In spite of claims to the contrary, science is not value free. Science itself represents a value. Moreover, the value of a science which claims to be value free, and not concerned about the social effects or utility of its efforts, is being questioned.

Ethical and value systems

We face the problem of finding a generally acceptable system of ethics or set of values, if such exists. The general conclusion of most of those who have been concerned with this problem is that no generally acceptable or universal system of values or ethics exists. Values and ethics, it is claimed, are relative. Or the position may be taken that there are a number of different systems, with no adequate basis for choosing among them. Lowe (1959), for example, identifies four different categories of value systems: naturalism, culturalism, theism, and humanism. Since these systems, it is stated, involved differences which cannot be resolved, Lowe concludes that 'there is no single professional standard to which his [the psychologist's] values can conform'. Psychology, he says, cannot accept one of these sets of values because it then would no longer be a science but would become a social movement.

There are several apparent flaws in this argument. In the first place, as already indicated, science is not above values and ethics, and cannot be if it is to be an inherent part of society. Its goals are its values, and must also be accepted as values by society. Second, it may be questioned whether there are numerous different sets or systems of ethics and values. The four categories of Lowe may be reduced to two: natural or humanistic and supernatural or theistic. Third, these categories are simply presumed sources of values. In the one case it is assumed that values arise naturally from the experience of human beings living together. In the second case it is assumed that systems of ethics or values are revealed, supernaturally, to man, as in the stone tablets given to Moses or the gold tablets given to Joseph Smith. Fourth, the systems of ethics arising at different times in different societies, or revealed at different times to seers, prophets or other religious leaders are not basically different or in unresolvable conflict. While it is true that there are some values which vary at different times and among different cultures, there are also some basic universal values upon which the religious leaders and philosophers of all times and cultures appear to agree.

Two questions follow from the above. First, what are the basic or universal values, and what is their origin and bases? Second, what is the relation of these values to a science of psychology?

There appear to be at least two basic values which transcend time and cultures. There no doubt have been certain brief times and certain (small) groups where these values have been absent, and of course there have been and are individuals who ignore or fail to subscribe to them. But these values appear to have been subscribed to by the major religions and philosophies of all times and cultures. The first of these is respect for the individual. In its ultimate form it is respect for human life; in its broader form it is respect for the human person. Aspects of this respect include respect for the rights of the individual to autonomy, freedom of choice, and freedom to act within the context of the rights of others, and freedom from invasion of privacy. In a positive sense, respect involves a concern for others, a caring and compassion. In its highest form it is manifested in love, or *agapé*.

The second value is a basic honesty in human relations. All ethical systems appear to include the condemnation of deception, dishonesty, trickery. In our current philosophy of existentialism the term 'authenticity' is used. Others speak of transparency (Jourard, 1964).

These values are not simply the product of the thought of religious leaders and philosophers. They are the products of the experience of men living together in society. Without the observance of these values, or their implementation at least at a minimal level, society could not survive. Respect for life, in some degree and in some situations, is necessary for the survival of the race. The infant needs someone to provide it with a minimal degree of caring or love for his physical survival. The individual needs a minimum of caring and love from others if he is to become a person or develop a self. If there is not a minimal level of honesty in a society, a basis for trust in others, the social order would collapse.

Skinner appears to accept the survival of the group or culture as the ultimate goal. He writes: 'If a science of behavior can discover those conditions of life which make for the ultimate strength of men, it may provide a set of 'moral values' which, because they are independent of the history and culture of any one group, may be generally accepted' (1953, p. 445). Again, he says: 'Eventually the practices which make for the greatest biological and psychological strength of the group will survive' (Skinner, 1955).

Values and science

Bronowski, in *Science and Human Values* (1955) proposes that values develop from science. Science is the pursuit of truth, which implies honesty. It requires independence and freedom, and the right to dissent. It implies democracy, including tolerance and respect for others and their views. Thus, he writes, 'The values of science turn out to be the recognizably human values' (Bronowski, 1956, p. 32). For Bronowski, these values derive from the methods of science. It is no doubt true that they can be derived from science, in that they are necessary for its methods. But this does not mean that they originated from science. These values arose before the development of the scientific method, and make possible the existence of science.

The relationship of science to human values is complex. From one point of view, values are outside of science. They are chosen by society in some manner, directly or indirectly, at various levels or by various groups. Thus the employers or supporters of science determine the objectives of scientific research, and thus set the values of scientific endeavor. It might appear that at an ultimate level there is agreement that the survival of the race is generally or universally accepted as the objective of science. But it is conceivable that this could be rejected and the annihilation of man would be the objective of science. Further, physical survival is a minimal objective. The quality of life must be considered. In *Walden Two* everyone is productive and happy, though (except for the controller) completely controlled without being aware of it. For Skinner, this is utopia. Many would not agree that this is utopia. Certainly there are other possibilities. Presumably man is flexible and can be changed or molded into a variety of forms, both biologically and psychologically. How do we decide what man will become, and who decides? Are there no limits to what he can become? Is there nothing inherent in man's nature which influences, if not determines, what he should become?

Values and humanism

This suggests another point of view regarding human values. Man's nature, including his potentialities, may be a source from which values can be derived. Certain values may be inherent in man's biological and psychological nature and needs. Whatever is necessary to meet man's need or drive for biological survival becomes a value. Even for physical survival of the individual the care or love of another human being is necessary, as indicated earlier. It is relatively simple to determine what is needed for physical survival, and these become values to the individual and to society. The need for survival is an inherent characteristic of the organism. A society which chose to frustrate this drive, or to annihilate itself, would be denying the inherent nature of man.

At the psychological level it is not so obvious what the inherent nature, needs, and potentials of man are. What is the psychological equivalent to the physical drive to survive and to nurture the growth and development of the body? If man has a physical nature doesn't he also have a psychological nature, and if so, what is it?

Clearly, we do not have agreement on this. Is it inherent in man to strive for happiness or productivity? But if there is a drive to develop the potentials of the physical organism through activity, isn't there also a drive in man to develop his psychological potentials? And if there is, then what are these potentials?

Here we come, finally, to humanistic psychology, which has been concerned with these questions. Humanistic psychology is not a homogeneous discipline, or perhaps even a discipline in its present stage of development, certainly not as behavior modification is — or at least was until quite recently, since it appears that behaviorism has been changing so much (cf. Bandura, 1974) that it probably no longer should be called behaviorism if the word is to have any historical meaning. Thus, while I am apparently identified as humanistic in my orientation, as indicated by my being asked to present the humanistic position, and while I do consider myself as a humanistic psychologist, I wish to enter a disclaimer that I represent humanistic psychology.

Humanistic psychology assumes that as there is a drive in the organism to develop its physical potential, so there is a corresponding drive to develop its psychological potential. Indeed, these may be only two manifestations of a single drive — to preserve and enhance the self, of which the body is a part (Combs and Snygg,1959). Several terms have been used to refer to the person who is moving towards the enhancement of the self or the process of self-enhancement. These include self-realization, self-fulfillment, the fully functioning person and, most widely used, self-actualization, a term apparently first used in this context by Goldstein (1939). It would appear that if we could reach agreement on the nature of this process or the description of a self-actualizing person we would achieve two important things: (1) we would have a statement of a goal which would be more than a theoretical, philosophical or theological construct, but would be anchored in the biological nature of man, and (2) this goal would be a criterion against which we could measure the desirability or acceptability of man's behavior toward man. Acceptable and desirable behaviors would be those which facilitate the self-actualization of other persons.

There appears to be some agreement, at least among humanistically oriented psychologists, about the nature of the self-actualizing process or at least about the characteristics of self-actualizing persons.

Self-actualization as a value

The description of the adequate self or personality given by Combs and Snygg (1959, p. 246) provides a basis for a description of a self-actualizing person. Such a person perceives himself in positive ways (as competent?); he has a positive self-concept. He accepts himself. He also accepts others. The adequate person is open to his experiences, and is able to accept into awareness all his perceptions, without distortion or rejection. Behaviorally he manifests more efficient behavior, since he is not handicapped by defensiveness. Being secure, he can take chances, and is thus capable of spontaneous and creative behavior. He is independent, finding that his own feelings, beliefs and attitudes are adequate guides to his behavior. Finally, Combs and Snygg describe the adequate person as compassionate: not being defensive, he can relate closely to others without hostility and fear.

Rogers' concept of the fully functioning person (Rogers, 1959, 1961) is similar to the adequate person of Combs and Snygg. The fully functioning person has three main characteristics: (a) he is open to his experience, to all stimuli, external and internal, and does not have to be defensive or to distort his experience, (b) he lives existentially — that is, he is constantly in process, and is flexible and adaptable; (c) his behavior is determined from within — the locus of control is internal. Since the fully functioning person is open to his experience, all relevant available data influences his behavior. Some relevant data may be missing, so that behavior is not always perfect, but the presence of constant feedback leads to correction.

Maslow has provided the most extensive description of the self-actualizing person. While his work is well known, it would appear that many writers who refer to it have perhaps not recently read it, since it often appears to be misrepresented. It therefore appears to be desirable to summarize it in some detail.

Maslow, on the basis of a study of persons (living and dead) selected as being self-actualizing persons on the basis of a general definition, described the self-actualizing person as follows, as compared to ordinary or average people (Maslow, 1956):

1. *More efficient perception of reality and more comfortable relations with it*. This characteristic includes the detection of the phony and dishonest person and the accurate perception of what exists rather than a distortion of perception by one's needs. Self-actualizing people are more aware of their environment, both human and nonhuman. They are not afraid of the unknown and can tolerate the doubt, uncertainty, and tentativeness accompanying the perception of the new and unfamiliar. This is clearly the characteristic described by Combs and Snygg, and Rogers, as awareness of perceptions or openness to experience.
2. *Acceptance of self, others, and nature*. Self-actualizing persons are not ashamed or guilty about their human nature, with its shortcoming, imperfections, frailties,

and weaknesses. Nor are they critical of these aspects of other people. They respect and esteem themselves and others. Moreover, they are honest, open, genuine, without pose or facade. They are not, however, self-satisfied but are concerned about discrepancies between what is and what might be or should be in themselves, others, and society. Again, these characteristics are those which Kelly, Rogers, and Combs and Snygg include in their descriptions.

3. *Spontaneity.* Self-actualizing persons are not hampered by convention, but they do not flout it. They are not conformists, but neither are they anti-conformist for the sake of being so. They are not externally motivated or even goal-directed — rather their motivation is the internal one of growth and development, the actualization of themselves and their potentialities. Rogers and Kelly both speak of growth, development and maturation, change and fluidity.

4. *Problem-centering.* Self-actualizing persons are not ego-centered but focus on problems outside themselves. They are mission-oriented, often on the basis of a sense of responsibility, duty, or obligation rather than personal choice. This characteristic would appear to be related to the security and lack of defensiveness leading to compassionateness emphasized by Combs and Snygg.

5. *The quality of detachment; the need for privacy.* The self-actualizing person enjoys solitude and privacy. It is possible for him to remain unruffled and undisturbed by what upsets others. He may even appear to be asocial. This is a characteristic that does not appear in other descriptions. It is perhaps related to a sense of security and self-sufficiency.

6. *Autonomy, independence of culture and environment.* Self-actualizing persons, though dependent on others for the satisfaction of the basic needs of love, safety, respect and belongingness, 'are not dependent for their main satisfactions on the real world, or other people or culture or means-to-ends, or in general, on extrinsic satisfactions. *Rather they are dependent for their own development and continued growth upon their own potentialities and latent resources.*' Combs and Snygg, and Rogers, include independence in their descriptions, and Rogers also speaks of an internal locus of control.

7. *Continued freshness of appreciation.* Self-actualizing persons repeatedly, though not continuously, experience awe, pleasure, and wonder in their everyday world.

8. *The mystic experience, the oceanic feeling.* In varying degrees and with varying frequencies, *self-actualizing persons have experiences of ecstasy, awe, and wonder* with feelings of limitless horizons opening up, followed by the conviction that the experience was important and had a carry-over into everyday life. This and the preceding characteristic appear to be related and to add something not in other descriptions, except perhaps as it may be included in the existential living of Rogers.

9. *Gemeinschaftsgefuhl. Self-actualizing persons have a deep feeling of empathy, sympathy, or compassion for human beings in general.* This feeling is, in a sense, unconditional in that it exists along with the recognition of the existence in others of negative qualities that provoke occasional anger, impatience, and disgust. Although empathy is not specifically listed by others (Combs and Snygg include compassion), it would seem to be implicit in other descriptions including

acceptance and respect.
10. *Interpersonal relations. Self-actualizing people have deep interpersonal relations with others.* They are selective, however, and their circle of friends may be small, usually consisting of other self-actualizing persons, but the capacity is there. They attract others to them as admirers or disciples. This characteristic, again, is at least implicit in the formulations of others.
11. *The democratic character structure.* The self-actualizing person does not discriminate on the basis of class, education, race, or color. He is humble in his recognition of what he knows in comparison with what could be known, and he is ready and willing to learn from anyone. He respects everyone as potential contributors to his knowledge, merely because they are human beings.
12. *Means and ends.* Self-actualizing persons are highly ethical. *They clearly distinguish between means and ends* and subordinate means to ends.
13. *Philosophical, unhostile sense of humor.* Although the self-actualizing persons studied by Maslow had a sense of humor, it was not of the ordinary type. Their sense of humor was the spontaneous, thoughtful type, intrinsic to the situation. Their humor did not involve hostility, superiority, or sarcasm. Many have noted that a sense of humor characterizes people who could be described as self-actualizing persons, though it is not mentioned by those cited here.
14. *Creativeness.* All of Maslow's subjects were judged to be creative, each in his own way. The creativity involved here is not special-talent creativeness. It is a creativeness potentially inherent in everyone but usually suffocated by acculturation. *It is a fresh, naïve, direct way of looking at things.* Creativeness is a characteristic most would agree to as characterizing self-actualizing persons.

The resistance of some writers to the concept of self-actualization appears to be related to some misconceptions or misunderstanding regarding its nature or meaning.

One objection to self-actualization appears to be the belief that it is inimical to individuality. This view would seem to represent the self-actualizing person as a collection of traits, which are the same for all self-actualizing persons, and which manifest themselves in standard, identical behaviors. It is true that self-actualizing persons have many common characteristics or behaviors. Since it involves the actualization of individual potentials, it allows for the fact that different individuals have different potentials, as well as different interests. More will be said about this later. As Maslow (1962, p. 196) noted, since self-actualization is the actualization of a self, and since no two selves are alike, individuals actualize themselves in different ways.

A second widespread notion is that a self-actualizing person is antisocial, or at least asocial or self-centered.

The idea that the self-actualizing person is, or can be, antisocial was stated in 1958 by E.G. Williamson. Pointing out that human nature is potentially both good and evil, and that:

> man seems to be capable both of becoming his 'best' bestial and debasing self, as well as those forms of 'the best' that are of high excellence,' he contends that it cannot be accepted that 'the nature

> or form of one's full potential and self-actualization will thus be the 'best possible' or the 'good' form of human nature' (Williamson, 1965, p.195).

While one could contend that counseling would provide conditions for the actualizing of one's 'best' potential, Williamson questions the 'implicit assumption that the "best" potentiality will be actualized under optimum counseling relationships' (Williamson, 1965). He appears to believe that counseling, by accepting self-actualization as its goal, is in danger of encouraging 'growth through demolishing all barriers restricting free development in any and all directions, irresponsibly and without regard for the development of others' (Williamson, 1950). He questions the assumptions that 'any and all forms of growth contain within themselves their own, and sufficient, justification', and asks 'Do we believe that the fullest growth of the individual inevitably enhances the fullest growth of all other individuals?' (Williamson, 1958).

Skinner (1975) assumes that self-actualization is a selfish process: 'We see a concern for the aggrandizement of the individual, for the maximizing of credit due him, in the self-actualization of so-called humanistic psychology'.

Bandura (1974) also presents a negative view of self-actualization:

> Behavioral theorists, however, recognize that 'self-actualization' is by no means confined to human virtues. People have numerous potentialities that can be actualized for good or ill. Over the years, man has suffered considerably at the hands of self-actualized tyrants. A self-centered ethic of self-realization must therefore be tempered by concern for the social consequences of one's conduct.

Some humanistically oriented psychologists appear to share this view. Maddi (1973a), criticizing self-actualization as the good life, writes 'Actualization will tend to take place without the aid of socialization. Indeed, society is usually regarded, in this view, as an obstruction, because it forces individuals into molds, roles, conventions that have little to do with their own unique potentialities. The best thing society can do is impinge upon the individual as little as possible.' In another place (Maddi, 1973b), he writes:

> According to Rogers . . . what blocks individuals is society, in the form of persons and institutions reacting with conditional positive regard and therefore being too judgmental to be facilitative of self-actualization . . . The definition of the good life involved emphasizes spontaneity rather than planfulness, openness rather than critical judgment, continual change rather than stability, and an unreflective sense of well-being. Enacting this, one would more likely live in the woods than enter public life.

Smith (1973) sees self-actualization as including undesirable, or antisocial, behaviors: 'and the problem of evil remains: people may realize their potentialities in ways that are humanly destructive, of others if not of themselves'.

Even White (1973) views self-actualization as self-centered or selfish. Recognizing that Maslow included 'focusing on problems outside oneself and being concerned with the common welfare' in the concept of self-actualization he questions its inclusion: 'To call working for the common welfare "self-actualization" instantly falsifies it into something done for one's own satisfaction'. Thus it is apparent that he views self-actualization as self, or selfish, satisfaction. 'I ask readers to observe carefully,' he writes, 'whether or not self-actualization, in its current use by psychological counselors and others, is being made to imply anything more than adolescent preoccupation with oneself and one's impulses.' This, in my opinion is an unfair and unwarranted characterization of counselors who accept the concept of self-actual ization.

The implicit assumption in this conception of self-actualization is that there is an inevitable conflict between the individual and society, and that the full development (or self-actualization) of individuals is inimical to the self-actualization of other individuals.

The formulations by Rogers of the self-actualizing person deal with this issue. Individuals live, and must live, in a society composed of other individuals. He can actualize himself only in interaction with others. Selfish and self-centered behavior would not lead to experiences which would be self-actualizing (or satisfying) in nature. The self-actualizing person 'will live with others in maximum possible harmony, because of the rewarding character of reciprocal positive regard' (Rogers, 1959, pp. 234–6). 'We do not need to ask who will socialize him, for one of his own deepest needs is for affiliation and communication with others. As he becomes more fully himself, he will become more realistically socialized' (Rogers, 1961, p. 194). He is more mature, more socialized in terms of the goal of social evolution, though he may not be conventional or socially adjusted in a conforming sense. 'We do not need to ask who will control his aggressive impulses, for when he is open to all his impulses, his need to be liked by others and his tendency to give affection are as strong as his impulses to strike out or to seize for himself. He will be aggressive in situations in which aggression is realistically appropriate, but there will be no runaway need for aggression' (Rogers, 1959, p. 251). The self-actualizing person needs to live in harmony with others, to love and to be loved to meet his own needs, to be a self-actualizing person. Thus, the self-actualizing person provides the conditions for the self-actualization of others, rather than being a negative social influence.

It would appear that some of this confusion about the nature of self-actualization is a matter of semantics. But is also in part a matter of how one views the nature of man. If man is viewed as innately bad or depraved, then self-actualization would involve the development of socially negative characteristics. If man is viewed as innately good, then this would not occur. If man is viewed as neither, or if he is viewed as essentially good but with potential for evil — for selfishness, for hurting others, for aggression — then it becomes important to know the conditions which lead to the expression of such behaviors on the one hand, and on the other hand those conditions which lead to the development of positive behaviors which facilitate the development of the positive self-actualizing behaviors in others.

Aggression has long been considered an instinct. Adler originally proposed that aggression was the single basic motive or instinct of man (Ansbacher and Ansbacher, 1956, p. 34). The strength and practical universality of aggression argue for its innateness. However, many have questioned its innateness or instinctiveness. Anthropologists have found societies with little trace or evidence of aggression. Ashley Montagu writes:

> My own interpretation of the evidence, strictly within the domain of science, leads me to the conclusion that man is born good and is organized in such a manner from birth as to need to grow and develop his potentialities for goodness . . . [The view that aggressiveness is inherited] is not scientifically corroborated. In fact, all the available evidence gathered by competent investigators indicates that man is born without a trace of aggressiveness (Montagu, 1962).

He refers to Lauretta Bender's finding that hostility in the child is a symptom complex resulting from deprivation in development. Charlotte Buhler, in her studies of infants, also found that there is

> evidence of a primary orientation toward 'reality' into which the baby moves with a positive anticipation of good things to be found. Only when this reality appears to be hurtful or overwhelming does the reaction become one of withdrawal or defense (Buhler, 1961, p. 71).

Maslow also declares that impulses of hate, jealousy, hostility, and so on are acquired. 'More and more,' he writes, 'aggression is coming to be regarded as a technique or mode of compelling attention to the satisfaction of one's need' (Maslow, 1949). There is no instinct of aggression that seeks expression or discharge without provocation or without regard to circumstances.

In other words, aggression is not primary but is a reaction to deprivation, threat, or frustration. This is the frustration-aggression hypothesis put forward in 1939 by the Yale anthropologist Dollard and his psychologist associates (Dollard, et al., 1939). A more general term for the stimuli that provoke aggression is threat. Aggression is universal because threat, in some form or other, is universal. The psychoanalyst Bibring, in criticizing Freud's theories, questions 'whether there are any phenomena of aggression at all outside the field of the ego-preservative functions' and notes 'the empirical fact that aggressiveness appears only or almost only when the life instincts or the ego instincts are exposed to harm' (Bibring,1958). A popular novel purporting to demonstrate the innateness of aggressiveness in man inadvertently supports the view that aggression is the result of threat, since the development of aggression in the group of castaway boys occurs under conditions of fear and feelings of being threatened (Golding, 1955).

There is evidence that man is inherently good in the continual striving toward an ideal society, with the repeated and independent development of essentially similar religious and ethical systems whose ideals have withstood the test of time. In spite of deprivation, threat, and frustration, these ideals have been held and practiced by many individuals. Mankind has developed systems of government and law that, though imperfectly, especially in their applications, represent these ideals.

It might actually be argued that goodness or cooperation has a survival value (Montagu, 1950), and that innate aggression would be selectively eliminated by evolution. If there were not an inherent drive toward good in man, or if aggression were innate, it is difficult to understand how the human race could have continued to survive. The potential for good has survived in the face of continued threat and frustration. When we can reduce deprivation and threat, the manifestations of good will increase and aggression will decrease. It is important to add that aggression does not include assertive behavior, initiative behavior, nor even much of competitive behavior. The confusion of these kinds of behavior with aggression has perhaps contributed to the belief that aggression is innate.

The conditions for self-actualization

If aggressive behaviors are the result of threat, then the absence of threat should lead to the expression of positive behaviors toward others. Here we can find some suggestions from experience and research in counseling or psychotherapy, particularly what is called client-centered or relationship therapy, since this approach accepts as its goal the development of more self-actualizing persons and appears to have developed at least some of the conditions which lead to this goal.

Three conditions which have been identified and studied are empathic understanding, respect, warmth, concern or caring, and therapeutic genuineness. These conditions hardly need to be elaborated upon, since they have become so well known through the writing of client-centered therapists and researchers. Extensive research (see Truax and Carkhuff, 1967; Carkhuff, 1969; Truax and Mitchell, 1971) indicates that these conditions, when provided at an adequate level in the psychotherapy relationship, are related to a wide variety of positive outcomes which include the aspects of self-actualization. Included among these outcomes appear to be the conditions themselves. Thus, persons who are treated with empathic understanding, respect, and therapeutic genuineness or honesty respond with similar behaviors.

The operation of such influences on others can be viewed, at least in part, from a behavioristic frame of reference. The process clearly involves modeling, which is claimed by the behaviorists as a behavioristic method. The process may also be viewed as involving reinforcement. The conditions can be considered to be the reinforcers of the similar behavior, or more broadly, of a wide variety of positive behaviors (Patterson, 1974, pp. 131–41). It can be argued that, in behavioristic terms, the most potent reinforcer of human behavior is a good human relationship.

If this is so, then is there not the possibility of the human relationship — of empathy, respect and honesty — to control and manipulate others for selfish purposes against the best interests of others? However, there appears to be an inbuilt protection in the nature of a good human relationship against excessive control or manipulation. The conditions of a good human relationship are not effective, at least in the long run, unless they are real and genuine. Real respect for another is inconsistent with the exploiting of the other for one's own selfish purposes. In addition, when there is the awareness that another is attempting to manipulate, that another is lacking in respect, then resistance to being controlled or changed arises. Thus respect for another prevents one from attempting to manipulate another, and awareness of lack of respect in another prevents one from being manipulated.

Summary
Our objective has been the attempt to develop a basis for evaluating efforts to influence and control human behavior. Currently those who are engaged in behavior modification are under scrutiny. But there are other behavior influencers whose behaviors also have serious ethical implications, including those active in the group movement. The increasing concern about ethical practices and the rights of individuals appears to signal the beginning of a new social era, in which the individual or person is coming into his own.

Most of those behaviorists who are concerned about the ethical justification of their objectives accept presumed social norms as criteria. This is an inadequate or unacceptable criterion. It accepts the status quo, and attempts to induce conformity to it. This attitude is the basis for the contention that counseling or psychotherapy is an instrument of social control for maintaining the establishment (Halleck, 1971).

The problem is to derive bases for, and a statement of, a generally acceptable set of values or ethical system by which we can evaluate psychological methods or techniques for influencing or changing behavior. The argument that there are no universal values and that all values are relative is rejected. It is argued that there are some values which are not time- or culture-bound, and that these relate to the nature of man and the conditions for his survival and development. Two such basic values are respect and honesty. These values derive from the experience of men living together, and presumably could be supported by scientific study of groups and societies. These values are not only necessary for physical survival and development, but for psychological survival and development. The concept of self-actualization is developed to encompass the individual's development and exercise of his psychological potentials. Some misconceptions of the nature of self-actualization are noted. The adherence to the two basic values of respect and honesty, together with empathic understanding, are necessary conditions for the development of self-actualizing persons. It is noted that there is considerable support for this statement in research in counseling or psychotherapy.

We thus have a concept which provides a criterion for a system of ethics, and a goal toward which the influence of human behavior can be directed. Specific methods of control can be evaluated in terms of their consistency with the desired outcome. Thus, for example, since autonomy is a characteristic of self-actualizing persons, then methods which take over the control of the individual's behavior and deny him autonomy or independence and responsibility for his own behavior are unacceptable, except in cases where the person has clearly demonstrated his inability to be responsible for his own behavior and interferes with the rights of others.

It is not asserted that a complete basis for a system of ethics has been provided. It is only suggested that a foundation has been provided for a system which should be acceptable not only to humanistic psychologists but to those who accept science as a value.

References

Ansbacher, H. L., and Ansbacher, R. (Eds.) (1956) *The individual psychology of Alfred Adler*. New York: Basic Books.

Bandura, A. (1969) *Principles of behavior modification*. New York: Holt, Rinehart and Winston.

Bandura, A. (1974) Behavior theory and the models of man. *American Psychologist*, 29, pp. 859–69.

Beit-Hallahmi, B. (1974) Salvation and its vicissitudes: Clinical psychology and political values. *American Psychologist*, 29, pp. 124–9.

Bibring, E. (1958) The development and problems of the theory of instincts. In Stacy, C. L. and Martino, M. F. (Eds.) *Understanding human motivation*. Cleveland: Howard Allen. Pp. 474–98.

Bronowski, J. (1956) *Science and human values*. New York: Julian Messner. (Harper and Row Torchbooks, 1959.)

Buhler, C. (1961) *Values in psychotherapy*. New York: Macmillan-Free Press.

Carkhuff, R. R. (1969) *Helping and human relations, Vol. 1; Selection and training, Vol. Il; Practice and research*. New York: Holt, Rinehart and Winston.

Cattell, R. B. (1948) Ethics and the social sciences. *American Psychologist*, 3, pp. 193–8.

Combs, A. W., and Snygg, D. (1959) *Individual behavior*. 2nd Ed. New York: Harper and Row.

Commager, H. S. (1975) The school as surrogate conscience. *Saturday Review*, January 11, pp. 54–7.

Creegan, R. F. (1958) Concerning professional ethics. *American Psychologist*, 13, pp. 272–5.

Davison, G. C. (1968) Systematic desensitization as a counterconditioning process. *Journal of Abnormal and Social Psychology*, 73, pp. 91–9.

Dollard, J., Doob, L. W., Miller, N. E., Mowrer, O. H., and Sears, R. R. (1939) *Frustration and aggression*. New Haven: Yale University Press,.

Golding, W. (1955) *Lord of the flies*. New York: Coward McCann.

Goldstein, K. (1939) *The organism*. New York: American Book. (Boston: Beacon Press, 1963.)

Halleck, S. L. (1971) *The politics of therapy*. New York: Science House.

Jourard, S. M. (1964) *The transparent self*. New York: Van Nostrand Reinhold.

Krasner, L. (1962) Behavior control and social responsibility. *American Psychologist*, 17, pp. 199–204.

Lazarus, A. (1971) *Behavior therapy and beyond*. New York: McGraw-Hill.

Lowe, C. M. (1959) Value orientations: An ethical dilemma. *American Psychologist*, 14, pp. 687–93.

Maddi, S. (1973a) Creativity is strenuous. *The University of Chicago Magazine*, September-October, pp. 18–23.

Maddi, S. (1973b) Ethics and psychotherapy: Remarks stimulated by White's paper.

The Counseling Psychologist, 4 (2), pp. 26–36.

Maslow, A. H. (1949) Our maligned human nature. *Journal of Psychology*, 20, pp. 273–8.

Maslow, A. H. (1956) Self-actualizing people: A study of psychological health. In C. E. Moustakas (Ed.) *The self: Explorations in personal growth*. New York: Harper and Row.

Maslow, A. H. (1962) *Towards a psychology of being.* Princeton, N. J.:Van Nostrand Reinhold

Michael, J., and Meyerson, L. (1962) A behavioral approach to counseling and guidance. *Harvard Educational Review*, 32, pp. 382–402.

Montagu, A. (1950) *On being human*. New York: Henry Schuman.

Montagu, A. (1962) *The humanization of man*. Cleveland: World Publishing.

Muller, H. J. (1958) Human values in relation to evolution. *Science*, 127, pp. 625–9.

Patterson, C. H. (1974) *Relationship counseling and psychotherapy*. New York: Harper and Row.

Reppucci, N. D., and Saunders. J. T. (1974) Social psychology of behavior modification: Problems of implementation in natural settings. *American Psychologist*, 29, pp. 649–660.

Robinson, D. N. (1973) Therapies: A clear and present danger. *American Psychologist*, 28, pp. 129 –33.

Rogers, C. R. (1959) A theory of therapy, personality, and interpersonal relationships as developed in the client-centered framework. In S. Koch (Ed.) *Psychology*: *A study of a science: Vol. 3, Formulations of the person and the social context*. New York: McGraw-Hill, pp. 184–256.

Rogers, C. R. (1961) *On becoming a person*. Boston: Houghton Mifflin.

Skinner, B. F. (1948) *Walden Two*. New York: Macmillan.

Skinner,B. F. (1953) *Science and human behavior*. New York: Macmillan.

Skinner, B. F. (1955) The control of human behavior. *Transactions of the New York Academy of Sciences,*17, pp. 547–551.

Skinner, B. F. (1975) The steep and thorny way to a science of behavior. *American Psychologist*, 30, pp. 42–49.

Smith, M. B. (1973) Comment on White's paper. *The Counseling Psychologist*, 4, (2), pp. 48–50.

Trotter, S., and Warren, J. (1974) Behavior modification under fire. *American Psychological Association Monitor*, 5 (4), p. 1.

Truax, C. B., and Carkhuff, R. R, (1967) *Toward effective counseling and psychotherapy*. Chicago: Aldine.

Truax, C. B., and Mitchell, K. M. (1971) Research on certain therapist interpersonal skills. In Bergin, A. E. and Garfield, S. L. (Eds.) *Handbook of psychotherapy and behavior change: An empirical analysis*. New York: Wiley.

White, R. W. (1973) The concept of healthy personality: What do we really mean? *The Counseling Psychologist*, 4 (2), pp. 3 –12.

Williamson, E. G. (1950) A concept of counseling. *Occupations*, 29, pp. 182–9.

Williamson, E. G. (1958) Value orientation in counseling. *Personnel and Guidance Journal*, 37, pp. 520–8.

BEHAVIORAL SCIENCE AND HUMANISTIC CONCERNS 29

Clearly, we are witnessing a change in our society, a change which, I believe, has tremendous implications for science and research as well as for applied psychology. This change involves the recognition of the importance of values, of goals, of ends as well as means. No longer can we adopt an 'anything goes attitude' — an attitude that more technology, more objectivity, more and greater control of behavior are *ipso facto* good.

The traditions of empiricism and pragmatism are changing. William James and the narrow behaviorists are no longer representatives of the American Way. We have become concerned about not just what works, how we can control behavior, but with questions of the nature of the objectives, outcomes, and goals. We are entering an era of concern for the individual — to which we have always given lip-service. This concern extends to individuals who are inmates of our institutions — mental patients, prisoners — as well as subjects of research.

So we seem to be in need of a new ethic, or a new basis for ethics. Can we look to psychology for a basis for an ethic of man's treatment of man? Why not? But 'psychology cannot tell people how they ought to live their lives'. So says Bandura — and as I read it, he does not mean that psychology is not able to do so, but should not do so. This is probably the only statement which he makes in his excellent APA presidential address with which I would take issue (Bandura, 1974).

If psychology is concerned with the study of human behavior and with the consequences of the behavior of one person on another, then it should have something to say about how people should behave if they are to contribute positively to the lives and development of other persons.

But wait — what do we mean by positive? Aren't we here introducing a value judgment? And aren't values outside of science? And isn't psychology a science? This is the dilemma we have been caught up in — a problem which I have attempted to deal with in my major paper (Patterson, 1978) but which I am not sure I dealt with in an adequate way. I'm not sure anyone else has adequately done so — even Bronowski (1956) in his stimulating little essay on 'Science and human values'. Bandura (1974), a few sentences after making the statement just quoted, seems to

Presented at a conference on 'Moral and Ethical Implications of Behavior Modification', University of Wisconsin-Madison, March 20–1, 1975.

say something quite different. 'As a science concerned about the social consequences of its applications, psychology must also fulfill a broader obligation to society by bringing influence to bear on public policies to ensure that its findings are used in the service of human betterment.' So science is concerned about human betterment, and presumably has some ideas about what it involves.

But how can science, an inanimate, intangible construct, be concerned? It is scientists who are concerned — at least some of them. Perhaps here is the key. Science is an abstract, hypothetically neutral construct. But it exists only, as Rogers has somewhere noted, in the minds of men. It not only can be used for good or ill, but, if it is used at all, it must be used for good or ill. Scientists have some responsibility for how it is used. It has been assumed that science is good. But its results, or the results of its application, are not necessarily good, and the scientists, if not science, bear some responsibility for its possible uses.

Now, until recently, most behaviorists have not been particularly concerned about how behavior modification is used. They have regarded themselves as technicians, in the employ of others who make the decisions about what their techniques are used for. But others, and society, regard them not only as scientists but as appliers of science, and put some responsibility on them for the way in which, and the ends for which, their techniques are used.

As I noted in my major paper (Patterson, 1978), behaviorists have given little consideration to the criteria for choosing target behaviors. Winett and Winkler (1972) conducted a survey of the target behaviors accepted in studies involving normal classrooms. The title is revealing: *Current behavior modification in the classroom: Be still, be quiet, be docile*. One study reviewed, by D. R. Thomas, W. C. Becker, and V. M. Armstrong (1968), entitled 'Production and elimination of disruptive classroom behavior by systematically varying the teacher's behavior', classified behaviors as appropriate and inappropriate. The latter, the inappropriate behaviors, included getting out of seat, standing up, walking around, running, hopping, skipping, jumping, moving chairs, racking chairs, tapping feet, rattling papers, carrying on a conversation with other children, crying, singing, whistling, laughing, turning head or body toward another child, showing objects to another child, and looking at another child. What is then left to do? Not much! Appropriate behaviors included attending to the teacher, raising hand and waiting for the teacher to respond, working in seat on a workbook, following in a reading text. Now some of the undesirable behaviors no doubt would interfere with learning. But it is clear what the concept of education and learning is in such a classroom — education is teacher-controlled, learning is passive. Obviously, we are a long way from recognizing the concepts of learning developed by Piaget and others often identified as humanistic psychologists, which recognize the necessity of activity and interpersonal interaction if real learning is to occur. Are behaviorists so enamored of conformity and so ignorant of the nature of the learning of human beings in natural environments — or have they indeed become technicians at the service of traditional school administrators and teachers?

Here, no doubt, there will be objections that I have misrepresented behaviorists. But what is a behaviorist? At the present time, there is no single or simple answer to this question. We have all kinds of behaviorists, from the radical behaviorist (Watson and Skinner) through the more conventional behaviorists, to the social learning or cognitive behaviorists (e.g. Bandura). This is certainly not a homogeneous group. In fact, they are so different, e.g. Skinner and Bandura, that to use the same term, behaviorism, to designate them is confusing and misleading. In effect, the behaviorists have been annexing area after area of psychology and subsuming it under the term 'behaviorism'. And now, wonder of wonders, we have humanistic behaviorists or behavioral humanists (Thoresen, 1973). It becomes difficult if not impossible to pin down just what the essence of behaviorism is. If one tries to find out what behaviorists have in common, it seems to boil down to the claim that they have a monopoly on the scientific method, so that what anyone else does is not scientific.

If one looks beneath this, there seems to be a basic attitude or assumption shared by those I would define as behavioristic — and this would not include Bandura and perhaps some of the so-called behavioral humanists or humanistic behaviorists. As a matter of fact, this attitude or assumption is related to the claim of being scientific, or to the concept of science held by behaviorists — and by most other psychologists except the humanistic psychologists. This is the view that the causes of behavior are wholly external to the person, except for the fixed genetic or constitutional causes, or limitations. Thus the person is similar to the objects of study in the physical sciences, that is, he becomes an object, to be controlled and manipulated by external stimuli and contingencies. It is this which I believe is a source of ethical problems in behavior modification. Absorption in the control and manipulation of behaviors easily leads to lack of concern about the desirability of outcomes and neglect of the interests and rights of subjects as persons. A behavioral humanism, or a humanistic behaviorism, would seem to still be tied to methods which fail to give adequate respect to the person even if he is being manipulated toward humanistic objectives. When a behaviorist writes that 'the individual person cannot be treated as an inanimate object to be manipulated, but must be viewed as a dynamic, active organism, (Thoresen, 1973, p. 398) then it would seem that the appellation 'behaviorist' is inappropriate.

But does this mean that the methods of behavior modification and behavior control, which are admittedly effective (though only maximally so when the control of the environment is complete) should not be used with human beings? Some have argued that if manipulation and control are restricted to positive reinforcement, and aversive consequences are not applied, then there is no ethical problem. But the ethical problem is not limited to the means of control. Nor is it limited to the objectives of control. It inheres in the fact of control itself. To be sure, as Skinner emphasizes, control is ubiquitous. But much of it is open and obvious. It exists with the knowledge of those being subject to it. It can be argued, then, that attempts to control others without their knowledge is unethical. But is knowledge sufficient? In research with human beings, emphasis is being placed upon the importance of informed consent by subjects in experiments. Should not this requirement of informed consent be extended beyond research to all who are subject to attempts to control or alter their behavior? This has become an issue in the use of behavior modification in institutions, especially correctional institutions. Knowledge and informed consent would seem to be minimal ethical requirements for the practice of behavior modification techniques. But beyond this there is the concern with the objectives and outcomes of behavior modification, which I have attempted to deal with in my formal paper.

There are two aspects which I did not touch upon, however, since they did not fit easily into the organization of my paper. One is the obligation of those engaged in research and demonstrations of behavior modification to the staff of the agencies and institutions in which they are engaged in such projects. Some disillusionment and resentment are being created in some of these situations, such as classrooms in schools. There are now numerous studies involving the modification and control of classroom behavior. The standard pattern of such projects is familiar. First, observation establishes a baseline for the behaviors to be modified. Then a program for changing behaviors is instituted, usually involving the use of extrinsic reinforcers or a token system. Then, to demonstrate that it is the program which is responsible for the resulting changes in behavior, the reinforcers are withdrawn, and, lo and behold, the behavior drops back to the baseline. Reinforcements are then resumed and behavior improves again. At this point, the demonstration is complete, or data for a publishable article, complete with graphs, are available, so the project is dropped. But what then happens? Without continued reinforcement, behavior regresses again, and the teacher is left with a classroom situation which may be worse than at the beginning, because she is confused and frustrated. Are there not ethical implications in such research and demonstration projects? In addition, the fact that the behavior changes do not persist, and do not transfer to other classrooms, but are tied to the reinforcements or token system, are practical limitations which are not adequately recognized by the enthusiastic salesmen of behavior modification. The talk about intrinsic reinforcers taking over and maintaining the behaviors is just talk.

Operant behaviors, which become objects of extrinsic reinforcement, presumably arise in part at least from internal motivations. If such behaviors are deemed desirable, they can be tied to external stimuli or artificial rewards. But is it the behavior *per se*, or the internally motivated or produced behavior which is desired? Behavior modification, in tying behavior to extrinsic reinforcers, does not necessarily assure the continuance of the behavior when the extrinsic reinforcers are removed. Intrinsic reinforcers do not automatically develop.

The argument, that if control does not involve aversive consequences at any time, it is acceptable (which is Skinner's argument), is inadequate. There are other consequences of control besides those which Skinner calls aversive which are or may be undesirable or ethically questionable. Some of these may be considered side effects. Thus, the control of some persons by others leads to dependence of the controlled upon the controllers. Some would consider dependence an undesirable consequence or outcome. Dependence is related to lack of freedom. Now I know freedom is a dirty word to many behaviorists. But the sense or feeling of freedom appears to be a value even to Skinner, since he presents as an asset in *Walden Two* (Skinner, 1948) the fact that its inhabitants feel they are free even though they are not. They are in fact happy slaves, but slaves nevertheless. Of equal if not more relevance is the fact that they have been deceived into feeling they are free. Skinner appears to have no compunctions about this.

There is something specious in arguing that certain kinds of control are bad, and other kinds of control are humanistic, when they are used to achieve goals arbitrarily selected as good or desirable by the behaviorists. All attempts to subject others to control toward objectives arbitrarily chosen by the controller deprive the controlled of some of his rights as a human being. Skinner (1971), admitting that while a science of behavior treats a person as an object, at the same time denies that it dehumanizes him because it regards him as 'an object of extraordinary subtlety and complexity'. But he is an object, nevertheless, or at best an organism whose behavior is determined by external forces, who can only react or respond to such forces, with no influence on his own behavior. This is in fact a highly simplified, not a complex, view of man. One might argue that, if man is not such a simplified organism at the mercy of his genetic and environmental history, no harm is done. But this fails to recognize the power of beliefs and expectations on behavior. If man is viewed as an object to be controlled, then we will create an environment which will conform to this view, in which behavior will be controlled by others. Those who are controlled will see themselves as an object to be controlled. But the paradox is that the controllers do not share this view as applying to themselves. Who controls the controllers? Are they in fact, as Skinner states, controlled by those they control? It is of course true that influence is reciprocal. But one becomes involved in a circle if the controlled control the controllers.

That behavior is not entirely determined by its immediate consequences can be substantiated by many examples of everyday experience. It is illustrated by the experience of behaviorists themselves when they persist in efforts at behavior modification, as in their work with autistic children, with little if any positive reinforcement of their efforts. Can it be that it is only the behavior of behaviorists which is not controlled by the immediate environment?

This possibility is suggested by the writing of Skinner about man controlling or shaping his environment, which, paradoxically, supposedly controls man's behavior. But it is apparently the behaviorists who will control the environment as the means of controlling the behavior of others, without their knowledge or consent. That is, of course, exactly what *Walden Two* is. By what right, and according to what ethics, should the behaviorists exercise this control? What is the ethics of leading others to believe they have no freedom or cannot control their own behavior, while the behaviorists do not accept such beliefs about their own behavior? By what right or ethics do those who appropriate for themselves the designation 'behavioral scientists' take on the governance of mankind? Does the appropriation of the term 'humanistic' — in a narrow, restricted sense — give them this right?

References
Bandura, A. (1974) Behavior theory and the models of man. *American Psychologist*, 29, pp. 859–69.
Bronowski, J. (1956) *Science and human values*. New York: Julian Messner.

(Harper & Row Textbooks, 1959).

Patterson, C. H. (1978) Humanistic concerns and behavior modification. In L. Beutler and R. Greene (Eds.) *Special problems in child and adolescent behavior.* Westport, Conn.: Technomic Publishing Co. Pp. 187–215.

Skinner, B. F. (1948) *Walden Two.* New York: Macmillan.

Skinner, B. F. (1971) In *The Humanist*, 31, No. 4.

Thomas, D. R., Becker, W. C., and Armstrong, V. M. (1968). Production and elimination of disruptive classroom behavior by systematically varying the teacher's behavior. *Journal of Applied Behavior Analysis*, 1, pp. 34–45.

Thoresen, C. E. (1973). Behavioral humanism. In Thoresen, C. E. (Ed.) *Behavior modification in education.* Chicago: National Society for the Study of Education, University of Chicago Press. Pp. 385–421.

Winett, R. A., and Winkler, R. C. (1972). Current behavior modification in the classroom: Be still, be quiet, be docile. *Journal of Applied Behavioral Analysis*, 5, pp. 499–504.

THE SOCIAL RESPONSIBILITY OF PSYCHOLOGY

30

The theme for this 77th Annual APA Convention is 'Psychology and the Problems of Society'. Psychologists, along with many other people, have become intensely aware that we do not live in the best of all possible worlds, that in fact the world is a pretty miserable place for many if not most human beings. That things could be better, few will deny. The discrepancy between what is, and what could be ,can and should be, narrowed if not eliminated. Surely psychology has something to offer to a society torn with strife, with individuals and groups demanding changes which will provide, or which they think will provide, a better life. Many psychologists are urging that the profession become more active in solving society's problems, and that individual psychologists become activists as well.

The bases for the current concern with social engineering in psychology seems to me to be two. First is the increasing recognition that man is a social being and must be seen in a social framework. The second is the recognition that environmental influences are important in determining behavior. A corollary of this is the realization that many persons today are the victims of unfavorable, even intolerably bad environmental conditions which have psychological implications. Psychologists — especially counseling and clinical psychologists — are concerned about people, and thus want to do something about this state of affairs. To many, helping individuals is no longer satisfying, since it is possible to help only a few. However, if the problems of individuals are not their problems, but originate in society, so that the individual has no control over the solution to his problem, the frustration of the psychologist is understandable.

It is thus contended, to quote Peterson (1968, p. 91), that 'changes of a cultural kind can be of much more general and lasting benefit than any individual treatment, however effective the latter may be'. Let us ignore the obvious overgeneralization of this statement and admit that there are many individuals whose problems derive from harmful social conditions that should and must be changed.

This is not, of course, a new problem; it is only that psychologists have become

First published in *The Counseling Psychologist*, 1969, 1, 4, pp. 97–100. ©1969 Division of Counseling Psychology. Reprinted by permission of Sage Publications/ Corwin Press, Inc. (Presented at the 77th Annual Convention, the American Psychological Association, Washington, D. C., September 1, 1969.)

more acutely aware of the problem and of the need to do something about it. Psychologists are Johnny-come-latelys to the scene. Sociologists have for more than half a century been concerned about the social origins of emotional disturbances or behavioral disorders, to use the new term. For example, in 1936, L. K. Frank published an article entitled 'Society as the Patient' (1936). Social psychiatry has been on the scene for at least a couple of decades. This has led to such approaches as the interpersonal therapy of Sullivan, milieu therapy, and the therapeutic community. And, as Peterson (1968, p. 50) notes,

> sociological change operations have also been addressed to the more general organization of social systems in the community at large, and to the preventive and therapeutic effects of the way societies function as a whole. Community mental health and community psychology have been employed as terms to designate social actions of this kind.

Peterson discusses the terms used to refer to this effort, such as social psychiatry and community psychology, and suggests that social engineering would be preferable, in part because it is 'neutral about professional hegemonies among those who are to do the work' (1968, p. 51). Others than the professions have of course been concerned — social reformers, politicians and statesmen, and now college youth, blacks, and the disadvantaged themselves.

It cannot be denied, now that we have fully recognized what Sullivan and the sociologists have been emphasizing, that we should be concerned about doing something about it. But the point is that the problem is one that requires the efforts of many groups. Psychologists have neither the total answer nor the total responsibility, no matter how arrogant they may feel about their knowledge or how guilty they may feel about their past failure to assume any responsibility. Psychology is not going to be the knight in shining armor riding up at the last minute to provide the solution to the problem. The reform of society is not the sole responsibility of psychology. Psychology has no monopoly, nor even any special expertise here. Other professions — anthropology, sociology, political science — have at least as much if not more to contribute to effective methods of social change since these disciplines have been concerned with the actions of large groups while psychology has been concerned mainly with the study of small group activities. And, of course, when it comes to the actual change process, it is mainly through nonprofessionals — politicians, statesmen, social reform organizations, etc. — that change occurs. Psychologists certainly may be active here, but as individual citizens rather than as representatives of a profession.

To quote Peterson again (1968, p. 237),

> the question no longer is whether social scientists and professional mental health workers should be involved in social engineering and the control of human behavior, but how much and what kind of engagement is appropriate. The politicians, financiers, and others who direct our society are not likely to deliver authority and power to professional do-gooders without reservation and sometimes

without a fight. Even if they would, it is undesirable that they should. The design of a democratic society must never be dictated by a single group.

The question is, what is the responsibility of psychology and psychologists; how can they contribute most effectively to positive social change? Individual therapy is not enough, and it does not — except perhaps indirectly to some extent — correct the social determinants of individual disorder.

The solution which is being suggested by many counseling and clinical psychologists is the abandonment of individual counseling or psychotherapy. The doors of the clinic and consulting room should be closed — but without the therapist and client being left inside. Everyone, it seems, should be moving out into the community. But it is never very clear just what they are to do there. Some seem to be advocating that they march in picket lines, lead or start riots, or at least engage in social movements as an activist.

Now all these things may be appropriate for a psychologist as an individual and as a citizen. Perhaps it is not too much to expect that all citizens with a professional education should be involved in some way in the effort to better social conditions. But we should not expect that psychologists as psychologists must be activists, and identify themselves by carrying signs saying, 'I am a psychologist'. And there are many ways in which individuals can work toward social improvement. Everyone should not be expected to do it in the same way, or in ways which activists think they should. Nor should those psychologists who do not choose to be activists be made to feel that they are no longer psychologists. There are some who seem to want to redefine the position description of the counseling psychologist to include some such statement as 'Every counseling psychologist must walk in at least one picket line a week'. There seems to be confusion between the obligations of a psychologist as a psychologist, and as a citizen.

In my earlier paper (Patterson, 1969), my plea was that psychology not abandon psychotherapy, individual or group, for unknown, untried activities or espouse social action as the only desirable or respected activity for a psychologist. I am still of this opinion. There are of course other methods than psychotherapy for changing or modifying individual and group behavior. Psychotherapy is probably appropriate for a small percentage of those with problems. But other methods, which usually involve more direct intervention and control, raise problems involving ethical and social values which have not been adequately faced by the behaviorists. In spite of the propaganda that the client determines the goals, this is not always the case. I have become concerned about the increasing number of reports of intervention in the lives of individuals and groups where the goals have been selected and imposed by the experimenter. It must also be remembered that much of the immediate social environment is a psychological environment and the client is part of it, and has some responsibility to change his own environment as well as some ability to do so if he is helped through individual or group therapy. It is still worth emphasizing that self-initiated and self-controlled change may be more desirable than change induced and directed by an outside agent.

This is not to deny that some environments — or some aspects of the environment — cannot be changed by the individual. Certainly psychologists — as well as social workers, teachers, parents, etc. — have some responsibility for changing environments for those unfortunate individuals who cannot do so for themselves. It is also true that there are some aspects of the environment that are harmful for large numbers of individuals, and these require large-scale social changes. But this is where the psychologist as a professional reaches his limits as far as direct change is concerned, though within the limits of an institution, such as the school, he has a professional responsibility for attempting change

This leads to the suggestion of three ways in which psychology can make its contribution — its unique professional contribution — to our social problems.

1. First, the movement towards involvement in the social systems in which people are immediately and directly involved is desirable. This includes the primary groups to which the client belongs, usually limited to the family in our present society, and other groups such as schools, mental hospitals, and clinics. Changes in the operation of these institutions are clearly necessary.

    I cannot help but introduce one of my peeves here in the suggestion that before psychologists take over the reform of society they first ought to do something about changing practices in institutions where they have been working for years — clinics, mental hospitals, public schools and schools for the retarded. Instead of spending most of their time administering tests, diagnosing and evaluating clients and writing lengthy reports of their findings which are of no value to anyone, psychologists should engage in treatment and other efforts to change behavior. The tremendous waste of time and money in the ritual of testing and diagnosis should be of concern to a socially conscious psychologist and could well become a social scandal if it were exposed by someone like Martin Gross.

    Perhaps we should move toward the 'social intervention centers' proposed by Albee, which would be staffed by special education teachers, social welfare workers, counselors, psychologists and psychiatrists. The latter two would be teachers and researchers, as well as supervisors and consultants, and also social activists, pushing for changes in the community environment to make it less dehumanizing. But two things must be noted here. First, individual and group counseling should be available for those who need it. Second, the limits of the effectiveness of individuals in achieving broad social changes must be recognized, or the frustration involved could lead to the need for psychotherapy by the psychologists and psychiatrists.

2. Psychology and psychologists, on the basis of their professional knowledge, should serve as consultants to government bodies engaged in the implementation of social changes at all levels of government. For too long has government neglected to consult the social sciences, while implementing the technology of the physical sciences with little concern for their psychological consequences. The establishment of a National Social Science Foundation becomes important here, and psychologists interested in social change should press for such a foundation.

3. But perhaps the most direct and, in the long run, most effective contribution of psychology is in the area of fostering the development of good interpersonal relationships. When the problems of the production and distribution of material goods and services have been solved, when we no longer have poor nations or poor minorities, slums, or hunger, we will still have the problems of living together. This would seem to be the area in which psychology would have responsibility. Beyond the conditions necessary for physical survival and optimum physical functioning, man's needs are psychological in nature. The conditions for optimum psychological functioning need to be determined and made available for every individual. This calls for research and the dissemination of the results of research through teaching. As a matter of fact, we now know at least some of the conditions for good human relationships. The preoccupation of the behaviorists with technology and techniques for behavior change may delay the recognition of the basic problem as one of human relations. Given enough time they will eventually reach this stage. Their need to discover everything for themselves all over again — such as that behavior is influenced by its consequences, and that direct teaching is effective in changing specific behaviors — is delaying progress. Their skepticism of the results of learning by experience rather than by experiment, even though the human experience numbers thousands of years of real life compared to a few hours of a laboratory situation, is another obstacle. But we now know, on the basis of considerable research, as well as experience, the basic conditions of good interpersonal relationships. And if these conditions existed universally, the personal psychological problems which now require counseling or psychotherapy could be eliminated. The stimuli which lead to psychologically desired behavior are social — they emanate from other persons. If we wish to control the results of these stimuli, then, in the best behavioral tradition, we should change the stimuli to which the individual is subjected. This means the changing of people so that they will provide good interpersonal relationships for others. If we know some of the principles and conditions of such relationships then it behooves us to teach them to everyone in our society. An illustration of such teaching is the training of police in New York City as family intervention specialists by Bard and Berkowitz (Bard, 1969). If we were successful in this task, then we would have no more need for counseling or psychotherapy. This, ultimately, is the social responsibility of the psychologist.

References

Bard, M. (1969) Expanding psychology's impact through existing community institutions. *American Psychologist*, 24, pp. 610–12.

Frank, L. K. (1936) Society as the patient. *American Journal of Sociology,* 42, pp. 335–44.

Patterson, C. H. (1969) What is counseling psychology? *Journal of Counseling Psychology*, 16, pp. 23–9.

Peterson, D. R. (1968) *The clinical study of social behavior*. New York: Appleton-Century-Crofts.

Psychology and Social Responsibility

31

If concern about psychology and social responsibility is any indication, then psychology has come of age as a significant and relevant field of activity. For it is only as psychology can make a difference to society that social concern in relation to psychology has any meaning. Until recently, it might have been said with considerable, if not absolute, truth that psychology made no difference and had no relevance.

The event or series of events in psychology which indicate that psychology can or does make a difference is the discovery, or rediscovery, of the methods and techniques of behavior control which are encompassed by the term 'behavior modification'. While it may be true that the degree of control of behavior in actual social, or real-life situations is not as great as may appear to be the case, it is considerable and will no doubt increase. Moreover, as Miller (1969) notes, the public sees psychology as being significant in the control of human behavior and is reacting with concern about this. It is clear that psychology is becoming relevant to society.

Responsible control of behavior

The behaviorists (many if not most of them) recognize that with ability to control comes responsibility. The pure scientist, professing interest not in application but only in so-called 'laws of behavior', may deny that any responsibility is involved. Yet science is commonly defined not simply or only as understanding, but to include prediction and control.

Miller (1969) would eliminate control as a goal of science, and perhaps this can and should be done. Control may be in the realm of application and technology rather than science — witness the title of Skinner's book on the application of operant conditioning to education, *The Technology of Teaching* (Skinner, 1968). But the knowledge underlying understanding and prediction can be used to control, and the question remains, what responsibility does psychology have for the use of its knowledge to control people?

There is another responsibility which many are demanding that psychology accept. Since psychology is concerned with individual and social behavior, and

First published in *Professional Psychology*, 1972, 3, pp. 3–10. Reprinted by permission of the American Psychological Association.

since the major problems which we face are problems of human behavior, why, it is asked, isn't psychology providing solutions, or at least concentrating research on these problems? Further, it is asked, why isn't psychology involved in applying what we already know, by social action or social programs, or even political action and programs?

Social responsibility

It would appear that psychology as a science has some responsibility to point out the social implications or consequences of research findings to the public as well as to colleagues. *Psychology Today*, though not an official publication of APA, is perhaps an outcome, to some extent, of this sense of responsibility. The inauguration of the Behavior section in *Time* magazine was, I am told (A. Brayfield, personal communication 1970), the result of a suggestion by APA. Certainly psychology, through APA or through its representatives, should provide information, consultation, and even advice to governmental and social organizations, and it has of course done so for a long time. But should psychology make the decisions? Most would feel that the answer to this question is 'no', that governmental or political organizations, as representative of society, make the decisions. But some believe that psychology officially, or the APA, should actively attempt to influence these decisions.

The science and the profession of psychology are supported by society, and this fact has some relevance for psychology's actions and its responsibilities.There are those who feel that science, including psychology, should be given a free hand, a *carte blanche*, by society, with no restrictions and no questions asked. To a great extent, society has done this.

But behavioral scientists do not function in a void, but in a society which supports them. It would appear that society has some right to influence, to some extent at least, the nature of the research which it supports. The industries which support research and development staffs ask that the research which they perform be relevant to the company. What is relevant is, of course, not always clear and obvious, so there is, and should be, considerable leeway, allowing for pure research as well as applied research. If the saying, 'He who pays the piper calls the tune', is not strictly applicable, at least he who pays the piper might suggest a program.

Walker (1969) begins his paper by stating that 'experimental psychology is a social enterprise'. He continues:

> Science is a social enterprise . . . Science flourishes to the extent to which it receives social support, and its products have profound social consequences . . . I believe that the individual scientist should take social value into consideration in choosing his problems, and I believe his colleagues should take social value into consideration in judging the merit of his work.

He concludes that '. . . experimental psychology must find a means of stepping up its attack on pressing social problems'.

The APA Board of Scientific Affairs (1970) recently stated:

> We should be aware of the fact that the academic community bears a

responsibility to the society which supports it, and should welcome the opportunity to apply our techniques and methodology toward the solutions of problems which are common to all of us who live in and benefit from this society.

This is all rather general. The problem is to convert the general statements to specifics upon which most psychologists could agree. Some of the current confusion about psychology and social responsibility seems to be a result of a failure to distinguish between the responsibility of psychology as a science and profession and of the American Psychological Association as its representative, of the individual psychologist as a scientist or professional and of the individual psychologist as a citizen. The following is an attempt to provide a preliminary statement upon which most psychologists can agree.

Responsibilities of psychology as a science and a profession
Psychology as a science and a profession, and the APA as its representative, has responsibilities of three kinds.

1.To consider social relevance, in terms of the social and psychological problems facing man, in its research efforts. There is no demand here that some research problems or even research areas will be defined as appropriate for research, and other problems or areas defined as not acceptable. No individual psychologist should be coerced to engage in a particular kind of research. Rather, research on relevant social problems should be encouraged. Such research by individuals has been discouraged, perhaps unintentionally, by a number of factors operating in psychology. One of these has been the existence of a kind of hierarchy of prestige or recognition, which places experimental laboratory research at the top. The emphasis on methodology, at the expense of attacking significant problems, is perhaps an aspect of this factor. So-called 'clean' research designs are emphasized. In the study of complex social problems much exploratory work is necessary. Such work is often not rewarded; it is difficult if not impossible to publish.

Reward
I am suggesting that the reward system should be changed, thus encouraging more research on socially significant but difficult problems. There is no suggestion experimental laboratory research be eliminated, or even decreased, but only that research on difficult social problems be recognized as scientific and encouraged.

Information
2. Psychology has a responsibility to disseminate information resulting from its research. We are concerned now about the storage and retrieval of scientific information. We need to become concerned about its dissemination, not only or mainly to other psychologists, but to users and consumers. If the individual producer of research is not always or completely responsible for interpreting the results of his research in terms of its implications for individual and social living, then the profession itself is. This is, of course, an obligation felt by some for some time,

and APA has given it some consideration.

Miller (1969) speaks of 'giving psychology away'. In a sense, psychology belongs to the people, so that we have nothing to give away. Every man is a psychologist. By virtue of the fact that each is a living, experiencing person he is something of an expert on living, at least on living his own life. In a sense in which each person cannot become his own physicist or physician, he can, and should, become his own psychologist.

The method for giving psychology to the people is through education. Miller (1969) discusses the education of adults in psychological principles and skills. But while this may be useful in dealing with some existing problems, more than this is necessary if we are to prevent problems or create a society which is not crippled by recurring problems. We now teach psychology in every college. It is taught in some high schools. But if every man is to develop a usable knowledge of psychology, it must be taught to everyone, and at an early age. Psychology, in the form of principles of good human relationships, must be taught in the elementary school. Education, in the long run, is more lasting and more effective than political pressure.

Use of knowledge

3. The third responsibility of psychology is to become actively involved in the use of psychological knowledge and the results of research and, even beyond this, to point out and encourage the use of such knowledge. The use of psychological knowledge and research results cannot wait upon the discovery of their relevance by others, and their application cannot be left to others. Knowledge and results which have implications for existing governmental and social policies and for the development of policies and programs which will foster human welfare must be brought to the attention of agencies and individuals in a position to do something. There has been a hesitancy to initiate programs of advice and consultation because of a feeling or belief that there is little definite knowledge, that the results of research are limited, restricted, and not generalizable to real social problems. Yet there is considerable knowledge, and as Rieff (1970) notes, it has been put to use in periods of war.

Psychology as a science and a profession, and APA as its representative, should make available advice and consultation. Of course, advice and consultation have been given, but almost always it has been the result of requests for help from agencies or government officials, rather than having been initiated by APA. Too often requests are not forthcoming where they should be. For too long has government neglected consulting the social sciences, while implementing the technology of the physical sciences with little if any concern for their psychological consequences. The establishment of a National Social Science Advisory Committee should be supported by psychology. A bill to establish a Council of Social Advisers has been proposed by Representative Mondale and supported by APA.

In none of these responsibilities is political action involved, and I do not advocate that APA become politically oriented. It cannot do so and still remain a scientific and a professional organization. But it can do much of value, in the ways indicated above, without political action. It can commit itself to the human use of psychology and to facilitating and fostering the development of man through the use of psychological knowledge.

Responsibilities of individual psychologists

It is difficult, if not impossible, to separate individual professional responsibility from the responsibility of a science or a profession. The question of the social responsibility of psychologists *as psychologists* appears to lead to responsibilities similar to those for psychology as a science and a profession. Individuals, in a sense, implement the general responsibilities. Here the problem posed by Miller (1969, 1970) about agreement on appropriate social (or political) action enters. The confusion between scientific and professional responsibilities and human and citizenship responsibilities arises. The responsibility of psychologists as psychologists is not the same as their responsibilities as citizens and human beings. Some psychologists, just as they seem to want APA to become a political organization, seem to be insisting that psychologists as psychologists should engage in social and political activities.

In academic circles it has been accepted practice that faculty members are free to participate in political and social activities, but as individuals, not as representatives of the university. Letters to the editors of newspapers, for example, are not signed with the writer's academic rank and position unless they deal with matters within his area of expertise.

Rieff (1970) expresses well the criterion for distinguishing between activities which are professionally based and those which are citizen — or humanity — based:

> If there is no empiric component at all, there is no basis for a professional decision . . . Participation as a professional under those circumstances might be irresponsible and misleading, giving rise to the impression that the psychologist's opinion is somehow 'better' than someone else's or rests on some foundation other than political preference.

The responsible psychologist should avoid stating or implying that his actions, opinions, or recommendations are based upon psychological knowledge when this is in fact not the case. However, it is not always easy to determine the extent of psychological knowledge, and whether it is sufficient for a professional decision or recommendation. There are matters on which there may be honest differences of opinion.

The psychologist as a psychologist

Now, recognizing that actions as a professional psychologist must be based upon some special knowledge or expertise, what are the kinds of actions which might be taken? Psychologists as psychologists would appear to have the following responsibilities, which follow those of the profession and its professional association.

1. The professional psychologist should consider social relevance as a factor

— one factor — in his choice of research problems. No one should be discouraged from seeking support for any kind of research he desires to do. The importance of so-called 'basic' or 'pure' research must be recognized and emphasized. Individual psychologists must have as much freedom of choice as possible in choosing research problems. But society can encourage, through providing support for, the kind of research it wants.

2. The professional psychologist has a responsibility for the interpretation and dissemination of the results of his research. This is a difficult and delicate area. Many psychologists feel that their obligation ends with the publication of the results of their research in scientific journals. Most are cautious — perhaps overcautious — about generalizing results or about developing the practical implications of their research. Many feel that the consideration of applications is something best done by those who are in a position to develop applications. Others feel that this is a place for a middleman.

Perhaps there is need for a middleman here. Perhaps the profession and APA have more responsibility here than the individual psychologist. But if research has a clear social relevance, the individual psychologist should feel some responsibility for pointing this out. Certainly he should, and probably would, object to misinterpretations or misuse by others. Perhaps if research is socially relevant, elements in society — such as the press — will seek out the researcher for his opinions and recommendations. Some researchers avoid this, or refuse comment, claiming that it would be simply the expression of opinion. But considered opinions, based upon research or special knowledge, are legitimate. Such opinions should be better than those of the uninformed layman.

3. It goes without saying that individual psychologists should be willing to advise and consult on professional matters. There seems to be no problem here at least as long as someone — government or industry — is willing to pay for such consultation. Perhaps there should be more willingness to provide consultation on a no-fee basis to small local groups and organizations. But no doubt much of this is being done by psychologists as citizens rather than formally as psychologists.

'Heal thyself'
4. I have made the suggestion (Patterson, 1969) that before taking over the reform of society, psychologists ought to begin doing something about psychological practices in the institutions in which they are working. I was referring then to psychologists in mental hospitals, schools for the retarded, clinics, and public schools, which are hardly operated on the basis of the best psychological principles. Many psychologists are engaged in introducing changes in such institutions. This activity has been designated social engineering.

But it seems to me that psychologists as individuals have a responsibility beyond this; psychologists working in any institution have a responsibility to apply their knowledge of psychology to the operation of the institution. This applies to universities and colleges, research institutes and centers, industry — wherever psychologists work. One would be hard put to discern any difference between the operation of a psychology department in a university and the physics department.

The psychologist as a citizen and as a person

Just as there is overlap between the responsibilities of organized psychology and individual psychologists, so is there between individual persons as psychologists and as citizens. Psychology consists of individual psychologists, and every psychologist is also a citizen and a human being. The responsibilities of psychologists as citizens, however, cannot be as simply and as easily delineated as responsibilities of the profession or of psychologists as psychologists. There is much more freedom or variability. Individual attitudes, preferences, beliefs, and opinions are free to operate here. This is the source of at least some of the confusion and disagreement among psychologists. It appears that some psychologists are advocating or insisting that psychologists and psychology engage in activities that are appropriate for psychologists as citizens, but perhaps not for psychologists as psychologists or for organized psychology.

Since there is so much individual freedom and individual difference in the activities of psychologists as citizens, it is not possible to list or discuss all possible activities or kinds of activities which might be considered responsibilities. But I would like to consider aspects of the responsibilities of psychologists as citizens, particularly as it relates to their behavior as psychologists.

1. The psychologist has all the rights and responsibilities of any citizen. These include the right, indeed the obligation, to express his beliefs and opinions regarding social problems, to engage in social action, and to attempt to persuade others to his beliefs and opinions and to act with him. One would expect that psychologists, in view of their scientific training, would be rational in their opinions and actions and would avoid attempting to gain acceptance of their opinions and beliefs by identifying or representing themselves as psychologists. Psychologists of like mind can join together to form social action organizations. Perhaps there is a need for a group with some such name as 'Psychologists for Social Action' to meet the needs of psychologists who wish more organized action than APA can engage in. But such organizations are not, and should not be, represented as psychological organizations.

2. Since psychologists recognize the existence of wide individual differences, and of the rights of individuals to their own opinions and beliefs, those psychologists who choose extreme forms of social action should recognize that others, who may even feel as strongly as they do about social situations, may elect to express themselves or contribute to social change in other ways. Some psychologists appear to be taking the position that every psychologist should be active in particular ways, even to engaging in protest behavior such as marching or picketing.

Social conscience and/or personal conscience

But there are different ways in which individuals, including psychologists, can meet the demands of their social consciences. Some will feel that their greatest contribution to social change is in devoting all their time and energy to their work, whether it is research, teaching, or some field of applied or professional psychology. The scientist who devotes his entire time and energy to his work, neglecting everything else, including his family, is the extreme case, but nevertheless this is his right.

Walker (1969) suggests there may be conflict between being a scientist and a social activist: 'If a man is to be a social activist, it is difficult for him to be a scientist. If a man is to be a scientist, he has little time and energy for social activism.'

Myers (1970) questions this concept. But there are a number of points that should be made. First, time is limited, and there is not time for everything. Choices must be made, and each individual has the right to determine how he will spend his time. Second, there are differences in the effectiveness with which individuals can function in social, civic, and political activities. Many scientists, by temperament, are perhaps very ineffective in this area. Third, as was indicated earlier, a particular individual may contribute more through his work than through other avenues.

These are my current thoughts about the social responsibilities of psychology and psychologists. It is difficult, if not impossible, to separate responsibilities definitively into those of (a) psychology as science and profession through APA, (b) the individual psychologist as a psychologist, and (c) the psychologist as a citizen. It is a complex problem, and there have been changes in viewpoint in many psychologists, including myself. Psychologists, like many others, are becoming more socially conscious. Perhaps this will continue, and we will move closer to the position of the activists in psychology who are demanding more action from their professional organizations. I have attempted to present what I think is a reasonable position which should be acceptable to most psychologists. While I am willing to allow individual psychologists to go further than I would go, I also ask that they be willing to allow me — and others — to contribute to social progress in our own way, without being made to feel that we are inadequate as citizens and as psychologists.

References

American Psychological Association Board of Scientific Affairs. (1970) 'Interaction.' *APA Monitor*, 1, (3), p. 2.

Miller, G. A. (1969) Psychology as a means of promoting human welfare. *American Psychologist*, 24, pp. 1063–75.

Miller, G. A. (1970) Comment on Rieff. *Professional Psychology*, 1970,1, pp. 327–8.

Myers, W. A. (1970) Presidential addresses of Miller and Walker. *American Psychologist*, 25, pp. 469–70.

Patterson, C. H. (1969) The social responsibility of psychology. *The Counseling Psychologist*, 1, pp. 97–100.

Rieff, R. (1970) Psychology and public policy. *Professional Psychology*, 1, pp. 315–24.

Skinner B. F. (1953) *Science and human behavior.* New York: Macmillan.

Skinner, B. F. (1968) *The technology of teaching.* New York: Appleton-Century-Crofts.

Walker, E. L.(1969) Experimental psychology and social responsibility. *American Psychologist*, 24, pp. 862–8.

MULTICULTURAL COUNSELING FROM DIVERSITY TO UNIVERSALITY

32

The multicultural movement in counseling began some 30 years ago. An early statement was Wrenn's (1962) article *The Culturally Encapsulated Counselor*. But the movement gained momentum from observations that 'minority-group clients receive unequal and poor mental health services' (S. Sue, 1977, p. 616). They were, it was claimed, underserved and poorly served. S. Sue cited as examples reports by Yamamoto, James, and Palley (1968) and others. S. Sue later (1988) referred to the President's Commission on Mental Health (1978), as had others before. It appeared in S. Sue's study that minority clients were more likely to receive supportive treatment than were White clients. S. Sue found, however, that Black clients and Native Americans 'were heavily overrepresented' in the community mental health centers he studied in Seattle, although Chicanos and Asian American clients were heavily underrepresented (S. Sue and McKinney, 1975; S. Sue, McKinney, Allen, and Hale, 1974). The failure-to-return rate (after the first session) was over 50% for Blacks, Native Americans, and Asian Americans; the Chicano rate was 42%, and the White rate was 30%. Blacks were the only group who received differential treatment, more often becoming inpatients and less often provided group and marital therapy (see also Wu and Windle, 1980).

Mays and Albee (1992) recently summarized their observations as follows:

> Members of ethnic minority groups are neither users of traditional psychotherapy nor purveyors of psychotherapy in anything like their proportion in the population . . . The pattern of usage should not be confused with levels of need or helpseeking for emotional problems. In general, ethnic minorities experience a higher proportion of poverty and social stressors typically regarded as antecedents of psychiatric and psychological disorders than Whites . . . Yet, in spite of the preponderance of these events in their lives, ethnic minorities are often underserved by high quality mental health resources (Wu and Windle, 1980, pp. 552–3).

First published in *Journal of Counseling and Development*, 1996, 74, pp. 227–31. Reprinted by permission. No further reproduction authorized without written permission of the American Counseling Association.

Early concern focused on minority groups in the United States (D. W. Sue, 1978). Publications on these groups mushroomed. D. W. Sue's book *Counseling the Culturally Different* (1981a) contained chapters on Asian Americans, Black Americans (by Elsie Smith), Hispanics (by R. Ruiz), and American Indians (by E. H. Richardson). A special issue of the journal *Psychotherapy*, on psychotherapy with ethnic minorities (Dudley and Rawlins, 1985), included articles on these groups (see also Atkinson, Morten, and D. W. Sue, 1993). D. W. Sue and D. Sue (1990) included chapters on American Indians, Asian Americans, Black Americans, and Hispanic Americans.

But multiculturalism expanded to include other groups: various subcultures, racial groups, gender groups, economic groups including the poor (see Goldstein, 1973). Curiously, little has been written about counseling in other cultures outside the United States. The book *Counseling Across Cultures* edited by Pedersen, Lonner, and Draguns (1976), did include some material on this topic.

The assumption was quickly made that a form of counseling that had been developed in the United States (and other Western countries) for upper-middle-class White clients was inappropriate for other groups, even within the same general culture. Pedersen (1976), in an early review, wrote that 'each cultural group requires a different set of skills, unique areas of emphasis, and specific insights for effective counseling to occur' (p. 26).

Perspectives on inadequacies of mental health services for minority groups

Many reasons have been advanced for the inadequacies of mental health services for ethnic minority groups, such as a lack of bilingual counselors and counselors who are members of the minority group, discrimination, or prejudice in counselors. S. Sue (1988) cited as one of the most frequent criticisms of counseling with minority clients 'the lack of therapists who can communicate and understand the values, lifestyles, and backgrounds of these clients'. S. Sue and Zane (1987) wrote that:

> the most important explanation for the problem in services delivery involves the inability of therapists to provide culturally responsive forms of treatment. The assumption, and a good one, is that most therapists are not familiar with the cultural background and styles of the various ethnic minority groups and have received training primarily developed for Anglo, or mainstream, Americans (Bernal and Padilla, 1982; Chunn, Dunston, and Ross-Sheriff, 1983; Wyatt and Parham, 1985). (p. 37).

In his early review Pedersen (1976) wrote,

> There is increasing evidence that the trained counselor is not prepared to deal with individuals who come from different racial, ethnic or socioeconomic groups whose values, attitudes, and general lifestyles are different from and threatening to his own (Padilla, Boxley, and Wagner, 1973, p. 35).

And Mays and Albee (1992) referred to 'the cultural insensitivity' of traditional psychotherapy and 'a failure of the profession of psychology to develop and promote relevant and adequate mental health services for this population' (p. 554).

Because every client belongs to numerous groups, it does not take much imagination to recognize that the number of combinations and permutations of these groups is staggering. Attempting to develop different theories, methods, and techniques for each of these groups would be an insurmountable task. Yet attempts have been made, limited to a few of the major ethnic-cultural groups.

There are numerous publications attempting to remedy the lack of knowledge about ethnic, racial, and cultural groups. The literature is replete with the characteristics of these groups and how to treat or not treat them (e.g. D. W. Sue, 1981a; D. W. Sue and D. Sue, 1990; Vontress, 1981). Pedersen (1976) in his early review reported that:

> Native American Indian culture presents its own unique requirements for effective counseling. When counseling Native American Indian youth, the counselor is likely to be confronted by passively nonverbal clients who listen and absorb knowledge selectively. A counselor who expects counselees to verbalize their feelings is not likely to have much success with Native American clients. The Native American is more likely to withdraw and, using the advice he has received, work out the problems by himself. The Native American is very conscious of having to make his own decisions and is likely to resent being pushed in a particular direction by persons seeking to motivate him or her (p. 30).

Ridley (1984) stated that Black clients distrust White counselors and do not self-disclose: 'Thus both the clinical and research evidence converge in portraying a black client who, as a therapeutic participant, is generally reluctant to disclose intimately to a white therapist' (p. 1236). Ridley's statement on self-disclosure in Blacks applies to other groups as well, including Asian Americans. Yet not all Blacks are non-self-disclosing, nor are all Asian Americans. S. Sue and Zane (1987) noted that 'many Asian American clients who were unacculturated seemed quite willing to talk about their emotions and to work with little structure' (p. 39). Trimble (1976) noted that 'the Indian is not accustomed to self-analysis nor is there a familiarity with the process of discussing with a non-Indian one's emotional conflicts' (p. 79). Meadow (1982) recommended that counselors de-emphasize the necessity for self-disclosure with Hispanic clients. D. W. Sue (1981a) wrote that counselors who 'value verbal, emotional and behavioral expressiveness as goals in counseling are transmitting their own values' (p. 38; see also D. W. Sue and D. Sue, 1990, p. 38). It appears that lack of self-disclosure is not necessarily an inability to do so but rather a reluctance to do so in certain situations with certain persons.

A second characteristic of certain (many) ethnic minority groups is the desire for a structured relationship in which the counselor is cast as an expert, giving advice and solutions to problems (D. W. Sue and D. Sue, 1990; S. Sue and

Morishima, 1982; Szapocznik, Santisteban, Kurtines, Hervis and Spencer, 1982; Vontress, 1976, 1981). Many clients from ethnic minority groups are dependent, desiring a therapist who is active, authoritative, directive, and concrete (Atkinson, Maruyama, and Matsui, 1978; Leong, 1986; D. W. Sue, 1981b; S. Sue and Zane, 1987; Trimble, 1976, 1981). It is usually stated that such clients need counselors who provide these conditions. However, it would be more accurate to say that they *want or prefer* such therapists. Virtually all of the research on the preferences of minority groups toward counseling has been conducted with participants who compose small, unrepresentative samples — not actual clients — and involve statements regarding the kind of counselor the participants would like if they were to go to a counselor.

Yet, the almost universal recommendation is that counselors use techniques that 'fit' the presumed characteristics of clients. Basic to this is 'the assumption that different cultural and subcultural groups require different approaches' (D. W. Sue and D. Sue, 1990, p. 161). Listing five publications (including Ridley, 1984), these authors wrote:

> All seem to endorse the *notion* [italics added] that various racial groups may require approaches or techniques that differ from white Anglo-Saxon middle-class clients. Indeed, the belief held by many cross-cultural scholars is that minority clients tend to prefer and respond better to directive than nondirective approaches, and that counselling approaches which are active rather than passive are more effective, that a structured, explicit approach may be more effective than an unstructured, ambiguous one, and that minority clients may desire a counselor who self-discloses his/her thoughts or feelings (Atkinson, Maruyama, and Matsui, 1978; Berman, 1979; Dauphinais, Dauphinais, and Rowe, 1981; Ivey, 1986; D. W. Sue, 1978; Szapocznik et al., 1982) (D. W. Sue and D. Sue, 1990, p. 160).

Problems with a technique orientation to multicultural counseling
There has been a plethora of publications recommending that 'culturally sensitive,' 'culturally relevant', and 'culturally appropriate' techniques be developed (e.g. D. W. Sue, 1989, 1990, 1991; D. W. Sue et al., 1982; D. W. Sue and D. Sue, 1990). There are a number of problems with the attempt to provide information and knowledge about ethnic minority groups and to recommend specific methods or techniques to fit these characteristics.

First, descriptions of the various groups are generalizations, describing the modal (abstract average) person. The result is the proliferation of stereotypes, a danger that a number of writers recognize. S. Sue (1983) cited Campbell (1967) who 'warned that the finding of actual differences between groups often leads to exaggerated stereotyped images of these differences' (p. 585). S. Sue (1983) was one of the first to point out the existence of wide individual differences within each group. In statistics when within-group variance is great compared with between-group variance, it becomes difficult, if not impossible, to assign individuals to groups or to differentiate among groups.

A note about the emphasis on value differences among cultures is relevant here. There are, to be sure, some value differences. But it needs to be pointed out that the word *values* is used too indiscriminately. Many so-called value differences among groups are actually customs, lifestyles, social norms or habits, and preferences. There are many values that are common to many different groups, and some universal values (Patterson, 1989b). Brown (1991) wrote that 'universals exist, they are numerous . . . It will be irresponsible to continue shunting these questions to the side, fraud to deny that they exist' (see pp. 142–156).

Second, the assumptions regarding the characteristics of ethnic minority groups leads to the self-fulfillment prophecy. If clients from other cultural groups are believed to be non-self-disclosing, dependent, in need of structure, direction, advice, and so on, then they will be treated as if these things are true, and they will respond to confirm the counselor's beliefs. It is thus assured that standard or traditional approaches will not be effective.

Third, the assumption that the counselor's knowledge of the culture of his or her client will lead to more appropriate and effective therapy has not been borne out. S. Sue and Zane (1987) stated that 'recommendations that admonish therapists to be culturally sensitive and to know the culture of the client have not been very helpful' (p. 37). They continued as follows:

> The major problem with approaches emphasizing either cultural knowledge or culture-specific techniques is that neither is linked to particular processes that result in effective psychotherapy . . . Recommendations for knowledge of culture are necessary but not sufficient for effective treatment . . . The knowledge must be transformed into concrete operations and strategies (p 39).

Fourth, perhaps the greatest difficulty with accepting assumptions about the characteristics and so-called needs of clients from differing cultures is that they will lead to failure, or lack of success, in counseling. The active, authoritative, directive, controlling counselor, providing answers and solutions to the client's problems, has not been considered competent or effective for many years. To provide this kind of treatment (it would not be called counseling) to clients from other cultures would be providing poor or second-class treatment.

Fifth, D. W. Sue (1981a, p. 38) and D. W. Sue and D. Sue (1990, p. 40) referred to 'the belief in the desirability of self-disclosure'. But client self-disclosure is more than desirable — it is necessary for client progress. D. W. Sue and D. Sue (1990) appeared to recognize its importance, referring to self-disclosure as an 'essential' condition, 'particularly crucial to the process and goals of counseling, because it is the most direct means by which an individual makes himself/herself known to another (Greene, 1985; Mays, 1985)' (p. 77). Vontress (1976, 1981) recognized it as 'basic to the counseling process' (p. 53). Ridley (1984) wrote that 'nondisclosure means that a client forfeits an opportunity to engage in therapeutic self-exploration . . . The result will most surely be nontherapeutic' (p. 1237).

Modifying or adapting counseling to the presumed needs or desires of ethnic minority clients cannot lead to abandoning those things that are essential for therapeutic progress. Ho (1985) recognized this: 'There is a limit on the degree to which the fundamental psychological-therapeutic orientation [the Western model] can be compromised' (p. 1214). To attempt to apply all the techniques that have been suggested in working with ethnic minority clients is to water down the counseling process until it is no longer effective in any meaningful sense of counseling. Although clients may be pleased or satisfied with such treatment and may even receive some immediate, temporary help, therapy that includes goals such as client independence, responsibility, and ability to resolve his or her own problems is not achieved.

Culture-specific techniques for people in all the innumerable groups who may come to a counselor for help have not been clearly specified, described, or matched with the groups to which they apply. More important, there is little if any research support for the effectiveness of the theorized differential techniques or methods.

S. Sue (1988) noted that 'considerable controversy exists over the effectiveness of psychotherapy for ethnic minority groups . . . Despite the strongly held opinions over the problems ethnic clients encounter in receiving effective services, empirical evidence has failed to consistently demonstrate differential outcomes for ethnic and White clients . . . Most treatment studies have failed to show differential outcomes on the basis of race or ethnicity of clients' (pp. 301–2), once clients enter and continue in treatment.

The solution to counseling with members of minority groups

What then, is the solution to the problem of counseling with members of minority groups? It is certainly not that traditional counseling, that is, counseling as competently practiced in our current society, be abandoned.

Early on, before the emphasis on specific techniques for different groups, several writers listed a number of counselor characteristics or attitudes as being necessary. Wohl (1976, p. 187) noted that McNeill (1965, p. vii) emphasized that the healing function includes a caring and concern on the part of the healer. And discussing Pande (1968), Wohl wrote that 'therapy provides a special, close, love relationship' (p. 189). Stewart (1976), at the same time, emphasized the importance of warmth, genuineness, and especially empathy. Torrey (1970, 1972), according to Pedersen (1976),

> identified the expectations of troubled contrast culture clients and the personal qualities of a counselor as being closely related to the healthy change, accurate empathy, and nonpossessive warmth and genuineness that are essential to effective mental health care (p. 30).

Vontress (1976) emphasized the importance of rapport as 'the emotional bridge between the counselor and the counselee . . . Simply defined, rapport constitutes a comfortable and unconstrained mutual trust and confidence between two persons' (p. 45). He appeared to include empathy in rapport. Richardson (1981) listed the following among the ways of working with American Indian clients: listen, be accepting, respect their culture, be natural, be honest, honor their presence, and do not be condescending. Vontress (1976) also commented on counselor training that:

> . . . what is needed most are affective experiences designed to
> humanize counselors . . . Few counselors ever ask what they can do
> to change themselves; few want to know how they can become better
> human beings in order to relate more effectually with other human
> beings who, through the accident of birth, are racially and ethnically
> different (p 62).

Unfortunately, the emphasis on techniques has overshadowed attention to the nature of the relationship between the counselor and the client. It now appears that this preoccupation with techniques is fading and that it is being recognized that counselor competence inheres in the personal qualities of the counselor. The competent counselor is one who provides an effective therapeutic relationship. The nature of this relationship has long been known and is the same regardless of the group to which the client belongs.

There are five basic counselor qualities that are essentials of all effective counseling (Rogers, 1957).

1. Respect for the client: This includes having trust in the client and assumes that the client is capable of taking responsibility for himself or herself (including during the therapy process), and capable of making choices and decisions and resolving problems — moreover, he or she should be allowed to do so, as a right.

2. Genuineness: Counseling is a real relationship. The counselor does not assume a role as an all-knowing expert, operating on the client with a battery of techniques. The counselor is not an impersonal, cold, objective professional, but a real person.

3. Empathic understanding: Empathic understanding is more than a knowledge of the client based on knowledge of the groups to which he or she belongs. It requires that the counselor be able to use this knowledge as it applies or relates to the unique client, which involves entering into the client's world and seeing it as he or she does. 'The ability to convey empathy in a culturally consistent and meaningful manner may be the crucial variable to engage the client' (Ibrahim, 1991, p. 18). The only way in which the counselor can enter the world of the client is with the permission of the client, who communicates the nature of his or her world to the counselor through self-disclosure. Thus, client self-disclosure is the *sine qua non* for counseling. Counselor respect and genuineness facilitate client self-disclosure.

4. Communication of empathy, respect, and genuineness to the client: The conditions must be perceived, recognized and felt by the client if they are to be effective. This becomes difficult with clients who differ from the therapist in culture, race, socioeconomic class, age, and gender. Understanding of cultural differences in verbal and nonverbal behaviors (D. W. Sue, 1989; D. W. Sue and D. Sue, 1990) can be very helpful here.
   [D. W. Sue and D. Sue (1990) conceded that 'qualities such as respect and acceptance of the individual, unconditional positive regard, understanding the problem from the individual's perspective, allowing the client to explore his or

her own values, and arriving at an individual solution are core qualities that may transcend culture' (p. 187).

These counselor qualities are not only essential for effective counseling, they are also the elements of all facilitative interpersonal relations. They are neither time-bound nor culture-bound.]

5. Structuring: There is another element in all counseling that is of particular importance in intercultural counseling. It appears to have been recognized by few writers. Vontress (1976) is one who did, and his statement bears repeating:

> On the whole, disadvantaged minority group members have had limited experiences with counselors and related therapeutic professionals. Their contacts have been mainly with people who tell them what they must and should do . . . Relationships with professionals who place major responsibility upon the individual for solving his own problems are few. Therefore, the counselor working within such a context should structure and define his role to clients; that is he should indicate what, how, and why he intends to do what he will do . . . Failure to structure early and adequately in counseling can result in unfortunate and unnecessary misunderstanding (p. 47) (see also S. Sue and Zane, 1987, pp. 41–43).

[And, it might be added, failure to structure may also result in failure of the client to continue. Structuring is necessary whenever a client does not know what is involved in the therapeutic relationship — how the counselor will function and what is expected of the client — or holds misconceptions about the process.]

There appears to have been the beginning of a change in the literature on multicultural counseling that could portend a return to a recognition of the basic nature of counseling as an interpersonal relationship. Patterson (1978) earlier had proposed such a view of multicultural therapy or counseling. Recently, change was introduced by the statement of Pedersen (1990) that 'to some extent all mental health counseling is multicultural' (p. 94). This was followed by his statement that 'we are moving toward a genuine theory of multiculturalism' (Pedersen, 1991, p. 6). He continued, 'The obvious differences in behavior across cultures are typically over emphasized, whereas the more difficult to discover similarities of expectations are typically underemphasized' (p. 9). Vontress (1988) earlier had emphasized the common humanness of all clients. Ibrahim (1991) also accepted multicultural counseling as generic. Speight, Myers, Cox, and Highlen (1991) stated it clearly: 'All counseling is cross-cultural or multicultural because all humans differ in terms of cultural backgrounds, values or lifestyle . . . Multicultural counseling is redefined as basic to all forms of helping relationships. All counseling is multicultural in nature' (pp. 29, 31). Unfortunately, the statement of standards of the Association for Multicultural Counseling and Development (D. W. Sue, Arredondo, and McDavis, 1992) does not adequately recognize this core of counselor competence.

All clients, as previously noted, belong to multiple groups, all of which influence the client's perceptions, beliefs, feelings, thoughts, and behavior. The counselor must be aware of these influences and of their unique blending or fusion in the client if counseling is to be successful.

The current overemphasis on cultural diversity and culture-specific counseling leads to (a) a focus on specific techniques (or skills as they are now called), with the counselor becoming a chameleon who changes styles, techniques, and methods to meet the presumed characteristics of clients from varying cultures and groups and (b) an emphasis on differences among cultures and their contrasting worldviews. This approach ignores the fact that we are rapidly becoming one world, with rapid communication and increasing interrelations among persons from varying cultures, leading to increasing homogeneity and a worldview representing the common humanity that binds all human beings together as one species.

Vontress (1979) proposed an existentialist philosophical view of cross-cultural counseling, a 'philosophical orientation that transcends culture' (p. 117). Freeman (1993), citing Pedersen's (1991) proposal for a search for a framework that recognizes the complex diversity of a plural society and, at the same time, suggests bridges of shared concern that bind culturally different persons to one another, developed such a framework that includes the universal and the specific in therapy. Though she does not make this point, the universal is the process, and the specific deals with the content in therapy.

If multicultural counseling is generic, and if all counseling is multicultural, then it becomes possible to develop a universal system of counseling (Patterson, 1989a, 1995).

References

Atkinson, D. R., Maruyama, M., and Matsui, S. (1978) Effects of counselor race and counseling approach on Asian Americans' perceptions of counselor credibility and utility. *Journal of Counseling Psychology*, 25, pp. 76–83.

Atkinson, D. R., Morten, G., and Sue, D. W. (1993) *Counseling American minorities: A cross-cultural perspective*. (4th ed.) Dubuque, IA: Brown.

Bernal, M. E., and Padilla, A. M. (1982) Status of minority curricula and training in clinical psychology. *American Psychologist*, 37, pp. 78–87.

Brown, D. E. (1991) *Human universals*. Philadelphia, PA: Temple University Press.

Campbell, D. T. (1967) Stereotypes and the perception of group differences. *American Psychologist*, 22, pp. 817–29.

Chunn, J. C., Dunston, P. J., and Ross-Sheriff, E. (1983) (Eds.) *Mental health and people of color: Curriculum development and change*. Washington, DC: Howard University Press.

Dauphinais, R., Dauphinais, L., and Rowe, W. (1981) Effects of race and communication style on Indian perceptions of counselor effectiveness. *Counselor Education and Supervision*, 21, pp. 72–80.

Dudley, G. R., and Rawlins, M. L. (1985) (Eds.) Psychotherapy with ethnic minorities [Special issue]. *Psychotherapy*, 22, (2).

Freeman, S. (1993) Client-centered therapy and diverse populations. *Journal of*

Multicultural Counseling and Development, 21, pp. 248–54.

Goldstein, A. R (1973) *Structured learning therapy: Toward a psychotherapy for the poor*. New York: Academic.

Greene, B. A. (1985) Considerations in the treatment of Black patients by White therapists. *Psychotherapy*, 22, pp. 389–93.

Ho, D.Y. F. (1985) Cultural values and professional issues in clinical psychology: The Hong Kong experience. *American Psychologist,* 40, pp. 1212–18.

Ibrahim, F. A. (1991) Contribution of cultural worldview to generic counseling and development. *Journal of Counseling and Development*, 70, pp. 13–19.

Leong, F. T. (1986) Counseling and psychotherapy with Asian-Americans. *Journal of Counseling Psychology*, 33, pp. 196–206.

Mays, V. M. (1985) The Black American and psychotherapy: The dilemma. *Psychotherapy*, 22, pp. 379–88.

Mays, V. M., and Albee, G. W. (1992) Psychotherapy and ethnic minorities. In D. K. Freedheim (Ed.), *History of psychotherapy.* (Pp. 552–70). Washington, DC: American Psychological Association.

McNeill, J. T. (1965) *A history of souls*. New York: Harper and Row.

Meadow, A. (1982) Psychopathology, psychotherapy, and the Mexican-American patient. In E. E. Jones and S. J. Korchin (Eds.), *Minority mental health.* (Pp. 331–61). New York: Praeger.

Padilla, E. R., Boxley, A., and Wagner, N. (1973) The desegregation of clinical psychology training. *Professional Psychology*, 4, 259–63.

Pande, S. (1968) The mystique of Western psychotherapy: An Eastern interpretation. *Journal of Nervous and Mental Diseases*, 146, pp. 425–32.

Patterson, C. H. (1978) Cross-cultural or intercultural counseling or psychotherapy. *International Journal for the Advancement of Counseling*, 1, pp. 231–47.

Patterson, C. H. (1989a, December) *A universal system of psychotherapy*. Keynote speech presented at the Southeast Asian Symposium on Counseling and Guidance in the 21st Century, Taipei, Taiwan.

Patterson, C. H. (1989b) Values in counseling and psychotherapy. *Counseling and Values*, 33, pp. 164–76.

Patterson, C. H. (1995) A universal system of psychotherapy. *Person-Centered Journal*, 2, (1), pp. 54–62.

Pedersen, P. (1976) The field of intercultural counseling. In P. Pedersen, W. J. Lonner and J. G. Draguns (Eds.), *Counseling across cultures* . (Pp. 17–41). Honolulu, Hl: University Press of Hawaii.

Pedersen, P. B. (1990) The multicultural perspective as a fourth force in counseling. *Journal of Mental Health Counseling*, 12, pp. 93–5.

Pedersen, P. B. (1991) Multiculturalism as a generic approach to counseling. *Journal of Counseling and Development*, 70, pp. 6–12.

Pedersen, P. B., Lonner, W., and Draguns, J. (1976) (Eds.). *Counseling across cultures*. Honolulu, Hl: University Press of Hawaii.

President's Commission on Mental Health. (1978) *Report to the President*. Washington, DC: U. S. Government Printing Office.

Richardson, E. H. (1981) Cultural and historical perspectives in counseling

American Indians. In D. W. Sue (Ed.), *Counseling the culturally different: Theory and practice* . (Pp. 216–55). New York: Wiley.

Ridley, C. R. (1984) Clinical treatment of the non-disclosing Black client. *American Psychologist*, 39, pp. 1234–44.

Rogers, C. R. (1957) A note on 'The nature of man'. *Journal of Counseling Psychology*, 4, pp. 199 –203.

Speight, S. L., Myers, L. J., Cox, C. l., and Highlen, R. S. (1991) A redefinition of multicultural counseling. *Journal of Counseling and Development*, 70, pp. 29–36.

Stewart, E. C. (1976) Cultural sensitivities in counseling. In P. Pedersen, W. J. Lonner, and J. Draguns (Eds.), *Counseling across cultures* (Pp. 98–122). Honolulu, HI: University Press of Hawaii.

Sue, D. W. (1978) Eliminating cultural oppression in counseling: Toward a general theory. *Journal of Counseling Psychology*, 25, pp. 419–28.

Sue, D. W. (1981a) *Counseling the culturally different: Theory and practice*. New York: Wiley.

Sue, D. W. (1981b) Evaluating process variables in cross-cultural counseling and psychotherapy. In A J. Marsella and P. Pedersen (Eds.), *Cross-cultural counseling and psychotherapy*. New York: Pergamon.

Sue, D. W. (1989, December) *Cultural specific techniques in counseling: A counseling framework.* Paper presented at the Southeast Asia Symposium on Counseling and Guidance in the 21st Century, Taipei, Taiwan.

Sue, D. W. (1990) Culture specific techniques in counseling: A conceptual framework. *Professional Psychology: Research and Practice*, 21, pp. 424–33.

Sue, D. W. (1991) A model for cultural diversity training. *Journal of Counseling and Development*, 70, pp. 99–105.

Sue, D. W., Arredondo, R., and McDavis, R. J. (1992) Multicultural counseling competencies and standards: A call to the profession. *Journal of Counseling and Development*, 70, pp. 477–88.

Sue, D. W., Bernier, J. E., Durran, A., Feinberg, L., Pedersen, P., Smith, E. J., and Velasquez-Nuttall, E. (1982) Position paper: Cross-cultural counseling competencies. *The Counseling Psychologist* ,10 (2), pp. 45–52.

Sue, D. W., and Sue, D. (1990) *Counseling the culturally different: Theory and practice* . (2nd ed.) New York: Wiley.

Sue, S. (1977) Community mental health services to minority groups: Some optimism, some pessimism. *American Psychologist*, 32, pp. 616–24.

Sue, S. (1983) Ethnic minorities in psychology: A re-examination. *American Psychologist*, 38, pp. 583–92.

Sue, S. (1988) Psychotherapeutic services for minorities: Two decades of research findings. *American Psychologist*, 43, pp. 301–8.

Sue, S., and McKinney, H. (1975) Asian Americans in the community mental health system. *American Journal of Orthopsychiatry*, 45, pp. 111–18.

Sue, S., McKinney, H., Allen, D., and Hale, J. (1974) Delivery of community mental health services to Black and White clients. *Journal of Consulting and Clinical Psychology*, 42, pp. 794–801.

Sue, S., and Morishima, J. K. (1982) *The mental health of Asian Americans.* San

Francisco, CA: Jossey-Bass.

Sue, S., and Zane, N. (1987) The role of culture and cultural techniques in psychotherapy. *American Psychologist*, 42, pp. 37–45.

Szapocznik, J., Santisteban, D., Kurtines, W. M., Hervis, O. E., and Spencer, E. (1982) Life enhancement counseling: A psychosocial model of services for Cuban elders. In E. E. Jones and S. J. Korchin (Eds.) *Minority mental health*. New York: Praeger.

Torrey, E. F. (1970, March) *The irrelevancy of traditional mental health services for urban Mexican-Americans*. Paper presented at the meeting of the American Orthopsychiatric Association, San Francisco, CA.

Torrey, E. F. (1972) *The mind game: Witch doctors and psychiatrists*. New York: Emerson Hall.

Trimble, J. E. (1976) Value differences among American Indians: Concerns for the concerned counselor. In P. Pedersen (Ed.), *Counseling across cultures* . (Pp. 65–81). Honolulu, Hl: University Press of Hawaii.

Trimble, J. E. (1981) Value differences and their importance in counseling American Indians. In P. Pedersen, J. G. Draguns, W. J. Lonner, and J. E. Trimble (Eds.), *Counseling across cultures*. (2nd ed.) Honolulu, Hl: University Press of Hawaii.

Vontress, C. E. (1976) Racial and ethnic barriers in counseling. In P. Pedersen, W. J. Lonner, and J. Draguns (Eds.), *Counseling across cultures*. (Pp. 42–64). Honolulu, HI: University Press of Hawaii.

Vontress, C. E. (1979) Cross-cultural counseling: An existential approach. *The Personnel and Guidance Journal*, 58, pp. 117–22.

Vontress, C. E. (1981) Racial and ethnic barriers in counseling. In P. Pedersen, J. S. Draguns, W. J. Lonner, and J. E. Trimble (Eds.), *Counseling across cultures*. (2nd ed.) Honolulu, Hl: University Press of Hawaii.

Vontress, C. E. (1988) An existential approach to cross-cultural counseling. *Journal of Multicultural Counseling and Development*, 16, pp. 73–83.

Wohl, J. (1976) Intercultural psychotherapy: Issues, questions, and reflections. In P. Pedersen, W. J. Lonner, and J. Draguns (Eds.), *Counseling across cultures* . (Pp. 184–207). Honolulu, Hl: University Press of Hawaii.

Wrenn, C. G. (1962) The culturally encapsulated counselor. *Harvard Educational Review*, 32, pp. 111-119.

Wu, I. H., and Windle, C. (1980) Ethnic specificity in the relative minority use and staffing of community mental health services. *Community Mental Health Journal*, 16, pp. 156–68.

Wyatt, G. E., and Parham, W. D. (1985) The inclusion of culturally sensitive issue materials in graduate school and training programs. *Psychotherapy*, 22, pp. 461–8.

Yamamoto, J., James, T. C., and Palley, N. (1968) Clinical problems in psychiatric therapy. *Archives of General Psychiatry*, 19, pp. 45–9.

THE PRIMARY PREVENTION OF PSYCHOLOGICAL DISORDERS: A PERSON-CENTERED/CLIENT-CENTERED PERSPECTIVE

33

If we could raise one generation of children with unconditional love, there would be no Hitlers. Elizabeth Kubler-Ross (Phillips, 1991, p. 11)

Introduction

The thesis of this paper derives from the conviction that the essence of psychotherapy is a relationship characterized by empathy, respect or compassion, and therapeutic genuineness (see Rogers, 1957). This relationship is best characterized by *agapé*, or love. The consistent loving, caring relationship has long been identified with client-centered therapy.

That the basis of psychotherapy is love has been recognized by many writers. Gordon Allport (1950) nearly 50 years ago, wrote: 'Love is incomparably the greatest psychotherapeutic agent' (p. 80). Thirty years ago Arthur Burton wrote: 'After all research on psychotherapy is accounted for, psychotherapy still resolves itself into a relationship best subsumed by the word love' (Burton, 1967, pp. 102–3). The object relations theorists Guntrip (1953) and Fairbairn (1954) used the word *agapé* to summarize the therapy relationship: 'This kind of parental love . . agapé . . . is the kind of love the psycho-analyst and psychotherapist must give the patient because he did not get it from his parents in sufficient measure or in a satisfactory form' (Guntrip, 1953, p.125). Patterson (1970,1974) independently began using the term *agapé* to summarize the therapy relationship.

If the source of psychosocial emotional disorders is the absence or lack of love, and if love is the cure for such disorders, then it follows that the primary prevention of such disorders would be the providing of unconditional love to all infants and children. The conditions for successful psychotherapy are the conditions for normal infant and human development.

Love and its deprivation in infancy

While love is important throughout life for the well-being of the individual, it is

With Suzanne Hidore. *The Person-Centered Journal,* 1997, 4, pp. 8–17. Adapted from Chapter 10 of *Successful Psychotherapy: A Caring, Loving Relationship* by C. H. Patterson and Suzanne C. Hidore. Published by Jason Aronson Inc. Northvale, N. J. 1997. Reprinted here with permission.

particularly important, indeed absolutely necessary, for the survival of the infant, and for providing the basis for the normal psychological development of the individual. The presence of at least one caregiver providing unconditional love for every infant (and young child) will prevent the occurrence of most social-psychological pathology. References are cited later to support this premise. Pathology deriving from neurological or biochemical sources would not be included. Burton (1972), while discouraging the search for a single overriding trauma causing emotional disturbance, nevertheless states that 'the basic pathogen is, for me, a disordered maternal or caretaking environment rather than any specific trauma as such' (p.14). Disruptive behaviors related to the influence of peer pressures would decrease and eventually disappear, since peers would (1) be less likely to be disturbed and (2) their influence would be reduced or eliminated since their peers would be secure and not vulnerable to such pressure. Other than neurological and biochemical disorders (some of which might be genetically based), such disruptive behaviors as existed would derive from the deprivation of the biological needs for existence; frustration of such needs could lead to aggressive and antisocial behaviors. But in a society permeated by love, such needs would be met — where there is love there will be bread.

We define love as an attitude that is expressed through empathic understanding, respect and compassion, acceptance, and therapeutic genuineness, or honesty and openness toward others. In more personal — as distinguished from therapy — relationships, love may be defined as

> that which satisfies our need to receive and bestow affection and nurturance: to give and be given assurance of value, respect, acceptance, and appreciation; and to feel secure in our unity with, and belonging to a particular family, as well as the human family (Walsh, 1991, p. 9).

Early recognition of importance of infant and early childhood influences

A hundred years ago Freud emphasized the importance of infancy and early childhood on later development and psychological disturbance. Early on he attributed neuroses to the early trauma of being sexually molested. But a few years later he changed his views, concluding that it was not actual sexual experiences of seduction, but false memories and fantasies that were the cause (the Oedipal complex). Attention to the importance of real experiences of the infant and child was thus deflected to unreal or imagined experiences.

The object relations school of psychotherapy emphasizes the importance of the infant's and child's relationship with a primary care person: 'whatever a baby's genetic endowment, the mother's ability or failure to "relate" is the *sine qua non* of psychic help for the infant. To find a good parent at the start is the basis of psychic health' (Guntrip, 1975, p. 156).

During the 1940s several psychoanalytic therapists published reports of the effects of real experiences on children. The term 'maternal deprivation' was applied to these experiences. In 1937 Levy (1937) published a study of children separated from their mothers at an early age. Lauretta Bender and Stella Chess, working in the child psychiatric service at Belleview Hospital in New York, reported on children who experienced emotional deprivation during their early years (Karen, 1994; Bender and Yarnell,1941).

Children in hospitals, even for brief periods of separation from their mothers, and children in institutions were found to be psychologically disturbed (Bakwin, 1942; Bowlby, 1959, 1973). In 1945 Rene Spitz (1945, 1946) reported on his experience with children in a foundling home, comparing them with children in the nursery of a penal institution. The physical conditions in the foundling home were better then those in the penal institution, but the illness and death rates were higher. Although developmentally the foundling home infants were superior, after a year of institutionalization they were inferior to those in the prison setting. Within two years, 37 % of the foundling home children were dead; all the prison children were alive five years later. The difference between the two settings was that in the prison the children's mothers cared for them, while in the foundling home the children were cared for by professional nurses.

John Bowlby became interested in the influence of the early environment on children in the late 1930s, and published his first paper in 1940 (Bowlby, 1940). In 1944 he published a paper reporting on 44 children, ages six to sixteen who were young thieves (Bowlby, 1944). The mothers of these children were described by social workers as 'immoral, violent and nagging', 'extremely anxious, fussing, critical', ' drunken and cruel', 'did not want the child', 'unstable and jealous', etc. One common objective factor was prolonged early separations of the child and mother, separations where the child had never developed a true attachment, and after separation had no opportunity to develop a true attachment.

In a study conducted for the World Health Organization, Bowlby (1951) surveyed the field and earlier studies. This survey included the work of Dorothy Burlingham and Anna Freud (1944) with children evacuated from London during the war whose behavior deteriorated in the absence of their mothers. Bowlby's survey showed that the behaviors and psychological disturbances of children subject to maternal depravation and separation were many and varied. In addition to the thievery observed by Bowlby, these disturbances included: indifference, incorrigibility, hostility, lack of any feeling or empathy for others — affectionless and detached (characteristic of a psychopathic personality).

The conditions leading to such behaviors, in addition to early, even brief, and later, longer separation from the mother, include lack of or early loss of mother-love, and the emotional quality of the home, even before the child's birth. Bowlby referred to the British style of parenting — cold, impatient, demanding. But such an atmosphere of child rearing was not limited to Britain. For much of the first half of this century child rearing in the United States followed Watson's (1928) approach:

> Treat them as though they were young adults. Dress them, bathe them with care and circumspection. Let your behavior always be objective and kindly firm. Never hug and kiss them, never let them sit on your lap. If you must, kiss them once on the forehead when they say good night. Shake hands with them in the morning. Give

them a pat on the head if they have made an extraordinary good job
of a difficult task (pp. 81–2).

Of course not all, or even most, mothers and fathers followed the British and
Watson precepts — fortunately so, considering the effects of such a program. The
need for love in the normal development of infants and children would appear to
be obvious.

The human infant is helpless and obviously unable to meet its needs for food,
clothing, and shelter. In addition to the meeting of these needs, the infant needs
more. It needs a nurturing, caring, compassionate caretaker who provides love.
For the infant, love is communicated primarily through touch — stroking, cuddling,
massaging, kissing. Walsh (1991) notes that 'even the behaviorist John Watson
believed that love was an innate human emotional need that is fed by the tactile
stimulation an infant receives as it snuggles in its mother's arms' (p.12). This care
is 'neurologically critical during the sensitive period in which the neural pathways
are being laid down' (Walsh, 1991, p. 44).

Somatosensory deprivation — lack of touch, movement, massage, etc. —
appears to be a basic cause of many physical and psychological disturbances.

Barry Stevens (Rogers and Stevens,1967) writes about an incident when her
husband was in charge of a pediatric ward in a New York hospital in the twenties.

> There was an infant whom none of the doctors could find anything
> wrong with, but all of them agreed the infant was dying. My husband
> spoke privately to a young nurse who loved babies. He swore her to
> secrecy before telling her what he wanted her to do. The secret was,
> 'Take care of this baby as if it were your own. Just love it.' At that
> time love was nonsense even to psychologists . . . The baby took
> hold. All the doctors agreed on that (p. 31).

Recently a number of hospitals have been conducting experiments with hospitalized
infants. Walsh (1991) refers to an AP news story (Associated Press, 1988) that
reported on a volunteer program at St. Luke's Roosevelt Medical Center in New
York, that takes abandoned, neglected infants and those born drug-addicted or
with AIDS. Although given good physical care, they received no touching or
stimulation, lying listless, and in time not even reacting to sound. But, when
volunteers held them, stroked, and cuddled them they became alert, smiling, cooing,
and reacting to stimuli.

At the University of Miami Medical School, psychologist Tiffany Field
conducted an extensive study of premature infants (Ackerman,1990). The infants
were stroked and massaged by nurses and volunteers three times daily. The
massaged infants gained weight faster, became more active and alert, were more
responsive to stimuli, and were discharged from the hospital sooner than
nonmassaged infants. Follow-up found that the massaged infants were larger and
had fewer physical problems. They also did better in tests of mental and motor
ability. Touch is a powerful expression of caring. Deprivation of this caring results
in retarded physical and psychological development.

Walsh (1991) writes that there is a growing momentum among anthropologists, endocrinologists, physiologists, psychiatrists, psychologists, neuropsychologists, and others, to recognize the role of mothers in

the critical task of humanizing the species . . . modern neurophysiology is reaffirming Freud's belief in the centrality of the mother's role in making us human . . . love . . . is a biological and psychological necessity (p. 37).

It is important to note that unloving behavior such as aggressive physical and verbal behavior toward children is disruptive of healthy development (Cohen and Brooks, 1995). Hitting, slapping, beating, and yelling even when justified as punishment have a causal effect on the development of delinquency through modeling coercive and aggressive behavior (McCord, 1995). Children learn the very interpersonal behaviors which the punishment is usually designed to suppress (Cohen and Brooks, 1995). Caretaker behavior need not be extreme to cause behavior disorders. According to Maughan, Pickles, and Quinton (1995), 'Harsh and coercive parenting, even when it falls short of overt abuse, can have serious negative effects' (p. 34). The use of sarcasm ('I'm gonna break your legs if you don't settle down'), scare tactics ('Stop that or I will lock you in the attic with the ghosts'), belittling the child ('You're so stupid'), or labeling and rejecting the entire child for one act ('You are a bad boy for running across the street') can have detrimental effects on the healthy development of children (Cochrane and Myers, 1980). Baumrind (1980), evaluating the research, concludes that 'caretakers play a determining role in the ways their children develop . . . caretakers can have a determining effect on children's intelligence, character, and competence' (p. 640).

Ainsworth (1979), who with Bowlsby spent much of her life studying mother-infant attachment, notes that while

it is an essential part of the growth plan of the human species — as well as that of many other species — for an infant to become attached to a mother figure, this figure need not be the natural mother but can be anyone who plays the role of principal caregiver (p. 932).

Baumrind (1980) states that 'there is no evidence of a biological need for an exclusive primary bond, and certainly not a bond to a particular person because she happens to be the child's biological mother' (p. 645). But 'a primary commitment cannot be shared, although the care itself can and should be. Someone must, when no one else will, provide the attention, stimulation, and continuous personal relationship without which a child is consigned to psychosis, psychopathy, or marasmus' (p. 645). And fathers, men, can be principal caregivers, especially if they are socialized to give appropriate nurturing behaviors.

Consequences of love deprivation
The effects of being deprived of love are harmful to adults and devastating to children. 'Individuals deprived of love become emotionally barren as they plod through dark lives' (Walsh, 1991, p. 8). 'Without love there can be no healthy

growth or development' (Montagu, 1981, p. 93).

Walsh (1991) opens his discussion of the effects of absence of a loving infant and early childhood environment with a general statement: 'The human infant can be molded and cultivated into a decent and caring adult, or its development can be distorted horribly in a way no nonhuman animal can have its nature altered by experiences that occur within its species' (p. 8). He then proceeds to document this statement. The innate potentials of the infant or child, the inherent drive towards the actualization of these potentials in a process of self-actualization, can be inhibited and distorted by the absence of a nurturing environment of unconditional love. Furthermore, these human potentials can be nearly or totally destroyed by abuse of the caretaking relationship.

The Neuroses

The various neuroses originate in some form of emotional deprivation, resulting in a lack of satisfaction of the basic human needs for affection, security, respect, and self-esteem. The child's need for love has been thwarted by parents who are emotionally cold, controlling, and unloving. The neurotic engages in attempts to meet his or her needs for love and respect in ways that often turn other people off. Neurotics are unable to offer the love and respect which would lead to reciprocation by others. Henderson (1982) studied the neurotic person's difficulty of forming attachments. Though they desperately desire such attachments, and engage in care-eliciting behavior, involving crying (in children), attempts to draw sympathy and 'please love me' appeals, this behavior is not successful. Walsh (1991) relates this to Maslow's deficit love, an abnormal craving for love.

Depression and Suicide

One of the symptoms of depression is thoughts of suicide. However, depression itself is an amorphous category of emotional disturbance. What has been called marasmus in infants is probably similar to depression in older persons. While there appears to be an increasing awareness of biochemical, and even genetic factors in depression, it is still the case that depression is usually precipitated by environmental events, particularly the loss of a loved one. And it is possible that biochemical abnormalities are the result of psychosocial experiences. Akiskal and McKinney (1975), for example, suggest that rejection, lovelessness, and lack of relatedness leads to reduced brain catecholines resulting in the behavioral disturbances characteristic of depression. Certainly, there are depressions that are the result of psychosocial factors rather than biochemical or genetic factors, though a genetic predisposition may be present in some cases. The evidence, at this time, is not consistent or absolutely definitive.

Suicide appears to be clearly related to psychosocial factors. Durkheim (1951), a French sociologist, noted the relation between social anomie and suicide. Suicide is higher in urban areas, among the unmarried and divorced, and among those living isolated lives. Among children, those who attempt suicide are more likely to have experienced abuse and neglect (Rosenthal and Rosenthal, 1984) Adolescents who attempt suicide are usually isolated from their friends and family.

Walsh (1991) reports a study in which he and a colleague found suicide attempts among juvenile delinquents related to love-deprivation.

Schizophrenia

As in the case of depression, there is evidence of brain malfunctioning and genetic factors in many of those diagnosed as schizophrenic. But there are wide differences among those with this diagnosis. While the concept of schizophrenogenic mother is no longer accepted, there are psychosocial factors present; it is difficult, however, to discern cause-effect relationships, even though PET and CAT scans show brain abnormalities. Drugs (chlorpromazine and recently clozapine) relieve or remove the symptoms in many schizophrenics.

Seymour Kety (see Walsh, 1991), a researcher on the genetics of schizophrenia, points out that we cannot dismiss environmental factors which can precipitate, intensify, or ameliorate symptoms. Love deprivation is viewed by many as an environmental factor, that may operate by affecting chemical factors in the brain. Walsh (1991) cites studies by Robert Heath on Harlow's love-deprived monkeys that found brain disturbances. Walsh concludes that 'schizophrenia may very well be the result of the effects of early childhood experiences on the mechanisms of neurotransmitter metabolism for individuals with a schizophrenic predisposition' (p.124). Lack of care and parental love, experienced as coldness and rejection, lead to passivity, isolation and suspicion (Buss, 1966). Studies of the onset of schizophrenia find this isolation and lack of responsiveness prior to the onset. Walsh (1991) points out that genetic factors in parents may influence parenting behavior. In addition, the authors note that some attention should be given to historical psychosocial factors in parental behavior. What quality of caretaking experience did the parents have themselves as children and how did that experience influence the parents' ability to love their children? The interactions of genetics, brain chemistry and environmental factors are complex, but in the trend toward biologizing schizophrenia, environmental factors cannot be ignored.

Sociopathy and Criminality

Statements reminding us of the importance of early love in antisocial behavior abound. A Public Broadcasting System radio program recently quoted a former Los Angeles gang member as saying: 'Kids aren't born bad. Kids are bad because they can't find love.' Anthropologist Ashley Montague (1970) writes: 'Show me a murderer, a hardened criminal, a juvenile delinquent, a psychopath, or a "cold fish" and in almost every case I will show you a tragedy that has resulted from not being properly loved during childhood' (p. 46). Research studies cited by McCord (1995) point to aggressive parental behaviors such as hitting, slapping, and beating as contributors to the development of juvenile delinquency. Lance Morrow (1992), in a *Time* magazine essay, came to the conclusion that 'it is usually the want of love that makes children vicious and sends them out of control' (p. 68).

Not all criminal behavior is the result of lack of love, of course. Walsh (1991) estimates that about ten % of habitual criminals are psychopaths, or sociopaths. They come from loveless homes, characterized by neglect, rejection, and abuse.

Not having experienced love for themselves, they may have difficulty feeling love for others. In some cases, children have had to alienate themselves from their own hurt at being unloved, from their feelings of unworthiness and eventually self-rejection. To protect themselves from those negative feelings, they have alienated themselves to some degree from all feelings. Thus they have a diminished capacity to feel sympathy or empathy for others, and are able to engage in cruelty toward others without personally feeling consequences. They have little or no capacity for empathy.

Empathic development always occurs through interaction with others. Hoffman (1982) outlined developmental progression of empathic awareness beginning at birth with a reactive cry. This is a response when newborn babies hear the cry of other babies. The ability to take the role of another, according to Hoffman, begins around the age of two or three when a child can understand that others have feelings which differ from his/her own. Another step toward empathic potential comes with the development of language. Although there is probably no one critical window of time for development of empathy, it would be reasonable to predict that a child who does not experience being loved would have few experiences for positive identification of self and others, and would be less likely to develop the capacity for empathy. Aggression, violence and cruelty may be committed without limits when there is no development of empathic understanding with others.

Walsh (1991, pp. 141–6) presents evidence that deprivation of love affects the functioning of emotional centers of the brain, leading to disruptive behaviors. 'In fact, the physiological line of thought reasons that socialization and the development of conscience (the internalized control of behavior) are largely a function of autonomic conditioning in childhood' (Walsh, 1991, p. 147). That early experiences can affect brain structure as well as function is becoming clear. Weil (1985) notes 'that experiences induce neurophysiological structuring is increasingly recognized' (p. 336; see also Rourke, Bakker, Fiske, and Strang, 1983). Whatever the interrelationships and relative weights of genetic, neurological, and psychological factors, sociopathic criminals appear to share some abnormalities in all these areas; genetic factors contribute susceptibility to the influence of other factors.

Not all parents are good nurturers, or to use Winnicott's (1965) term 'good enough mothers'. Not all parents can or will love their infants. But it is not possible to remove infants or children from such parents, unless and until there is evidence of abuse. Early intervention, beginning before the birth of the child, can have positive effects with some of these parents. Intervention later to repair the effects of neglect and abuse has not been highly effective (Parens and Kramer, 1993). It is possible that there is a critical period for the bonding of the necessary relationship with a caretaker.

What can be done?
Ideally, every infant and young child should have at least one principal caretaker who can and will provide the unconditional love necessary for normal physical and psychological development. This is clearly a tremendous task, and society is probably not yet ready, or able, to provide such care. Yet while it may be impossible

in our world society to assure a loving caregiver for every infant and child, the desirability, indeed the necessity, of doing so must be recognized, and steps taken toward its achievement. Walsh (1991) notes that while there are agencies charged with assuring a minimal level of food and shelter (though not successfully doing this for all citizens), 'there are no similar institutions monitoring the nation's love needs, nor is there likely to be any time soon' (p. 52).

Steps that can, and should, be taken include the following:

1. Ratification by the United States of the United Nations Convention on the Rights of the Child (United Nations General Assembly, 1989). This convention was adopted by the 159 Member States of the UN General Assembly on November 20, 1989, and has been ratified by 54 nations, but not by the United States. This convention includes the right of the child to affection, love, and understanding in a family, unless it is in the best interests of the child to remove the child from the parents.
2. Prenatal care, including preventing malnutrition in mothers, and education in infant needs and care can be increased. Here, the United States is behind some other countries.
3. Modification of hospital practices and extension of the programs to provide infant stimulation through massaging and other contacts by touch, by the mother/ father and by other hospital personnel.
4. Providing maternal — and paternal — leave from employment on, and for a period following, the birth of a child. Desirably this should be paid leave, so that those with low incomes could afford it. The United States has lagged behind other countries. Over 100 countries provided this, before the United States, even though the United States was a signatory to the United Nations Convention in the Elimination of all Forms of Discrimination Against Women that includes an agreement 'to introduce maternity leave with pay or comparable social benefits without loss of former employment' (Walsh, 1991, p. 53). In 1993, the United States finally joined the other developed countries when the family leave legislation was passed by the Congress and signed by President Clinton.
5. Provide person-centered theory based education to parents and potential parents about effective parenting behavior and the provision of love.
6. Provide education to the public concerning the devastation of abuse. Part of the problem of abuse is that the issue has been avoided. From the time when Sigmund Freud bowed to the pressure of professional shunning to our own times when abuse is still denied as fantasy, human abuse reminds us too poignantly of our own fears. In avoiding our own sorrow we have allowed children to live the terror of abuse and to pass their inheritance to the following generations.
7. Encourage the awareness of the media (television/video programming, print and internet) as influences on interpersonal behavior, especially on modeling effective behavior for parenting roles, conflict resolution, and the provision of love.

Conclusion

This paper presents just a sampling of the voluminous evidence that the level of love in infancy and early childhood is the source of much, if not most, psychosocial disturbance and disorder. Love is a powerful prophylactic. The logical solution of the problem is startlingly simple: The provision of a safe and loving caregiver for every infant and child. The actual implementation of this solution is admittedly difficult. It requires focus and intent. Educational models built on client-centered/person-centered theory can contribute to healthy social roles and behaviors which promote more effective love of children. Therapists can facilitate person-centered theory based education through school and college classes, organizational presentations, and community discussions. There are isolated efforts being made toward the goal of creating more loving environments for children, and thus there is some hope that with recognition of its importance, more will be done.

References

Ackerman, D. (1990) *A natural history of the senses.* New York: Random House.

Ainsworth, M. D. (1979) Infant-mother attachment. *American Psychologist.* 34, pp. 932–7.

Akiskal, H., and McKinney, W. (1975) Overview of recent research in depression. *Archives of General Psychiatry,* 32, pp. 285–305.

Allport, G. W. (1950) *The individual and his religion.* New York: Macmillan.

Associated Press News Service (1988, September 18) Wanted: Someone to love babies, if only for an hour. *Idaho Press-Tribune*, p. D1.

Bakwin, H. (1942) Loneliness in infants. *American Journal of Diseases of Children,* 63, pp. 30–40.

Baumrind, D. (1980) New directions in socialization research. *American Psychologist,* 35, pp. 639–52.

Bender, L., and Yarnell, H. (1941) An observation nursery: A study of 250 children in the psychiatric division of Belleview Hospital. *American Journal of Psychiatry,* 97, pp. 1158–74.

Bowlby, J. (1940) The influence of early environment in the development of neuroses and neurotic character. *International Journal of Psycho-Analysis, 1,* pp. 154–78.

Bowlby, J. (1944) Forty-four juvenile thieves: Their characters and homelife. *International Journal of Psycho-Analysis,* 25, pp. 19–52.

Bowlby, J. (1951) *Maternal care and mental health.* Geneva: World Health Monograph Series (2).

Bowlby, J. (1959) Separation anxiety. *International Journal of Psycho-Analysis,* 41, pp. 89–113.

Bowlby, J. (1973) *Attachment and Loss. Vol. 2. Separation.* New York: Basic Books.

Burlingham, D., and Freud, A. (1944) *Infants without families.* London: Allen and Unwin.

Burton, A. (1967) *Modern humanistic psychotherapy.* San Francisco: Jossey-Bass.

Burton, A. (1972) *Interpersonal psychotherapy.* Englewood Cliffs, NJ: Prentice-Hall.

Buss, A. (1966) *Psychopathology*. New York: Wiley.

Cochran, C. T., and Myers, D. V. (1980) *Children in crisis*. Beverly Hills: Sage Publications.

Cohen, P., and Brooks J. S. (1995) The reciprocal influence of punishment and child behavior disorder. In McCord, J. (Ed.) *Coercion and punishment in long-term perspectives*. (Pp. 154–64) Cambridge: Cambridge University Press.

Durkheim, E. (1951) *Suicide*. Glencoe, Il.: Free Press.

Fairbairn, W. A. D. (1954) *An object-relations theory of the personality*. New York: Basic Books.

Guntrip, H. (1953) The therapeutic factor in psychotherapy. *British Journal of Medical Psychology*, 26, pp. 115–32.

Guntrip, H. (1975) My experience of analysis with Fairbairn and Winnicott. *International Review of Psycho-Analysis*, 2, pp. 145–56.

Henderson, S. (1982) The significance of social relationships in the etiology of neuroses. In C. Parkes, and 1. Stevenson-Hinkle (Eds.) *The place of attachment in human behavior*. New York: Basic Books.

Hoffman, M. L. (1982) Development of prosocial motivation: Empathy and guilt. In N. Eisenberg (Ed.) *The development of prosocial behavior*. (Pp. 281–313) New York: McGraw-Hill.

Karen, R. (1994) *Becoming attached*. New York: Warner.

Levy, D. (1937) Primary affect hunger. *American Journal of Psychiatry*, 94, pp. 643–52.

Maughan, B., Pickles, A., and Quinton, D. (1995) Parental hostility, childhood behavior, and adult social functioning. In McCord, J. (Ed.) *Coercion and punishment in long-term perspectives*. (Pp. 34–58) Cambridge: Cambridge University Press.

McCord, J. (1995) *Coercion and punishment in longterm perspectives*. Cambridge: Cambridge University Press.

Montagu, A. (1970) A scientist looks at love. *Phi Beta Kappan*.

Montagu, A. (1981) *Growing young*. New York: McGraw-Hill.

Morrow, L. (1992, May 11) Video warriors in Los Angeles. *Time*, p. 68.

Parens, H., and Kramer, S. (Eds.) (1993) *Prevention in mental health*. New York: Jason Aronson.

Patterson, C. H. (1970) A model for counseling and other facilitative interpersonal relationships. In W. H. Van Hoose and J. J. Pietrofesa (Eds.) *Counseling and guidance in the twentieth century*. (Pp. 169–92) Boston: Houghton Mifflin.

Patterson, C. H. (1974) *Relationship counseling and psychotherapy*. New York: Harper and Row.

Phillips, C. (1991, August 11) To be whole again. *Parade Magazine*, pp. 10–12.

Rogers, C. R. (1957) The necessary and sufficient conditions of therapeutic personality change. *Journal of Consulting Psychology*, 21, 95–103.

Rogers, C. R., and Stevens, B. (1967) *Person to person: The problem of being human*. Lafayette, CA: Real People Press.

Rosenthal, R., and Rosenthal, S. (1984) Suicidal behavior in preschool children. *American Journal of Psychiatry*, 141, pp. 520–4.

Rourke, B. P., Bakker, J. D., Fiske, I. L., and Strang, J. D. (1983) *Child neuropsychology*. New York: Guilford.

Spitz, R. A. (1945) Hospitalism. In R. S. Eissler, (Ed.)*The psychoanalytic study of the child (Vol. l)* New York: International Universities Press.

Spitz, R. A. (1946) Hospitalism: A follow-up report. In R. S. Eissler, (Ed.)*The psychoanalytic study of the child (Vol.ll)*. New York: International Universities Press.

United Nations (UN) General Assembly (1989; November 17) Adoption of a convention on the rights of the child. New York: Author.

Walsh, A. (1991) *The science of love*. Buffalo, NY: Prometheus Books.

Watson, J. B. (1928) *Psychological care of infant and child.* New York: Norton.

Weil, A. P. (1985)Thoughts about early pathology . *Journal of the American Psychoanalytic Association,*33, pp. 335–52.

Winnicott, D. W. (1965) *The maturational processes and the facilitating environment*. New York. International Universities Press.

THE CURRENT STATE AND THE FUTURE OF CIVILIZATION

34

Psychotherapy is concerned with mitigating individual psychological pain and suffering. But there is the broader question of the state and future of our civilization. It is not, of course, a new problem. Over 20 years ago, Rogers (1973) referred to his 'concerns about our very sick society and the near fatal illnesses of our culture' (p. 378). We are clearly not living in the best of all possible worlds. There are a number of indications of the decline of our civilization. It has been said that each society contains within itself the seeds of its demise. I can do little more here than to enumerate some of these.

1. *Overpopulation.* There is no question that, without control, sooner or later we will reach a condition where the world's resources will no longer be able to support its people. The debate can only concern the time when this occurs. The planet's resources are limited, and science cannot make something out of nothing. In the past, disease, wars, famines, and pestilence have controlled population. Henry Kendall (1994), a Nobel Laureate in physics, has said that if population was not controlled in a humanitarian way nature would do so in its inhumane way. It appears that nature is being aided by genocide in some areas of the world.

2. *Pollution.* We are polluting our environment at an increasing rate. Providing clean air and water will become a growing problem. And again, the question is not whether or not this is a major problem but when the earth will become uninhabitable if we do not now begin to control pollution.

3. *Global warming.* The greenhouse effect, leading to global warming, is real. The industrialized nations, using fossil fuel, are filling the atmosphere with an increasing layer of carbon dioxide, but efforts at reducing the emissions are blocked by the energy and automobile lobbies. Again, it is only a matter of time before climatic changes will disastrously affect millions of people.

4. *Extreme diversity.* In addition to environmental problems, we are beset by

Extract from the Leona Tyler Award Address: *Some Thoughts on Reaching the End of a Career.* Presented at the 1995 American Psychological Association Annual Convention. Extracted from *The Counseling Psychologist*, 1996, 24, pp. 336–47. © 1995, Division of Counseling Psychology. Reprinted by permission of Sage Publications/Corwin Press, Inc.

increasing social problems. Diversity is the theme of the day and is being praised and encouraged but there can be too much of a good thing. Our society is splintering and polarizing into innumerable racial, ethnic, tribal, national, social, religious, political, and other groups, many of them in extreme opposition to each other. Extreme diversity leads to divisiveness; we are experiencing this in many areas, leading to legislative gridlock, ethnic cleansing, and other violence between groups. Extreme multiculturalism focuses on, and magnifies, differences, polarizing and pitting one group against another. Yet we are all of the same species, fundamentally like one another, and we live in one world. With instant communication and world trade we could become one community, a global village, if the common good replaced efforts of separate groups to monopolize our resources.

5. *Increasing violence.* The increase of violent crime and personal and group violence in our society is well documented. Terrorism is widespread in the world. Violence of group against group, including genocide, is almost of epidemic proportions. There is no single world war, but a series of wars throughout the world. Ethnic, racial, and national hatreds appear to be deepseated, ready to break out with minimal provocation. And violence of individual against individual is widespread.

6. *Our criminal justice system is overloaded and ineffective*, costing billions of dollars a year. Our adversarial legal system was devised to discover the truth and provide justice. In practice, it has evolved into an elaborate game, with the goal of each side to win at all costs, including the suppression of the truth. A juror dismissed from the O. J. Simpson case is reported to have said, 'I see a situation where truth is not the issue.' One of the prosecution lawyers, Christopher Darden, disgusted and ashamed of the spectacle, referred to 'this supposed truth-seeking process'. The selection of jurors is manipulated to attempt to seat those who might be easily influenced. Our juries are hardly composed of peers. The most competent persons are exempt from, or are able to avoid, jury duty (Adler,1994a,b). Issues are settled by technicalities. Criminal lawyers build their reputations by winning jury verdicts for clients whom they know are guilty.

7. *Our system of representative democracy has deteriorated* to a struggle for legislation favorable to particular interest groups. Virtually all legislation is compromised to benefit particular groups. Government is corrupted by the money of special interest groups. It might be said that we have a government of the political action committees (PACs), by the PACs, and for the PACs. It is often said that we have the best government money can buy. Local, state, and regional groups are benefited rather than the country as a whole.

8. *Our vaunted economic system of capitalism fails us in many ways.* It can only continue to exist with increasing consumption and greater use and destruction of our resources. We are urged to buy more, use more, and discard more, so that industry can show increasing production, sales, and profits. We fluctuate between feast and famine — prosperity and depression. The gap between the rich and the poor increases. Business and industry do not provide enough jobs

paying living wages, above the poverty line. The result is that society must take on the support of the jobless through welfare. One out of every three people on the planet lives in abject poverty.

Adam Smith declared that the engine of capitalism is self-interest. He used the wrong term — the correct one is greed. The government spends billions of dollars a year regulating business and industry to protect consumers from dishonesty and fraud, and to preserve competition. With the advent of capitalism in Russia and China, greed is becoming endemic in those countries. Fraud and corruption are rampant in business, industry, and government throughout the world.

This is only a sketch of the problems facing our society and our civilization. It is a disturbing picture. The barbarians are not at the gate — they are here among us. Economic considerations — money — take precedence over preservation of the environment and health, and of human survival. The four horsemen of the apocalypse are here: War (or violence), famine, pestilence, and disease. Add to them three more — poverty, pollution, and greed.

The future looks bleak indeed. There are two scenarios for the end of the world, in addition to the second coming of Christ that some believe in. The first involves the destruction of our environment, of the planet on which we depend for our lives. We are well on the way to killing our world. Carl Sagan (1994) has said that 'due to our own action and inactions and the misuse of technology, we live in an extraordinary moment — the first time that a species on Earth has become able to wipe itself out'. His suggestion that we colonize other planets is fantasy. We would have to export everything necessary for life from the earth — even our air and water.

Nor can we depend on science to save us. Science cannot provide air, water, and food when the natural sources of these are exhausted. Pollution and global warming can be solved, but only if action is taken in time. But science is conservative. It is bound to the 5% or 1% solution. That is, it will reject the null hypothesis only at the 99% or 95% level of certainty. There is great danger in accepting the null hypothesis when it is false. More research, more evidence, is required, it is said. So we procrastinate. But by the time enough evidence is available, it could well be too late to reverse the processes of pollution and global warming. We have the intelligence but not the will to act when we are not immediately threatened.

This scenario appears to be moving toward its conclusion. We are rapidly depleting the earth's resources. Its flora and fauna are being decimated. As my daughter's gorilla T-shirt puts it, 'Extinction is forever'.

The second scenario for the end of the world involves humanity's self-destruction. We seem to be on the way to this, with racial and ethnic hatreds leading to undeclared wars and genocide. Add to this the acts of terrorism by religious and political fanatics. Violence is endemic in our society. Is there any hope for a future in which all beings can live together? 'Can't we,' as Rodney King asked, 'all just get along?'

The seventh horseman of the apocalypse, greed, runs rife among us. One columnist (Terrell, 1994) wrote that 'greed is the thing that will destroy the world, not the bomb.' Human inhumanity suggests that the human race has not evolved far enough for us to live together peaceably. Are violence and greed inherent in human nature, as it has evolved in the struggle for existence?

Certainly the potential is there. But the expressions of violence and greed are fostered by certain environmental conditions. Early primitive societies were characterized by cooperation when struggling against the environment to obtain sufficient food in both hunting and fishing and agricultural societies. Violence, aggression, and greed occur under conditions of deprivation, frustration, and threat, when there are those who have and those who have not. It appears that violence and greed could be minimized in a society in which the necessities of life are distributed equitably, when the needs of all of its members for food, clothing, shelter, and health are met.

However, besides the potentially negative elements in human nature there are positive elements. Evidence for such elements surfaces in times of natural and human-caused disasters. Barbra Streisand, in the final concert of her 1994 tour introduced the song 'People Who Need People' as follows; 'This has been a year filled with natural disasters. And it has been amazing how in times of catastrophe people come together and forget their differences and help one another.' Then she ended by saying: 'Do we always need a catastrophe to remind us that we are all just people?' Will we end up huddled together facing the extinction of the human race by a natural or human-made catastrophe to reach the tie that binds?

We need not end that way. Roger Sperry (who died in April 1993) was a physiological psychologist and also a humanistic psychologist. He wrote about a cognitive revolution (Sperry, 1993, 1994). He quoted Skinner as saying that 'the more we learn about human behavior the less and less promising appear the prospects' (Sperry, 1993, p. 878). But Sperry then continued:

> I see a possible ray of hope in psycho!ogy's cognitive revolution and what it could mean in bringing new perspectives, beliefs and values — in short new mind-sets and a new way of thinking — much needed if humanity is to survive the next century. (Sperry, 1993, p. 878).

Of today's mounting global ills, he wrote,

> including the vicious spiral of mounting population, pollution, energy demands, environmental degradation, urban overcrowding and associated crime . . . will not be cured merely by applying more and better science and technology . . . A major reconception of the human venture is called for (p. 883).

In Sperry's new paradigm, causation is turned upside down or, rather, it becomes a reciprocal process. Brain activity leads to emergent mental states that become new elements in consciousness. They, in turn, have a primacy in determining what a person is and does.

These renovations of the cognitive revolution provide a new way of

> knowing and understanding, a unifying new vision in which some
> see a rational solution to our global predicament in the form of more
> realistic guidelines, beliefs and values to live and govern by (Sperry,
> 1993, p. 880).

> The great challenge ahead . . . is to take this paradigm gained, put it
> into action, and turn humankind's self-destructive course around
> before it is too late (Sperry, 1994, p. 10).

This paradigm is not really new. It is inherent in the humanistic psychology movement of the past few decades. However, Sperry's argument is convincing and provides an answer to a strict behaviorism and a theoretical physiological-neurological foundation for humanistic psychology.

Nevertheless, if Sperry is correct, this process has been in operation for some time, in fact, over the history of the human race. So far it has not led to the kind of world Sperry and others desire. Can we hope that it will lead to the necessary changes in human beliefs and behaviors in the near future?

Something more is needed. Cognition is not enough. In addition to the potential for violence and greed in human beings, there is also the potential for positive behaviors. Human beings are social animals, and an essential element for being social, and thus human, is concern for others. A concern for others was essential in the development of the race. Early primitive societies, both hunting and fishing and agrarian societies, depended on cooperation and sharing for survival. The infant depends on others, parents or parent surrogates, for survival, requiring parental love and compassion.

Thus it is argued that altruism is a part of human nature (Batson, 1990). Humans are not entirely egoistic but have the capacity for being caring and compassionate without getting anything tangible in return. Empathy appears to develop naturally in children at three to four years of age.

So we have come full circle, from the idea that the essence of psychotherapy is love to the recognition that the preservation of life and our civilization depends on love. Over 75 years ago, Maria Montessori (1917) wrote that 'it is love which preserves the human species, and not the struggle for existence' (p. 326). Viktor Frankl (1985) has said that 'the salvation of man is through love and in love' (*Man's Search for Meaning*, p. 57). Eric Hoffer (1979) argued that the survival of the species depends on human compassion. The popular song of a few years ago had it right: 'What the World Needs Now is Love Sweet Love'.

Let us hope that William James (1902) was being prophetic when over 90 years ago he wrote, 'I saw that the foundation principle of the worlds, of all the worlds, is what we call love' (p. 391).

References

Adler, S. J. (1994). *The jury*. New York: Times Books.

Adler, S. J. (1994b). Lawyers' poker: Stacking the Marcos jury. *Wall Street Journal*, Sept. 14, pp. B1, B12.

Batson, C. D. (1990). How social an animal? The human capacity for caring. *American Psychologist*, 45, 336–46.

Frankl, V. E. (1985) *Man's search for meaning*. New York: Washington Square Press.

Hoffer, E. (1979) In *Saturday Review*, November 11.

James, W. (1902) *Varieties of religious experience*. New York: Modern Library.

Kendall, H. (1994) In *Time*, September 5, p. 53.

Montessori, M. (1917) *Spontaneous activity in education*. New York: Stokes.

Rogers, C. R. (1973) Some new challenges. *American Psychologist,* 28, 379–87.

Sagan, C. (1994) *Pale blue dot: A vision of the human future in space*. New York: Random House.

Sperry, R. W. (1993) The impact and promise of the cognitive revolution. *American Psychologist*, 48, pp. 878–85.

Sperry, R W. (1994) A powerful paradigm made stronger. *Psychological Science Agenda*, October, 10, pp. 11–13.

Terrell, B. (1994) *Asheville Citizen-Times*, October, 18.

Index of Names

Main Subject Index

The new introduction to Person-Centred counselling from its origins to current developments in theory and practice

LEARNING AND BEING IN PERSON-CENTRED COUNSELLING
A TEXTBOOK FOR DISCOVERING THEORY AND DEVELOPING PRACTICE

Tony Merry *with additional material by Bob Lusty*
ISBN 1 898059 24 1   156x234   pp. 180+iv   £13.00

THIS BOOK IS a complete rewrite and extended version of the successful *What is Person-Centred Therapy* by Tony Merry and Bob Lusty previously published by the Gale Centre. At almost twice the size of the original, it contains new, up-to-date material and offers in-depth discussion of all aspects of person-centred counselling in theory and practice.

The coverage of the topics is innovative, comprehensive and thorough. Tony Merry is renowned for his straightforward and accessible writing style, making *Learning and Being in Person-Centred Counselling* suitable for a wide variety of readers.

Augmenting the clear presentation, the book is brought to life by many suggestions for exploring and developing person-centred values, qualities, attitudes and skills.

LEARNING AND BEING IN PERSON-CENTRED COUNSELLING is recommended for:
- certificate and diploma in counselling trainees and tutors;
- undergraduate psychology students and lecturers;
- nurses and social workers in training;
- those on vocational and professional helping professions-related courses;
- trainees on integrative, cognitive or psychodynamic courses;
- anyone seeking input on contemporary person-centred theory and practice.

CHAPTERS INCLUDE
- Human nature, actualisation and the development of the person;
- A theory of counselling;
- Developing person-centred values, skills, qualities and attitudes;
- Training issues: client work and personal development;
- Supervision;
- Working and being in groups;
- Resources;

TONY MERRY teaches at the University of East London on postgraduate and undergraduate courses in counselling and counselling psychology. He is author of several books and articles on counselling. He co-founded the British Association for the Person-Centred Approach in 1989 and is currently editor of *Person-Centred Practice* and the *Universities Psychotherapy Association Review*. He has contributed to workshops and other person-centred events in Europe, including several with Carl Rogers in England, Ireland and Hungary in the 1980s.

Bob Lusty worked closely with Tony Merry at the University of East London for over 20 years. He is now in private practice as a counsellor and supervisor.

Person-Centred Approach
& Client-Centred Therapy
Essential Readers
Series editor Tony Merry

Person-Centred Therapy: *A Revolutionary Paradigm*

Jerold D. Bozarth 1998 ISBN 1 898059 22 5 234 x 156 pp 204 + vi £15.00

Jerold D. Bozarth is Professor Emeritus of the University of Georgia, where his tenure included Chair of the Department of Counseling and Human Development, Director of the Rehabilitation Counseling Program and Director of the Person-Centered Studies Project.

In this book Jerold Bozarth presents a collection of twenty revised papers and new writings on Person-Centred therapy representing over 40 years' work as an innovator and theoretician. Divided into five sections,

- Theory and Philosophy
- Applications of Practice
- Implications
- The Basics of Practice
- Research

this important book reflects upon Carl Rogers' theoretical foundations, emphasises the revolutionary nature of these foundations and offers extended frames for understanding this radical approach to therapy. This book will be essential reading for all with an interest in Client-Centred Therapy and the Person-Centred Approach.

• • •

Experiences in Relatedness:
Groupwork and the Person-Centred Approach
edited by **Colin Lago** and **Mhairi MacMillan**
1999 ISBN 1 898059 23 3 234 x 156 pp 182+iv £15.00

This book is an international collection of specially commissioned papers. Contributors include Ruth Sandford (USA); Peggy Natiello (USA); John K. Wood (Brazil); Peter Figge (Germany); Irene Fairhurst, Tony Merry, John Barkham, Alan Coulson and Jane Hoffman (UK). This is the first substantial book within the person-centred tradition on group work since Carl Rogers' *Encounter Groups.* Topics include the history of the development of small and large group work within the PCA, theoretical principles of person-centred groupwork, working with issues of sexuality and sexism, the use of the group in training and groups, organisations, and the Person-Centred Approach.

The authors have uniquely caught the spirit of the person-centred approach in their various writing styles, which combine personal expression with disciplined reflections on experience. References to research studies sit comfortably alongside personal testimonies, philosophical reflections are underpinned by a wide range of references from other disciplines.

• • •

Women Writing in the Person-Centred Approach
edited by **Irene Fairhurst**
1999 ISBN 1 898059 26 8 234 x 156 pp. 217+ii £15.00

Edited by the co-founder of the British Association for the Person-Centred Approach (BAPCA), this book is the first anthology of women's writings informed by and focusing on the Person-Centred Approach. This uniquely themed collection includes contributions from all over the world, representing the wide range of developments in client-centred therapy and the person-centred approach.

In person-centred counselling and psychotherapy training courses, women outnumber men by about eight to one, yet in our literature the opposite is the case. This book is not written specifically for women, or about women — it redresses the balance — it is a place for women with something to say, to meet together, and for some, to find their voice. Twenty-one papers from an impressive international list of contributors.